D1220774

RHYTHMS OF
LEARNING

VISTA SERIES

VOLUME 4

A Life for the Spirit:
Rudolf Steiner in the Crosscurrents of Our Time

Henry Barnes

A Western Approach to Reincarnation and Karma:
Selected Lectures & Writings by Rudolf Steiner

Edited and Introduced by
René Querido

Art as Spiritual Activity:
Rudolf Steiner's Contribution to the Visual Arts

Edited and Introduced by
Michael Howard

RHYTHMS OF LEARNING

*What Waldorf Education Offers
Children, Parents & Teachers*

SELECTED LECTURES BY

RUDOLF STEINER

EDITED AND INTRODUCED BY

ROBERTO TROSTLI

C Anthroposophic Press

Introductions copyright © 1998 Roberto Trostli
Lectures copyright © 1998 Anthroposophic Press

Published by Anthroposophic Press
3390 Route 9, Hudson, NY 12534
www.anthropress.org

The lectures in this book are from the *Rudolf Steiner Gesamtausgabe* [Collected Works of Rudolf Steiner], published by Rudolf Steiner Verlag, Dornach, Switzerland. Some of the lectures for this edition were newly translated by Robert Lathe and Nancy Whittaker; the remainder were revised from previously published material.

Library of Congress Cataloging-in-Publication Data

Steiner, Rudolf, 1861–1925.
    [Lectures. English. Selections]
    Rhythms of learning : what Waldorf education offers children, parents & teachers / selected lectures by Rudolf Steiner ; edited and introduced by Roberto Trostli.
       p. cm. — (Vista series ; v. 4)
    Includes bibliographical references and index.
    ISBN 0-88010-451-1 (pbk.)
    1. Waldorf method of education.   2. Anthroposophy.
I. Trostli, Roberto.   II. Title.   III. Series.
LB1029.W34S7362513   1998
371.39—dc21   98-20641
                                                              CIP

10 9 8 7 6 5 4 3 2

All rights reserved. No part of this book may be reproduced in any form without the written permission of the publisher, except for brief quotations included in critical reviews and articles.

Printed in the United States of America

SOURCES

The essay "The Education of the Child in the Light of Spiritual Science," is from part 1 of *The Education of the Child and Early Lectures on Education*, copyright 1996 by Anthroposophic Press, Inc. Translated by George and Mary Adams, it appeared originally in German in the journal *Lucifer-Gnosis* (nr. 33) as "Die Erzieuhung des Kindes vom Geschictspunkte der Geisteswissenschaft." It is included in vol. 34 in the Collected Work of Rudolf Steiner, published by Rudolf Steiner Verlag, Dornach, Switzerland, 1987.

"The Four Temperaments" [Das geheimnis der menschlichen temperamente] is lecture 4 in *Anthroposophy in Everyday Life*, copyright 1987 by Anthroposophic Press, Inc. Translated from German by Brian Kelly, it is included in *Wo und wie findet man den Geist?*, vol. 57 in the Collected Work.

"Understanding Children's Temperaments" is lecture 1 in *Discussions with Teachers*, copyright 1997 by Anthroposophic Press, Inc. Translated from German by Helen Fox and revised by the publisher, it is included in *Erziehungskunst. Seminarbesprechungen und Lehrplanvortrage*, vol. 295 in the Collected Work.

"Gratitude, Love, and Duty" is lecture 6 in *The Child's Changing Consciousness as the Basis of Pedagogical Practice*, copyright 1996 by Anthroposophic Press, Inc. Translated from German by Roland Everett and revised by the publisher, it is included in *Die Padagogische Praxis vom Gesichtspunkte geisteswissenschaftlicher Menschenerkenntnis*, vol. 306 in the Collected Work.

"Walking, Speaking, Thinking" is lecture 6 and "Nature Study in the Elementary School" is lecture 8 in *A Modern Art of Education*, published by Rudolf Steiner Press, London, 1981. Newly translated from German by Robert Lathe and Nancy Whittaker for this edition, they are included in *Gegenwärtiges Geistesleben und Erziehung*, vol. 307 in the Collected Work.

"The Child at Seven" is lecture 9 in *Soul Economy and Waldorf Education*, copyright 1986 by Anthroposophic Press, Inc. Translated from German by Roland Everett and revised by the publisher for this edition, it is included in *Die gesunde Entwickelung des Leiblich-Physischen als Grundlage der freien Entfaltung des Seelisch-Geistigen*, vol. 303 in the Collected Work.

"Teaching Children to Write" is lecture 5 and "Education through Art" is lecture 3 in *Practical Advice to Teachers*, published by Rudolf Steiner Press, London, 1976. Translated from German by Johanna Collis and revised by Anthroposophic Press for this edition, they are included in *Erziehungskunst. Methodisch-Didaktisches*, vol. 294 in the Collected Work.

"Teaching Arithmetic" is lecture 5 in *The Kingdom of Childhood*, copyright 1995 by Anthroposophic Press, Inc. Translated from German by Helen Fox and revised by the publisher, it is included in *Die Kunst des Erziehens aus dem Erfassen der Menschenwesenheit*, vol. 311 in the Collected Work.

"Zoology and Botany in the Elementary School" is lecture 8; "Teaching History" is lecture 12; and "An Introduction to Eurythmy" is in *The Renewal of Education*. Translated from German by Robert Lathe and Nancy Whittaker for this edition, they are included in *Die Erneuerung der Pädagogisch-didaktischen Kunst durch Geisteswissenschaft*, vol. 301 in the Collected Work.

"Teaching Geography" is lecture 11 and "The Child at Twelve" is lecture 8 in *Practical Advice to Teachers*, published by Rudolf Steiner Press, London, 1976. Translated from German by Johanna Collis and revised by Anthroposophic Press for this edition, they are included in *Erziehungskunst. Methodisch-Didaktisches*, vol. 294 in the Collected Work.

"Teaching in the Upper Grades" is an abbreviated version of lectures 2 and 3; "Working with Adolescents" is lecture 5 in *Education for Adolescents*, copyright 1996 by Anthroposophic Press, Inc. Translated from German by Carl Hoffmann, they are included in *Menschenerkenntnis und Unterrichtsgestaltung*, vol. 302 in the Collected Work.

This book is dedicated to

EKKEHARD PIENING

my friend and colleague,
who inspired me to become a Waldorf teacher

CONTENTS

FOREWORD

ROBERT MCDERMOTT

GENERAL EDITOR, VISTA SERIES

An experiment in its eighth decade, with more than sixty thousand students attending five hundred schools worldwide, Waldorf education is the largest and fastest growing independent, nonsectarian school movement in the world. The more than one hundred and fifty Waldorf schools in North America appear to be but the beginning of a rapid growth that will almost certainly be continued by the next generation. This volume is intended as a companion to educators and parents, both inside and outside the Waldorf school movement, who want to explore Steiner's intuitive and spiritual-scientific research concerning child development and, in particular, the positive and negative forces affecting that development in a culture that puts children at risk.

In addition to his several hundred lectures on the curricula and pedagogy that constitute the Waldorf approach to the education of young children and adolescents, Steiner published more than three hundred volumes of lectures for the education of adults. A thorough understanding of Steiner's teachings will suggest that all education, of children and adults alike, is compensatory. Called *spiritual science*, or *anthroposophy* ("human wisdom" and "wisdom of the human"), Steiner's teachings call for the cultivation of free, active, imaginal thinking deepened by affect and strengthened by will. From this kind of developed spiritual activity can flow a deep harmony between science and art, between personal and social transformation, and between insights and service on behalf of humanity and the Earth.

The self-education of adults is essential for the Waldorf approach to educating children, because Waldorf does not consist solely of methods, techniques, or structures, but rather the development of human capacities—those of the children but also, and more importantly, those of teachers and parents. Decades before the sensible slogan "it takes a village" became current, Steiner's lectures to Waldorf teachers and parents indicated the need for a deep and trusting collaboration between family and school on behalf of children. Rudolf Steiner was the first to bring to Western education the importance of rhythm and emulation, both of which are made possible by the child's teachers and parents. In this respect, Steiner's pedagogy complemented that of John Dewey and anticipated that of Maria Montessori, though it is far more developed than either.

In 1919, at the request of Emil Molt, Steiner created the first Waldorf school. The school that, in the early 1920s, Steiner guided tirelessly during the last five years of his life was built essentially on the moral, spiritual, and professional capacities of the teachers he selected, most of whom were not teachers at all but active in entirely different professions. Steiner delivered a series of lectures to those he had selected to be teachers so that they could more effectively approach their students out of their own inner resources.

The Waldorf curriculum emphasizes physical and emotional readiness; it engages the children's bodies and artistic sensibilities in all subjects, including academic ones. Scores of parents who do not share the affirmation of the spiritual life of the child, which is central to the Waldorf approach to education, are nevertheless committed to their children's Waldorf school, because they see its positive effects throughout the course of their children's development.

This book, consisting of a representative selection of Steiner's lectures on the child and education, along with helpful introductions by an accomplished Waldorf teacher, is intended for all teachers and parents devoted to a well founded and demonstrably effective approach to educating children. As will be evident, the Waldorf approach is precisely that—an approach, not a set of fixed answers, principles, or procedures. Because of his stupendous capacity to see into the souls of modern, Western children and adults, Steiner articulated countless recommendations, or indications, none of which were intended to be accepted on faith. Steiner was a spiritual empiricist, and he urged his students and readers to be no less so.

Ideally, teachers and parents alike will increasingly join the effort to find the most effective approaches to each pedagogical challenge, each child, each relationship, each lesson, and each hour of the day. The relationship of science to art, of temperaments to pedagogy, of healthy rhythms to the clamor of contemporary society, aesthetic sensibility to rapidly developing computer technology, all require fresh and original responses by teachers and parents—and, as they mature, by students themselves. Steiner bequeathed a wide bookshelf of suggestions as well as a generation of teachers who constitute a living lineage inspired directly by his words and presence on behalf of the lives of real children in the first Waldorf school in Stuttgart. These influences are worthy of the respect accorded them by Waldorf teachers worldwide, but it is equally important to emphasize that there is no handbook and no rules. Waldorf teaching requires creativity, with each teacher committed to a lifelong apprenticeship as artist in the medium of education. Artistry is called for in the classroom, in parent conferences, in the task of revising social studies and natural science curricula, in search for greater collaboration among teachers, and in performing the complex work of school administration.

Almost all readers of Steiner tend to rely on his findings, and sometimes on his words as though holy writ, because his research was stunningly insightful and authoritative (never authoritarian). It has taken a great many Waldorf researchers to give local form and worldwide visibility to Steiner's research. Roberto Trostli, the editor of this volume, is one of the many Waldorf teachers in the United States who strives daily with his students, and in relation to his students' families and to the culture of which they are a part, to implement, and as necessary expand and revise the material in Steiner's lectures.

One of the strengths of this volume is the close relationship between the editor's introductions to Steiner's lectures and the lectures themselves. By virtue of his close reading of these and hundreds of similar lectures, and his thorough knowledge of the history of science as well as his deep appreciation of the arts (especially his experience as a musician), and his fidelity to the spiritual practices that Rudolf Steiner recommended, Roberto Trostli brings to this volume the fruits of his own research. In a successful Waldorf school such as The Hartsbrook School in Hadley, Massachusetts, where Roberto Trostli has been teaching the same class of 28 students for the past seven years, one's "own" research really means a combination of spiritual practice and close collaboration with striving colleagues in one's school, throughout the community of Waldorf schools, and with great teachers who combine spiritual and pedagogical depth.

Readers of this volume are invited to savor the depth of Steiner's understanding of the child and the process by which children, teachers, and parents can cooperate to enable children to realize their deepest capabilities and intentions. Steiner's insights and recommendations need to be tested by individuals and communities if children are to receive the healthy start they deserve. A culture so lacking in understanding of, and dedication to, the beginning and end of life seriously endangers the current generation of children, affluent ones as well as those who are economically disadvantaged. May this volume be so used as to give renewed meaning to Steiner's recommendation to Waldorf teachers that they receive the child in reverence, educate the child in love, and send the child forth in freedom.

* * * * * *

The VISTA SERIES has been generously supported by a grant from Laurance S. Rockefeller who, with respect to the spiritual dimension of human relationships, responsible business, conservation and ecology, has been an inspiring educator for at least six decades. He traces his commitment to education to the deep sense of responsibility instilled in him by his parents and to his joyful years as a student of the Lincoln School, an experimental "learning environment" created by the faculty of Teachers College of Columbia University according to John Dewey's approach to education.

PREFACE

This book has been seven years in the making. During those years, I have reread the lectures included in this volume many times, and every reading has yielded new perspectives and new insights. The introductions in this book have been rewritten repeatedly, for whenever I reviewed the previous year's work, I was no longer satisfied. My understanding of Rudolf Steiner's ideas had deepened, and my previous formulation seemed inadequate.

The longer I have been a Waldorf teacher, the more I have come to realize that Waldorf education is a work in progress. This may not be immediately apparent, because much of Waldorf education seems to hearken back to Rudolf Steiner rather than forward toward the future. On closer examination, however, it becomes apparent that Waldorf education is constantly growing, changing, and adapting to new circumstances and new needs.

Rudolf Steiner gave Waldorf teachers an invaluable legacy: a picture of the developing human being, a curriculum that addresses the stages of development, and a way of teaching that engages the whole human being. But in every lecture cycle, and in all of his conferences and conversations with the first Waldorf teachers, Steiner exhorted teachers to reinvent the art of pedagogy and to make it their own. He challenged them to do their own research and to develop their own approach. He knew that Waldorf education would stagnate unless teachers become artists in education He knew that teachers need to continue to grow and change through their pedagogical practice. He knew that Waldorf education will not meet the needs of students unless teachers are willing to commit themselves to inner development.

Throughout my career as a Waldorf teacher, I have striven to meet these challenges. I have had countless questions about Steiner's view of child development, about the Waldorf curriculum, and about Waldorf methods. I have attempted to find answers to these questions by delving deeply into Steiner's work and by collaborating with my colleagues in the Waldorf movement. Sometimes Rudolf Steiner's words proved immediately useful. Sometimes my colleagues had valuable ideas or advice. Most of the time, however, the answers to my questions became clearer only over time. Born out of reflection and meditation, tempered by experience, what arose in me went beyond answers. Truth emerged when I was ready to perceive it.

My attempt to come to terms with Steiner's ideas mirrors what has occurred in Waldorf education during the past eight decades. In Waldorf schools and in Waldorf teacher training institutes throughout the world, Steiner's ideas are studied and continually reexamined in the light of experience. In every Waldorf classroom, Waldorf education is constantly being recreated to meet the needs of those particular students.

Waldorf schools have always faced political, economic, and cultural challenges. As the Waldorf movement has expanded, it has had to deal with important issues, such as how to work more successfully with children with learning difficulties; how to make Waldorf education more accessible and affordable; how to develop better relationships within and outside the Waldorf school community; how to broaden Waldorf education's Eurocentric foundations; how to articulate more clearly Waldorf education's relationship to religion; how to develop new approaches to working with technology; how to work more closely with other educational movements; and how to administrate Waldorf schools more effectively.

In the coming decades, Waldorf education will have to continue to grow and change to adapt to the needs of the time. As Waldorf teachers and parents grapple with new issues and work together to meet new challenges, it is essential that they also continue to strengthen the basis of Waldorf education, which is the work of Rudolf Steiner. Without Steiner's continued inspiration and guidance, this new art of education cannot succeed.

This book strives to strengthen the foundations of Waldorf education by providing an introduction to Rudolf Steiner's educational philosophy. I have selected these particular lectures, because I believe they are the clearest and most straightforward of his hundreds of lectures on education. The reader who works through these introductory lectures will be well prepared to delve into Steiner's more difficult and esoteric works on education.

Writing this book required a measure of selflessness that was sometimes hard to muster. I found it a constant challenge to keep my point of view in the background so that it did not interfere or detract from Steiner's words. How strange that the process of continually trying to put myself aside resulted in a deeper level of insight and a broader perspective!

Most people who ponder Rudolf Steiner's words and take them to heart find that they begin to develop new capacities of imagination, inspiration, and intuition. It is my sincere hope that all who read this book will discover some of the treasures that I discovered and that they will use these precious gifts for the good of all.

Roberto Trostli

ACKNOWLEDGEMENTS

I would like to thank the following people: Robert McDermott for inviting me to work on this project. His faith and confidence in me helped me to keep working at what often seemed an impossible task. Douglas Sloan for his encouragement and his thoughtful and careful editing. My students and colleagues, past and present, for teaching me what I needed to learn. And most of all, my wife Donna Marie. Without her love and support, this book would not have been possible.

INTRODUCTION

A Seed for the Future

In the early decades of this century a seed was planted that has borne much fruit. It was planted in faith and in hope: faith in human beings' capacity to transform themselves and society; hope for the future of humanity and of the Earth. Out of an impulse toward social renewal the first Waldorf School was founded.

Waldorf education has now spread throughout the world, and during the last few decades so many new Waldorf schools have been founded that it is becoming difficult to keep track of how many there are. Waldorf schools form the largest independent, nonsectarian school system in the world, with more than 120 schools in North America, over 600 schools worldwide, and an estimated enrollment of 70,000 students.

Although they share a common philosophy and methodology, each Waldorf school is truly independent—no central organization determines that a Waldorf school should be established in a particular town or city. Rather, a group of parents who desire a Waldorf education for their children work together for a period of years to establish a social and financial base that will support a school.

Waldorf schools usually begin as a nursery or kindergarten; when conditions are right, new classes are added year by year until the school reaches its full complement of eight or twelve grades. Given that every Waldorf school has been founded independently and has had to overcome both internal difficulties and external challenges, the rapid growth of Waldorf schools reveals the eagerness with which this form of education is being sought by parents throughout the world.

The First Waldorf School

The first Waldorf School was founded in 1919 in Stuttgart, Germany, by Emil Molt, the director of the Waldorf Astoria Cigarette Factory. Molt's decision to found a school grew out of his concern for the future of Germany and the other Central European countries that had been devastated by the First World War. In those countries that had suffered from the physical destruction of the war, that were afflicted by millions of war casualties and prostrated by fears of imminent economic and political upheaval, the future seemed to hold little promise. Molt recognized that hope for Central Europe lay not with those who had experienced the war but with the new generation of schoolchildren. If they could leave behind the old modes of thought that had proved inadequate for the modern world and develop new capacities, perhaps they would be able to forge a brighter future.

If these children were to develop capacities that would allow them to transform society, however, they would need to be taught in a new way—a way that addressed their essential humanity, that enhanced their concern for other people, and that fostered a sense of responsibility for the Earth. This new generation would need an education that would not only challenge them intellectually, but would cultivate their artistic and social abilities as well. Above all, they would need an education that would nurture the capacities that would allow them to adapt to a rapidly changing world. Emil Molt knew the man who could develop a form of education to meet these needs: Rudolf Steiner.

Rudolf Steiner

Born in 1861 in Austria, Rudolf Steiner attended the Technical University in Vienna, where he became interested in the scientific works of Johann Wolfgang von Goethe. As a young man, Steiner edited Goethe's scientific writings and earned his doctorate in philosophy. Steiner's first major work, *Intuitive Thinking As a Spiritual Path: A Philosophy of Freedom*, was published in 1894 and established the foundation for the world-view known as anthroposophy.

In the early decades of the twentieth century, Steiner became increasingly well known throughout Europe as an author and lecturer. He published over 50 books and gave approximately 6,000 lectures, later published in 300 volumes. Their subjects include philosophy, the evolution of consciousness, the sciences, the arts, and education.

In 1919, at Molt's request, Steiner established the first Waldorf school. He developed the curriculum, gave practical courses in pedagogy, and worked with the faculty of the school until his death in 1925. Because of its philosophical and spiritual foundations, its unique curriculum and innovative teaching methods, the original Waldorf School quickly grew, gaining international recognition and inspiring the establishment of new Waldorf schools in Europe and throughout the world.

Waldorf Education: Education for the Whole Human Being

Three salient features characterize the Waldorf approach to education:

1) Waldorf education is based on a developmental approach that addresses the changing needs of the growing child and maturing adolescent.
2) Waldorf teachers strive to transform education into an art that educates the whole child—the heart and the hands as well as the head.
3) Waldorf schools are committed to developing capacities as well as skills so that their students will become self-aware, compassionate individuals with a sense of responsibility for the Earth.

The Developmental Approach

In Steiner's view, the process of human development unfolds in cycles of approximately seven years each. The curriculum and methods of Waldorf education are based on the recognition that during each of these stages, children need forms of instruction and specific subjects and activities that will encourage healthy development.

The education of the young child is based on imitation and example. Because young children soak up impressions of all that surrounds them, Waldorf teachers strive to provide their students with examples that are worthy of imitation in a setting that is full of beauty. Young children live in a world of deeds; to them, play is work and work is play. The Waldorf kindergarten therefore offers a wonderful array of imaginative and practical activities that nourish the children's imaginations and strengthen their will.

Whereas young children learn primarily through imitation, children of elementary school age learn through their feelings for those who teach them. The education of these older children is therefore based on discipleship and authority, and they need teachers whom they love and trust. The curriculum and methods of the elementary school address the changes of the growing child by beginning with a more imaginative and experiential approach and slowly leading the children into the world of concepts and ideas. The arts play a prominent role throughout the elementary school years, for artistic work engages the students' feelings and develops their creativity.

The education of high school students is based on respect and freedom; adolescents need to be taught by teachers who are experts in their fields. The Waldorf high school offers a rich and rigorous academic curriculum as well as a wide range of artistic and practical subjects. Throughout their high school years, students are challenged to develop their thinking and they are inspired to apply themselves in the world in meaningful ways.

The Class Teacher

One of the unique elements in a Waldorf school is the class teacher, who remains with the class for a period of years, ideally from first through eighth grade. The class teacher teaches all the core academic subjects—language arts, mathematics, history, geography, and the sciences—as well as many of the artistic subjects—drawing, painting, sculpture, music, speech, and drama.

When people first encounter the idea of a class teacher they typically ask: "What if a child doesn't get along with the teacher?" or,

"How can one person teach all those subjects from first through eighth grade?" These are legitimate questions that deserve consideration, although it should be mentioned that most parents who have had children in a Waldorf school for a number of years have found their initial concerns to be unfounded.

Children enter elementary school with tremendous eagerness and with boundless faith in the individuals who stand before them. Young children usually feel a natural and deep connection with their teacher because the teacher stands as a representative of humanity who, day by day, will lead the class into ever wider explorations of the world. By their sincere interest in each child and their genuine enthusiasm for each subject, class teachers try to prove themselves worthy of the children's confidence and love.

Unfortunately, teachers are not always blessed with the gifts of love and trust that children display in such abundance. If teachers find that they do not naturally relate well to certain children, they have the duty to understand what lies behind their feelings. More than understanding is needed, however; class teachers are expected to work on such difficulties within themselves until they have transformed them. The fact that they will face these children every day for many years provides both a context and an incentive to pursue such inner work with vigor.

Children are remarkably perceptive; they respond to the special efforts teachers make to work on themselves and to rise above their shortcomings. The children themselves help teachers in their inner tasks; through the children's response, the teachers' feelings for them are transformed, and the resulting relationship is enriched. Many teachers experience an extraordinary bond to those children with whom they have had difficulties and for whom they have had to struggle within themselves. This bond grows out of the teachers' striving, out of their inner work, and out of a child's response to these efforts. In an age where relationships so easily dissolve for lack of commitment, children are strengthened by the knowledge that their class teacher loves them, will stand by them, and will accompany them on this part of their journey through life. Such knowledge gives children faith in the power of human relationships to endure.

Throughout the years, class teachers use every opportunity to develop in their students a sense of the unity and interconnectedness of the world of knowledge. Each subject is taught with reference to other subjects, and the connections between them are revealed and developed. Although they must work to attain a basic foundation of knowledge in all subjects, class teachers need not be specialists in every field. More than expertise, it is the teachers' interest in, and enthusiasm for, the subject that inspires their students. Many teachers find that the subjects with which they are the least familiar are the ones they teach most successfully, because through their own learning process a magical ingredient enters their teaching.

Class teaching demands the continuing education of the teacher. Class teachers must become mathematicians as well as musicians, poets as well as painters, sculptors as well as scientists. Few teachers have a natural aptitude for all of these subjects, and as they work to refine their skills, teachers demonstrate to the children that much can be achieved through dedicated effort. In a time of increasing specialization and narrowness, the class teacher stands as an example before the children, confirming the children's belief that the possibility of understanding the world is within their grasp.

The Waldorf Method: Education as an Art

In his work with the teachers of the first Waldorf school, Steiner challenged his colleagues to transform education into an art. To this day, Waldorf teachers strive to meet this challenge—to become artists in education who can educate the whole human being, addressing the spirit, soul, and body of the child.

What does it mean to be an artist in education? Is it different from being an artist in another field? One salient feature of artistry is that artists achieve such a mastery over their medium that they are left free to create and to serve as the means for what seeks to express itself. How does this apply to teachers? What is their medium? Just as musicians work with melody, harmony, and rhythm, and painters with light, color, and form, teachers work with the curriculum, with their pedagogical methods, and, most of all, with the children whom they strive to educate. Especially in the elementary school their method derives directly from art; teachers use the arts—verbal, pictorial, musical, dynamic, and plastic—to achieve what only art allows: a connection between the subject and object, a sense of communion engendered in the feeling life of the child.

The Main Lesson

The main lesson in a Waldorf school is one of the canvases upon which the process of education as a work of art can be rendered. Every day, students in the elementary school and high school begin their studies in a main lesson—a double academic period during which the same subject is studied for a block of three to six weeks. The main lesson allows a class to become thoroughly involved in a subject, for these lessons include a lively presentation, a review and discussion of the previous day's study, and work on academic and artistic projects. Subjects such as history, geography, and the sciences are usually taught in one or two main lesson blocks per year, while subjects needing regular practice, such as English and mathematics, are supplemented by weekly classes as well.

The main lesson exhibits, in a kernel, many aspects of the Waldorf approach to education. Do we not first become involved in a new activity or field because of our feelings—feelings of curiosity, attraction, interest, or awe? Everyone who has ever experienced a vocation, a calling to perform a significant task, will recognize that this call came, not from thought or deliberation, but from the life of the soul. Only after the stage when the feelings are aroused do people stop and think about what they have experienced. A second stage then begins, and we further develop our interest by thinking. When we decide to pursue an interest and to find out more about it, we may plan a line of inquiry or follow a course of study. This second stage leads us into a third stage of involvement—that of action. As soon as we begin to be active in a new interest, we begin truly to reap the fruits of our involvement.

This sequence of activities—the stimulation of feeling, the development of thoughts, the spur to activity—is a natural learning process. Teaching according to this sequence insures that children will thoroughly learn what is taught, and that their love for the process of learning is strengthened.

How does this sequence apply to a main lesson block in the elementary school? Take Roman history in the sixth grade as an example. The block might begin with the story of Aeneas. As the teacher tells this story, the students' imaginations are stirred and they form living pictures of Aeneas as he carries his old father, Anchises, out of the burning town. They listen in suspense as the Trojans' ships are driven across the oceans by violent storms, they mourn as Dido sacrifices herself for this most perfect of men, and they rejoice as Aeneas founds the settlement of New Troy. Now that their curiosity and interest are awakened, students are eager to hear what became of that settlement. As they study the seven kings of Rome, they begin to realize that each had a purpose to fulfill, each accomplished a great task that helped prepare Rome to assert its power as a mighty civilization. As the weeks progress, the students continue to be caught up in the mighty drama of the stories, but the element of thought now figures more prominently in their studies. For the sixth graders, it is not enough to hear about the lives and adventures of great men and women, they want to know more about the Roman civilization: how people lived, what they thought, and what their great culture achieved. .

Throughout the main lesson block, students work on a wide variety of projects. They may learn to recite poems in Latin or to draw perfect Roman capitals. They might write their own accounts of the stories of the kings and heroes in the form of narratives, letters, poems, or plays. Pictures are drawn to illustrate their written work, elephants sculpted to bring Hannibal's invasion to life. A meeting of the Roman Senate might be held to try a case, and with lofty gestures and high rhetoric the sixth graders try to appeal to their classmates' faculty of reason and their love of justice. By the end of a four-week main lesson block, the sixth graders will have experienced the essence of early Roman history, and because the main lesson block allowed them to become totally involved in the subject, what they learned will be remembered lovingly for many years to come.

Engaging the Whole Child: The Rhythms of Learning

In the individual main lesson classes, the larger sequence described for the block is repeated in brief. Every day the main lesson begins with a reverential morning verse, followed by singing, recitation, and concentration exercises to focus the children on the tasks ahead. Now the teacher makes a presentation. Having become thoroughly familiar with the subject, the teacher brings a myth, a biography, or a historical event to life; this awakens interest and amazement for the various geographic regions of the Earth. Awe and wonder are inspired by the teacher's descriptions and demonstrations of the natural world and the physical processes of the universe. Bringing a subject to life is akin to performing a concerto. Every note, every phrase and nuance must be studied in order to be forgotten when the performance actually takes place. During the actual presentation, the teacher must be free to create—words must take wing, so that the images invoked by the teacher in the students' minds will be vivid and true. This part of the lesson stirs the students' feelings and engages them directly in the material by speaking to their hearts.

If making a presentation is akin to performing a concerto, conducting a review and discussion on the following day demands even greater artistry and insight, for now one has to be free enough to improvise. In the review the teacher works with what the students learned from the presentation of the previous day; the teacher brings what was experienced through the feelings into the light of thinking. The students may have been touched by a particular element in a story, or by a specific facet of a science experiment. During the review the teacher listens to what the students are really asking and steers the discussion into realms that may not have been planned, but that are obviously right. Here the teacher's knowledge of the class bears fruit; if the teacher has observed the students carefully and knows their needs, these unplanned moments can be used to help children grapple with their deepest questions and most pressing concerns. Yet the subject must not get lost in digressions, for, like a mighty theme, the essence of the lesson must sound forth so that the class will develop clear concepts of the material they have studied.

The presentation and review take, at most, one half of the main lesson. What do the students do in the remaining time? They work, thereby experiencing the subjects on another level. Herein lies the key to Waldorf education: something that has stirred the feelings and stimulated thoughts must be transformed into another level of experience—into deeds. If they can be creative deeds, the child's experience will be enriched a hundredfold. In Waldorf schools the arts are not taught for their own sake, but because they allow a child to experience a subject on a far deeper, richer level than the intellectual one.

Class teachers are fortunate in having all the arts at their disposal to involve the children more deeply in a subject. They must, however, first have schooled themselves sufficiently in the arts so that they can lead the children toward artistic experience. They need not be experts at drawing, but they need to have experienced the dynamic power of line and form; they need not be theatrical directors, but they need to have developed beautiful, clear speech and gestures; they need not be consummate artists in any medium, but they need to have schooled their eye, ear, hand, and heart so that they can recognize the beautiful and help their students in their desire to achieve it. Artistic experiences usually leave lasting impressions in a student's life. Information can be gathered or retrieved, but the experience of the subjects through individual work and through the arts builds a foundation in the soul that will enrich all further learning and the whole of a student's life.

Through these methods, Waldorf teachers seek to transform teaching into an art. Yet the greater artistry lies in the transformation of the art of teaching into true education, into the schooling of capacities, into a preparation for life.

Developing Capacities: Education for the Future

Waldorf teachers consider it their responsibility to prepare children for life, but for which aspects of life do we seek to prepare them? Should we teach our students the skills needed in contemporary life or those that will be needed in the future?

We live in a time of rapid change. Dramatic advancements in technology—especially in the field of communications—have so rapidly altered our way of life that we seem to have less and less in common with our forebears. We can only speculate about how much more the world will change in coming generations. We can be certain, however, that children now in school will live in a world in which much of what we experience today will be obsolete. We cannot prepare them for entering a new age by teaching them only about this one. Rather, we must prepare students by nourishing in them capacities that can serve them in unimaginable situations of the future.

What capacities do Waldorf teachers strive to nourish and draw forth from their students? First and foremost, the teachers work to foster the capacity to think clearly, logically, and creatively, and they work to guide the child toward self-knowledge. Second, there is the hope of engendering the capacity to feel deeply, to be sensitive to the beauties, the joys, the sorrows of this world, to experience compassion for others. Finally, teachers attempt to cultivate the strength and willingness to act, to do what must be done, and to work not only for oneself, but for the benefit of all humanity and for the Earth.

The education of these capacities is achieved not only through our rich curriculum and our teaching methods, but also through the attitude with which we, as teachers, approach the process of education itself. From the descriptions above it should be clear that we perceive education as a process of inner growth promoted by students' relationships with their teachers and peers, their exposure to a rich curriculum, and their work in the arts and in practical life. Graduates of Waldorf schools overwhelmingly attest that the education they received made a vital difference in their lives. They report that this difference derived largely from the teachers' values, from the teachers' fundamental respect for the individuality of each child, and from the teachers' willingness to serve and meet the needs of each child.

An approach to education can be only as effective as the capacities and dedication of the individuals who practice it. The most profound philosophy, interesting curriculum, and innovative teaching methods cannot succeed if teachers are not working on themselves. Whether in the preschool, elementary school, or high school, Waldorf education succeeds because the teachers try, consciously and constantly, to develop themselves, to transform themselves into self-aware, compassionate individuals who can translate their ideas into ideals and their ideals into practice.

The rapid spread of Waldorf education in this century is more than a social fact: it is a testament to the power of an ideal and the striving of men and women who are working for the development of the human being, the transformation of society, and the renewal of the Earth.

References throughout the introductory essays of each chapter use the following abbreviations when referring to Rudolf Steiner's writings and lecture courses:

(ALT): *Anthroposophical Leading Thoughts*

(BT): *Balance in Teaching*

(CCC): *The Child's Changing Consciousness As the Basis of Pedagogical Practice*

(DT): *Discussions with Teachers*

Education as a Force for Social Change

(EA): *Education for Adolescents*

(EOTC): *The Education of the Child and Early Lectures on Education*

(FHE): *The Foundations of Human Experience* (also translated as *Study of Man*)

(GL): *The Genius of Language*

(HV): *Human Values in Education*

(KC): *The Kingdom of Childhood*

(LE): *A Lecture on Eurythmy*

(MA): *A Modern Art of Education*

(ES): *An Outline of Esoteric Science* (also translated as *An Outline of Occult Science*)

(PA): *Practical Advice to Teachers*

(RE) *The Renewal of Education*

(SE): *Soul Economy and Waldorf Education*

(SG): *The Spiritual Ground of Education*

(SWS): *The Spirit of the Waldorf School*

(TH): *Theosophy*

(WEA): *Waldorf Education and Anthroposophy*

1

THE
FOUNDATIONS
OF WALDORF
EDUCATION

THE FOUNDATIONS for Waldorf education were laid by Rudolf Steiner more than a decade before the opening of the first Waldorf school in Stuttgart, Germany, in 1919. In his first lectures on education, given in 1906 and published as "The Education of the Child in the Light of Spiritual Science," Steiner described a type of education that could address the child at each stage of development. Waldorf education is based on Steiner's philosophy, which is called *anthroposophy*, "the wisdom of the human being." Steiner characterized anthroposophy as "a path of knowledge to guide the Spiritual in the human being to the Spiritual in the universe" (ALT, p. 13). Through study, meditation, and spiritual research, anthroposophists seek to investigate the deepest aspects of life, of humanity, and of the universe. Anthroposophy is not only a means of uniting us with the spiritual. It must also be practical and capable of providing fruitful solutions to the questions of daily life. One of the most urgent questions is education.

An education that truly addresses the needs of the developing child must be based on a thorough understanding of the stages of human development. In "The Education of the Child in the Light of Spiritual Science," Steiner describes the nature of the human being, characterizes the different stages of child development, and indicates how one can educate the child at each these stages.

The opening sections of Steiner's essay outline the anthropo-sophical view of the nature of the human being. This view may be difficult to understand or accept at first, for it is based on both sensible and supersensible perception. Steiner did not expect what he said to be believed or taken on faith, but hoped instead that people would develop the spiritual faculties that would allow them to explore the higher worlds hidden to everyday consciousness and to corroborate—or revise—what he presented. While most of us cannot experience directly what Steiner discovered through clairvoyant consciousness, we can penetrate what he presented with our intellects, relate to it with our feelings, and corroborate it through our life experience.

The Nature of the Human Being

According to Steiner, the human being is composed of various "members" or "bodies." When we use the word "body," most of us refer to something corporeal, but Steiner also uses this word to refer to higher, nonphysical aspects of the human being. Of our four "bodies," only the physical body can be perceived by our senses. Our three higher "bodies"—the "etheric body," the "astral body," and the I, or I-being—are not physical. Their presence can be perceived and experienced only through their effects on our bodies and our souls.

The first member of the human being is the physical body, which is subject to the physical and chemical laws and processes that govern the mineral kingdom. Although we often refer to our flesh and bones and our muscles and organs as our "physical body," the physical body is hard to perceive as such, for the physical substances of our bodies are permeated and organized by life forces and organic processes. Only at death is the purely physical body revealed.

Steiner called the second member of the human being the etheric body. He also named this body the *life body*, or *body of formative forces*, because it is this body that enables plants, animals, and humans beings to live and grow. Steiner characterizes this body as follows:

Human beings have this etheric or life-body in common with plants and animals. The life-body works in a formative way on the substances and forces of the physical body and thus brings about the phenomena of growth, reproduction, and inner movement of vital body fluids. It is therefore the builder and shaper of the physical body, its inhabitant and architect. The physical body may even be spoken of as an image or expression of the life-body. (p. 16)

According to Steiner, the third member of the human being is the "astral" body. This body is also called the "sentient body," for it allows us to perceive sensations, to experience emotions, to be conscious. Plants do not have an astral or sentient body. Although they are affected by their environment, the responses of plants manifest on the etheric level in terms of metabolism, growth, or reproduction. The astral body not only allows animals and human beings to perceive and respond to the external world, it also gives them the possibility of experiencing another world, an inner world.

The fourth member of the human being is unique to our species. We have the astral body in common with the animals, the etheric body in common with plants and animals, and the physical body in common with minerals, plants, and animals, but we also have a body—the I—which is absent in these other kingdoms. The I allows us to be conscious of ourselves, to experience ourselves as individuals; it allows us to refer to ourselves by the word *I*.

This little word "I," as used in our language, is a name that differs from all other names. Appropriate reflection on the nature of this name opens up an approach to understanding human nature in a deeper sense. Any other name can be applied to the corresponding object by all of us in the same way. Everyone can call a table "table" and a chair "chair." But this is not true when it comes to the name "I." No one can use it to mean someone else; we can only call ourselves "I." (TH, p. 49)

The I is the imperishable drop of divinity that lives within each human being. It allows us to experience the divine in the world and in ourselves, and it is our means to fulfill our uniquely human task—to develop fully the qualities of freedom, love, and responsibility. In the hidden Holy of Holies of the soul resides "the God who ... begins to speak when the soul recognizes itself as an I." (ES, p. 46)

Child Development

Waldorf education is based upon the recognition that the four bodies of the human being develop and mature at different times. The physical, etheric, and astral bodies provide the foundations of our existence, but as they develop, the higher bodies increasingly provide the basis for psychological and intellectual processes, which Steiner called soul functions. As they develop, the etheric body will serve as the foundation for our thinking, the astral body for our life of feeling, and the I for our independent will.

In "The Education of the Child in the Light of Spiritual Science," Steiner describes how human beings experience several "births" during the course of their lives. Although the birth of the physical body is the most apparent to our sense-perception, the trained observer may also be able to perceive the birth of the higher bodies—the etheric body, the astral body, and the I.

Prior to the birth of the physical body, the fetus lives in the mother's womb, which protects and nourishes it. During gestation, the unborn child does not come into independent contact with the physical world. Only at birth will the world begin to act upon the newborn baby. Gestation is a time of the profoundest process of physical development; the transformation from a fertilized ovum to new-born baby is truly miraculous. After birth, the child's physical development continues more slowly and is also affected by the child's environment.

Just as the physical body first develops in the physical sheath of the womb, the etheric body develops within an etheric sheath. During this development, it is protected from external influences and follows its own laws. During this time it works upon the physical body, adapting and refining the body so that it can serve as an instrument of soul and spirit.

Throughout our lives, the etheric body is intimately related to the physical body. Its forces are responsible for growth, circulation, metabolism, and other essential processes. Around the age of seven, however, the etheric body is ready to be "born." With this birth, some of the etheric forces, which have hitherto performed physiological functions, become available for psychological functions. How can we recognize this birth? According to Steiner, one of the indicators of the birth or emancipation of the etheric body is the loss of the child's baby teeth, which takes place at the age of seven. Up to this age, the forces of the etheric body were working like a sculptor, shaping, refining, and adapting the body for life processes to occur. The development of the adult teeth signals that these forces are no longer needed for physical functions. Now they can become increasingly available for thinking, for remembering, and for forming concepts. As teachers, we call upon these etheric forces; we strive to nourish, to develop, and to refine them, so that our students will develop living thoughts.

The astral body, which is responsible for our life of feeling, remains in its protective sheath until around the age of fourteen; it is "born" at puberty. Until that time, children's feelings are deeply bound up with their physical organization. Love and hate, joy and sorrow, pleasure and pain, all affect the child's breathing, circulation, digestion, and other essential processes. When the astral body is emancipated, the forces that served the processes of perception, sensation, and emotion become available for a new faculty of understanding referred to by Steiner as "judgment." During the high school years, teachers will help students to develop their judgment so that they will not be ruled by their sympathies and antipathies, but can exercise discrimination in the best sense of the word.

The I, which allows us to experience and express ourselves, undergoes the longest period of gestation. It is "born" at around the age of twenty-one. Prior to that time, the I is still intimately bound up with the will, which is active in organic processes, especially in our limbs and our metabolic system. After twenty-one, the I begins to be emancipated. One sign of this emancipation is that our impulses no longer necessarily serve only our physical or emotional needs, but can and should serve a higher purpose. The birth of the I allows us to begin to take responsibility for self-development and to manifest our intentions, our ideals, and our moral impulses in the world.

The curriculum and methods of Waldorf education are based on the recognition of the stages of human development summarized above. In the second part of "The Education of the Child in the Light of Spiritual Science," Steiner gives practical indications of how parents and teachers can work most fruitfully with the growing child.

Educating the Child at Each Stage of Development

The Preschool

The womb provides a perfect environment for the development of the unborn child. After birth, it is our responsibility to provide an environment that will continue to support the child's healthy and harmonious physical, emotional, and spiritual development.

> Just as nature causes the proper environment for the physical human body before birth, so after birth the educator must provide for the proper physical environment. The right physical environment alone works on the child in such a way that the physical organs correctly shape themselves. (p. 25)

Not only are the physical organs influenced and shaped by the child's physical environment, but the foundations for a child's emotional and spiritual capacities are established by the actions, words, and thoughts to which the child is exposed. Young children are innately imitative beings, so one must work to create an environment that is truly worthy of imitation. Above all, the young child needs to be surrounded by warmth and love, for "children who live in such an atmosphere of love and warmth, and who have around them truly good examples to imitate, are living in their proper element" (p. 29).

In "The Education of the Child in the Light of Spiritual Science," Steiner gives a few practical examples of how to work with young children. He speaks about the kinds of toys that will develop the child's imagination and emphasizes the importance of developing healthy instincts for food. He describes the effects of colors on the child's mood and mentions the value of children's songs. Waldorf parents and kindergarten teachers have developed these indications. The fruit of their labors is a holistic approach to child rearing and early childhood education that is truly nourishing to the child's body, soul, and spirit.

Elementary School

During the elementary school years, once the etheric body has been "born," teachers strive to nourish the child's emancipated etheric forces. Rudolf Steiner writes:

> We must be very clear about what works on the etheric body from the outside. The formation and growth of the etheric body means the shaping and developing of inclinations and habits, of the conscience, character, memory, and temperament. (p. 29)

How can we strive to develop the child's character? While young children learn primarily through imitation and example, the elementary school-age child should be educated through authority. In Steiner's view, authority does not mean compulsion or force; children naturally accept the right kind of authority without question, because they love and are loved by the person whom they hold in high regard.

Because children at this age yearn for pictures, imaginations, and allegories, they also need to hear about the great men and women of other ages and cultures. Likewise, the secrets of nature and the laws underlying human existence can be revealed through parables that children in the lower grades will grasp first with their feelings and then in the later grades with their intellects. Rudolf Steiner states:

At this time in childhood all perception must be spiritual. We should not be satisfied, for example, with presenting a plant, a seed, a flower to children only as it is perceived with the senses. Everything should become a parable of the spiritual. In a grain of corn there is far more than meets the eye. There is a whole new plant invisible within it. Children must comprehend in a living way with their feeling and imagination that something like a seed has more within it than is sense-perceptible. They must divine through feeling the secrets of existence. (p. 37)

Another way to work with the etheric body during elementary school is to develop the child's memory through rhythm, repetition, and imagination. Because the intellect—with its capacity for critical analysis, for logical deduction, and for discriminating judgment—is only born at puberty, Waldorf teachers strive to help their students in the lower grades develop living pictures of all that they study.

Until puberty children should be storing in their memories the treasures of thought on which humankind has pondered; later intellectual understanding may penetrate what has already been well imprinted in memory during the earlier years. *It is necessary for human beings to remember not only what they already understand, but to come to understand what they already know.* (p. 36)

High School

In elementary school, Waldorf teachers work to develop and deepen the students' experience of all the subjects of the curriculum. In high school, teachers work to help students penetrate with understanding what the students themselves have experienced. If between the ages of seven and fourteen, the child's astral body is nourished and allowed to grow and develop according to its own laws and rhythms, then after puberty it can be used in the service of thought.

With puberty the time has arrived when human beings are ripe for the formation of their own judgments about what they have already learned. Nothing is more harmful to children than to awaken independent judgment too early. Human beings are not in a position to judge until they have collected material for judgment and comparison in their inner life. If they form their own conclusions before doing so, their conclusions will lack foundation. (p. 41)

The elementary school years should be devoted to the process of gathering material for judgment. Students are introduced to a vast range of subjects—language and literature, mathematics, the sciences, history, and geography—which they will experience primarily through their feelings and their wills. This is the best preparation for a more intellectual approach to these subjects in the high school.

Thought must take hold in a living way in children's minds so that they first learn and then judge. What the intellect has to say about any matter should only be said when all the other faculties of the soul have spoken. Before then the intellect only has an intermediary part to play; its task is to comprehend what occurs and what is experienced in feeling, to receive it exactly as it is, not letting unripened judgment immediately come in and take over. (p. 42)

In elementary school, when students have faith and trust in authority, they naturally respect and accept what others have thought. In the high school, when students become increasingly able to judge and evaluate what they have learned, they will become capable of developing their own insights.

Steiner once expressed the goal of Waldorf education as follows: "Our highest endeavor must be to develop free human beings, who are able, of themselves, to bring purpose and direction to their lives." By working with the natural stages of human development, by addressing the whole human being, by helping our students develop clarity of thought, balance in feeling, and conscience and initiative in action, Waldorf teachers worldwide work to achieve this goal.

A Seed for the Future

Spiritual science, when called on to build up an art of education, can indicate all these things in detail.... For spiritual science is realistic and not gray theory; it is something for life itself. (p. 28)

More than a decade passed before Steiner was called on to speak about all these things in detail. In 1919, Emil Molt, director of the Waldorf Astoria Cigarette Factory, asked Steiner to establish a school for the workers' children. During the last weeks of the summer, Steiner worked with the prospective teachers to deepen their understanding of human nature by describing the stages of child development, teaching them the most effective methods for working with each age, and outlining the curriculum. A vast educational movement has sprung up from the first seeds sowed by Steiner when he lectured and published his essay on the education of children. Although Steiner was to give more than three hundred lectures on education, the philosophical basis, the essence of the curriculum, and the fundamental methods of Waldorf education are contained in this seminal essay, "The Education of the Child in the Light of Spiritual Science."

The Education of the Child
in the Light of Spiritual Science

An essay by Rudolf Steiner; originally appeared in the journal
Lucifer-Gnosis, *1907; translated by George and Mary Adams.*

Humankind has inherited much from past generations that contemporary life calls into question; thus, the numerous "current crises" and "demands of our time." How many such matters occupy the world's attention—social questions, women's issues, various educational concerns, health debates, questions of human rights, and so on? Human beings endeavor to come to terms with these problems in the most varied ways. There are countless numbers of people who appear with some remedy or program to solve—or at least partially solve—one or another of them. In the process, all sorts and shades of opinions are asserted: extremism, which casts a revolutionary air; the moderates, full of respect for what exists, but trying to evolve something new from it; and the conservatives, up in arms whenever any of the old institutions are tampered with. Aside from these main tendencies of thought and feeling there are all kinds of positions in between.

Viewing such matters with deeper vision only leads one to feel—indeed the impression is forced upon us—that our contemporaries are in the position of trying to meet the demands of modern life with completely inadequate methods. Many try to reform life without really recognizing life's foundations. But those who make proposals for the future must not be satisfied with only a superficial knowledge of life. They must investigate its depths.

Life in its wholeness is like a plant. The plant contains more than what it offers to external life; it also holds a future condition within its hidden depths. One who views a newly leafing plant knows very well that eventually there will also be flowers and fruit on the leaf-bearing stem. The plant already contains in its hidden depths the flowers and fruit in embryo. Nevertheless, how can simple investigation of what the plant offers to immediate vision reveal what those new organs will look like? This can be told only by one who has come to recognize the very nature and being of the plant.

Likewise, the whole of human life also contains within it the seeds of its own future; but if we are to tell anything about this future, we must first penetrate the hidden nature of the human being. Our age is little inclined to do this, but instead concerns itself with what appears on the surface, and believes it is walking on unsure ground when asked to penetrate what escapes outer observation.

It is definitely simpler in the case of the plant; we know that others of its kind have repeatedly borne fruit. Human life is present only once. The flowers it will bear in the future have never been there before, yet they are present within a human being in the embryo, even as the flowers are present in a plant that is still only in leaf. And there is a possibility of saying something of humankind's future, if once we penetrate beneath the surface of human nature to its real essence and being. The various ideas of reform current in the present age can become fruitful and practical only when fertilized by this deep penetration into human life.

Spiritual science, by its inherent character and tendency, has the task of providing a practical concept of the world—one that comprehends the nature and essence of human life. Whether what often passes as such is justified is not the point; what concerns us here is the true essence of spiritual science, and what it can be by virtue of its true essence. For spiritual science is not intended as a theory that is remote from life, one that merely caters to human curiosity or thirst for knowledge. Nor is it intended as an instrument for a few people who for selfish reasons would like to attain a higher level of development for themselves. No, it can join and work at the most important tasks of modern people and further their development for the welfare of humankind.[1]

---

1. It should not be inferred that spiritual science is only concerned with the greater questions of life. Spiritual science, as expressed here, is destined to provide a basis for the solution of the greater questions of humankind.

It is true that in taking on this mission, spiritual science must be prepared to face all kinds of skepticism and opposition. Radicals, moderates, and conservatives in every sphere of life are bound to meet it with skepticism, because in its beginnings it will scarcely be in a position to please any party. Its promises are far beyond the sphere of party movements—being founded, in effect, purely and solely on a true knowledge and perception of life. If people have knowledge of life, it is only out of life itself that they can take up their tasks. They will not draw up programs arbitrarily, for they will know that the only fundamental laws of life that can prevail in the future are those that prevail already in the present. The spiritual investigator will therefore of necessity respect what exists. No matter how great the need they may find for improvement, they will not fail to see the embryo of the future within what already exists. At the same time they know that in everything "becoming" there must be growth and evolution. Thus they will perceive the seeds of transformation and of growth in the present. They will invent no programs, but read them from what is already there. What they read becomes in a certain sense the program itself, for it bears within it the essence of development. For this very reason a spiritual-scientific insight into the being of humankind must provide the most fruitful and the most practical means for the solution of the urgent questions of modern life.

In the following pages we shall endeavor to prove this in relation to one particular question: the question of education. We shall not set up demands nor programs, but simply describe child-nature. From the nature of the growing and evolving human being, the proper viewpoint for Education will, as it were, result spontaneously.

If we want to perceive the nature of the evolving human being, we must begin by considering hidden human nature as such. What

---

1. *(continued)* At the same time it is no less true that spiritual science can bring help to every individual person wherever they find themselves in life; it can be a source from which we may draw the answers to the most common questions, from which we may draw comfort, strength, confidence for life, and work. Spiritual science can give strength for meeting the great life problems, and just as surely also for meeting the immediate needs of the moment, even in the apparently least significant matters of daily life.

sense observation learns to know in human beings, and what the materialistic concept of life would consider as the only element in human beings, is for spiritual investigation only one part, one member of human nature: that is, the physical body. This human physical body is subject to the same laws of physical existence and is built up of the same substances and forces as the world as a whole, which is commonly referred to as lifeless. Spiritual science, therefore, designates that humankind has a physical body in common with all of the mineral kingdom. And it designates as the *physical body* only what, in human beings, are those substances that mix, combine, form, and dissolve through the same laws that also work in the substances within the mineral world.

Now beyond the physical body spiritual science recognizes a second essential principle in the human being. It is the *life-body*, or *etheric body*. The physicist need not take offense at the term *etheric body*. The word *ether* in this connection does not mean the same as the hypothetical ether of physics.[2] It must simply be taken as a designation for what will be described here and now. Recently it was considered highly unscientific to speak of such an etheric body, although this was not the situation at the end of the eighteenth and during the first half of the nineteenth century. In that earlier time people would say to themselves, "The substances and forces at work in a mineral cannot, by themselves, form the mineral into a living creature. There must also be a peculiar "force" inherent in the living creature. They called this the *vital force* and thought of it somewhat as follows: the vital force works in the plant, the animal, and the human body, and produces the phenomena of life, just as magnetic force is present in the magnet that produces the phenomena of attraction. In the succeeding period of materialism, this idea was dispensed with. People began to say that living creatures are built up in the same way as lifeless creation; that the same forces are at work in both the living organism and in the mineral; that the same

---

2. *Ether* was at that time hypothesized by physicists to occupy all of space beyond our atmosphere, and was thought to account for the source of electromagnetic radiation throughout space. — ED.

forces merely work in a more complicated way and build a more complex structure.

Today, however, it is only the most rigid materialists who hold on to this denial of a life-force, or vital force. There are a number of natural scientists and thinkers who have been taught by facts of life to assume the existence of something like a vital force or life-principle. Thus modern science in its later developments is in a certain sense approaching what spiritual science says about the life-body. There is, however, a very important difference. From sense-perceptible facts modern science assumes, through intellectual considerations or inflections, a kind of vital force. This is not the method of genuine spiritual investigation that spiritual science adopts and on the results of which it bases its statements. It cannot be emphasized too often how great the difference is in this respect between spiritual science and today's modern science. For modern science considers sense experiences to be the foundation for all knowledge. Anything that cannot be built on this foundation is taken to be unknowable. From the impressions of the senses it draws deductions and conclusions. What goes on beyond them is rejected as lying "beyond the frontiers of human knowledge."

From the standpoint of spiritual science, such a view is like that of a blind person who only acknowledges as valid what can be touched and the conclusions deduced from the world of touch—a blind person who rejects the statements of seeing people as lying beyond the possibility of human knowledge. Spiritual science shows that human beings are capable of evolution, capable of bringing new worlds within their sphere by developing new organs of perception. Color and light are all around those who are blind. If they cannot see these things it is simply because they lack the proper organs of perception. Similarly, spiritual science asserts that there are many worlds around human beings who can perceive them only if they develop the necessary organs. Just as a blind person who has undergone a successful operation looks out at a new world, so through the development of higher organs human beings can come to know new worlds—worlds totally different from what our ordinary senses allow us to perceive.

Now whether one who is blind in body can be operated on or not depends on the constitution of the organs. But the higher organs whereby one can penetrate into the higher worlds are present in the embryo of every human being. Anyone can develop these organs who has the patience, endurance, and energy to apply the methods described in *How to Know Higher Worlds: A Modern Path of Initiation.*[3]

Spiritual science, therefore, would never say that there are definite frontiers to human knowledge. What it would rather say is that for human beings those worlds exist for which they have the organs of perception. Thus spiritual science speaks only of the methods whereby existing frontiers may be extended; and this is its position in terms of the investigation of the life-body or etheric body, and of everything specified in the following pages as still higher members of human nature. Spiritual science acknowledges that only the physical body is accessible to investigation using the bodily senses; and, from the perspective of this kind of investigation it would be possible, at most, by intellectual deductions to surmise the existence of a higher body. At the same time it tells how it is possible to open up a world where these higher members of human nature emerge for the observer, just as the color and the light of things emerge after an operation in the case of a person born blind. For those who have developed the higher organs of perception, the etheric or life-body is an object of perception and not merely an intellectual deduction.

Human beings have this etheric or life-body in common with plants and animals. The life-body works in a formative way on the substances and forces of the physical body and thus brings about the phenomena of growth, reproduction, and inner movement of vital body fluids. It is therefore the builder and shaper of the physical body, its inhabitant and architect. The physical body may even be spoken of as an image or expression of the life-body. In human beings the two are nearly—though by no means totally—equal in form and size. However, in animals, and even more so in the plants,

---

3. Anthroposophic Press, Hudson, NY, 1994.

the etheric body is very different in both form and extension from the physical.

The third member of the human body is called the *sentient* or *astral body.* It is the vehicle of pain and pleasure, of impulse, craving, passion, and so on—all of which are absent in a creature that consists of only the physical and etheric bodies. These things may all be included in the term *sentient feeling,* or *sensation.* The plant has no sensation. If in our time some learned people see that plants will respond by movement or some other way to external stimulus and conclude that plants have a certain power of sensation, they only show their ignorance of what sensation is. The point is not whether the creature responds to an external stimulus but whether the stimulus is reflected in an inner process such as pain or pleasure, impulse, desire, and so on. Unless we stick to this criterion, we would be justified in saying that blue litmus-paper has a sensation of certain substances, because it turns red through contact with them.[4]

Humankind, therefore, has a sentient body in common with the animal kingdom only, and this sentient body is the vehicle of sensation or of sentient life.

We must not make the same mistake as certain theosophical circles and imagine that the etheric and sentient bodies consist simply of substances that are finer than those present in the physical body. That would be a materialistic concept of these higher members of

---

4. It is necessary to stress this point, because in our time there is a great need for clarity on such matters. Many people obscure the distinction between a plant and a sentient being, because they are not clear about the true nature of *sensation.* If a being or thing responds in some way to an external stimulus, it is not therefore justified to say that it has a sensation of the impression. It can only be said to have sensation if it *experiences* the impression in its *inner life*—that is, if there is a kind of inward reflection of the outer stimulus. The great advances of the natural sciences in our time—for which a true spiritual investigator has the highest admiration—have nevertheless caused a lack of clarity concerning higher concepts. Some biologists do not know what sensation is and thus ascribe it to a being that has none. What they understand by sensation may well be ascribed even to non-sentient beings. What spiritual science must understand by sensation is completely different.

human nature. The etheric body is a *force-form*; it consists of active forces, and not of matter. The astral or sentient body is a figure of inwardly moving, colored, and luminous pictures. The astral body deviates in both size and shape from the physical body. In human beings it presents an elongated ovoid form in which the physical and etheric bodies are embedded. It projects beyond them—a vivid, luminous figure—on every side.[5]

Human beings also possess a fourth member of their being, and this fourth member is shared with no other earthly creature. It is the vehicle of the *human I*, or self. The little word *I*—as used, for example, in the English language—is a name essentially different from any other name. To anyone who ponders rightly on the nature of this name, an approach to the perception of true human nature is opened up immediately. All other names can be applied equally by everyone to what they designate. Everyone can call a table "table," and everyone can call a chair "chair," but this is not true of the name "I." No one can use this name to designate another. Every human being can only call themselves "I"; the name "I" can never reach my ear as a description of myself. In designating oneself as I, one has to name oneself within oneself. Human beings who can say "I" to themselves are a world unto themselves. Those religions founded on spiritual knowledge have always had a feeling for this truth; hence they have said, "With the *I*, the *God*, who in lower creatures reveals himself only externally in the phenomena of the surrounding world, begins to speak internally. The vehicle of this faculty of saying "I," of the *I-faculty*, is the *body of the I*, the fourth member of the human being.[6]

---

5. A distinction must be made between human beings' experience of the sentient body within themselves and the perception of the sentient body by a skilled seer. What is referred to here is what is revealed of the sentient body to a developed spiritual eye.

6. The reader must not take offence at the expression "Body of the I." It is certainly not used in any grossly material sense. But in anthroposophical science there is no other possibility than to use the words of ordinary language; and as these are ordinarily applied to material things, they must, in their application to a spiritual science, first be translated into the spiritual.

This *body of the I* is the vehicle of the higher soul of humankind. With it human beings are the crown of all earthly creation. Now in human beings today the I is in no way simple in character. We may recognize its nature if we compare human beings at different stages of development. Look at an uneducated, so-called primitive person next to a typical European, or again compare the latter with a person of high ideals. They all have the faculty to say "I" of themselves; the body of the I is present in them all. But the so-called uneducated primitives, with their I, more easily follow passions, impulses, and cravings. The more highly formed Europeans say to themselves, I may follow certain impulses and desires, whereas others are held in check or suppressed altogether. Idealists have developed new impulses and new desires in addition to those originally present. All of this has taken place through the I working upon the other members of the human being. Indeed, this constitutes the special task of the I. Working outward from itself it has to ennoble and purify the other members of human nature.

In human beings who have reached beyond the condition where the external world first placed them, the lower members have changed to a greater or lesser degree under the influence of the I. When human beings are only beginning to rise above the animal, when their I is only just kindled, they are still like an animal insofar as the lower members of their being are concerned. The etheric or life-body is simply the vehicle of the formative forces of life, the forces of growth and reproduction. The sentient body gives expression only to those impulses, desires, and passions, which are stimulated by external nature. As human beings work their way up from this stage of development through successive lives or incarnations to higher and higher evolution, the I works upon the other members and transforms them. In this way the sentient body becomes the vehicle of purified sensations of pleasure and pain, refined wants and desires. And the etheric or life-body also becomes transformed. It becomes the vehicle of habits, of human beings' more permanent intent or tendency in life, of the temperament and memory. One whose I has not yet worked upon the life-body has no memory of experiences in life. One just lives out what has been implanted by Nature.

This is what the growth and development of civilization means for humanity. It is a continual working of the I on the lower members of human nature; this work penetrates all the way into the physical body. Under the influence of the I the whole appearance and physiognomy, the gestures and movements of the physical body, are altered. It is possible, moreover, to distinguish how the different ways of culture or civilization work on the various members of human nature. The ordinary factors of civilization work on the sentient body and permeate it with pleasures and pains, and with impulses and cravings that are different from what it had originally. Again, when a human being is absorbed in the contemplation of a great work of art the etheric body is being influenced. Through the work of art one divines something higher and more noble than is offered by the ordinary environment of the senses, and in this process one is forming and transforming the life-body. Religion is a powerful way to purify and ennoble the etheric body. Here is where the religious impulses have their tremendous purpose in human evolution.

What we call *conscience* is no more than the result of the I's work on the life-body through many incarnations. When people begin to perceive that they should not do one thing or another and when this perception makes a strong enough impression that the impression passes into the etheric body, conscience arises.

Now this work of the I on the lower members may be something that is either proper to the whole human race, or it may be entirely individual—an achievement of the individual I working on itself alone. In the former case the whole human race collaborates, as it were, in the transformation of the human being. The latter kind of transformation depends on the activity of the individual I alone, in and of itself. The I may become so strong that it transforms, through its very own power and strength, the sentient body. What the I then makes of the sentient or astral body is called *spirit-self* (or by the Eastern term, *manas*). This transformation is performed mainly through a process of learning, an enriching of one's inner life with higher ideas and perceptions.

The I can rise to an even higher task, one that belongs essentially to its own nature. This happens not only when the astral body is enriched but also when the etheric or life-body is transformed. People learn many things in the course of life, and if from some point we look back on our past, we can say to ourselves that we have learned much. But we can speak to a far lesser degree of a transformation in temperament or character during life, or of an improvement or deterioration in memory. Learning relates to the astral body, whereas the latter kinds of transformation relate to the etheric or life-body. It is thus not a happy image if we compare the astral body's degree of change during life with the progress of a clock's minute hand, and the transformation of the life-body with the hour hand's progress.

When people enter into a higher training—or *occult training*, as it is called—above all, it is important to take up this latter formation out of the I's very own power. Individually and with full consciousness, we have to work out the transformation of habits and temperament, character and memory; insofar as we work thus into the life-body, we transform it into what is called in spiritual-scientific terms, *life-spirit* (or, in the Eastern expression, *buddhi*).

At a still higher stage we come to acquire forces whereby we can work upon the physical body and transform it—transforming, for example, the circulation of the blood, the pulse. The amount of the physical body that is thus transformed becomes *spirit-body* (or, in the Eastern term, *atman*).

As a member of the whole human race or some section of it—for example, of a nation, tribe, or family—human beings also attain certain transformations of the lower parts of their nature. In spiritual science the results of this kind of transformation are known as the following: the astral or sentient body, transformed through the I, is called the *sentient soul*; the transformed etheric body is called the *intellectual soul*; and the transformed physical body the *spiritual soul*. We must not imagine that the transformations of these three members take place one after another in time. From the moment the I lights up, all three bodies undergo transformation simultaneously. Indeed, the work of the I does not become clearly perceptible to a person until a part of the spiritual soul has already been formed and developed.

......

From what has been said, it is clear that we may speak of four members of human nature: the *physical body*, the *etheric* or *life-body*, the *astral* or *sentient body*, and the *I-body*. The sentient soul, the intellectual soul, the spiritual soul, and beyond these the even higher members of human nature—spirit-self, life-self, spirit-human being—appear in connection with these four members as products of transformation. When speaking of the vehicles of human qualities, it is indeed only the first four members that are considered.

The educator works on these four members of the human being. Therefore, if we want to work in the right way we must investigate the nature of these parts of human beings. One must not imagine that they develop uniformly in human beings, so that at any given point in life—the moment of birth, for example—they are all equally developed; this is not the situation. Their development occurs differently in the different ages of a person's life. The correct foundation for education and for teaching involves a knowledge of these laws of development of human nature.

Before physical birth, growing human beings are surrounded by the physical body of another. They do not come into independent contact with the physical world. Their environment is the physical body of the mother, and it alone works on them as they grow and ripen. Indeed, physical birth consists in this: the physical mother-body, which has been as a protecting sheath, frees human beings, thus allowing the environment of the physical world to work thereafter directly on them. Their senses open to the external world, and in this way the external world gains an influence over human beings that was previously exercised by the physical envelope of the mother-body.

A spiritual understanding of the world, as represented by spiritual science, sees the birth of the physical body in this process, but not yet that of the etheric or life-body. Even as human beings are surrounded by the physical envelope of the mother-body until the moment of birth, so until the time of the change of teeth—until approximately the seventh year—they are surrounded by etheric and astral envelopes. It is only during the change of teeth that the etheric envelope liberates the etheric body. And an astral envelope remains until puberty when the astral or sentient body also becomes free on all sides, even as the physical body becomes free at physical birth and the etheric body at the change of teeth.[7]

Thus, spiritual science speaks of three births of human beings. Until the change of teeth certain impressions intended for the etheric body can no more reach it than the air and the struggle of the physical world can reach the physical body while it rests in the mother's womb.

Before the change of teeth occurs, the free life-body is not yet at work in human beings. Just as within the body of the mother the physical body receives forces not its own, gradually developing its own forces within the protecting sheath of the mother's womb, so also are the forces of growth until the change of teeth. During this first period the etheric body is only developing and shaping its own forces together with those—not its own—it has inherited. While the etheric body is thus working its way toward freedom, the physical body is already independent. The etheric body, as it liberates itself, develops and works out what it has to give to the physical body. The second teeth—that is, the person's own teeth—that take the place of those inherited, represent the culmination of this work. They are denser than anything else embedded in the physical body and thus appear last at the end of this period.

---

7. To argue that a child has memories before the change of teeth would indicate a misunderstanding of what is said here. We must understand that the etheric and astral bodies are present from the beginning; but they are within their protecting envelopes, which indeed allows the etheric body, for example, to evolve and manifest the qualities of memory very obviously before the change of teeth. Similarly, the physical eyes are also present before birth within the protecting envelope of the mother's womb and protected within the embryo. It is the same with the qualities carried by the astral body. Before the age of puberty one must nourish them while the astral body is still within a protecting envelope. It is one thing to nurture the inherent seeds of development in the astral body before puberty; it is another to expose after puberty the now independent astral body to influences in the outer world that it can receive and work on, unprotected by the surrounding envelope.

After this point the growth of the human physical body is brought about by one's own etheric body alone. But this etheric body is still under the influence of an astral body that has not yet escaped its protecting sheath. At the moment the astral body also becomes free, the etheric body concludes another period of its development; this conclusion is expressed in puberty. The organs of reproduction become independent because, from this time on, the astral body is free, no longer working inwardly, but openly and without its envelope, meeting the external world.

Just as the physical influences of the external world cannot influence the unborn child, so until the change of teeth one should not influence the etheric body with forces that are, for it, the same as the impressions of the physical environment are for the physical body. And in the astral body the corresponding influences should not be allowed influence until after puberty.

Vague and general phrases like "the harmonious development of all the powers and talents in the child," and so on, cannot provide the basis for a genuine art of education. A genuine art of education can only be built on true knowledge of human beings. Not that these phrases are incorrect, but basically they are as useless as saying about a machine that all its parts must be activated harmoniously. To work a machine you must approach it not with phrases and truisms but with real and detailed knowledge. Thus, what is important for the art of education is a knowledge of the members of the human being and of their various developments. We must know what part of the human being especially needs to be worked on at a certain age and how to work on it in the proper way. There is, of course, no doubt that a truly realistic art of education, such as that indicated here, will make its way slowly. This is, indeed, because of the whole mentality of our age, which will continue for a long time to consider facts of the spiritual world to be the empty talk of a wild imagination, while it takes vague and completely unreal phrases as the result of realistic thinking. Here, however, we shall describe unreservedly what will eventually come to be common knowledge, though many today might still consider it a figment of the imagination.

With physical birth the physical human body is exposed to the physical environment of the external world. Before birth it was surrounded by the protecting envelope of the mother's body. What the forces and fluids of the enveloping mother-body have done for it thus far, must from now on be done by the forces and benevolence of the external physical world. Before the change of teeth in the seventh year the human body has to accomplish a task on itself that is essentially different from the tasks of any other period of life. In this period the physical organs must form themselves into definite shapes; their whole structural nature must receive particular tendencies and directions. Growth takes place in later periods as well; but throughout the whole succeeding life growth is based on the forces developed in this first life-period. If true forms were developed, true forces would grow; if misshapen forms were developed, misshapen forms would grow. We can never repair what we have neglected as educators in the first seven years; just as nature causes the proper environment for the physical human body before birth, so after birth the educator must provide for the proper physical environment. The right physical environment alone works on the child in such a way that the physical organs correctly shape themselves.

Two "magic" words indicate how children enter into relationship with their environment. These words are *imitation* and *example*. The Greek philosopher Aristotle called human beings the most imitative of creatures. For no age in life is this truer than for the first stage of childhood, before the change of teeth. Children imitate what happens in their physical environment, and in this process of imitation their physical organs are cast in the forms that thus become permanent. "Physical environment" must, however, be understood in the widest sense imaginable. It includes not just what happens around children in the material sense, but everything that occurs in their environment—everything that can be perceived by their senses, that can work on the inner powers of children from the surrounding physical space. This includes all moral or immoral actions, all wise or foolish actions that children see.

It is not moralistic talk or wise admonitions that influence children in this sense, but it is, rather, what adults do visibly before their eyes. The effect of admonition is that it shapes the forms—not of the physical, but of the etheric body; and the etheric body, as we saw, is surrounded until the seventh year by a protecting etheric envelope, even as the physical body is surrounded before physical birth by the physical envelope of the mother-body. Everything that must evolve in the etheric body before the seventh year—ideas, habits, memory, and so on—all of this must develop "by itself," just as the eyes and ears develop within the mother-body without the influence of external light. The things that we read in Jean Paul's excellent educational work, *Levana* or *Science of Education*, is no doubt true. He says that travelers have learned more from their nurses in their first years of life than they will in all of their journeys around the world. Children, however, do not learn by instruction or admonition, but through imitation. The physical organs shape themselves through the influence of the physical environment. Good sight will be developed in children if their environment has the proper conditions of light and color, while in the brain and blood circulation the physical foundations will be laid for a healthy moral sense if children see moral actions in their environment. If before their seventh year children see only foolish actions in their surroundings, the brain will assume the forms that adapt it to foolishness in later life.

As the muscles of the hand grow firm and strong through doing the work for which they are suited, so the brain and other organs of the physical body of human beings are guided into the correct course of development if they receive the proper impressions from their environment. An example will best illustrate this point. You can make a doll for a child by folding up an old napkin, making two corners into legs, the other two corners into arms, a knot for the head, and painting eyes, nose, and mouth with blots of ink. Or you can buy the child what is called a "pretty" doll, with real hair and painted cheeks. We need not dwell on the fact that the "pretty" doll is of course hideous and apt to spoil the healthy aesthetic sense for a lifetime; for education, the main question is different. If the children have the folded napkin before them, they have to fill in from their own imagination what is necessary to make it real and human.

This work of the imagination shapes and builds the forms of the brain. The brain unfolds as the muscles of the hand unfold when they do the work they are suited for. By giving the child the so-called "pretty" doll, the brain has nothing more to do. Instead of unfolding, it becomes stunted and dried up. If people could look into the brain as a spiritual investigator can, and see how it builds its forms, they would certainly give their children only the toys that stimulate and enliven its formative activity. Toys with dead mathematical forms alone have a desolating and killing effect on the formative forces of children; on the other hand whatever kindles the imagination of living things works in the proper way. Our materialistic age produces few good toys. It is certainly a healthy toy, for example, that, with movable wooden figures, represents two smiths facing each other and hammering an anvil. These things can still be bought in rural areas. The picture books where the figures can be moved by pulling threads from below are also excellent and allow children themselves to transform a dead picture into a representation of living action. All of this causes a living mobility of the organs, and through such mobility the proper forms of the organs are built up.

Of course, these things can only be touched on here, but in the future, spiritual science will be called on to give the necessary indications in detail, which it is in a position to do. For it is not an empty abstraction, but a body of living facts that can provide guidelines for the conduct of life's realities.

A few more examples may be given. With regard to the environment, "nervous" children, that is, excitable children, should be treated differently from those who are quiet and lethargic. Everything comes into consideration, from the color of the room and the various objects that are generally around the child, to the color of the clothes they wear. One will often do the wrong thing if one does not take guidance from spiritual knowledge, for in many cases the materialistic idea will be the exact reverse of what is proper. Excitable children should be surrounded by and dressed in red or reddish-yellow colors, while lethargic children should be surrounded by blue or bluish-green shades of color. The important thing is the complementary color that is created within the child. In the case of red it is green, and in the case of blue, orange-yellow. This can be seen very easily by looking for awhile at a red or blue surface and then quickly looking at a white surface. The physical organs of the child create this contrary or complementary color, and this is what causes the corresponding organic structures that the child needs. If excitable children have a red color around them, they will inwardly create the opposite, the green; and this activity of creating green has a calming effect. The organs assume a tendency of calmness.

One thing must be thoroughly and fully recognized for this age in a child's life: the physical body creates its own scale of measurement for what is beneficial to it. It does this by properly developing craving and desire. Generally speaking, we may say that the healthy physical body desires what is good for it. In the growing human being, so long as it is the physical body that is important, we should pay the closest attention to what healthy, craving desire and delight require. Pleasure and delight are the forces that most properly enliven and call forth the organs' physical forms.

In this matter it is all too easy to do harm by failing to bring children into the proper physical relationship with their environment. This may happen especially in regard to their instincts for food. Children may be overfed with things that make them lose completely their healthy instinct for food, whereas by giving them the proper nourishment, the instinct can be preserved so that they always want what is wholesome for them under the circumstances, even a glass of water, and this works just as surely with what would do harm. Spiritual science, when called on to build up an art of education, can indicate all these things in detail, even specifying particular forms of food and nourishment. For spiritual science is realistic and not gray theory; it is something for life itself.

The joy of children in and with their environment must therefore be counted among the forces that build and shape the physical organs. They need teachers that look and act with happiness and, most of all, with honest unaffected love. Such a love that streams, as it were, with warmth through the physical environment of the children may be said to literally "hatch" the forms of the physical organs.

The children who live in such an atmosphere of love and warmth, and who have around them truly good examples to imitate, are living in their proper element. One should thus strictly guard against anything being done in the children's presence that they should not imitate. One should not do anything that one would then have to say to a child, "You should not do that." The strength of children's tendency to imitate can be recognized by observing how they paint and scribble written signs and letters long before they understand them. Indeed, it is good that they paint the letters first by imitation and only later learn to understand their meaning. For imitation belongs to the time when the physical body is developing, while meaning speaks to the etheric, and the etheric body should not be worked on until after the change of teeth, after the outer etheric envelope has fallen away. All learning associated with speech in these years should be especially through imitation. Children will best learn to speak through hearing; no rules or artificial instruction of any kind can be good for this.

It is important to realize the value of children's songs, for example, as a means of education in early childhood. They must make pretty and rhythmical impressions on the senses; the beauty of sound is of greater value than the meaning. The more alive the impression on eye and ear the better. Dancing movements in musical rhythm have a powerful influence in building up the physical organs, and this should also not be undervalued.

. . . . . .

With the change of teeth, when the etheric body lays aside its outer etheric envelop, the time begins when the etheric body can be worked on through external education. We must be very clear about what works on the etheric body from the outside. The formation and growth of the etheric body means the shaping and developing of inclinations and habits, of the conscience, character, memory, and temperament. The etheric body is worked on through pictures and examples—that is, through a child's carefully guided imagination. Just as before the age of seven we have to give the child the actual physical pattern to copy, so between the time of the change of teeth and puberty we must bring into the child's environment things that have the proper inner meaning and value. Growing children will now take guidance from the inner meaning and value of things. Whatever is filled with deep meaning that works through pictures and allegories is proper for these years. The etheric body will unfold its forces if a well-ordered imagination is allowed to take guidance from the inner meaning it discovers for itself in pictures and allegories—whether seen in real life or communicated to the mind. It is not abstract concepts that work in the right way on the growing etheric body, but rather what is seen and perceived—indeed, not with external senses, but with the mind's eye. Such seeing and perceiving is the proper means of education for these years.

For this reason it is most important that boys and girls should have for their teachers people who can awaken in them, as they observe them, the proper intellectual and moral powers. As *imitation* and *example* were, as it were, the magic words for education in the first years of childhood, for the years of this second period, the magic words are *discipleship* and *authority*. What children see directly in their educators with inner perception must, for them, become authority—not authority compelled by force, but authority that they accept naturally without question. Through this they will build up their conscience, habits, and inclinations. They will bring their temperament along an ordered path. They will look at things of the world through its eyes, as it were. The beautiful words of a poet who said, "Everyone must choose their heroes, in whose footsteps they will tread as they carve out their paths to the heights of Olympus," have special meaning during this time of life. Veneration and reverence are forces whereby the etheric body grows in the right way. If it were not possible during these years to look up to another person with unbounded reverence, one would have to suffer for this loss throughout all of later life. Where reverence is lacking, the living forces of the etheric body are stunted in their growth.

Picture to yourself how an incident such as the following works on the character of children. An eight-year-old boy hears of someone who is truly worthy of honor and respect. Everything he hears about him inspires holy awe in the boy. The day draws near when he will be able to see him for the first time. With trembling hand he lifts the latch of the door, behind which will appear before him, the person he reveres. The beautiful feelings that such an experience calls forth are among the lasting treasures of life. It is the happy person who, not only in the solemn moments of life but continually, can look up to one's teachers and educators as natural and unquestioned authorities.

Beside these living authorities who embody, as it were, intellectual and moral strength for children, there should also be those they can only apprehend with the mind and spirit, who likewise become their authorities. The outstanding people of history, life stories of great men and women—allow these to determine the conscience and the direction of the mind. Abstract moral maxims are not useful yet; they can only begin to have a beneficial influence when, at the age of puberty, the astral body liberates itself from its astral mother-envelope.

Especially in history lessons, teachers should direct their teaching as indicated. When telling all kinds of stories to little children before their change of teeth, our aim cannot be more than to awaken delight, liveliness, and a happy enjoyment of the story. But after the change of teeth we have to remember something else in selecting material for stories—that is, that we are placing before boys and girls pictures of life that will arouse a spirit of emulation in the soul.

It should not be overlooked that bad habits may be overcome completely by pointing to appropriate examples that shock or repel the child. Reprimands give but little help, at best, in the matter of habits and inclinations. If, however, we show the living picture of a person who has given way to a similar bad habit and allow the child to see where such an inclination actually leads, this will work on the young imagination and go a long way toward uprooting the habit. One fact must always be remembered—that abstract ideas do not influence the developing etheric body but rather, living pictures that are seen and comprehended inwardly. The suggestion that has just been made certainly needs to be carried out with great tact so that the effect is not reversed and results in the very opposite of what was intended. When telling stories everything depends on the art of telling. Word-of-mouth narration cannot, therefore, simply be replaced by reading.

In another connection, for the period between the change of teeth and puberty, it is important to present living pictures—or symbols, as it were—to the mind. It is essential that the secrets of nature, the laws of life, be taught to children, not in dry intellectual concepts, but as far as possible in symbols. Parables of the spiritual connections of things should be brought before the souls of children in such a way that behind the parables they divine and feel, rather than understand intellectually, the underlying law in all existence. "Everything passing is but a parable," must be the maxim guiding all of our education during this time. It is of vast importance for children that they receive the secrets of nature in parables before they are brought before their souls as "natural laws" and so on. An example may serve to make this clear. Let us imagine that we want to tell a child of the immortality of the soul, of the coming forth of the soul from the body. The way to do this is to use a comparison—for example, the butterfly coming out of the chrysalis. As the butterfly soars up from the chrysalis, so after death the human soul comes forth from the house of the body. No one can properly understand this fact in intellectual concepts who has not first received it through such a picture. By a parable such as this we speak not just to the intellect but to the feelings of children, to their whole soul. Children who have experienced this will approach the subject with a completely different mood of soul when later it is taught to them in the form of intellectual concepts. It is a very serious matter indeed for anyone who is not first given the ability to approach the problems of existence through feeling. It is therefore essential that educators have at their disposal parables for all the laws of nature and secrets of the world.

Here we have an excellent opportunity to observe the effects that spiritual-scientific knowledge works to affect in life and practice. When teachers come before their children in class, ready with the parables they "made up" out of an intellectual materialistic way of thinking, in general, they will make little impression upon them, for teachers first have to puzzle out the parables for themselves with all their intellectual cleverness. Parables that first have to be condescended to have no convincing effect on those who listen to them. When one speaks in parables and pictures, it is not just what is spoken and shown that works on the hearer, but a fine spiritual stream that passes from the one to the other, from the one who gives to the one who receives. If the one who tells does not have the warm feeling of belief in the parable, no impression will be made on the other. For true effectiveness, it is essential to believe in one's parables as one does in absolute realities. And this can only be so when one's thought is alive with spiritual knowledge. Take, for example, the parable we have been speaking of. True students of spiritual science need not torment themselves to get it out. For them it is reality. In the coming forth of the butterfly from the chrysalis they see at work, on a lower level of being, the very same process that is repeated, on a higher level, at a higher stage of development, when the soul comes forth from the body. They believe in it with all their might; and this belief streams, as it were, unseen from speaker to hearer, carrying conviction. Life flows freely, unhindered, back and forth from teacher to pupil. But for this it is necessary that teachers draw from the full fountain of spiritual knowledge. Their words, everything that comes from them, must have feeling, warmth, and color from a truly spiritual-scientific way of thought.

A wonderful prospect is thus opened throughout the field of education. If it will only let itself be enriched from the well of life that spiritual science contains, education will also be filled with life and understanding. There will no longer be the groping so prevalent now. All art and practice of education that does not continually receive fresh nourishment from roots such as these is dry and dead. The spiritual-scientific knowledge has appropriate parables for all the secrets of the world—pictures taken from the very being of the things, pictures not first made by human beings, but put in place by the forces of the world within things themselves, through the very act of their creation. Therefore this spiritual knowledge must form the living basis for the whole art of education.

A force of soul that has particular value for this period of human development is memory. The development of the memory is connected with the shaping of the etheric body. Since this shaping occurs so that the etheric body becomes liberated between the change of teeth and puberty, so this is also the time for conscious attention from outside toward the growth and cultivation of the memory. If what is due to human beings at this time has been neglected, their memory will always have less value than it would have had otherwise. It is not possible to make up for later what was left undone.

In this connection many mistakes can be made through an intellectual, materialistic way of thinking. An art of education based on such a way of thought easily arrives at a condemnation of what is mastered simply by memory. It will often place itself untiringly and emphatically against the mere memory training, and will employ the subtlest methods to ensure that children commit nothing to memory that they do not intellectually understand. Yes, and after all, how much has really been gained by such intellectual understanding? A materialistic way of thought is so easily led to believe that any further penetration into things beyond intellectual concepts that are, as it were, extracted from them, simply does not exist; only with great difficulty will it fight its way through to the perception that other forces of the soul are at least as necessary as the intellect to comprehend things. It is no mere figure of speech to say that people can understand with their feeling, their sentiment, their inner disposition, as well as with their intellect. Intellectual concepts are only one way we have for understanding things of this world, and only to the materialistic thinker do they appear as the sole means. Of course there are many who do not consider themselves materialists, who nevertheless consider an intellectual conception of things to be the only kind of understanding. Such people perhaps profess an idealistic or even spiritual outlook. But in their souls they relate themselves to it in a materialistic way, for the intellect is in effect the soul's instrument for understanding what is material.

We have already alluded to Jean Paul's excellent book on education; a passage from it relating to this subject of the deeper foundations of the understanding may well be quoted here. Indeed, Jean Paul's book contains many golden words on education, and deserves far more attention than it has received. It is of greater value for the teacher than many of the educational works currently held in highest regard. One passage follows:

Have no fear of going beyond the childish understanding, even in whole sentences. Your expression and the tone of your voice, aided by the child's intuitive eagerness to understand, will light up half the meaning and with it, in the course of time, the other half. With children as with the Chinese and people of refinement, the tone is half the language. Remember, children learn to understand their own language before they ever learn to speak it, just as we do with Greek or any other foreign language. Trust to time and the connections of things to unravel the meaning. A child of five understands the words "yet," "even," "of course," and "just." But now try to explain these—not just to the child, but to the father! In the one word "of" there lurks a little philosopher! If an eight-year-old child with developed speech is understood by a child of three, why do you want to narrow your language to the little one's childish prattle? Always speak to a child some years ahead—do not those of genius speak to us centuries ahead in books? Talk to one-year-olds as if they were two, to two-year-olds as if they were six, for the difference in development diminishes in inverse ratio with age. We are far too prone to credit teachers with all that children learn. We should remember that the children whom we have to educate bear half their world within them, all there and ready-taught—that is, the spiritual half, including, for example, the moral and metaphysical ideas. For this very reason, language, equipped as it is with material images alone, cannot give the spiritual archetypes; all it can do is to illumine them. The very brightness and decisiveness of children should give us brightness and decisiveness when we speak to them. We can learn from their speech as well as teach them through our own. Their word-building is bold, yet remarkably accurate! For example, I have heard the following expressions used by children three or four: "the barreler" (for the maker of barrels); "the sky-mouse" (for the bat); "I am the looking-through person" (standing behind a telescope); "I'd like to be a gingerbread eater"; "he joked me down from the chair"; "see how one o'clock it is?"

It's true that our quotation refers to something other than our immediate subject; but what Jean Paul says about speech has its value in the present connection also. Here there is also an understanding that precedes intellectual comprehension. Little children receive the structure of language into the living organism of their souls and, for this process, do not require the laws of language formation in intellectual concepts. Similarly, for the cultivation of the memory, older children must learn much that they cannot master with their intellectual understanding until years later. Those things are afterward best apprehended in concepts that have first been learned simply from memory during this period of life, just as the rules of language are best learned in a language one can already speak. So much talk against "mindless rote learning" is simply materialistic prejudice. Children, for example, only need to learn the essential rules of multiplication in a few given examples, for which no apparatus is necessary—the fingers are much better for the purpose than any apparatus—they are then ready to get to work and memorize the whole multiplication table. Proceeding in this way, we shall be acting with due regard for growing children's nature. However, we shall be offending against their nature if, at the time when the development of the memory is the important thing, we are calling too much on the intellect.

The intellect is a soul-force only born with puberty, and we should not try to influence it in any way externally before this time. Until puberty children should be storing in their memories the treasures of thought on which humankind has pondered; later intellectual understanding may penetrate what has already been well imprinted in memory during the earlier years. *It is necessary for human beings to remember not only what they already understand, but to come to understand what they already know*—that is, what they have acquired by memory in the way the child acquires language. This truth has a wide application. First there must be an assimilation of historical events through the memory, then the apprehension of them in intellectual concepts; first the faithful commitment to memory of geographical facts and then an intellectual understanding of the connections between them. In a certain sense, understanding things through concepts should proceed from the stored-up treasures of the memory. The more children know in memory before they begin to understand through intellectual concepts the better.

There is no need to emphasize the fact that these things apply only to the period of childhood we are concerned with here, and not later. If at some later age in life one has occasion to take up a subject for any reason, then of course the opposite may easily be the correct and most useful way of learning it, though even here much will depend on the mentality of the person. During the time of life we are now concerned with, however, we must not dry up a child's mind and spirit by filling it with intellectual conceptions.

Another result of materialistic thinking may be seen in the lessons that are based too exclusively on sense-perception. At this time in childhood all perception must be spiritual. We should not be satisfied, for example, with presenting a plant, a seed, a flower to children only as it is perceived with the senses. Everything should become a parable of the spiritual. In a grain of corn there is far more than meets the eye. There is a whole new plant invisible within it. Children must comprehend in a living way with their feeling and imagination that something like a seed has more within it than is sense-perceptible. They must divine through feeling the secrets of existence. One cannot object that pure perception of the senses is obscured in this way—on the contrary, by going no further than what the senses observe, we stop short of the whole truth. For full reality consists of the spirit as well as the substance, and there is no less need for faithful and careful observation when bringing all the faculties of the soul into play, than when only the physical faculties are employed. If people could only see, as the spiritual investigator sees, the desolation achieved in soul and body by instruction based on external perception alone, they would never insist on it as strongly as they do. In the highest sense, what good is it that children have been shown all possible varieties of minerals, plants, and animals, and all kinds of physical experiments, if nothing further is connected with teaching these things—that is, to make use of the parables that the world offers to awaken a feeling for the secrets of the spirit?

Certainly a materialistic way of thinking has little use for what has been said here, and spiritual investigators understand this all too well. But they also know that the materialistic way of thought will never produce a truly practical art of education. As practical as it appears to itself, materialistic thinking is impractical when what is needed is to enter into life in a living way. In the face of reality, materialistic thought is fantastic—although, indeed, to a materialistic thinker spiritual-scientific teachings, adhering as they do to the facts of life, can only appear fantastic. There will no doubt be many obstacles yet to overcome before the principles of spiritual science—which are, in fact, born from life itself—can make their way into the art of education. It cannot be otherwise. At the present time the truths of this spiritual science can only seem strange to many people. Nevertheless, if they are indeed true, they will become part of our life and civilization.

· · · · · ·

Teachers can have the tact to meet any occasion that arises only when they have a conscious and clear understanding of how various subjects and methods of education work in the proper way on growing children. They have to know how to treat the various faculties of the soul—thinking, feeling, and willing—so that their development can react on the etheric body, which during this time between the change of teeth and puberty can attain more and more perfect form under external influences.

By a proper application of fundamental educational principles during the first seven years of childhood, the foundation is laid for the development of a strong and healthy *will*; for a strong and healthy will must have its support in well-developed forms of the physical body. Then, from the change of teeth on, the etheric body that is now developing must bring to the physical body the forces whereby it can make its forms firm and inwardly complete. Whatever makes the strongest impression on the etheric body also works most powerfully toward consolidating the physical body. The strongest of all the impulses that can work on the etheric body come from the feelings and thoughts through which human beings consciously divine and experience their relationship to the Eternal Powers—that is, they come from religious experience. Never will a person's will— nor as a result a person's character—develop in a healthy way, if one cannot during this period of childhood receive religious impulses deep into the soul. How people feel their place and part in the universal whole will be expressed in the unity of their life of will. If they do not feel linked with strong bonds to a divine-spiritual, their will and character must remain uncertain, divided, and unsound.

The world of *feeling* is developed in the proper way through parables and pictures, which we have spoken of, and especially through the pictures of great men and women, taken from history and other sources and brought before children. A correspondingly deep study of the secrets and beauties of nature is also important for the proper formation of the world of feeling. Last but not least, there is the cultivation of a sense of beauty and the awakening of the artistic feeling. The musical element must bring to the etheric body the rhythm that will then enable it to sense in everything the rhythm otherwise concealed. Children who are denied the blessing of having their musical sense cultivated during these years will be the poorer because of it for the rest of their lives. If this sense were entirely lacking, whole aspects of the world's existence would necessarily remain hidden, nor should the other arts be neglected. The awakening of the feeling for architectural forms, for molding and sculpting, for line and design, for color harmonies—none of these should be left out of the plan of education. No matter how simple life must be under certain circumstances, the objection can never be valid that the situation does not allow something to be done in this way. Much can be done with the simplest resources, if only the teacher has the proper artistic feeling, joy, and happiness in living, a love of all existence, a power and energy for work—these are among the lifelong results of the proper cultivation of a feeling for beauty and art. The relationship of person to person—how noble, how beautiful it becomes under this influence! Again, the moral sense is also being formed in children during these years through the pictures of life placed before them, through the authorities whom they look up to—this moral sense becomes assured if children, from their own sense of beauty, feel that the good is beautiful, and also that the bad is ugly.

Thought in its proper form, as an inner life lived in abstract concepts, must still remain in the background during this period of childhood. It must develop of itself, as it were, without external influences, while life and the secrets of nature are being unfolded in parable and picture. Thus between the seventh year and puberty, thought must be growing, the faculty of judgment ripening, in among the other experiences of the soul; so that after puberty is reached, young people may be able to form independently their own opinions about the things of life and knowledge. The less direct the influence is on the development of judgment in earlier years, and the more a good indirect influence is exercised through the development of the other faculties of soul, the better it is for all of later life.

Spiritual-scientific insights afford the true foundations, not just for spiritual and mental education, but also for physical education. This can be illustrated by referring to children's games and gymnastic exercises. Just as love and joy should permeate children's surroundings in the earliest years of life, so through physical exercises the growing etheric body should experience an inner feeling of its own growth, of its continually increasing strength. Gymnastic exercises, for example, should be such that each movement, each step, gives rise to the feeling within a child: "I feel growing strength within me." This feeling must take hold in the child as a healthy sense of inner happiness and ease. To think out gymnastic exercises from this perspective requires more than intellectual knowledge of human anatomy and physiology. It requires an intimate intuitive knowledge of the connection between a sense of happiness and an ease of positions and movements of the human body—a knowledge that is not merely intellectual, but permeated with feeling. Those who arrange such exercises must be able to experience in themselves how one movement and position of the limbs produces a happy and easy feeling of strength, while another, as it were, an inner loss of strength. To teach gymnastics and other physical exercises with these things in mind, the teacher will need what only spiritual science—the spiritual-scientific habit of mind—can give. They do not need to see directly into the spiritual worlds themselves, but they must have the understanding to apply in life what springs only from spiritual knowledge. If the knowledge of spiritual science were applied in practical spheres such as education, the idle talk that such knowledge has to be proved first would quickly disappear. Those who apply it correctly will find that the knowledge of spiritual science proves itself in life by making life strong and healthy. They will see it is true because it is valid in life and practice, and in this they will find a proof stronger than all the logical, so-called scientific arguments can afford. Spiritual truths are best recognized in their fruits and not by what is called a proof, no matter how scientific; indeed, such proof can never be more than logical skirmishing.

At the age of puberty the astral body is first born. Henceforth the astral body in its development is open to the outside world. Therefore, now we can approach the child only from the outside, with everything that opens up the world of abstract ideas, the faculty of judgment, and independent thought. It has already been pointed out how, until this time, these faculties of soul should be developing free from outer influence within the environment provided by the education that is proper to the earlier years, even as the eyes and ears develop free from outer influence within the organism of the mother. With puberty the time has arrived when human beings are ripe for the formation of their own judgments about what they have already learned. Nothing is more harmful to children than to awaken independent judgment too early. Human beings are not in a position to judge until they have collected material for judgment and comparison in their inner life. If they form their own conclusions before doing so, their conclusions will lack foundation. Educational mistakes of this kind are the cause of all narrow one-sidedness in life, and all barren creeds based on a few scraps of knowledge, ready on this basis to condemn ideas experienced and proven by humankind often throughout long ages.

One's ripeness for thought requires that one has learned to be full of respect for what others have thought. There is no healthy thought that has not been preceded by a healthy feeling for the truth, a feeling for the truth supported by faith in authorities accepted naturally. If this principle were observed in education there would no longer be as many people who all too quickly imagine themselves ripe for judgment, and spoil their own power to receive openly and without bias the general impressions of life. Every judgment that is not built on a sufficient foundation of gathered knowledge and experience of soul throws a stumbling block in the way of those who form it. For having once pronounced a judgment on a matter, we are thereafter influenced by this judgment. We no longer receive the new experiences we would if we had not already formed a judgment about it. Thought must take hold in a living way in children's minds so that they first learn and then judge. What the intellect has to say about any matter should only be said when all the other faculties of the soul have spoken. Before then the intellect only has an intermediary part to play; its task is to comprehend what occurs and what is experienced in feeling, to receive it exactly as it is, not letting unripened judgment immediately come in and take over. For this reason, until puberty children should be spared all theories about things; the main consideration is that they should simply meet the experiences of life, receiving them into their souls. Certainly they can be told what various people have thought about this and that, but exercises of judgment, too early, about one view or another must be avoided. Thus, children should receive people's opinions with the feeling power of the soul. Without jumping to a conclusion or taking sides with this or that person, they should be able to listen to all, saying to themselves: "So and so said this, and another said that." The cultivation of such a mind in a boy or girl certainly demands the exercise of great tact from teachers and educators; but tact is just what spiritual-scientific thought offers.

All we have been able to do is to unfold a few aspects of education in the light of spiritual science. And this alone was our intention—to indicate how great the task is that the impulse of spiritual-science must fulfill in education for the culture of our time. Its power to fulfill the task will depend on the spread of an understanding for this way of thinking in wider and wider circles. For this to happen, however, two things are necessary. First, people should relinquish their prejudices against spiritual science. Anyone who honestly pursues it will soon see that it is not the fantastic nonsense that many today consider it to be. We are not making any reproach against those who hold this opinion; for everything that the culture of our time offers tends, on a first acquaintance, to make one consider the adherents of spiritual science to be fantastic dreamers. Superficial consideration can reach no other judgment, for in the light of it, spiritual science with its claim to be a science of the spirit will appear to be in direct contradiction to everything that modern culture gives to humankind as the foundation of a healthy view of life. Only a deeper consideration will reveal that the views of the present day are in themselves deeply contradictory and will remain so as long as they are without a spiritual-scientific foundation. Indeed, by their very nature they call out for such a foundation and cannot in the long run exist without it.

The second thing that is needed concerns the healthy cultivation of spiritual science itself. Only when it is perceived in spiritual-scientific circles everywhere that the point is not merely to theorize about the teachings, but to let them bear fruit in the most far-reaching way in all the relationships of life—only then will life itself open up to spiritual science with sympathy and understanding. Otherwise people will continue to consider it a variety of religious sectarianism for a few cranks and enthusiasts. If, however, it performs positive and useful spiritual work, the spiritual science movement cannot in the long run be denied intelligent recognition.

2

TEACHER
AND CHILD

The Temperaments: A Key to Understanding Human Nature

THE PRIMARY TASK of a Waldorf teacher is to understand the
human being in body, soul, and spirit. From this understanding will
grow the approach, the curriculum, and the methods of an education capable of addressing the whole child. How can teachers
develop this understanding? In lecture six of *Human Values in Education*, Rudolf Steiner states:

> Where is the book in which the teacher can read about what
> teaching is? The children themselves are this book. We
> should not learn to teach out of any book other than the one
> lying open before us and consisting of the children them-
> selves. In order to read in this book, however, we need the
> widest possible interest in each individual child, and nothing
> must divert us from this. (p. 116)

Teachers who develop this kind of interest will begin to decipher
the script of human nature. A tool that can help us in that process
is the knowledge of the temperaments. Few people today refer to
the temperaments, for modern psychology has developed other
ways of viewing personality types. In classical and medieval times,
however, the system of the temperaments was widely known, and
human beings were classified as sanguine, phlegmatic, melancholic,
or choleric according to the predominance of one of four essential
fluids, or "humors." These humors—*blood, phlegm, bile,* and *gall*—

were thought to determine a person's constitution, disposition, and behavior. In the early years of this century, Steiner reclaimed, expanded, and refined this view of the temperaments, and he presented the results of his research in a number of lectures, two of which are included in this chapter.

According to Steiner, our lives are the confluence of two streams: the stream of the past and the stream of the future. The stream of the past is connected with a person's family and therefore with the forces of heredity. This stream is expressed primarily by the physical and etheric bodies. The stream of the future is connected with a person's individuality and with destiny; these find their expression through the astral body and the I. Our temperament mediates between these two streams; it allows us to reconcile our hereditary characteristics with our destiny. In "The Four Temperaments," Steiner states:

> Temperament stands between the things that connect a human being to an ancestral line, and those the human being brings out of earlier incarnations. Temperament strikes a balance between the eternal and the ephemeral. And it does so in such a way that the essential members of the human being ... enter into a very specific relationship with one another. (p. 58)

In the anthroposophic view, each of the four members of our being fulfills both physiological and psychological functions, depending on our age and stage of development. The member of our being that predominates determines the physical and emotional tendencies that form the foundation for our temperament.

In "The Four Temperaments," Steiner describes the basis for the temperaments in an adult: if the physical body predominates, a person will have a melancholic temperament; if the etheric body predominates, a person will have a phlegmatic temperament; the predominance of the astral body manifests itself as a sanguine temperament; and the predominance of the I results in a choleric temperament.

In the child, the temperaments have a different basis, and this can be confusing for someone who is trying to understand this way of viewing the human being. If the physical body predominates, the child will have a phlegmatic temperament; if the etheric body predominates, the child will be sanguine; the astral body predominates in a choleric child; while the predominance of the I results in a melancholic temperament. Steiner summarizes the differences between the basis for the temperament of the adult and the child in the fifth lecture of *Discussions with Teachers* as follows:

> Human beings are extremely complicated. There is a definite relationship in them between the I and the physical body, and also between the etheric and astral bodies. Hence the predominance of one can become a predominance in another during human life. For example, in the case of the melancholic temperament, the predominance of the I becomes a predominance in the physical body, and in a choleric person ... the preponderance of the astral becomes a preponderance of the I. (pp. 56–57)

How does one's temperament change as one grows older? According to Steiner, each stage of life is colored by a particular temperament. Childhood is a time of sanguinity; adolescence is choleric; adulthood is a time of melancholia; and old age is phlegmatic. Within this general progression, one's individual temperament remains unchanged. What does change, however, is the basis for the temperament. Thus, the melancholic child tends to remain melancholic as an adult, but the basis for the melancholia changes from a predominance of the I to the predominance of the physical body.

Whatever the basis for the temperament, each of the temperaments displays certain typical characteristics both in childhood and adulthood. These characteristics may not always be obvious, because everyone embodies some aspects of each of the four temperaments. Typically, one of the temperaments tends to predominate and thus expresses some distinctive traits, but it is important to remember that a person rarely displays all of the characteristics listed in any one description.

Cholerics are usually energetic, forceful, and assertive. They are natural leaders, for they are decisive and courageous and have great warmth of heart. Cholerics can also be stubborn or willful, and tend to become short-tempered or impatient with anyone or anything that holds them back. They typically work hard and are determined to achieve their goals no matter what obstacles stand in their way.

Phlegmatics tend to be slow and steady. They love order, repetition, and physical comfort. Phlegmatics generally do not become easily interested or involved in something, but once they begin they become thoroughly engaged and will stick with a task until it is done. Phlegmatics tend to be patient, even-tempered, loyal, steadfast, and dependable.

Sanguines are usually graceful and full of life. They notice and respond to everything and everyone in their environment. They move quickly from one impression or experience to the next and rarely remain with anything for long. They can therefore be restless, distractible, or fickle. Sanguines tend to be sociable, for they are personable, vivacious, and light-hearted.

Most melancholics are introspective, thoughtful, and insightful people. They take everything to heart and are often sad or despondent. Although melancholics may be self-involved, they also have a great capacity for sympathy, for they can identify deeply with another person's struggles or pain. Melancholics tend to be very perceptive about people and situations, and they are well able to articulate their thoughts and feelings.

This brief overview does not do justice to the subtleties of an individual's temperament, for everyone has a blend of temperaments, and everyone's temperament expresses itself slightly differently. We must also remember that our temperament is not the only defining aspect of our being. Our character, personality, and individuality also express themselves powerfully in all that we are and do. As one studies the temperaments, however, one will begin to appreciate that many truths are revealed by this way of looking at human nature.

Knowledge of the temperaments is extremely useful to teachers, for it allows them to structure lessons that will appeal to various kinds of children. For example, when we tell seventh graders the biography of Galileo, the cholerics will probably identify with Galileo's personality, with this man of scintillating intellect and indomitable will. The melancholics are likely to empathize with Galileo's personal and professional struggles; undoubtedly they will feel compassion for the blind old scientist who lives out the final years of his life under house arrest with orders not to express his views on astronomy. The sanguines are likely to appreciate the details of courtly life in Italy in the sixteenth and seventeenth centuries, and they will probably be fascinated by Galileo's many difficult relationships that led inexorably toward his confrontation with the Church. The phlegmatics will be impressed by Galileo's perseverance; despite his many setbacks, he continued working diligently on his research, recording his observations in meticulous detail.

Understanding the temperaments also allows Waldorf teachers to help their students achieve greater inner balance. One might think that this would be done by trying to counter the child's tendencies—for instance, by making a sanguine stick to a task or forcing a choleric to give in, by cheering up a melancholic or drawing out a phlegmatic. Anyone who has tried such methods knows how ineffective they are. Steiner suggests that we do the opposite: we should work with the temperament to help children overcome the one-sidedness that their temperament might create. Although there are no recipes for working with human beings, Steiner gave very helpful indications for working effectively with children of different temperaments.

Choleric children admire strength, competence, and authority, and they benefit from having a relationship with people whom they can respect and esteem. Cholerics respect a person who is in command of every situation and who knows what to do in every instance. Such a person can stand up to the choleric children and meet them with objectivity and firmness, thereby helping the cholerics develop self-control. Choleric children need an environment that provides them with physical challenges. By pitting themselves against physical obstacles, cholerics develop inner as well as outer strength, and they learn to moderate their impulsiveness and impetuousness.

Phlegmatic children do not easily become engaged with other people, but they benefit from being around people who are interested in many things, for they slowly absorb those interests. As other peoples' interests find their reflection in the soul of the phlegmatic children, these children start to overcome their outer indifference and begin to awaken to the world. Strange as it may sound, phlegmatics benefit from being in surroundings and circumstances toward which apathy is an appropriate reaction. If phlegmatics dwell long enough in their phlegma, they will begin to be inwardly stirred to take outer action.

Although sanguine children have difficulty developing a deep interest in anything, their interest can be awakened by a particular person. Through admiration, love, and attachment for that person, the sanguine child develops the capacity for greater involvement. A sanguine child benefits from surroundings that are sanguine— full of objects of every variety. If these objects are unexpectedly withdrawn, the child's interest in these objects is intensified. An ever-changing environment can cause sanguine children to develop an inner yearning to be able to dwell on something or to explore it in greater depth; it therefore deepens their capacity to sustain their interest.

Melancholic children benefit from knowing people whose words and actions show that they too have had to endure hardship or a difficult destiny. When melancholics encounter the pain and suffering of another, they develop sympathy for that person and are led beyond their preoccupation with their own difficulties. Melancholic children are helped to overcome their melancholia by an environment that presents them with outer hindrances, which redirect their own inner suffering to outer circumstances.

In order for teachers to be able to respond to children in the various ways indicated above, they need to experience and explore their own temperament. They need to bring their temperament into greater balance, because a teacher's unbridled temperament can be harmful to a child. Everything that adults do makes an impression on the child's soul. These impressions work their way into the child's breathing, circulation, and metabolism and can affect that child's health in later life. Although Steiner did not discuss the effects of the teacher's temperament on the child in the lectures included in this chapter, he dealt with the theme at length in the first lectures of *The Roots of Education* and *The Essentials of Education*.

According to Steiner, teachers with an overly strong choleric temperament cause children to live in dread of their fury. This dread penetrates into the child's metabolism, and can lead to disorders of the metabolic system in adulthood. Teachers who are overly melancholic can be so preoccupied and self-involved that they behave coolly toward the children. This lack of warmth can cause disorders of the respiratory and circulatory systems in later life. Teachers who are overly phlegmatic and not sufficiently responsive to the children can cause a certain dullness to arise in the children. This manifests as nervous problems in adulthood. Sanguine teachers, who give themselves up to every impression, hastening from one thing to the next, fail to arouse sufficient inner activity in the child. This lack of inner activity can result in a lack of strength and vital force in adulthood. As teachers we therefore have a responsibility to strive to master ourselves, to bring ourselves into harmony and balance, so that we can promote the health and well-being of our students for the rest of their lives.

Waldorf teachers recognize that we affect our students not just through the curriculum and the subjects we teach them, not just by the methods we use, but by who we are. Every Waldorf teacher therefore wonders: Who am I to stand before my students as a representative of humanity? How can I, with all my faults and limitations, guide my students toward their higher selves? We must remember that what is most important to our students is not our achievements but our striving. Each of us is engaged in the process of becoming. Our students are often our teachers in this process, for they force us to face our shortcomings and limitations and inspire us to continue to strive to transform ourselves. By working on ourselves, we work on behalf of our students. By coming to know ourselves, we learn to know our students. Anthroposophy is a meditative path and a way of life that supports this striving. According to another of Steiner's lectures on the temperaments:

> We learn to know individual human beings in every way when we perceive them in the light of spiritual science. We even learn to perceive the child this way. Little by little we come to respect, or value, in the child the peculiarity, or enigmatic quality, of the individuality; we also learn how an individual must be treated in life, because spiritual science doesn't merely provide general, theoretical directions. It guides us in our relationship to the individual in the solving of the questions we need to solve. Such solutions require that we love the individual as we must, otherwise we merely fathom others with the mind. We must allow the other to work upon us completely. We must let spiritual scientific insight give wings to our feelings of love. That is the only proper soil that will yield true, fruitful, genuine human love; it is the basis from which we discover what we must look for as the innermost kernel in each individual.[1]

Developing the Virtues

Waldorf teachers consider the moral education of children to be one of their primary tasks. In "Gratitude, Love, and Duty," Steiner considers questions of ethical and social education and discusses how to cultivate these three fundamental human virtues.

Gratitude is the basis for religious feeling, and it is important that we cultivate this virtue in the young child. Young children are naturally religious, for they feel reverence for the cycle of the year and for the kingdoms of nature. The fact that young children unconsciously imitate their parents and teachers is an expression of

---

1. Lecture of January 19, 1909 (*The Four Temperaments*, Anthroposophic Press, Hudson, NY, 1968, p. 58).

their reverence for human beings and all they do. In this lecture, Steiner states that in order to instill gratitude in young children, we do not need to point out all the things for which they should be grateful. Rather, by striving to cultivate a mood of gratitude and by conducting ourselves accordingly, we will foster a deep-seated piety in the child, "not the kind that dwells on one's lips or in one's thoughts only, but a piety that will pervade the entire human being and that will be upright, honest, and true" (p. 76).

In the Waldorf kindergarten, teachers can cultivate gratitude in many ways. The room where the children work and play is beautiful and orderly. The furniture, decorations, and toys all reflect an attitude of respect and reverence for the natural world and for the work of human beings. Children say or sing grace before each meal, expressing reverence for the Earth and its gifts, and the seasonal activities and festivals foster a deep appreciation for the kingdoms of nature and for the cycle of the year.

Gratitude is the basis for love, and in the middle section of this lecture, Steiner describes how teachers can work with children of elementary school age to awaken their love for the world and for their fellow human beings.

During the early years of elementary school, children are deeply connected to the world through their feeling. The animals, plants, and stones, the sun, the moon, and the stars speak a language that they still understand. When we tell children nature stories and legends with a moral element, we awaken their appreciation for the natural world and deepen their love for all creation. After the twelfth year change, children begin to experience the world more through their thinking. Now the curriculum includes subjects such as geology, astronomy, physics, and chemistry, which can only be grasped fully through the power of thought. Because these subjects could so easily become dry or abstract, teachers need to cultivate an element of inner and outer grace, and they must strive to infuse their lessons with lightness and humor. By keeping their teaching alive and presenting lessons that engage the students fully, teachers can develop their students' interest in and love for the world. By infusing every word and deed with meaning, teachers can deepen their students' respect and appreciation for human beings and the work they do in the world.

Love for the world and for other human beings is the foundation for a sense of duty. In the high school, Waldorf teachers strive to engender a love for work and for the activities that give meaning to life.

> Love is something that extends to everything, is the innermost impetus for action. We ought to do what we love to do. Duty is to merge with love; we should like what we are duty-bound to do. (EA, p. 133)

Teachers can develop their students' sense of duty through their own example. How teachers approach their daily tasks and the collective responsibilities for governing the school acts powerfully upon the students. Since their inception, Waldorf schools have had a form of governance that differs greatly from that of other schools. Rather than relying on a headmaster or principal, the teachers themselves are responsible for the administration of the school. During the initial faculty conferences, Steiner introduced this collaborative, co-responsible principle of school administration in his opening remarks to those whom he would train as teachers at the original Waldorf school.

> We will organize the school not bureaucratically, but collegially, and will administer it in a republican way. In a true teachers' republic we will not have the comfort of receiving directions from the board of education. Rather, we must bring to our work what gives each of us the possibility and the full responsibility for what we have to do. Each one of us must be completely responsible. (FHE, p. 30)

In every Waldorf school, teachers meet weekly to study and deepen their understanding of the children, the curriculum, and the methods of Waldorf education. In schools that have reached a certain stage of stability and maturity, there is also a weekly meeting of the College of Teachers, a group of teachers who have made a commitment to work with anthroposophy as a path of self-development, who have committed themselves to work in the collegial manner described by Steiner, and who are committed to the destiny of their school. The College of Teachers is responsible for the school both as an organization and as an organism. It over-sees everything that is happening in the school in the pedagogical and the practical administrative realms, but it also tries to serve as a sense organ for the impulses that spiritual beings are trying to manifest through the work of the teachers and the school. Teachers who would help students develop the virtues of gratitude, love, and duty not only need to be masters of the art of teaching, they must develop themselves so they can serve their students and help them fulfill their destinies. In "Gratitude, Love, and Duty," Steiner says:

> Essentially, there is no education other than self-education, whatever the level may be. This is recognized in its full depth within anthroposophy, which has conscious knowledge through spiritual investigation of repeated Earth lives. Every education is self-education, and as teachers we can only pro-vide the environment for children's self-education. We have to provide the most favorable conditions where, through our agency, children can educate themselves according to their own destinies. (p. 88)

Steiner offered a great deal of guidance for those wishing to tread the path of self-development. He also suggested specific exer-cises and meditations for teachers to help them work more con-sciously on the Earth on behalf of the spiritual powers. The key to this process of self-development is selflessness, for it is only by becoming so selfless that the highest powers can manifest them-selves in us, that the teacher can truly serve the child.

The Four Temperaments

LECTURE BY RUDOLF STEINER

Berlin, March 4, 1909

It has frequently been emphasized that humanity's greatest riddle is itself. Both natural and spiritual science ultimately try to solve this riddle—the former by understanding the natural laws that govern our outer being, the latter by seeking the essence and purpose inherent in our existence. Now as correct as it may be that humanity's greatest riddle is itself, it must also be emphasized that each individual human being is a riddle, often even to itself. Every one of us experiences this in encounters with other people.

Today we shall be dealing not with general riddles, but rather with those posed to us by every human being in every encounter, and these are just as important. For how endlessly varied people are! We need only consider temperament, the subject of today's lecture, in order to realize that there are as many riddles as there are people. Even within the basic types known as the temperaments, such variety exists among people that the very mystery of existence seems to express itself within these types. Temperament, that fundamental coloring of the human personality, plays a role in all manifestations of individuality that are of concern to practical life. We sense something of this basic mood whenever we encounter another human being. Thus we can only hope that spiritual science will tell us what we need to know about the temperaments.

Our first impression of the temperaments is that they are external, for although they can be said to flow from within, they manifest themselves in everything we can observe from without. However, this does not mean that the human riddle can be solved by means of natural science and observation. Only when we hear what spiritual science has to say can we come closer to understanding these peculiar colorations of the human personality.

Spiritual science tells us first of all that the human being is part of a line of heredity. A person displays the characteristics that were inherited from father, mother, grandparents, and so on. These characteristics are then passed on to the following progeny. The human being thus possesses certain traits by virtue of being part of a succession of generations.

However, this inheritance gives us only one side of human nature. Joined to that is the individuality that is brought out of the spiritual world. This is added to what father, mother, and other ancestors are able to give. Something that proceeds from life to life, from existence to existence, connects itself with the generational stream. Certain characteristics can be attributed to heredity; on the other hand, as a person develops from childhood on, we can see unfolding out of the center of this being something that must be the fruit of preceding lives, something that could never have been only inherited from ancestors. We come to know the law of reincarnation, of the succession of earthly lives, and this is but a special case of an all-encompassing cosmic law.

An illustration will make this seem less paradoxical. Consider a lifeless mineral, say, a rock crystal. Should the crystal be destroyed, it leaves nothing of its form that could be passed on to other crystals. A new crystal receives nothing of the old one's particular form.[2] When we move on to the world of plants, we notice that a plant cannot develop according to the same laws as the crystal. It can only originate from another, earlier plant. Form is here preserved and passed on.

Moving on to the animal kingdom, we find an evolution of the species taking place. We begin to appreciate why the nineteenth

2. Translator's note: The reader may conclude from this remark—for it was, after all, a remark, not a published claim—that Steiner was ignorant of the concept of seed crystals. However, a likelier explanation is that Steiner, whose audience was very likely not a scientifically knowledgeable one, was simply indulging in a bit of rhetorical hyperbole. He doubtless knew that a seed crystal will hasten the crystallization process in a saturated salt solution, but this fact is not really relevant to his point, which comes out only gradually in this paragraph. His point is not that a newly-forming crystal *cannot* receive some contribution from a previously existing one, only that it *need* not; this is in contrast to living things, which require a progenitor.

century held the discovery of evolution to be its greatest achievement. In animals, not only does one being proceed from another, but each young animal during the embryo phase recapitulates the earlier phases of its species' evolutionary development. The species itself undergoes an enhancement.

In human beings not only does the species evolve, but so does the individual. What a human being acquires in a lifetime through education and experience is preserved, just as surely as are the evolutionary achievements of an animal's ancestral line. It will someday be commonplace to trace a person's inner core to a previous existence. The human being will come to be known as the product of an earlier life. The views that stand in the way of this doctrine will be overcome, just as was the scholarly opinion of an earlier century, which held that living organisms could arise from nonliving substances. As recently as three hundred years ago, scholars believed that animals could evolve from river mud, that is, from nonliving matter. Francesco Redi, an Italian scientist, was the first to assert that living things could develop only from other living things.[3] For this he was attacked and came close to suffering the fate of Giordano Bruno.[4] Today, burning people at the stake is no longer fashionable. When someone attempts to teach a new truth—for example, that psychospiritual entities must be traced back to earlier psychospiritual entities—such a person probably won't be burned at the stake, but will more likely be dismissed as a fool. But the time will come when the real foolishness will be the belief that the human being lives only once, that no enduring entity unites with a person's inherited traits.

Now an important question arises: How can something originating in a completely different world, that must seek a father and a mother, unite itself with physical corporeality? How can it clothe itself in the bodily features that link human beings to a hereditary chain? How does the spiritual-psychic stream, of which a human

3. Francesco Redi, 1626–1697. Refuted spontaneous generation of living beings out of mud.
4. Giordano Bruno, 1548–1600. Italian philosopher, Dominican monk, burned at the stake as heretic. Taught that the world is infinite in space and time and filled with innumerable suns.

being forms a part through reincarnation, unite itself with the physical stream of heredity? The answer is that a synthesis must be achieved. When the two streams combine, each imparts something of its own quality to the other. In much the same way that blue and yellow combine to give green, the two streams in the human being combine to yield what is commonly known as temperament. Our inner self and our inherited traits both appear in it. Temperament stands between the things that connect a human being to an ancestral line, and those the human being brings out of earlier incarnations. Temperament strikes a balance between the eternal and the ephemeral. And it does so in such a way that the essential members of the human being, which we have come to know in other contexts, enter into a very specific relationship with one another.

Human beings as we know them in this life are beings of four members. The first, the physical body, they have in common with the mineral world. The first supersensible member, the etheric body, is integrated into the physical and separates from it only at death. There follows as third member the astral body, the bearer of instincts, drives, passions, desires, and of the ever-changing content of sensation and thought. Our highest member places us above all other earthly beings as the bearer of the human I, which endows us in such a curious and yet undeniable fashion with the power of self-awareness. These four members we have come to know as the essential constituents of a human being.

The way the four members combine is determined by the flowing together of the two streams upon a person's entry into the physical world. In every case, one of the four members achieves predominance over the others, and gives them its own peculiar stamp. Where the bearer of the I predominates, a choleric temperament results. Where the astral body predominates, we find a sanguine temperament. Where the etheric or life body predominates, we speak of a phlegmatic temperament. And where the physical body predominates, we have to deal with a melancholic temperament. The specific way in which the eternal and the ephemeral combine determines what relationship the four members will enter into with one another.

The way the four members find their expression in the physical body has also frequently been mentioned. The I expresses itself in the circulation of the blood, and so in the choleric the predominant system is that of the blood. The astral body expresses itself physically in the nervous system; so in the sanguine, the nervous system holds sway. The etheric body expresses itself in the glandular system; hence the phlegmatic is dominated physically by the glands. The physical body as such expresses itself only in itself; thus the outwardly most important feature in the melancholic is the physical body. This can be observed in all phenomena connected with these temperaments.

In the choleric, the I and the blood system predominate. Cholerics come across as people who must always have their own way. Their aggressiveness, everything connected with their forcefulness of will, derives from their blood circulation.

In the nervous system and astral body, sensations and feelings constantly fluctuate. Any harmony or order results solely from the restraining influence of the I. People who do not exercise that influence appear to have no control over their thoughts and sensations. They are totally absorbed by the sensations, pictures, and ideas that ebb and flow within them. Something like this occurs whenever the astral body predominates, as, for example, in the sanguine. Sanguines surrender themselves in a certain sense to the constant and varied flow of images, sensations, and ideas since in them the astral body and nervous system predominate.

The nervous system's activity is restrained only by the circulation of the blood. That this is so becomes clear when we consider what happens when a person lacks blood or is anemic, in other words, when the blood's restraining influence is absent. Mental images fluctuate wildly, often leading to illusions and hallucinations.

A touch of this is present in sanguines. Sanguines are incapable of lingering over an impression. They cannot fix their attention on a particular image nor sustain their interest in an impression. Instead, they rush from experience to experience, from percept to percept. This is especially noticeable in sanguine children, where it can be a source of concern. The sanguine child's interest is easily kindled, a picture will easily impress, but the impression quickly vanishes.

We proceed now to the phlegmatic temperament. We observed that this temperament develops when the etheric or life body, as we call it, which regulates growth and metabolism, is predominant. The result is a sense of inner well-being. The more human beings live in their etheric body, the more they are preoccupied with their own internal processes. They let external events run their course while their attention is directed inward.

In melancholics we have seen that the physical body, the coarsest member of the human organization, becomes master over the others. As a result, melancholics feel they are not master over their body, that they cannot bend it to their will. The physical body, which is intended to be an instrument of the higher members, is itself in control, and frustrates the others. Melancholics experience this as pain, as a feeling of despondency. Pain continually wells up within them because the physical body resists the etheric body's inner sense of well-being, the astral body's liveliness, and the I-being's purposeful endeavor.

The varying combinations of the four members also manifest themselves quite clearly in external appearance. People in whom the I predominates seek to triumph over all obstacles, to make their presence known. Accordingly their I stunts the growth of the other members; it withholds from the astral and etheric bodies their due portion. This reveals itself outwardly in a very clear fashion. Johann Gottlieb Fichte, that famous German choleric, was recognizable as such purely externally.[5] His build revealed clearly that the lower essential members had been held back in their growth. Napoleon, another classic example of the choleric, was so short because his I had held the other members back.[6] Of course, one cannot generalize that all cholerics are short and all sanguines tall. It is a question of proportion. What matters is the relation of size to overall form.

In the sanguine the nervous system and the astral body predominate. The astral body's inner liveliness animates the other mem-

---

5. Johann Gottlieb Fichte, 1762–1814. German Idealist philosopher.
6. Napoleon Bonaparte, 1769–1821. French ruler and emperor 1804–1814 and 1815.

bers, and makes the external form as mobile as possible. Whereas the choleric has sharply chiseled facial features, the sanguine's are mobile, expressive, changeable. We see the astral body's inner liveliness manifested in every outer detail, for example, in a slender form, a delicate bone structure, or lean muscles. The same thing can be observed in details of behavior. Even one who is not clairvoyant can tell from behind whether someone is choleric or sanguine; one does not need to be a spiritual scientist for that. When you observe the gait of a choleric, you notice that a choleric plants each foot so solidly that it would seem to bore down into the ground. On the other hand, the sanguine has a light, springy step. Even subtler external traits can be found. The inwardness of the I, the choleric's self-contained inwardness, expresses itself in eyes that are dark and smoldering. The sanguine, whose I has not taken such deep root, who is filled with the liveliness of the astral body, tends by contrast to have blue eyes. Many more such distinctive traits of these temperaments could be cited.

The phlegmatic temperament manifests itself in a static, indifferent physiognomy, as well as in plumpness, for fat is due largely to the activity of the etheric body. In all this the phlegmatic's inner sense of comfort is expressed. The gait is loose-jointed and shambling, and the manner timid. Phlegmatics seem somehow to be not entirely in touch with their surroundings.

The melancholic is distinguished by a hanging head, as if the strength necessary to straighten the neck was lacking. The eyes are dull, not shining like the choleric's; the gait is firm, but in a leaden rather than a resolute sort of way.

Thus you see how significantly spiritual science can contribute to the solution of this riddle. Only when one seeks to encompass reality in its entirety, which includes the spiritual, can knowledge bear practical fruit. Accordingly, only spiritual science can give us knowledge that will benefit the individual and all humankind. In education, very close attention must be paid to the individual temperaments, for it is especially important to be able to guide and direct them as they develop in the child. But the temperaments are also important to our efforts to improve ourselves later in life. We do well to attend to what expresses itself through them if we wish to further our personal development.

The four fundamental types I have outlined here for you naturally never manifest themselves in such pure form. Every human being has one basic temperament, with varying degrees of the other three mixed in. Napoleon, for example, although a choleric, had much of the phlegmatic in him. To truly master life, it is important that we open our souls to what manifests itself as typical. When we consider that the temperaments, each of which represents a mild imbalance, can degenerate into unhealthy extremes, we realize just how important this is.

Yet, without the temperaments the world would be an exceedingly dull place, not only ethically, but also in a higher sense. The temperaments alone make all multiplicity, beauty, and fullness of life possible. Thus in education it would be senseless to want to homogenize or eliminate them, but an effort should be made to direct each into the proper track, for in every temperament there lie two dangers of aberration, one great, one small. One danger for young cholerics is that they will never learn to control their temper as they develop into maturity. That is the small danger. The greater is that they will become foolishly single-minded. For the sanguine the lesser danger is flightiness; the greater is mania, induced by a constant stream of sensations. The small danger for the phlegmatic is apathy; the greater is stupidity, dullness. For the melancholic, insensitivity to anything other than personal pain is the small danger; the greater is insanity.

In light of all this it is clear that to guide the temperaments is one of life's significant tasks. If this task is to be properly carried out, however, one basic principle must be observed, which is always to reckon with what is given, and not with what is not there. For example, if a child has a sanguine temperament, it will not be helped by elders who try to flog interest into the child. The temperament simply will not allow it. Instead of asking what the child lacks, in order that we might beat it in, we must focus on what the child has, and base ourselves on that. And as a rule, there is one thing that will always stimulate the sanguine child's interest. However flighty the child might be, we can always stimulate interest in a particular personality. If we ourselves are that personality, or if we bring the child together with someone who is, the child cannot but develop an interest. Only through the medium of love for a personality can the interest of the sanguine child be awakened. More than children of any other temperament, the sanguine needs someone to admire. Admiration is here a kind of magic word, and we must do everything we can to awaken it.

We must reckon with what we have. We should see to it that the sanguine child is exposed to a variety of things in which a deeper interest is shown. These things should be allowed to speak to the child, to have an effect upon the child. They should then be withdrawn, so that the child's interest in them will intensify; then they may be restored. In other words, we must fashion the sanguine's environment so that it is in keeping with the temperament.

The choleric child is also susceptible of being led in a special way. The key to this child's education is respect and esteem for a natural authority. Instead of winning affection by means of personal qualities, as we try to do with the sanguine child, we should see to it that the child's belief in the teacher's ability remains unshaken. The teacher must demonstrate an understanding of what goes on around the child. Any showing of incompetence should be avoided. The child must persist in the belief that the teacher is competent, or all authority will be lost. The magic potion for the choleric child is respect and esteem for a person's worth, just as for the sanguine child it is love for a personality. Outwardly, the choleric child must be confronted with challenging situations. The choleric must encounter resistance and difficulty, lest life become too easy.

The melancholic child is not easy to lead. With a melancholic, however, a different approach may be applied. For the sanguine child the approach is love for a personality; for the choleric, it is respect and esteem for a teacher's worth. By contrast, the important thing for the melancholic is that the teachers be people who have in a certain sense been tried by life, who act and speak on the basis of past trials. The child must feel that the teacher has known real pain. Let your treatment of life's details be an occasion for the child to appreciate what you have suffered. Sympathy with the destinies of others furthers the melancholic's development. Here, too, one must reckon with what the child has. The melancholic has a firmly rooted capacity for suffering, for discomfort, that cannot be disciplined out. However, it can be redirected. We should expose the child to legitimate external pain and suffering, so that the child learns there are outer things that can engage the capacity for experiencing pain. This is the essential thing. We should not try to divert or amuse the melancholic, for to do so only intensifies the despondency and inner suffering; instead, the melancholic child must be enabled to see that objective occasions for suffering exist in life. Although we must not carry it too far, redirecting the child's suffering to outside objects is what is called for.

The phlegmatic child should not be allowed to grow up alone. Although naturally all children should have playmates, for phlegmatics it is especially important that they have them. Their playmates should have the most varied interests. Phlegmatic children learn by sharing in the interests, the more numerous the better, of others. Their playmates' enthusiasms will overcome their native indifference toward the world. Whereas the important thing for the melancholic is to experience another person's destiny, for the phlegmatic child it is to experience the whole range of a playmate's interests. The phlegmatic is not moved by things as such, but an interest arises when he sees things reflected in others, and these interests are then reflected in the soul of the phlegmatic child. We should bring into the phlegmatic's environment objects and events toward which "phlegm" is an appropriate reaction. Impassivity must be directed toward the right objects, objects toward which one may be phlegmatic.

From the examples of these pedagogical principles, we see how spiritual science can address practical problems. These principles can also be applied to oneself, for purposes of self-improvement. For example, a sanguine gains little by self-reproach. Our minds are in such questions frequently an obstacle. When pitted directly against stronger forces such as the temperaments, they can accomplish little. Indirectly, however, they can accomplish much. Sanguines, for example, can take their sanguinity into account, abandoning self-exhortation as fruitless. The important thing is to display sanguinity under the right circumstances. Experiences suited to a short attention span can be brought about through thoughtful planning. Using thought in this way, even on the smallest scale, will produce the requisite effect.

Persons of a choleric temperament should purposely put themselves in situations where rage is of no use, but rather only makes them look ridiculous. Melancholics should not close their eyes to life's pain, but rather seek it out; through compassion they redirect their suffering outward toward appropriate objects and events. If we are phlegmatics, having no particular interests, then we should occupy ourselves as much as possible with uninteresting things, surround ourselves with numerous sources of tedium, so that we become thoroughly bored. We will then be thoroughly cured of our "phlegm"; we will have gotten it out of our system. Thus does one reckon with what one has, and not with what one does not have.

By filling ourselves with practical wisdom such as this, we learn to solve that basic riddle of life, the other person. It is solved not by postulating abstract ideas and concepts, but by means of pictures. Instead of arbitrarily theorizing, we should seek an immediate understanding of every individual human being. We can do this, however, only by knowing what lies in the depths of the soul. Slowly and gradually, spiritual science illuminates our minds, making us receptive not only to the big picture, but also to subtle details. Spiritual science makes it possible that when two souls meet and one demands love, the other offers it. If something else is demanded, that other thing is given. Through such true, living wisdom do we create the basis for society. This is what we mean when we say we must solve a riddle every moment.

Anthroposophy acts not through sermons, exhortations, or catechisms, but through the creation of a social groundwork upon which human beings can come to know each other. Spiritual science is the ground of life, and love is the blossom and fruit of a life enhanced by it. Thus, spiritual science may claim to lay the foundation for the human being's most beautiful goal—a true, genuine love for humankind.

Understanding Children's Temperaments

LECTURE BY RUDOLF STEINER

Stuttgart, August 21, 1919

My dear friends, in these afternoon sessions I shall speak informally about your educational tasks—about the distribution of work in the school, arrangement of lessons, and so on. For the first two or three days we will have to deal mainly with the question of our relationship to the children. When we meet the children we very soon see that they have different dispositions, and despite the necessity of teaching them in classes, even large classes, we must consider their various dispositions. First, aside from everything else, we will try to become conscious of what I would say is ideal necessity. We need not be too anxious about classes being too full, because a good teacher will find the right way to handle this situation. The important thing for us to remember is the *diversity* of children and indeed of all human beings.

Such diversity can be traced to four fundamental types, and the most important task of the educator and teacher is to know and recognize these four types we call the temperaments. Even in ancient times the four basic types—the *sanguine, melancholic, phlegmatic,* and *choleric* temperaments—were differentiated. We will always find that the characteristic constitution of each child belongs to one of these classes of temperament. We must first acquire the capacity to distinguish the different types; with the help of a deeper anthroposophical understanding we must, for example, be able to distinguish clearly between the sanguine and phlegmatic types.

In spiritual science we divide the human being into *I-being, astral body, etheric body,* and *physical body.* In an ideal human being the harmony predestined by the cosmic plan would naturally predominate among these four human principles. But in reality this is not so with any individual. Thus it can be seen that the human being, when given over to the physical plane, is not yet really complete; education and teaching, however, should serve to make the human being complete. One of the four elements rules in each child, and education and teaching must harmonize these four principles.

If the I dominates—that is, if the I is already very strongly developed in a child, then we discover the melancholic temperament. It is very easy to err in this, because people sometimes view melancholic children as though they were especially favored. In reality the melancholic temperament in a child is due to the dominance of the I in the very earliest years.

If the astral body rules, we have a choleric temperament. If the etheric body dominates, we have the sanguine temperament. If the physical body dominates, we have the phlegmatic temperament.

In later life these things are connected somewhat differently, so you will find a slight variation in a lecture I once gave on the temperaments.[7] In that lecture I spoke of the temperaments in relation to the four members of the adult. With children, however, we certainly come to a proper assessment when we view the connection between temperament and the four members of the human being as I just described. This knowledge about the child should be kept in the back of our minds as we try to discover which temperament predominates through studying the whole external bearing and general habits of the child.

If a child is interested in many different things, but only for a short time, quickly losing interest again, we must describe such a child as sanguine. We should make it our business to familiarize ourselves with these things so that, even when we have to deal with a great many children, we can pick out those whose interest in external impressions is quickly aroused and as quickly gone again. Such children have a sanguine temperament.

Then you should know exactly which children lean toward inner reflection and are inclined to brood over things; these are the melancholic children. It is not easy to give them impressions of the

7. "The Four Temperaments" in *Anthroposophy in Everyday Life*, Anthroposophic Press, Hudson, NY, 1995.

outer world. They brood quietly within themselves, but this does not mean that they are unoccupied in their inner being. On the contrary, we have the impression that they are active inwardly.

When we have the opposite impression—that children are not active inwardly and yet show no interest in the outer world, then we are dealing with the phlegmatic children.

And children who express their will strongly in a kind of blustering way are cholerics.

There are of course many other qualities through which these four types of temperament express themselves. The essential thing for us during the first few months of our teaching, however, is to observe the children, watching for these four characteristics so that we learn to recognize the four different types. In this way we can divide a class into four groups, and you should gradually rearrange the seating of the children with this goal in mind. When we have classes of boys and girls, we will have eight groups, four groups of boys and four of girls—a choleric, a sanguine, a phlegmatic, and a melancholic group.

This has a very definite purpose. Imagine that we are giving a lesson; during our teaching we will sometimes talk to the children and at other times show them things. As teachers we must be conscious that when we show something to be looked at, it is different from judging it. When we pass judgment on something we turn to one group, but when we show the children something, we turn to another. If we have something to show that should work particularly on the senses, we turn with particular attention toward the sanguine group. If we want the children to reflect on what has been shown, we turn to the melancholic children. Further details on this matter will be given later. But it is necessary to acquire the art of turning to different groups according to whether we show things or speak about them. In this way what is lacking in one group can be made good by another. Show the melancholic children something that they can express an opinion about, and show the sanguine something they can look at; these two groups will complement each other in this way. One type learns from the other; they are interested in each other, and one supplies what the other lacks.

You will have to be patient with yourselves, because this kind of treatment of children must become habit. Eventually your *feeling* must tell you which group you have to turn toward, so that you do it involuntarily, as it were. If you did it with fixed purpose you would lose your spontaneity. Thus we must come to think of this way of treating the different tendencies in the temperaments as a kind of habit in our teaching.

Now you should not hurry the preparation of your lessons, but be sure to truly strengthen yourselves for the work. I do not mean that you should spend the limited time at your disposal in a lot of detailed preparation, but nevertheless you can only make these things your own if you ponder over them in your souls. It will thus be our task to concern ourselves in a truly practical way with the *teacher's* attitude to the temperamental tendencies of children. So now we will divide the work among you as follows. I will ask one group to concern themselves with the sanguine temperament, a second group with the phlegmatic, a third with the melancholic, and the fourth with the choleric. And then, in our free discussions tomorrow, I would like you to consider the following questions: first, how do you think the child's own temperament is expressed? Second, how should we deal with each temperament?

With regard to the second question I have something more to say. You can see from the lecture I gave some years ago that, when we want to help a temperament, the worst method is to foster the opposite qualities in a child. Let's suppose we have a sanguine child; when we try to train such a child by driving out these qualities, we provide a bad treatment. We must work to understand the temperament, to go out to meet it. In the case of the sanguine child, for example, we bring as many things as possible to the attention of the child, who becomes thoroughly occupied, because in this way we can work with the child's propensities. The result will be that the child's connection with the sanguine tendency will gradually weaken and the temperaments will harmonize with each other. Similarly, in the case of the choleric child we should not try to prevent ranting and raging, but endeavor to meet the child's needs properly through some external means. Of course it is often not so easy to allow a child to have a fling in a fit of temper!

You will find a distinct difference between phlegmatic and choleric children. A phlegmatic child is apathetic and is also not very active inwardly. As teachers you must try to arouse a great deal of sympathy within yourselves for a child of this type, and take an interest in every sign of life in such a child; there will always be opportunities for this. If you can only find your way through to the apathy, the phlegmatic child can be very interesting. You should not however express this interest, but try to appear indifferent, thus dividing your own being in two, as it were, so that inwardly you have real sympathy, while outwardly you act so that the child finds a reflection in you. Then you will be able to work on the child in an educational way.

With the choleric child, on the other hand, you must try to be indifferent inwardly, to look on cooly when the child is in a bad temper. For example, if the child flings a paint jar on the floor, be as phlegmatic and calm as possible outwardly during such a fit of temper—imperturbable! On the other hand, you should talk about these things with the child as much as you can, but not immediately afterward. At the time you must be as quiet as possible outwardly and say with the greatest possible calm, "Look, you threw the paint jar." The next day when the child is calm again, you should talk about the matter with the child sympathetically. Speak about what has been done and offer your sympathy and understanding. In this way you will compel the child to repeat the whole scene in memory. You should then also calmly judge what happened, how the paint jar was thrown on the floor and broke in pieces. By these means very much can be done for children who have a temper. You will not get them to master their temper in any other way.

This will guide you in dealing with the two questions we will consider tomorrow. We will arrange it so that each of you can present what you have to say. Make short notes on what you have thought of and we will talk about what you have prepared. Time must always be allowed for the teaching faculty to discuss these and similar matters. In discussions of this kind, which have a more democratic character, a substitute must be found for a dictatorial leadership like that of a headmaster, so that in reality every individual teacher can always share in the affairs and interests of the others. So tomorrow we will begin with a discussion. As a starting point I would like to give you a kind of diagram to work from.

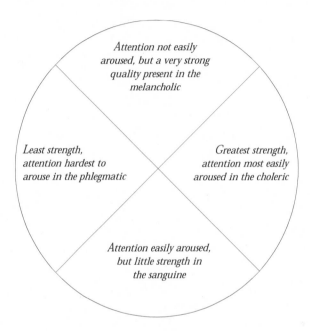

Whenever people express themselves in any way, you can tell from their dispositions whether they perceive things strongly or weakly; and further, whether they perceive and feel more strongly what is outside themselves or within their own inner situation. We must also notice whether such people are changeable or not. People either persevere at something and change very little, or show less perseverance and change greatly. This is how the various temperaments differ.

When you have observed such things you will understand certain indications about the temperaments in this diagram. Sanguine and phlegmatic temperaments are frequently found together, and you will see that they are next to each other in the diagram. You will never find a phlegmatic temperament passing easily into the choleric. They are as different as the North and South Poles. The melancholic and sanguine temperaments are also polar opposites. The temperaments that are next to each other merge into one another and mingle; so it will be good to arrange your groups as follows: if you put the phlegmatics together it is good to have the cholerics on the opposite side, and to let the two others, the melancholies and sanguines, sit between them.

All these things bring us back to what I spoke of this morning.[8] The inner life, the life of soul, is the most significant aspect in the child. Teaching and education depend on what passes from the soul of the teacher to the soul of the child.

We cannot overestimate what takes place in the hidden links that pass from one soul to another. There is, for example, a remarkable interplay between souls when you remain calm and indifferent around a choleric child, or when you have inner sympathy toward a phlegmatic child. In this way your education of the child through your own inner soul mood will have a truly supersensible quality. Education occurs because of what you are, or rather, let's say, what you make of yourself when you are with the children. You must never lose sight of this.

But children also influence each other. And that is the remarkable thing about this division into four groups of similar temperaments; when you put those that are alike together, it does not have the effect of intensifying their temperamental tendencies but of reducing them. For example, when sanguine children are put together in one group, they do not intensify each other's sanguinity but tone it down. And when in your lessons you turn to the choleric

---

8. See *The Foundations of Human Experience* (previously *Study of Man*), Anthroposophic Press, Hudson, NY, 1996 and *Practical Advice to Teachers,* Rudolf Steiner Press, London, 1988 (at the end of the first lectures in each). In addition to these lectures and discussions with the teachers, Rudolf Steiner was giving other lectures simultaneously in order to prepare for the opening of the school the following month. See *The Spirit of the Waldorf School: Lectures Surrounding the Founding of the First Waldorf School, Stuttgart–1919*, Anthroposophic Press, Hudson, NY, 1995 (these lectures began August 24, 1919).

children, the sanguine profit from what you say, and vice versa. As a teacher you must allow your own soul mood to influence the children, while the children of like temperaments are toning down each other's soul moods. Talking and chattering together signifies an inner desire to subdue each other, even the chattering that goes on during the breaks. The cholerics will chatter less when sitting together than they would when sitting with children of other temperaments. We must avoid viewing and assessing these things externally....

Gratitude, Love, and Duty

LECTURE BY RUDOLF STEINER

Dornach, April 20, 1923

Questions of ethical and social education are raised when we consider the relationship between growing children and their surroundings. We will consider these two issues today—even though briefly and superficially, due to the shortness of time. Once again, the kernel of the matter is knowing how to adapt to the individuality of the growing child. At the same time, you must remember that, as a teacher and educator, you are part of the social setting, and that you personally bring the social environment and its ethical attitudes to the growing pupil. Again, pedagogical principles and methods must be formed so that they offer every opportunity of reaching the child's true nature—one must learn to know the child's true nature according to what has been shown here briefly during the last few days. As always, much depends on *how* one's material is brought to the students during their various ages and stages.

Here we need to consider three human virtues—concerning, on the one hand, the child's own development, and on the other hand, what is seen in relation to society in general. They are three fundamental virtues. The first concerns everything that can live in the *will to gratitude*; the second, everything that can live in the *will to love*; and third, everything that can live in the *will to duty*.

Fundamentally, these are the three principal human virtues and, to a certain extent, encompass all other virtues.

Generally speaking, people are far too unaware of what, in this context, I would like to term gratitude or thankfulness. And yet gratitude is a virtue that, in order to play a proper role in the human soul, must grow with the child. Gratitude is something that must already flow into the human being when the growth forces—working in the child in an inward direction—are liveliest, when they are at the peak of their shaping and molding activities. Gratitude is something that has to be developed out of the bodily-religious relationship I described as the dominant feature in the child from birth until the change of teeth. At the same time, however, gratitude will develop very spontaneously during this first period of life, as long as the child is treated properly. All that flows, with devotion and love, from a child's inner being toward whatever comes from the periphery through the parents or other educators—and everything expressed outwardly in the child's imitation—will be permeated with a natural mood of gratitude. We only have to act in ways that are worthy of the child's gratitude and it will flow toward us, especially during the first period of life. This gratitude then develops further by flowing into the forces of growth that make the limbs grow, and that alter even the chemical composition of the blood and other bodily fluids. This gratitude lives in the physical body and must dwell in it, since it would not otherwise be anchored deeply enough.

It would be very incorrect to remind children constantly to be thankful for whatever comes from their surroundings. On the contrary, an atmosphere of gratitude should grow naturally in children through merely witnessing the gratitude that their elders feel as they receive what is freely given by their fellow human beings, and in how they express their gratitude. In this situation, one would also cultivate the habit of feeling grateful by allowing the child to imitate what is done in the surroundings. If a child says "thank you" very naturally—not in response to the urging of others, but simply by imitation—something has been done that will greatly benefit the child's whole life. Out of this an all-embracing gratitude will develop toward the whole world.

The cultivation of this universal gratitude toward the world is of paramount importance. It does not always need to be in one's consciousness, but may simply live in the background of the feeling life, so that, at the end of a strenuous day, one can experience gratitude, for example, when entering a beautiful meadow full of flowers. Such a subconscious feeling of gratitude may arise in us whenever we look at nature. It may be felt every morning when the Sun rises, when beholding any of nature's phenomena. And if we only act properly in front of the children, a corresponding increase in gratitude will develop within them for all that comes to them from the people living around them, from the way they speak or smile, or the way such people treat them.

This universal mood of gratitude is the basis for a truly religious attitude; for it is not always recognized that this universal sense of gratitude, provided it takes hold of the whole human being during the first period of life, will engender something even further. In human life, love flows into everything if only the proper conditions present themselves for development. The possibility of a more intense experience of love, reaching the physical level, is given only during the second period of life between the change of teeth and puberty. But that first tender love, so deeply embodied in the inner being of the child, without as yet working outward—this tender blossom will become firmly rooted through the development of gratitude. Love, born out of the experience of gratitude during the first period of the child's life, is the love of God. One should realize that, just as one has to dig the roots of a plant into the soil in order to receive its blossom later, so one has to plant gratitude into the soul of the child, because it is the root of the love of God. The love of God will develop out of universal gratitude, as the blossom develops from the root.

We should attend to these things, because in the abstract we usually know very well how they should be. In actual life situations, however, all too often these things turn out to be very different. It is easy enough, in theory, to say that people should carry the love of God within themselves—and this could not be more correct. But such demands, made abstractly, have a peculiar habit of never seeing the light of day in practice.

I would like to return to what I said during one of the last few days. It is easy enough to think of the function of a stove in the following way: You are a stove and we have to put you here because we want to heat the room. Your categorical imperative—the true categorical "stove-imperative"—tells you that you are obliged to heat the room. We know only too well that this in itself will not make the slightest difference in the temperature of the room. But we can also save our sermonizing, and, instead, simply light the stove and heat it with suitable logs. Then it will radiate its warmth without being reminded of its categorical imperative. And this is how it is when, during various stages of childhood, we bring the right thing to children at the right time.

If, during the first period of life, we create an atmosphere of gratitude around children, and if we do something else, of which I shall speak later, then, out of this gratitude toward the world, toward the entire universe, and also out of an inner thankfulness for being in this world at all (which is something that should ensoul all people), the most deep-seated and warmest piety will grow—not the kind that lives on one's lips or in thought only, but piety that will pervade the entire human being, that will be upright, honest, and true. As for gratitude, it must grow; but this can happen with the intensity necessary for such a soul and spiritual quality only when it develops from the child's tender life-stirrings during the time from birth to its change of teeth. And then this gratitude will become the root of the love of God. It is the foundation for the love of God.

Knowing all this will make us realize that, when we receive children into the first grade, we must also consider the kinds of lives they have led before reaching school age. There should really be direct contact with the parental home—that is, with what has happened before the child entered school. This contact should always be worked for, because teachers should have a fairly clear picture of how the present situation of children was influenced by their social conditions and the milieu in which they grew up. At school, teachers will then find plenty of opportunities to rectify any possible hindrances. For this to happen, however, knowledge of the child's home background, through contact with the parents, is of course absolutely essential. It is necessary that teachers can observe how certain characteristics have developed in a child by simply watching and imitating the mother at home. To be aware of this is very important when the child begins schooling. It is just as much part of teaching as what is done in the classroom. These matters must not be overlooked if one wants to build an effective and properly based education.

We have already seen that, in the years between the child's change of teeth and the coming of puberty, the development of a sense for the authority of the teacher is both natural and essential. The second fundamental virtue, which is love, then grows from that when the child is in the process of also developing the physical basis of love. But one must see love in its true light, for, because of the prevailing materialistic attitudes of our time, the concept of love has become very one-sided and narrow; and because a materialistic out-look tends to see love only in terms of sexual love, it generally traces all manifestations of love back to a hidden sexuality. In an instance of what I called "amateurism squared" the day before yesterday, we find, if not in every case, that at least many psychologists trace human traits back to sexual origins, even if they have nothing what-soever to do with sex. To balance such an attitude, the teacher must have acquired at least some degree of appreciation for the universal nature of love; for sexual love is not the only thing that begins to develop between the child's second dentition and puberty, but also love in its fullest sense, love for everything in the world. Sexual love is only one aspect of love that develops at this time of life. At that age one can see how love of nature and love for fellow human beings awaken in the child, and the teacher needs to have a strong view of how sexual love represents only one facet, one single chapter in life's book of love. If one realizes this, one will also know how to assign sexual love to its proper place in life. Today, for many people who look at life with theoretical eyes, sexual love has become a kind of Moloch who devours his own offspring, inasmuch as, if such views were true, sexual love would devour all other forms of love.

The way love develops in the human soul is different from the way gratitude does. Gratitude has to grow with the growing human being, and this is why it has to be planted when the child's growing forces are at their strongest. Love, on the other hand, has to *awaken*. The development of love really does resemble the process of awakening, and, like awakening, it has to remain more in the region of the soul. The gradual emergence of love is a slow awakening, until the final stage of this process has been reached. Observe for a moment what happens when one awakes in the morning. At first there is a dim awareness of vague notions; perhaps first sensations begin to stir; slowly the eyelids struggle free of being closed; gradually the outer world aids one's awakening; and finally the moment arrives when that awakening passes into the physical body.

This is also how it is with the awakening of love—except that, in the child, this process takes about seven years. At first love begins to stir when sympathy is aroused for whatever is taught during the early days at school. If we begin to approach the child with the kind of imagery I have described, we can see how love especially comes to meet this activity. Everything has to be saturated with this love. At that stage, love has a profoundly soul-like and tender quality. If one compares it with the daily process of waking up, one would still be deeply asleep, or at least in a state of sleeping-dreaming. (Here I am referring to the child's condition, of course—the teacher must not be in a dream, although this appears to happen all too often!) This condition then yields to a stronger jolt into wakefulness. And in what I described yesterday and the day before about the ninth and tenth years—and especially in the time leading up to the twelfth year—love of nature awakens in the child. Only then do we see it truly emerging.

Before this stage, the child's relationship to nature is completely different. A child then has a great love for all that belongs to the fairyworld of nature, a love that has to be nourished by a creative and pictorial approach. Love for the realities in nature awakens only later. At this point we are faced with a particularly difficult task. Into everything connected with the curriculum at this time of life (causality, the study of lifeless matter, an understanding of historical interconnections, the beginnings of physics and chemistry) into all of this, the teacher must introduce—and here I am not joking, but speak very earnestly—the teacher must introduce an element of *grace*. In geometry or physics lessons, for example, there is every need for the teacher to allow real grace to enter into teaching. All lessons should be pervaded with an air of graciousness, and, above all, the subjects must never be allowed to become sour. So often, just during the ages from eleven and a half, or eleven and three-quarters, to fourteen or fifteen, work in these subjects suffers so much by becoming unpalatable and sour. What the pupils have to learn about the refraction and reflection of light or about the measurement of surface areas in a spherical calotte, is so often spoken of not with grace, but with an air of sourness.

At just this time of life the teacher must remember the need for a certain "soul-breathing" in the lessons, which communicates itself to the pupils in a very strange way—soul-breathing must be allowed for. Ordinary breathing consists of inhaling and exhaling. In most cases, or at least on many occasions, teachers, in their physics and geometry lessons, only breathe out with their souls. They do not breathe in, and the out-breath is what produces this acidity. I am referring to the out-breathing of soul expressed in dull and monotonous descriptions, which infuses all content with the added seriousness of inflated proportion. Seriousness does have its place, but not through exaggeration.

On the other hand, an in-breathing of soul brings an inherent sense of humor that is always prepared to sparkle, both within and outside the classroom, or whenever an opportunity arises for teachers and pupils to be together. The only possible hindrance to such radiating humor is the teachers themselves. The children certainly would not stand in its way, nor would the various subjects, provided they were handled with just the right touch during this particular age. If teachers could feel at home in their subjects to the degree that they were entirely free of having to chew over their content while presenting lessons, then they might find themselves in a position where even reflected light is likely to crack a joke, or where a spherical skullcap might calculate its surface area with a winning smile. Of course, jokes should not be planned ahead, nor should they be forced on the classroom situation. Everything should be tinted with spontaneous humor, which is inherent within the content, and not artificially grafted onto it. This is the core of the matter. Humor has to be found in things themselves and, above all, it should not even be necessary to search for it. At best, teachers who have prepared their lessons properly need to bring a certain order and discipline into the ideas that will come to them while teaching, for this is what happens if one is well prepared. The opposite is equally possible, however, if one has not prepared the lessons adequately; one will feel deprived of ideas because one still has to wrestle with the lesson content. This spoils a healthy out-breathing of soul and shuts out the humor-filled air it needs. These are the important points one has to remember at this particular age.

If teaching follows its proper course in this way, the awakening of love will happen so that the student's soul and spirit are properly integrated into the human organization during the final stage of this awakening—that is, when the approach of puberty begins. This is when what first developed so tenderly in the child's soul, and then in a more robust way, can finally take hold of the bodily nature in the right and proper way.

Now you may wonder what teachers have to do to be capable of accomplishing their tasks as described. Here we have to consider something I would like to call the "social aspect" of the teaching profession, the importance of which is recognized far too little. Too often we encounter an image that a certain era (not ancient times, however) has associated with the teaching profession, whose members are not generally respected and honored as they should be. Only when society looks upon teachers with the respect their calling deserves, only when it recognizes that the teachers stand at the forefront of bringing new impulses into our civilization—not just in speeches from a political platform—only then will teachers receive the moral support they need to do their work. Such an attitude— or perhaps better still, such a sentiment—would pave the way toward acquiring a wider and more comprehensive view of life. This is what the teachers need; they also need to be fully integrated into life. They need more than just the proper qualifications in educational principles and methods, more than just special training for their various subjects; most of all teachers need something that will renew itself again and again: a view of life that pulsates in a living way through their souls. What they need is a deep understanding of life itself; they need far more than what can pass from their lips as they stand in front of their classes. All of this has to flow into the making of a teacher. Strictly speaking, the question of education should be part of the social question, and it must embrace not just the actual teaching schools, but also the inner development of the teaching faculty.

It should be understood, at the same time, that the aims and aspirations for contemporary education, as presented here, are in no way rebellious or revolutionary. To believe that would be a great misunderstanding. What is advocated here can be introduced into the present situation without any need for radical changes. And yet, one feels tempted to add that it is just this social aspect of education that points to so many topical questions in life. And so, I would like to mention something, not because I want to agitate against present conditions, but only to illustrate, to put into words, what is bound to come one day. It will not happen in our current age, so please do not view what I am going to say as something radical or revolutionary.

As you know, it is customary today to confer a doctorate on people who, fundamentally speaking, have not yet gained any practical experience in the subjects for which they are given their degree, whether chemistry, geography, or geology. And yet, the proof of their knowledge and capacity would surely have to include the ability to pass their expertise on to other candidates, of teaching them.[9] And so a doctor's degree should not really be granted until a candidate has passed the practical test of teaching and training others who wish to take up the same vocation. You can see great wisdom, based on instinctive knowledge, in the popular expression; for, in the vernacular, only a person capable of healing, capable of giving tangible proof of healing abilities, is called a "doctor." In this

---

9. The word *doctor* is derived from *docere*, the Latin verb meaning "to teach." — TRANS.

instance the word *doctor* refers to someone engaged as a practical healer, and not just to a person who has acquired specialized medical knowledge, however comprehensive this might be.

Two concepts have arisen gradually from the original single concept—that of educating as well as that of healing. In more distant times, teaching or educating was also thought of as including healing. The process of educating was considered synonymous with that of healing. Because it was felt that the human being bore too many marks of physical heredity, education was viewed as a form of healing, as I have already mentioned during a previous meeting here. Using the terminology of past ages, one could even say teaching was considered a means of healing the effects of original sin. Seen in this light, the processes of healing, set in motion by the doctor, are fundamentally the same as those of teaching, though in a different realm of life. From a broader perspective, the teacher is as much of a healer as a doctor. And so the weight the title "doctor" usually carries in the eyes of the public could well become dependent on a general awareness that only those who have passed the test of practical experience should receive the honor of the degree. Otherwise, this title would remain only a label.

However, as I have already said, this must not be misunderstood as the demand of an instigator for the immediate present. I would not even have mentioned it except in a pedagogical context. I am only too aware of the kind of claims that are likely to be listened to in our times, and the ones that inevitably give the impression one is trying to crash through closed doors. If one wants to accomplish something in life, one must be willing to forgo abstract aims or remote ideals, the attempted realization of which would either break one's neck or bruise one's forehead. One must always try to remain in touch with reality. Then one is also justified in using something to illustrate certain needs of our time, even if these may only be fulfilled in the future; for what I have spoken of cannot be demanded for a very long time to come. It may help us to appreciate, nevertheless, the dignity within the social sphere that should be due the teaching profession. I have mentioned all of this because it seemed important that we should see this question in the proper light. If teachers can feel moral support coming from society as a whole, then the gradual awakening of love in the young will become the close ally of their natural sense of authority, which must prevail in schools. Such things sometimes originate in very unexpected places.

Just as the love of God is rooted in gratitude, so genuine moral impulses originate in love, as was described. For nothing else can be the basis for truly ethical virtue except a kind of love for humankind that does not allow us to pass our fellow human beings without bothering to know them, because we no longer have an eye for what lives in them—as happens so easily nowadays. The general love toward all people is the love that reaches out for human understanding everywhere. It is the love that awakens in the child in the time between the change of teeth and puberty, just as gratitude has grown between the child's birth and the loss of the first teeth. At school, we must do everything we can to awaken love.

How are children affected by what happens in their immediate surroundings during the first period of life—that is, from birth to the change of teeth? They see that people engage in all kinds of activities. But what children take in are not the actual accomplishments in themselves, for they have not yet developed the faculty to perceive them consciously. What they do perceive are meaningful gestures. During this first period of life we are concerned with only a childlike understanding of the meaningful gestures they imitate. And from the perception of these meaningful gestures the feeling of gratitude develops, from which the gratitude-engendered will to act arises.

Nor do children perceive the activities happening in their environment during the subsequent years, between the change of teeth and puberty—especially not during the early stages of this period. What they do perceive—even in the kinds of movements of the people around them—no longer represents the sum total of meaningful gestures. Instead, events begin to speak to the children, become a meaningful language. Not just what is spoken in actual words, but every physical movement and every activity speaks directly to the child during this particular time. It makes all the difference, therefore, whether a teacher writes on the blackboard:

Leaf

Or writes the same word thus: *Leaf*

Whether the teacher writes the figure seven like this: 7

Or like this: 7

Whether it is written in an artistic, in a less-refined, or even in a slovenly way, makes a great difference. The way in which these things affect the child's life is what matters. Whether the word *leaf* is written in the first or second way (see above), is a meaningful language for the child. Whether the teacher enters the classroom in a dignified manner, or whether the teacher tries to cut a fine figure, speaks directly to the child. Likewise, whether the teacher is always fully awake to the classroom situation—this will show itself in the child's eye by the way the teacher handles various objects during the lessons—or, during wintertime, whether it could even happen that the teacher absent-mindedly walks off with the blackboard towel around his or her neck, mistaking it for a scarf—all of this speaks volumes to the child. It is not so much the outer actions that work on the child, but what lives behind them, whether unpleasant and ugly, or charming and pleasant.

In this context, it is even possible that a certain personal habit of a teacher may generate a friendly atmosphere in the classroom, even if it might appear, in itself, very comic. For example, from my thirteenth to eighteenth year I had a teacher—and I always considered him to be my best teacher—who never began a lesson without gently blowing his nose first. Had he ever started his lesson without doing so, we would have sorely missed it. I am not saying that he was at all conscious of the effect this was having on his pupils, but one really begins to wonder whether in such a case it would even be right to expect such a person to overcome an ingrained habit. But this is an altogether different matter. I have mentioned this episode only as an illustration.

The point is, everything teachers do in front of children at this stage of life constitutes meaningful language for them. The actual words that teachers speak are merely part of this language. There are many other unconscious factors lying in the depths of the feeling life that also play a part. For example, the child has an extraordinarily fine perception (which never reaches the sphere of consciousness) of whether a teacher makes up to one or another pupil during lessons or whether she or he behaves in a natural and dignified way. All this is of immense importance to the child. In addition, it makes a tremendous difference to the pupils whether teachers have prepared themselves well enough to present their lessons without having to use printed or written notes, as already mentioned during our discussion. Without being aware of it, children ask themselves: Why should I have to know what the teachers do not know? After all, I too am only human. Teachers are supposed to be fully grown up, and I am only a child. Why should I have to work so hard to learn what even they don't know?

This is the sort of thing that deeply torments the child's unconscious, something that cannot be rectified once it has become fixed there. It confirms that the sensitive yet natural relationship between teachers and students of this age can come about only if the teachers—forgive this rather pedantic remark, but it cannot be avoided in this situation—have the subject completely at their fingertips. It must live "well-greased" in them— if I may use this expression— but not in the sense of bad and careless writing.[10] I use it here in the sense of greasing wheels to make them run smoothly. Teachers will then feel in full command of the classroom situation, and they will act accordingly. This in itself will ensure an atmosphere where it would never occur to students to be impudent.

---

10. In German, "very untidy writing" is often referred to as *Geschmier,* a "smear on the page." The verb *schmieren* also means "to grease." — TRANS.

For that to happen among children of ten, eleven, or twelve would really be one of the worst possible things. We must always be aware that whatever we say to our pupils, even if we are trying to be humorous, should never induce them to give a frivolous or insolent reply. An example of this is the following situation: A teacher might say to a student who suddenly got stuck because of a lack of effort and attention, "Here the ox stands held up by the mountain." And the pupil retorts, "Sir, I am not a mountain."[11] This sort of thing must not be allowed to happen. If the teachers have prepared their lessons properly, a respectful attitude will emerge toward them as a matter of course. And if such an attitude is present, such an impertinent reply would be unthinkable. It may, of course, be of a milder and less undermining kind. I have mentioned it only to illustrate my point. Such impudent remarks would destroy not only the mood for work in the class, but they could easily infect other pupils and thus spoil a whole class.

Only when the transition from the second life period to the third occurs, is the possibility given for (how shall I call them now in these modern times?) young men and young women to observe the activities occurring around them. Previously the meaningful gesture was perceived, and later the meaningful language of the events around the child. Only now does the possibility exist for the adolescent to observe the activities performed by other people in the environment. I have also said that, by perceiving meaningful gestures, and through experiencing gratitude, the love for God develops, and that, through the meaningful language that comes from the surroundings, love for everything human is developed as the foundation for an individual sense of morality. If now the adolescent is enabled to observe other people's activities properly, love of work will develop. While gratitude must be allowed to grow, and love must be awakened, what needs to evolve now must appear with the young person's full inner awareness. We must have enabled the

---

11. The German saying "*Wie der Ochs Corm Berg stehen.*" It means literally "to stand there like the ox facing the mountain." It is a very common saying, and it can also be translated as "to be completely out of one's depth," "to be nonplussed." — TRANS.

young person to enter this new phase of development after puberty with full inner awareness, so that in a certain way the adolescent comes to find the self. Then love of work will develop. This love of work has to grow freely on the strength of what has already been attained. This is love of work in general and also love for what one does oneself. At the moment when an understanding for the activities of other people awakens as a complementary image, a conscious attitude toward love of work, a love of "doing" must arise. In this way, during the intervening stages, the child's early play has become transmuted into the proper view of work, and this is what we must aim for in our society today.

What part do teachers and educators have to play in all of this? This is something that belongs to one of the most difficult things in their vocational lives. For the best thing teachers can do for the child during the first and second life period is to help what will awaken on its own with the beginning of puberty. When, to their everlasting surprise, teachers witness time and again how the child's individuality is gradually emerging, they have to realize that they themselves have been only a tool. Without this attitude, sparked by this realization, one can hardly be a proper teacher; for in classes one is faced with the most varied types of individuals, and it would never do to stand in the classroom with the feeling that all of one's students should become copies of oneself. Such a sentiment should never arise—and why not? Because it could very well happen that, if one is fortunate enough, among the pupils there might be three or four budding geniuses, very distinct from the dull ones, about whom we will have more to say later. Surely you will acknowledge that it is not possible to select only geniuses for the teaching profession, that it is certain that teachers are not endowed with the genius that some of their students will display in later life. Yet teachers must be able to educate not only pupils of their own capacity, but also those who, with their exceptional brightness, will far outshine them.

However, teachers will be able to do this only if they get out of the habit of hoping to make their pupils into what they themselves are. If they can make a firm resolve to stand in the school as selflessly as possible, to obliterate not only their own sympathies and antipathies, but also their personal ambitions, in order to dedicate themselves to whatever comes from the students, then they will properly educate potential geniuses as well as the less-bright pupils. Only such an attitude will lead to the realization that *all education is, fundamentally, a matter of self-education.*

Essentially, there is no education other than self-education, whatever the level may be. This is recognized in its full depth within anthroposophy, which has conscious knowledge through spiritual investigation of repeated Earth lives. Every education is self-education, and as teachers we can only provide the environment for children's self-education. We have to provide the most favorable conditions where, through our agency, children can educate themselves according to their own destinies.

This is the attitude that teachers should have toward children, and such an attitude can be developed only through an ever-growing awareness of this fact. For people in general there may be many kinds of prayers. Over and above these there is this special prayer for the teacher:

> Dear God, bring it about that I—inasmuch as my personal ambitions are concerned—negate myself. And Christ make true in me the Pauline words, "Not I, but the Christ in me."

This prayer, addressed to God in general and to Christ in particular, continues: "… so that the Holy Spirit may hold sway in the teacher." This is the true Trinity.

If one can live in these thoughts while in close proximity to the students, then the hoped-for results of this education can also become a social act at the same time. But other matters also come into play, and I can only touch on them. Just consider what, in the opinion of many people, would have to be done to improve today's social order. People expect better conditions through the implementation of external measures. You need only look at the dreadful experiments being carried out in Soviet Russia. There the happiness of the whole world is sought through the inauguration of external programs. It is believed that improvements in the social sphere depend on the creation of institutions. And yet, these are the least significant factors within social development. You can set up any institutions you like, be they monarchist or republican, democratic or socialist; the decisive factor will always be the kind of people who live and work under any of these systems. For those who spread a socializing influence, the two things that matter are a loving devotion toward what they are doing, and an understanding interest in what others are doing.

Think about what can flow from just these two attributes; at least people can work together again in the social sphere. But this will have to become a tradition over ages. As long as you merely work externally, you will produce no tangible results. You have to bring out these two qualities from the depths of human nature. If you want to introduce changes by external means, even when established with the best of intentions, you will find that people will not respond as expected. And, conversely, their actions may elude your understanding. Institutions are the outcome of individual endeavor. You can see this everywhere. They were created by the very two qualities that more or less lived in the initiators—that is, loving devotion toward what they were doing, and an understanding interest in what others were doing....

3

THE WALDORF KINDERGARTEN

The World of the Young Child

THE FIRST SEVEN YEARS of life are a time of tremendous growth and transformation. Having left the spiritual worlds, the child begins the journey of incarnation, and the soul and spirit have to struggle to adapt to the vessel of the body. During the first three years of life, the child faces the monumental challenges of learning to walk, to speak, and to think. In the following years, countless other capacities and skills will need to be developed in order for the child to become independent. The education of the young child is a particularly challenging endeavor, for it demands that parents and teachers penetrate both the spiritual and the practical tasks of leading the child into earth existence. In *Foundations of Human Experience*, Rudolf Steiner summarized this endeavor:

> The task of education, understood in a spiritual sense, is to bring the soul-spirit into harmony with the temporal body. They must be brought into harmony and they must be tuned to one another, because when the child is born into the physical world they do not yet properly fit each other. The task of the teacher is to harmonize these two parts to one another. (p. 39)

The Nature of the Young Child

Although young children are earthly beings, to a certain extent they are still cosmic beings. Living as they do between these two worlds, they need to find a relationship to time. This relationship is developed through the etheric body, which is working on the physical body to make it into a suitable instrument for the child's later life. The etheric body is a body working through time, and etheric processes are always rhythmical.

Young children respond strongly to rhythm, and they are tremendously helped when there is rhythm and regularity in their lives. Waldorf kindergartens therefore build a strong rhythmic element into their program. In all Waldorf kindergartens each day has a rhythm. The morning might begin with a period for play and work followed by circle time, consisting of verses, nursery rhymes, songs, and circle games. Next comes a session of outdoor play, and the morning session ends with a nature story or a folk or fairy tale. Each week has its rhythm as well—there is one day for baking, another for painting, a third for crafts, and so on. Seasonal activities such as harvesting grain, planting bulbs, tapping maple trees, or gathering nuts serve to deepen the children's awareness of the world around them. Seasonal festivals, which celebrate the bounty of the autumn or the advent of spring foster a connection to the cycle of the year. Through such activities, which are taken up rhythmically, a child's feeling for the cycles of life and of nature is strengthened. In later years this feeling may sustain a sense of well-being and a sense of connection to the natural world.

Young children also have an intimate connection to their surroundings, and everything they encounter makes a deep impression on them. Because they are so sensitive and receptive, one might conceive of young children as sense organs that perceive the world with their whole being.

What is localized as a sense in adult ears, however, is spread out through the entire organism of a young child. For that reason, children do not differentiate between spirit, soul, and body. Everything that affects a child from outside is recreated within. Children imitatively recreate their entire environment within themselves. (p. 91)

Since the surroundings in which children are raised and educated affect them deeply, great care must be taken to create an environment that is nourishing to the senses. Waldorf teachers therefore strive to create an environment where order and beauty prevail. The walls of the kindergarten are usually painted with luminous washes of watercolor; the window curtains are made from plant-dyed fabric; sturdy tables and chairs are constructed of solid wood; and most of the imaginative toys and playthings are handcrafted from natural materials. These beautiful surroundings are simple and calming, and the sense impressions that they engender promote the child's physical growth and health. Because the materials used in the kindergarten are natural and real, they help the child develop a healthy relationship to the material world.

Young children not only perceive and respond to their environment, they also reflect and express the gesture of their surroundings and of the people in their lives. This places a great responsibility on the adults responsible for raising and educating the child: they must be worthy of imitation. In lecture two of *The Kingdom of Childhood*, Steiner says:

> These are the things that matter most for young children. What you say, what you teach, does not yet make an impression, except insofar as children imitate what you say in their own speech. But it is what you *are* that matters; if you are good this goodness will appear in your gestures; and if you are bad-tempered this also will appear in your gestures—in short, everything that you do yourself passes over into the children and makes its way within them. This is the essential point. Children are wholly sense-organ, and react to all the impressions of the people around them. Therefore the essential thing is not to imagine that children can learn what is good or bad, that they can learn this or that, but to know that everything that is done in their presence is transformed in their childish organisms into spirit, soul, and body. The health of children for their whole life depends on how you conduct yourself in their presence. The inclinations that children develop depend on how you behave in their presence. (pp. 17–18)

The education of young children is therefore largely a matter of the adult's own self-education. We must become ever more conscious of ourselves and committed to our strivings; we must work to transform ourselves so that the children in our care will be nourished by the truth, beauty, and goodness living in our thoughts, words, and deeds. This work is supported by the path of inner development suggested by Steiner.

Why are young children such imitative beings? According to Steiner, this trait is a continuation of the child's pre-birth experiences. Before birth, the spirit of the child is united with angelic and other spiritual beings, whose impulses are expressed in and through the child. After the child is born, the child still responds to and expresses impulses from without; this becomes imitation.

The realization that we as human beings continue the work of the angels, the archangels, and even higher spiritual beings can fill us with awe and inspire a feeling of gratitude.

> This feeling is essential in a teacher and educator, and it should be instinctive in anyone entrusted with nurturing a child. Thus, the foremost thing to strive for in spiritual knowledge is gratitude that the universe has given a child into our keeping. (SG, p. 57)

Imitation can take several forms. A young child might imitate someone's actions directly. If a teacher is carding and spinning wool, for example, a child might also want to card and spin. Children might also imitate in their play the actions that they have encountered. For instance, a group of children might join together to form a moving company. They will pack up the toys in the kindergarten into a moving van that they have made of some chairs and boards and drive it to another land. Children also imitate our inner attitude. Kindergarten teachers therefore try to pervade everything they do with care. This will be reflected in the way they place an object on the seasonal table, or the way they put the toys away at clean-up time and make sure all the babies are tucked in and don't have any cold toes sticking out. If parents and teachers approach common life tasks such as cooking or cleaning with reverence and care, children will develop a deep respect for work and for material things. If, however, such tasks are done quickly and sloppily, this will be reflected in children's difficulties in finding meaning in life.

Through imitation, children become human beings and learn the three fundamental capacities that distinguish the human being from the animals: to walk upright, to speak, and to think. In "Walking, Speaking, Thinking," Steiner describes how children develop these three capacities, and he indicates how parents and teachers can affect this process.

According to Steiner, *"the real secret of human development is that what is ensouled or made spiritual at a particular stage in life is later revealed physically, often after many years"* (p. 105). How we approach the child during these early years can therefore determine the child's future health.

Because children have a natural impulse to raise themselves upright and to walk, these activities need not be forced or aided by artificial means. Parents can best help their children learn to walk through loving guidance and gentle assistance. This will "create health-giving forces in the children that will reveal themselves as a healthy metabolism when those children reach fifty or sixty years of age" (p. 104).

Speaking is a further refinement of the child's limb activity, for "all the nuances of speech arise from the forms of movement. Life consists first of gestures; those gestures are then inwardly transformed into the source of speech" (p. 105). Adults can best help the child learn to speak by cultivating a deep inner truthfulness. Speaking in an artificial or childish manner should be avoided, for children want to learn the speech of adults and inwardly resent and reject baby talk. According to Steiner, children who learn to speak by imitating the spirit of truth in the adults around them will be strengthened in their respiratory system later in life.

The ability to think evolves from the capacity for speech. The best help we can give young children in learning to think is to bring clarity and precision into our own thoughts. If we are inconsequent in our thinking, if we confuse children by giving orders and then reversing ourselves, we may not only impair the child's ability to think but may lay the foundation for nervous diseases in adulthood.

The capacities for walking, speaking, and thinking establish the foundation of our humanity. Walking establishes our relationship to the world, speech allows us to communicate with our fellow human beings, thought gives us the capacity to know ourselves. We serve the whole of a child's life if we cultivate the inner qualities that will help in the proper acquisition of these capacities.

Learning through Play

Young children love to play. Through play, they enter the activities of the adults around them. The best kind of activities for kindergarten children are therefore those that allow them to engage, on a child's level, in the work of adults. In the kindergarten, "we should not allow the children to do anything, even in play, that is not an imitation of life itself " (KC, p. 118). In the Waldorf kindergarten, children are offered the possibility of participating in the traditional activities that might take place in a home: cooking and baking, cleaning and washing, sewing and ironing, gardening and building. Because these activities are done rhythmically, they create a feeling of well-being and a sense of security in the child. Because they are real, they help a child become grounded in the realities of life. Because they serve a purpose and are filled with meaning, they help the child enter more fully into life at a later age.

The materials and toys in a Waldorf kindergarten stimulate the children to use their powers of imagination and fantasy. As these powers are developed, children become able to transform natural materials into any kind of toy. They can use pieces of wood that have been left in their natural shapes as tools, musical instruments, telephones, vehicles, tickets to a performance, food for a feast, or the gold and jewels of a buried treasure hidden by pirates.

If one observes children playing with toys that have a great deal of detail, one can see that there is a different quality to the play. Whereas an "unfinished" toy leaves children free to exert their imaginations, a "finished" toy ties the child to a certain group of activities. If, for instance, children are given a toy yellow taxi cab, they are likely to limit their play to activities involving a taxi. If, however, they are given a plain wooden car, it can serve many different purposes: a racing car or moving van, a sight-seeing bus or a tractor trailer, the caboose of a freight train or an ambulance. The possibilities are endless, limited only by the children's imagination.

However much they may seem fascinated by toys that are realistic, children have an inner antipathy toward such playthings, because they cannot imbue such objects with the living powers of imagination. In "Walking, Speaking, Thinking," Steiner says that to give children such toys is a form of inner punishment. In another lecture on early childhood, he says that playing with building blocks has far-reaching affects on the development of the child's imagination, for it begets an atomistic-materialistic mentality that always wants to put bits and pieces together in predictable, limited ways. These statements should challenge us to find toys and playthings that will be nourishing to our children, that stimulate their imagination and develop the sources of creativity and intellectual capacities that will develop in later years.

Paradoxical as it may seem, we help children lay the foundations for capacities of thought by letting them dwell in the dreamy state that is engendered through imaginative play. In lecture thirteen of *The Renewal of Education*, Steiner speaks about the importance of this kind of play.

> During the time between birth and the change of teeth, we acquire the forces of our still unborn spirituality through the activity of playing and through what is enacted before our eyes in such a dreamlike way. They are unborn because they have not yet been absorbed by the physical body. As I have told you, the forces that have been building up the child's physical organism become independent of the body after the change of teeth and become the forces for thinking and ideation. During the change of teeth something is being withdrawn, as it were, from the child's physical body. However,

by contrast, the forces that flow through the activities of a child at play have yet to anchor themselves to earthly life and its practical tasks; they have not yet incarnated in the child's physical organism.

This means we are confronted with two different forces at this time: those working through the child's body, which after the change of teeth are transformed into the capacity of forming concepts that can be remembered; and other forces active within the child's soul and spiritual sphere, hovering lightly and etherically above the child, pervading play activities just as dreams pervade our sleep during our lives. For the child, the activity of these latter forces develops not only during sleep, but also while awake—when the child plays. In this way these forces become outer reality.

However, what is being developed through this outer reality begins to recede after the seventh year. Just as the germinating forces in the plant recede during leaf and petal formation and reappear only when the fruit is forming, so also the forces that pervade the playing child reappear approximately in the twenty-first or twenty-second year as powers of intellect that enable the human being to gather free and independent life experiences. (RE, pp. 168–169)

The curricula of many modern kindergartens include various kinds of readiness activities that prepare children for formal learning. In some kindergartens, children are even taught the rudiments of reading, writing, and arithmetic. Waldorf kindergartens also prepare children for the academic challenges of elementary school, but they do so by engaging the will through meaningful life activities, by cultivating the feelings through the arts, and by stimulating creativity and fantasy through imaginative play. Waldorf kindergarten teachers do not place premature academic demands on their students. Rather, they allow the children's intellectual faculties to unfold naturally so that by the time children enter the elementary grades, they are ready and eager to experience new forms of learning.

Awakening Reverence

Young children are imbued with a natural piety, for they view the world with wonder and they give themselves fully to every experience. Waldorf kindergarten teachers try to keep alive children's natural sense of wonder and their sense of oneness and unselfconscious participation with the world. This is done by surrounding the children with a mythic consciousness, one that affirms the living reality of the elements and creatures of the natural world; the children greet Father Sun in their morning verse and give thanks to Mother Earth at snack time; gentle Prince Autumn must make way for King Winter with his blustery moods, and lovely Princess Spring is warmly welcomed by all.

In the Waldorf kindergarten, the child's sense of reverence is fostered and deepened through activities, stories, and festivals that enable children to participate in the cycle of the year. In the autumn, for example, the classroom might be decorated with stalks of corn and sheaves of ripened grain. Bouquets of bright-hued leaves and autumn flowers sparkle here and there, adding color and fragrance to the room. The seasonal table might be draped with red and golden silks on which pumpkins and gourds are displayed; a little squirrel is hiding acorns, and a gnome peeks out of a small hollow stump. The morning circle time includes songs and poems that express the bounty of the year. The children might learn a finger play to a verse such as, "Way up high in the apple tree, two little apples are smiling at me. I shook that tree as hard as I could; Down came the apples—umm, they were good!" or play a circle singing game such as "Old Roger." Apples are plentiful and the children may make applesauce or apple crisp or an apple pie with a fancy latticed crust. They might create little boats out of walnut shells and sail them down the stream, or dip leaves in beeswax and hang them in the windows. The season might culminate with an autumn festival to which the parents are invited. The children wear bright colored capes and autumn crowns and their faces glow with excitement and joy. The teacher tells a story; parents as well as children are transported to another time, another place. Then everyone gathers in a circle and voices rise in a song of thankfulness and praise before the harvest feast is served. Fortunate are the children whose experience of the season has been enriched in so many ways!

The seeds of reverence sown in the kindergarten and early elementary grades yield fruits that may ripen much later in life.

> If one observes children who, through proper upbringing, have developed a natural reverence for the adults around them, and if one follows them through their various phases of life, one may discover that their feelings for reverence and devotion in childhood gradually transform during the years leading to old age. As adults, such persons may have a healing effect on others, so that through their mere presence, tone of voice, or perhaps a single glance they spread inner peace to others. Their presence can be a blessing, because as children they have learned to venerate and to pray in the right way. No hands can bless in old age, unless in childhood they have been folded in prayer. (RE, p. 65)

Working with young children is extraordinarily challenging, for it demands that teachers work out of the very essence of their being and be willing to put themselves aside in the service of the child. Teachers who choose to work in the kindergarten must be willing to ask themselves:

> What must I do to obliterate, as far as possible, my personal self in order to keep those entrusted to my care from being burdened by my subjective nature? How should I act so that I do not interfere with the children's destiny? And, above all, how can I best educate the children toward human freedom? (SE, pp. 107–108)

Although the responsibilities of working with young children are immense, the rewards are boundless; the seeds that are sown during these early years will sprout and grow, and their blossoms and fruit will enrich the rest of the children's lives.

Walking, Speaking, Thinking:

Milestones in the Life of the Young Child

LECTURE BY RUDOLF STEINER

Ilkley, August 10, 1923

What I have presented thus far should not result simply in some theory about the necessity for a new form of education, but in a new attitude toward education. In the previous lectures, I wanted to speak less to the intellect and more to the heart. That is most important for the teacher since, as we have seen, we must base the art of education upon a thorough understanding of the human being.

For some time now, whenever people discuss the art of education we hear that it is the child that is important. There are numerous pedagogical directives, in a certain sense, theoretical commands, about what we should do with the child. However, we can never develop the teacher's complete devotion to the profession of education in that way. That is possible only when the educator is capable of penetrating all of human nature in body, soul, and spirit.

Those who have living ideas about the human being of the sort I have described will find that those ideas are transformed directly into will. Teachers will learn in a practical way from hour to hour how to answer a most important question.

But who asks that question? It is the children themselves. Thus, the most important thing is to learn how to read the children. A genuinely practical understanding of the human being in body, soul, and spirit guides us in learning how to really read children.

It is difficult to speak about the so-called Waldorf School pedagogy, as that pedagogy is not actually something we can learn or discuss. The Waldorf School pedagogy is purely practical, and we can describe it only through examples—that is, how in one situation or another, how for one need or another, that pedagogy is practiced.

How we practice the pedagogy itself is a direct result of experience. When we start from this attitude, we always assume that an appropriate understanding of the human being is present in the teacher. If that is the case, then pedagogy and teaching are, in a certain sense, very general social questions, since the education of the child should actually begin immediately after birth. That means humanity as a whole is responsible for education, every family and every group of people—something that an understanding of the nature of children before the change of teeth before the age of seven, teaches us. Jean Paul, a German writer, said something really wonderful when he said that people learn more about life in their first three years than they do in three years at the university.

It is, in fact, true that primarily the first three years, and then the remaining years before the age of seven, are the most important for the general development of the human being. A child is a very different human being at a later age. During those first years, a child is actually an organ of sense perception. The problem is that people do not normally imagine intensively enough the importance of that fact. We need to make very drastic statements if we are to reveal the full truth of that thought.

Later in life, people taste what they eat with their mouths or gums or on their tongues. Their taste is localized in their heads, so to speak. That is not the case with children, particularly during the first years of life. Taste has an effect upon their entire organism. Children can taste their mother's milk and their first foods right into their limbs. What later takes place only on the tongue happens for the young child throughout the entire organism. In a certain sense, the child lives by tasting everything encountered. In this regard, there is something quite animalistic in young children; however, we should never imagine what is animalistic in a child as the same as what is animalistic in animals. What is animalistic in young children is, in a certain sense, at a higher level. A human being is never an animal, not even as an embryo—in fact, there least of all. We can clarify such ideas by comparing them with something else.

If you have ever looked with some insight into natural processes say, at a herd of cows, how they graze in a meadow or field, then lie down and take care of their digestion, each cow devoted, in a certain way, to the whole world, then you may have gotten some impression of what actually goes on in the animal. An entire universe, an extract of cosmic happening, is underway in the animal, and the animal experiences the most wonderful visions while it is digesting. Digesting is the most important means of understanding in animals. While the animal is digesting, it devotes itself in a dreamy, imaginative way to the entire world.

That seems overstated, but the most curious thing is that it is not at all overstated. It, in fact, corresponds to reality. If we now raise that picture a step, the result is the experience of the young child in the physical functions. Taste accompanies all physical functions. And just the same way that taste accompanies all physical functions, something else, which is later localized only in the eyes and ears, exists throughout the entire organism of the child.

Imagine how wonderful an eye is, how it receives something full of color formed outside and creates a picture within, which is how we see. That is localized, it is separate from the totality of our experiences. We comprehend with our intellect what the eye creates in this wonderful way. The intellect makes it into a kind of shadow picture. It is just the same with the wonderful processes that are localized in the ears of adults. What is localized as a sense in adult ears, however, is spread out through the entire organism of a young child. For that reason, children do not differentiate between spirit, soul, and body. Everything that affects a child from outside is re-created within. Children imitatively recreate their entire environment within themselves.

Now that we have looked at things from that perspective, we need to look at how children learn three important activities during the first years, that is, how they learn to walk, to speak, and to think. During their first years, children learn these three capacities that are so important for the remainder of their lives.

I would call "learning to walk" a kind of abbreviation, a shorthand form of something that is much more comprehensive. Because learning to walk is most obvious to us, we say children learn to walk. However, learning to walk is directly connected with putting ourselves into a state of balance in relation to the entire spatial world. As children, we seek to stand up. We seek to bring our legs into such a relationship to gravity that we then have our balance. We seek to do the same with our arms and hands. Our entire body thus achieves an orientation. Learning to walk means finding our direction in space, that is, placing our organism into a spatial orientation to the world.

It is important for us to see properly that a young child is an imitative, sense-perceptive being, since, during their first years, children must learn everything through imitation—that is, by imitating what occurs in their surroundings.

It is clear to everyone how the child's organism develops its own strengths of orientation, how the human organism tends to bring itself into a vertical position and not remain in a horizontal position, as with crawling, and to bring the arms into a similar balance with the spatial world. All of that is an inherent characteristic of the young child and arises out of the organism's own impulses, so to speak.

If, as teachers, we bring even the slightest compulsion into the real desires of human nature, if we do not leave human nature free and act only as assistants, then we spoil the human organism for all of earthly life. If we use some improper external actions to force the child to begin to walk, if we do not simply help the child, but instead force the child to walk or stand up, we ruin the child's life right up until death. In particular, we ruin the child's life when he or she reaches old age. What is important in properly educating a child is not to look simply at the present, but to look at the entirety of the child's life until death. We need to understand that the seeds of a person's entire earthly life exist in the person during childhood.

Since a child is an extraordinarily subtly organized organ of sense perception, he or she is receptive not only to the physical influences of the surroundings, but also to the moral influences, in particular, the influences of thoughts. As paradoxical as that may seem to today's materialistically thinking people, children perceive what we think when we are near them. As parents or teachers, it is important that when we are near young children we not only avoid doing things we should not do in front of children, but also that our thoughts and feelings, which the children feel, be inwardly true and moral. A child forms its being not just according to our words or deeds, but also according to our attitudes, our thoughts, and our feelings. During the first period of childhood, until the age of seven, the most important thing for education is the child's surroundings.

We now come to the question of what we can do to guide or assist children who are learning to walk and orient themselves. It is important that, through spiritual science, we see the living relationships that we cannot see with a dead, unspiritual science.

Let us take a child who was forced to walk and to orient him- or herself in space in all kinds of ways because people felt it was the proper thing to do. Let us now look at that child who has reached the age of fifty or sixty. If nothing else has acted to correct it, under some circumstances we will see that this adult of fifty to sixty years old has all kinds of metabolic illnesses, rheumatism, gout, and so forth. Everything we do with children to force them into the vertical position and teach them to walk, even though we may do it only halfheartedly, goes so deeply into the spirit-soul that their spirits affect their physical bodies. Those forces that we create through very questionable means remain throughout the entirety of life, and, if they are not the proper forces, they reveal themselves later in physical illnesses.

All education of young children is also a physical training. You cannot separate physical education, since all spiritual and soul education has an effect upon children's physical bodies and is thus physical education. When you see children beginning to orient themselves in standing upright and beginning to walk, when you view with inner love the wonderful secret of the human organism that causes children to move from horizontal to the vertical, when you have a religious feeling and view with modesty the creative forces of God and how children begin to orient themselves in space, when you are someone who intimately loves the human nature of the children in that you love every expression of human nature—in other words, when you assist children in learning to walk and orient themselves—you create health-giving forces in the children that will reveal themselves as a healthy metabolism when those children reach fifty or sixty years of age, a time when people require some control over their metabolisms.

The real secret of human development is that what is ensouled or made spiritual at a particular stage in life is later revealed physically, often after many years. That is how it is with learning to walk. A child who is guided with love into learning how to walk will grow up to be a healthy human being. Using love in helping the child learn to walk is a good part of simple physical and health education.

Speaking develops out of the child's orientation in space. Modern physiology does not know much about that, but it does know a little. Physiology recognizes that although we act with our right hands, there is a certain area on the left-hand side of the brain that represents the source of speaking. Physiology, therefore, indicates a correspondence between the movements of the right hand and the so-called Broca's area in the left side of the brain. How the hand moves, how it gestures, and how strength enters it, enters the brain and forms the source of speech. That is but a small part of what science knows about the subject. The truth is, though, that speaking arises not just from the movements of the right hand, which correspond to a structure on the left-hand side of the brain,[1] but also out of the entire motor functions of the human being. How the child learns to walk and to orient itself in space, how it learns to transform those first dangling, uncontrolled movements of its arms into meaningful movements connected to the external world, all that transfers through unknown means to the inner organization of the human head. That inner organization makes its appearance as speech.

Those who can correctly comprehend such things realize that children who drag their feet voice their sounds, especially those made with the lips, differently than children with a firm step. All the nuances of speech arise from the forms of movement. Life consists

---

1. Among neurologists, it is currently a widely accepted observation that the area of speech appears in some individuals on the right side of the brain. — Trans.

first of gestures; those gestures are then inwardly transformed into the source of speech. Speech is thus a result of walking and the child's orientation in space. Much of how a child speaks depends on our loving help as a child learns to walk.

These are the subtle connections resulting from a genuine comprehension of the human being. It was not without reason that I went into such detail in the past days about how the spirit comes into the human constitution. In this way, we can bring the spirit to the physical body, since the physical body follows the spirit at each step if the spirit is brought to it in the proper way.

Children learn to speak by first using their entire organism. When you look at the situation, you will see that you first have external leg movements, which give rise to strong contours of speech. These are followed by arm and hand movements, which give rise to inflections in words and their forms. We can see that external movements become a flexibility of language within the child.

If to assist children in learning to walk, we need to provide guidance through love, then to assist them in learning to speak, we need to be inwardly quite true. Life's greatest untruths are created while the child is learning to speak, since the truth of speech is taken in through the physical organism.

Children to whom we always express ourselves truthfully as teachers will imitate their surroundings and learn to speak so that the subtle activity that continuously occurs as inhalation and exhalation will become firmer. We should not, of course, imagine these things as gross, but as very subtle. They have a very subtle existence, but they reveal themselves throughout life. We inhale oxygen and exhale carbon dioxide. Within our organism, we must transform oxygen into carbon dioxide through the breathing process. The world gives us oxygen and receives carbon dioxide from us. Whether we can properly transform oxygen into carbon dioxide depends upon whether we were treated truthfully or untruthfully by those in our surroundings while we were learning to speak. In this case, the spiritual is transformed completely into the physical.

One such untruth is our belief that we are doing something good when we reduce our language to that of a child's when we are around children. Unconsciously, a child does not want childish language. Children want to hear the genuine language of adults. We should, therefore, speak normally to children, not with some made-up childish language. Due to their incapacities, children will first imitate in a babbling way what we say to them, but we should not babble. That would be a major mistake. If we believe we must use babbling baby talk, we will ruin the children's digestive organs, as all spiritual things become physical and act formatively upon the physical organism. Everything we do spiritually with children is also a physical training, since children are nothing in themselves. An unhealthy digestive organ in later life is often due to incorrectly learning to speak.

Just as speaking comes from walking and gestures, from human movements, thinking develops from speaking. Just as we need to give loving assistance in helping children learn to walk, we should pay particular attention to truthfulness while they are learning to speak, since they inwardly recreate their surroundings. Since children are completely organs of sense perception and recreate the spiritual physically, we should emphasize clarity in our thinking, so they will develop proper thinking from speaking.

The worst thing we could do to a child would be to make a statement and then retract it and say something different, so that confusion arises. Using confused thinking in front of a child is the actual cause of what today's civilization calls nervousness. Why are so many people nervous? Because when, as children, they were learning to think after they had learned to speak, people near them did not think clearly and precisely.

The greatest errors in the behavior of the next generation are a true reflection of the previous generation. If you look later in life at the children you taught and notice what their vices are, those vices should give you cause to think about yourself. There is a very close connection between everything that occurs in the surroundings of children and what children express through the physical body. For young children, love as they are learning to walk, truthfulness as they are learning to speak, and clarity and firmness in their surroundings as they are learning to think become their physical constitution. The children's organs and vessels form according to the way love, truthfulness, and clarity develop in their environment.

Metabolic illnesses result from learning to walk without love. Digestive problems can result from untruthfulness while the child is learning to speak, and nervousness results from confused thinking in the child's surroundings.

If you look at how common nervousness is in the third decade of the twentieth century, you have to conclude that teachers were very confused around the beginning of the century. The confused thinking of that time appears as nervousness today. Furthermore, people's nervousness at the turn of the century is nothing more than a picture of confusion around 1870. We cannot look at these things and say that a physiological, hygienic, and psychological pedagogy existed, and that a doctor should have been brought in whenever the teacher needed to handle something in a healthy way. Instead, physiological pedagogy and school hygiene form a whole, and it is part of the teacher's mission to work with the effects of the spiritual upon the physical, sense-perceptive organism.

Since all people are teachers for children between birth and the age of seven, we face the social task of achieving a genuine understanding of the human being if humanity is not to regress, but instead move forward.

Our more humane age has justifiably eliminated a previously very common practice in schools, namely, beating and spanking. No one should accuse me of supporting beatings, but in our time there has been such great success in removing beatings from the schools because we pay more attention to externalities. We can see how physically harmful beatings are and the moral consequences arising from those beatings.

However, in our age so much oriented toward the physical and sense perceptible and so little oriented toward the spirit and the soul, we have brought a terrible form of beatings into education, a form people have no idea of because they look so little toward the spirit.

For example, modern mothers, and to a certain extent fathers, find it extremely important to give "beautiful dolls" to little girls, so that a little girl can play with such a beautiful doll. In spite of those good intentions, such beautiful dolls are horrible looking because they are so inartistic. Nevertheless, modern people often think a beautiful doll must have "real" hair, "real" make-up, and maybe even moveable eyes, so that when you lay the doll down, the eyes close, and when you pick it up again, the eyes look at you. There are even dolls that move. In short, we now give children toys that imitate life in a strange and inartistic way. Such dolls are simply characteristic examples. Our civilization is slowly creating all children's toys in a similar way. Such toys are a terrible inner beating of children. Just as children who are well-behaved in public can have a conventional upbringing and be beaten at home, so children do not reveal the antipathy toward beautiful dolls that lies deep within their souls. We force children to like them, but the unconscious forces within the children, their dislike of everything about the beautiful dolls, also play a strong role. As I will show in a moment, such things beat children inwardly.

If you take into consideration everything children experience in their simple thinking until the age of four or five, or even until the age of six or seven, while learning to stand up and walk, the result is a doll that you can make out of a handkerchief with a head on top and at most a couple of ink spots for eyes. In that doll you have everything young children can understand, as well as everything they can love. Such a doll presents the primitive characteristics of the human form, at least to the extent a young child can take in.

A child knows nothing more about human beings than that human beings stand up, that they have an up and a down, and that on top there is a head with a pair of eyes. In children's drawings, you will often find that they have drawn the mouth on the forehead. The position of a person's mouth is not entirely clear to young children. What a child can actually experience exists in a doll made from a handkerchief with a pair of ink spots on it. An inner creative force is active within young children. Everything they receive from their environment is translated into inner development, which includes the formation of organs.

If a child's father often expresses anger, that is, if at any moment something unmotivated could occur that would shock the child, then he or she experiences that too. The child experiences it in such a way that it is expressed in the breathing and the circulation. Since it is expressed in the breathing and the circulation, it works to form the lungs and the heart, in fact, the entire system of vessels. The child has that sculpted inner organization the rest of his or her life, a constitution that was formed by seeing the actions of the angry father.

What I just said is intended only to indicate how children have a wonderful inner formative force, and how they continuously work upon themselves as sculptors. If you give a child a doll made from a handkerchief, those sculpturally creative forces quietly move into the brain, that is, the forces acting upon the rhythmic system through breathing and blood circulation move gently into the brain to form it also. They shape the child's brain in much the way a sculptor works upon sculptural material with a subtle, light, spiritualized, and ensouled hand. There, everything proceeds through an organic development. Children look at a doll made from a handkerchief, and the formative forces arising from the rhythmic system begin to work upon the brain.

If you give a child a so-called beautiful doll, one that might even be able to move or move its eyes, one that is painted and has beautiful hair, if you give a child such a doll that looks so artistic but is actually quite terrible, the formative forces arising out of the rhythmic system, these sculpturally active forces that arise from the breathing and circulatory systems to form the brain, act like lashes from a whip. Everything a child cannot yet understand whips the brain. The brain is therefore thoroughly whipped, it is beaten in a terrible way. That is the problem with such beautiful dolls, and it is also the problem with much of children's play.

When we want to lovingly guide children's play, we need to be clear about how much of their inner developmental strengths are called upon. In this connection, our entire civilization sees things incorrectly. Our civilization has, for instance, created animism. A child hurts him- or herself on a table, then hits the corner of the table. People in our times say that the child gives the table life, imagines the table to be alive, to be a living thing. They say the child dreams life into the table and then hits the table.

That is not at all true. The child does not dream anything into the table. Instead, children dream life from living beings, from beings who actually live. It is not that children dream life into a table, but they dream life from actual living beings. When a child has injured itself, it hits back as a kind of reflex—since everything is still without life for a child, children do not dream life into a table. They behave in the same way toward animate and inanimate objects.

We can see how our civilization is unable to approach children properly through such quite reversed ideas. What is important is that we work really lovingly with children so that we guide them only with love toward what they, themselves want. For that reason, we should not beat children inwardly with beautiful dolls. We should live with the children and make a doll in the way they experience it inwardly.

It is the same with all play. Play requires a genuine understanding of the nature of the child. If we babble like a small child, if we reduce our language to that of a child and do not speak in a way children should hear, and in a way appropriate to our own nature, we present children with untruthfulness. However, while we should not place ourselves in a position of untruthfulness in speech, we should place ourselves specifically at the level of the children in connection with willed activities, that is, with play. If we do that, it will be clear that nowhere in its organic being does a child have what our modern civilization so adores, namely, intellectuality. For that reason, we may not bring anything influenced by intellect into children's play.

In a very natural way, children imitate in play what occurs in their surroundings. We seldom experience that children want to be, say, linguists, in play. It is certainly a rare experience for a four-year-old to want to be a linguist. However, under some circumstances, a child might want to be a chauffeur. Why? Because everything a chauffeur is can be seen. You can see that, and it makes a direct pictorial impression. But, what a linguist does makes no pictorial impression. It is not pictorial and completely passes by the child's life. We should bring into play only what does not pass by children unnoticed. All intellectual things do pass children by. What is it that we as adults need to properly guide children's play? We plow, we make hats, we sew clothing, and so forth. In all that, there is an orientation toward the practical, and what is intellectual lies in that orientation. Wherever we find a goal in life, we have penetrated it with the intellect.

On the other hand, though, everything in life, whether it is plowing or something else, say building a wagon or shoeing horses, aside from the fact that it is directed toward some goal, also exists in its outer form, in its simple exterior form. When you see a farmer guiding his plow through the furrows, quite aside from the goal of the activity we can feel, if I may use the expression, what lives in that picture. If we as adults can work our way through to comprehend what exists in something aside from its purpose, the result is what we can present to children in play. Our sense of aesthetics enables us to do that. In particular, by not pursuing the kind of beauty that today's beautiful dolls strive for, which is completely intellectual, but by going into what speaks to human feeling, we arrive at that primitive, genuinely enjoyable doll that looks more like this [a doll carved by a Waldorf School student], not the so-called beautiful doll. But this, of course, is something for older children.

What is important is that we, as educators, be able to see the aesthetics of work in the work itself, so that we can present that in the way we make toys. If we bring the aesthetics of work into the toys we make, then we approach what children actually want. In our civilization, we have become almost completely utilitarian, that is, intellectual, and therefore present children with all kinds of things we think up. What is important though, is that we do not present young children with things from later in life, things we think up. Instead, we want to give them things they can feel when they are older. That is what needs to be in toys. We may want to give a boy a toy plow, but it is important that we put what is formative and aesthetic in plowing into the toy. That is what fully develops the strength of human beings.

That is where many otherwise very good kindergartens have made major errors. The kindergarten Fröbel and others created with a genuine love of children needs to become clear that young children are imitative beings, but that they can imitate only what is not intellectualized. Therefore, we should not bring all kinds of thought-up activities into the kindergarten. All of these games, like pick-up sticks or braiding, that often play such an important role in kindergarten are simply thought up. In kindergarten, we should only do those things big people also do, not things specially thought up. People who really understand human beings are often overcome by a tragic feeling when they come into these well-intended kindergartens with such beautifully thought-up activities. On the one hand, there is such an endless amount of goodwill in these kindergartens, so much love of children; but on the other hand, no consideration is given to the fact that everything is so intellectual, that kindergartens should exclude everything that is thought up for children's play, and that kindergarten children should imitate only external adult activities.

Children that we train intellectually before the age of four or five take something really terrible into life: we bring them up to be materialists. The more you raise a child intellectually before the age of four or five, the more you create a materialist in later life. The brain develops so that the spirit lives within its form, but inwardly people have an intuition that everything is only material, because the brain has been taken over by intellectualism at such an early age.

If you want to educate people so that they understand the spiritual, you need to present the intellectual form of what is externally spiritual as late as possible. Even though it is very necessary, particularly in modern civilization, for people to be completely awake later in life, it is just as necessary to allow children to live in their gentle dreamy experiences as long as possible so that they grow slowly into life. They need to remain in their imaginations, in their pictorial capacities without intellectualism, as long as possible. In our modern civilization, if you allow the organism to be strengthened without intellectualism, children will later grow into the necessary intellectualism in the proper way.

If you beat a child's brain in the way I described, you will ruin the person's soul for the remainder of life. Just as you ruin a person's digestion through babbling, or a person's metabolism through learning to walk without love, in the same way, you ruin a person's soul when you beat a child from within. Thus, an ideal of our education must be to eliminate those beatings of the child's soul, that is, since the child is entirely a physical, soul, and spiritual being, to eliminate also the inner physical beatings. Which is to say, our ideal is to eliminate the so-called beautiful dolls and, most important of all, to bring play to the proper level.

I would like to conclude my remarks today by once again stating that we need to avoid what is erroneously spiritual, so that what is properly spiritual, namely the human being in its entirety, can make its appearance later in life.

4

THE FIRST
SCHOOL YEARS

From Whole to Part

DURING THE FIRST SEVEN YEARS of life, children go through a dramatic stage of development: they learn to walk, to talk, and to think, and their bodies grow and change at a rapid pace. According to Rudolf Steiner, this process of growth and development is a result of the work of the *etheric*, or "life body."[1] During these years, when the etheric body forms and organizes the physical body, it uses the inherited physical body as a model to form a person's more individual, "second" body, fashioning it into a suitable instrument for the person's life tasks. In lecture 8 of *Human Values in Education*, Steiner describes this process as follows:

> To begin with human beings receive their *first* physical body—if I may say it this way—from the forces of heredity. This is prepared by the father and mother. During the first seven years of life this physical body is cast off, but during this time it also serves as the model from which the etheric body can build up the second body. (HV, p. 146)

At around the age of seven, the etheric body completes its work in the physical sphere. Although the etheric body will continue to fulfill physiological functions throughout our lives, it now also

---

1. See "The Nature of the Human Being" on page 2.

becomes available for psychological functions. Rudolf Steiner pointed to the loss of the milk teeth as the developmental marker that signals that the etheric body is available to work in new ways. In lecture 3 of *The Roots of Education* he states:

> In actuality, what is it that causes the second teeth? It is the fact that, until this time, the etheric is almost completely connected with the physical body; and when the first teeth are forced out, something separates from the physical body.... When the etheric body is separated, what formerly worked in the physical body now works in the soul realm. (p. 48)

What kind of work does the etheric body do in the realm of soul? Just as it devoted itself to organic development and growth in the first seven years, the etheric body now develops and organizes our thoughts, our ideas, and our memories, and it lays the foundation for our conceptual life.

Because the etheric body is responsible for a child's intellectual development, it is imperative that Waldorf teachers understand the etheric body and how to work with it. We can begin to develop this understanding through study, observation, and meditation, but Steiner suggested that we deepen our understanding of the etheric body by sculpting and modeling in clay. When we sculpt, we are utilizing the same kind of forces the etheric body uses to form and mold the physical body.

> Anyone who really works at sculpture and enters its formative nature will learn to experience the inner structure of forms, and indeed the inner structure of just those forms with which the human body of formative forces is also working. (HV, p. 148)

Living Letters

Children in Waldorf schools learn very significantly through the arts. Because the arts engage our feelings, stimulate our imagination, and foster enthusiasm and joy, they allow the children's souls to grow and develop in healthy, harmonious ways. Young children are naturally artistic, imaginative, and creative. The arts provide the most appropriate means by which abstract, intellectual subject matter can be presented. The introduction to writing and reading well illustrates the artistic nature of the Waldorf approach.

As adults, we have a hard time remembering a time when we felt no connection to the written or printed word, yet young children feel no such connection, for writing and print are completely foreign to their nature. Many schools consider it necessary to teach children their letters before the change of teeth. Consequently, children often feel alienated from what they are required to learn and do. In lecture 5 of *The Spiritual Ground of Education*, Steiner develops this idea.

It is thoroughly unnatural to require a child during the sixth or seventh year to merely copy the signs that we, in this advanced stage of civilization, now use for reading and writing.

If you consider the letters we now use for reading and writing, you will realize that there is no connection between these letters and what a child of seven is naturally disposed to do. Remember, that when human beings first began to write they used painted or drawn signs that reproduced things or occurrences in the surrounding world. Or they wrote from will impulses, so that the forms of writing expressed processes of the will—cuneiform characters, for example. Today's entirely abstract form of letters, which the eye must gaze at or the hand form, arose from picture writing. When we confront a young child with such letters, we are bringing something alien, something that in no way conforms to the child's nature.

Let us be clear about what it means to "push" a foreign body into a child's organism. It is just as though a child, from the very earliest years, were being habituated to wearing very small clothes that do not fit, and therefore damage the child's organism. Today observation tends to be superficial, and people are even unaware of the damage done to the child's organism simply by introducing reading and writing in a wrong way. (pp. 61–62)

Because the letters are so foreign to a young child, Waldorf teachers strive to build a human and artistic bridge to the act of writing. Writing is therefore introduced through movement, gesture, sound, and image. In "The Child at Seven," Steiner describes how a child can experience the letter *L*, for instance, by running its form on the floor and then by "writing" it in the air. Only after children have experienced the form with their whole body and then their arms and hands, will the teacher begin to forge the link between the shape of the letter and its sound.

Letters can also be introduced through gestures that express their sound. A *W* can be derived from the undulating movement of a wave, or an *S* from the rushing movement of the wind. Such movements and gestures are refined in the study of eurythmy, where every sound is expressed in a specific way.[2]

The letters of the alphabet may also be introduced through pictures. Deriving the letter symbols from pictures mirrors the process by which the letters we use were developed. While research into the origins of the alphabet yields important insights, such research is not necessary for introducing the letters. Young children do not need to learn the history of the letters. They should have opportunities to experience the letters with the pictorial consciousness of earlier ages, when meaning and expression were found through images.

The image that contains the letter might be derived from a story told by the teacher or through a class conversation that draws on the children's life experience. Children are quickly able recognize the forms of the letters that live in a picture, for instance, an *M* made by the ridge of the twin mountain peaks and the *V* of the valley between them. Just as a letter's form can be found in a picture, the sound the letter makes can be found in the word. Working this way, from the whole to the part, is an essential ingredient of Waldorf teaching. In "Teaching Children to Write," Rudolf Steiner vividly demonstrates the process by which letters and sounds can be derived in this way.

Once the children have seen how a letter is derived from an image, they draw their own pictures that show the transformation of an

---

2. See "An Introduction to Eurythmy" on page 299.

object into a symbol. When they finally write the letter, using bright beeswax crayons to draw a beautifully formed capital letter against a glowing background, they infuse the skeletal symbol with life.

Whether letters have been introduced through movement, sounds, or pictures, children can also experience them by working on speech exercises, tongue twisters, and poetry. Because children are deeply musical, they enter readily and easily into the musical element of speech, relishing its rhythms and rhymes and enjoying its patterns and word plays. Such speech work deepens the child's relationship to language and serves as a foundation for writing and reading.

Writing and Reading

Since writing is developed out of drawing, children are allowed and encouraged to dwell in the pictorial and formative aspects of the letters. In this way, for several years writing remains an artistic activity. Parents who expect their children to be writing fluently in the early grades may become anxious about their children's lack of proficiency. In "The Child at Seven," Steiner discusses this slower approach.

> Some parents have expressed their anxieties about their children still being unable to write properly, even at the age of eight. We have to show them that our slower approach is really a blessing, because it allows the children to integrate the art of writing with their whole being. We try to convince parents that in our school children learn writing at the right age and in a far more humane manner than if they had to absorb something essentially alien to their own nature—alien because it represents the end product of a long cultural evolution. We must help our parents see the importance of an immediate and direct response within the child to the introduction of writing. Naturally we have to provide our pupils with the tools of learning, but we must always do so by adapting our content to the nature of the child. (p. 135)

Throughout elementary school, students write by hand rather than using typewriters or computers. Although this approach may seem anachronistic, we believe that young children benefit from developing the coordination and dexterity necessary for hand-writing before becoming dependent on a tool to simplify the process. In "The Child at Seven," Steiner shares his clairvoyant perceptions of what occurs when we type and comments on the effects of typing on health. Although such spiritual-scientific perceptions and conclusions might be difficult for some to accept, evidence suggests that they deserve careful consideration.

In Waldorf schools, reading is taught through writing, for children are most connected to the words that they have written themselves. From the copying of verses and simple sentences, students progress to writing and reading their own compositions and then to reading from the printed page. This approach to learning to read may take slightly longer, but it has incalculable educational benefits for the child. Parents may, however, worry about their children learning to read later than their peers in other kinds of schools. In lecture 4 of *The Child's Changing Consciousness and Waldorf Education*, Steiner addresses this point.

> But if one adopts this method in order to work harmoniously with human nature, it can become extraordinarily difficult to withstand modern prejudices. Naturally, pupils will learn to read a little later than expected today, and if they have to change schools they appear less capable than the other students in their new class. Yet, is it really justified that we cater to the views of a materialistic culture with its demands concerning what an eight-year-old child should know? The real point is that it may not be beneficial at all for such a child to learn to read too early. By doing so, something is being blocked for life. If children learn to read too early, they are led prematurely into abstractions. (CCC, p. 76)

In lecture 2 of *The Kingdom of Childhood* Steiner emphasizes how much better it is to learn to write and read late and he speaks of the spiritual benefits of waiting to develop these skills.

People will object that the children then learn to read and write too late. This is said only because it is not known today how harmful it is when the children learn to read and write too soon. It is a very bad thing to be able to write early. Reading and writing as we have them today are really not suited to the human being till a later age—the eleventh or twelfth year—and the more a child is blessed with not being able to read and write well before this age, the better it is for the later years of life. A child who cannot write properly at thirteen or fourteen (I can speak out of my own experience because I could not do it at that age) is not so hindered for later spiritual development as one who early, at seven or eight years, can already read and write perfectly. (KC, p. 26–27)

Most Waldorf students learn to read without any pressure or anxiety. Many students do not even need to be taught how to read, but learn on their own, naturally and joyfully. The Waldorf school environment is permeated by language and literature, and almost all of the subjects are first presented through the spoken word. As a result, our students develop a deep appreciation for language in all of its forms, and they become highly skilled in its many applications.

In the later elementary grades, the work in language arts becomes more complex and sophisticated. It includes drama and recitation, reading and discussion of literature of different genres, exercises in different forms of writing, and extensive work in grammar, vocabulary, and spelling. In the high school, teachers strive to refine the students' skills in expository and creative writing and to develop the students' appreciation and understanding of comparative literature. This work in language arts is all built on the foundation established in the first few months of school. It is for this reason that Steiner laid such emphasis on presenting the letters in a living way.

The Wonder of Numbers

In the early grades, language arts are taught very differently from mathematics. When the letters are taught in the ways that have been described, an imaginative picture slowly becomes more concrete; when the numbers and the mathematical operations are introduced, the child's concrete experiences are transformed into living concepts.

Steiner suggested that the study of numbers begin with the human being. Each of us is a unit, an indivisible whole; from this we derive the number one. We find the number two expressed by our hands and feet or by our eyes and ears. The number three may be found in the three major parts of our bodies: head, trunk, and limbs. To find the number four we can count our limbs; for five we can refer to the digits on each hand or the toes on each foot. By working in this way, the teacher can lead the children to the perception that we contain the world of numbers in our very being.

According to Steiner, former ages did not develop the numbers by adding one to another, but by dividing the whole into parts. The unit was considered the greatest number, for it contained all of the other numbers. Steiner asserted that by showing children how to derive numbers out of the whole and teaching them to work from the whole to the parts, we help them develop living concepts. In "Teaching Arithmetic," he states:

> The living thing is always a whole and must be presented as a whole first of all. It is wrong for children to have to put together a whole out of its parts, when they should be taught to look first at the whole and then divide this whole into its parts; get them first to look at the whole and then divide it and split it up; this is the right path to a living conception. (p. 161)

Once children have been introduced to the numbers, they can begin to explore the nature and quality of the numbers. They learn to recognize their archetypical qualities and discover how these qualities find their expression in the world. One is more than a number—it is a unifying principle that encompasses everything. Two, on the other hand, denotes duality, division, and opposition. Three has a dynamic quality, which mediates between opposites by harmonizing them, while four engenders stability by balancing opposites evenly. Each of the numbers up to seven has its own characteristics. Teachers might give descriptions and tell stories that bring the inner qualities of the numbers to light, and they will try to inspire their students to search for numbers and their revelations in the world of nature. The class might also recite verses about the numbers or play number games that bring out the essential character of the numbers.

After exploring the various qualities of numbers one to seven, students can experience their forms, using the same means that they employed to learn the shapes of the letters. Finally the children will write the numbers in their main lesson notebooks, illustrating each page with a representative picture. Students who have gone through this process will never consider numbers simply as abstractions or merely as marks upon a page; to them numbers are living entities with unique individual characteristics.

After considering the individual numbers, first graders move on to number patterns, beginning with moving and counting in rhythm. Children might walk a pattern that has alternating short and long steps, for instance: one-two-THREE, four-five-SIX, and so on. Or, they might stamp or clap when they come to a number that should be stressed. Such exercises might be couched in imaginative pictures of a number family, for example, where each number has its own temperament or character. This is a wonderful prelude to learning multiplication tables, which are initially derived from counting. They are then practiced with increasingly complex and challenging movements such as those employed in clapping games. Because children love anything that is rhythmical, they perform such counting drills with joy. Because they are using their bodies actively, number patterns and arithmetic facts are grounded in experience and do not remain cerebral.

The four arithmetic operations—adding, subtracting, multiplying, and dividing—are also introduced in the first grade. Steiner placed great emphasis on the introduction to these operations, for he asserted that the way children learn to think about them will help determine whether they will achieve true freedom of thought as adults.

Thinking has two major aspects: synthesis and analysis. When we synthesize, we add things together, building something up from parts; when we analyze, we separate or divide a whole into its parts. According to Steiner, the process of synthesizing does not leave a human being completely free. In lecture 10 of *The Renewal of Education* he explains:

> If I have to add two and five and three in order to find the total, I am not free, for the answer is fixed by an underlying law. But if I begin with the number ten, I can view it as consisting of nine and one or five and five; or I can arrange it into three, five, and two and so on. When analyzing, I am able to act with complete inner freedom, whereas when synthesizing, I am forced by outer circumstances to adapt my soul activity to an external necessity. (RE, p. 126)

Although children are much more disposed to analyzing than synthesizing, most modern educational practices stress synthesis over analysis, especially in the early grades. According to Steiner, such overemphasis may have profound implications for later life: if children's urge for analysis is not sufficiently satisfied, as adults they may become overly materialistic in their thinking.

> You all know how we suffer today from a materialistic worldview. You may object to my use of this expression, but I cannot help but experience it in this way. This materialistic attitude not only consists of people's acceptance of matter as the basis for everything, but also of attributing the whole world to the activity of atoms.... Matter is viewed as being composed of the smallest particles, as dependent on the activity of these particles and—this is the point—this way of thinking is then transferred to the realm of soul and spirit as well. Things have gone so far today that people view atomic theories as scientifically proven facts, failing to realize that they are mere hypotheses. Therefore, they take it for granted that the atom is the basis of all natural phenomena. How is

it possible that so many people have developed what one could call an inclination toward atomism? The reason is that their analytical faculty was underdeveloped in childhood. (RE, p. 127–128)

How can we use the process of analysis as the basis for learning the arithmetic operations? In "Teaching Arithmetic," Steiner states:

In your teaching you must not start with the single addenda, but start with the sum, which is the whole, and divide it up into the single addenda. Then you can go on to show that it can be divided up differently, with different addenda, but the whole always remains the same. By taking addition in this way, not as is very often done by having first the addenda and then the sum, but by taking the sum first and then the addenda, you will arrive at conceptions that are living and mobile. (p. 163)

Later in the lecture he demonstrates how this approach can be applied to subtraction, multiplication, and division. The process of solving problems that begins with the whole appeals to children, for such problems are true to the kinds of circumstances children encounter in their everyday lives. Not all arithmetic problems should be solved in this way. There are plenty of instances in life where synthesis is necessary and appropriate, and children need to develop the inner flexibility to work both analytically and synthetically. If, however, the arithmetic operations are introduced analytically, children will develop a form of thinking that is both mobile and concrete, capable of abstraction, but grounded in the realities of life.

Many Waldorf teachers also bring the arithmetic operations to life by personifying them through stories. They may present an arithmetic kingdom that is ruled by King Plus, whose patient work makes his kingdom thrive and prosper. Everything grows in abundance, and there is always a surplus. King Plus loves to accumulate and organize his wealth. He is happiest counting, storing, and putting everything in neat piles. King Plus's wife, Queen Minus, is deeply sensitive to the pain and suffering of others. She uses her vast wealth to help anyone in need, feeding the hungry, clothing the poor, healing the sick. Prince Times, their son, likes to figure out the quickest and easiest way to do things. Why add things one by one when it's so much more efficient to deal with them in groups? Their daughter, Princess Divide, likes to bring order into chaos. She organizes the goods in the warehouses in even piles so that everything can always be accounted for.

Through such stories the teacher seeks to bring these operations to life, developing the temperament of the characters, and therefore of the operations.[3] Addition is phlegmatic by nature, for the phlegmatic loves to add things, one to another, and has the perseverance to keep on counting. Subtraction is more melancholic in temperament. The melancholic feels loss deeply, but because of an ability to empathize with others, is often very generous. Multiplication is sanguine and loves speed and facility, having an eagerness to find the answer. Division is choleric and knows the best way to do things and is able to go to the heart of the matter without any fuss. Children enter eagerly into the imaginative content of such stories, but they do not take them literally. They sense that behind the persona of the characters lie the great truths about the nature of mathematical operations.

During the rest of elementary school, the study of mathematics becomes broader and more complex. It includes a wide variety of applications of the four operations, as well as fractions, mixed numerals, decimals, business mathematics, measurement, formulas, and substantial exposure to algebra and geometry. The high school curriculum includes algebra, geometry, trigonometry, and calculus. All of these subjects depend on the foundation established in the first grade. It is for this reason that Steiner spoke about the introduction to arithmetic in such detail and left teachers free to develop the rest of the curriculum out of that beginning.

---

3. See "The Temperaments: A Key to Understanding Human Nature" on page 44.

Children in Waldorf schools do not view mathematics as something difficult, onerous, or boring. They enter the world of number with interest, enthusiasm, and joy. Waldorf students develop a deep appreciation for mathematics, and when they go on to further studies, they do so with mobility of thought, with an eye for beauty, and with an understanding for the practical applications of mathematics in our lives.

The Child at Seven

LECTURE BY RUDOLF STEINER

Dornach, December 31, 1921

When the child begins to lose the first teeth, an important and far-reaching change is taking place, not just a physical event in the life of a human being, but also a metamorphosis of the entire human organization. A true art of education demands a thorough appreciation and understanding of this metamorphosis. What I have called the etheric body in our previous meetings, or the refined body of formative forces, is being freed from certain functions between the change of teeth and puberty. Previously the etheric body has been working directly into the child's physical body, but now it also begins to function in the realm of the child's soul, so that the physical body is gripped from within in quite a different manner than before.

Previously, the situation was more or less as described by materialists, who see in the physical processes of the human body the foundation of the human psyche. They view the soul and spirit as emanating from the physical and related to it much as the candle flame is related to the candle. And this is more or less correct for the young child up to the change of teeth. During these early years the soul and spiritual life of the child is entirely bound up with its physical and organic processes, which, like all physical and organic processes, at the same time have a soul and spiritual nature. All the shaping and forming of the body at that age is conducted from the head downward. This stage concludes when the second teeth are being pushed through in the head. At that time the forces working in the head cease to predominate, and soul and spiritual activities enter the lower regions of the body in the rhythmical activities of the heart and the breath. Previously these forces worked especially upon forming the child's brain, but they were also streaming down into the remaining organism, shaping and molding, and entering directly into the physical substances of the body, where they brought about physical processes.

All that changes with the coming of the second teeth, when certain of these forces begin to work more in the child's soul and spiritual realm, affecting especially the rhythmical movement of the heart and the lungs. They are no longer active to the same degree in the physical processes themselves, but now also work in the rhythms of breathing and blood circulation. One can observe this even physically, in that the child's breathing and pulse become noticeably stronger at this time. The child now has a strong desire to experience its emerging life of soul and spirit on waves of rhythm and beat within its own body, quite unconsciously of course. It has a real longing for this interplay of rhythm and beat in its own organism. Consequently adults must realize that whatever they bring to the child after the change of teeth has to be given with an inherent quality of rhythm and beat. Everything addressed to the child at this time must be imbued with these qualities. Educators have to be able to so live themselves into the element of rhythm and beat that whatever they bring will make an impact upon the child by allowing it to live in its own musical element.

All this is also the beginning of something else. If, at this stage, the rhythms of breathing and blood circulation are not treated in the right way, the resulting harm may extend irreparably into later life. Many weaknesses and unhealthy conditions of the respiratory and circulatory systems in adult life are the consequences of an incorrect education during these early school years. Through the change in the working of the child's etheric body, the limbs begin to grow rapidly, with the effect that the life of the muscles and bones, of the entire skeleton, begins to play a predominant role. The life of the muscles and bones strives to become attuned to the rhythms of breathing and blood circulation. At this stage the child's muscles vibrate in sympathy with the rhythms of breathing and blood circulation, so that the entire being of the child takes on a musical character. Whereas previously the child's inborn activities were akin to those of a sculptor, now the inner musician begins to work, albeit beyond the child's consciousness. It is essential for teachers to realize they are dealing with a natural, though unconscious musician when the child enters the first grade. We must meet these inner needs of the child, which demand a somewhat similar treatment, metaphorically speaking, to that of a new violin responding to being played, adapting itself to the characteristic pattern of the violinist's sound waves. Through maltreatment, a violin may be ruined once and for all. But in the case of the living human organism, principles harmful to its growth may be implanted, which will increase and develop until eventually they can ruin the entire life of the individual concerned.

When you have embarked on the study of the human being, which throws light both on educational principles and on methods, you will find that the characteristic features just indicated occupy roughly the time between the change of teeth and puberty. You will also discover that this period again falls into three smaller phases: The first lasts from the change of teeth until approximately the end of the ninth year, the second until roughly the end of the twelfth year, and the third from the thirteenth year until sexual maturity has been reached.

If you observe how the child lives entirely in a musical element, you can also gain insight into how these three phases differ from each other. During the first phase, that is until approximately the end of the ninth year, the child wants to experience everything that comes toward it within its own inner rhythms—in what belongs to beat and measure. It will relate everything to the rhythms of breath and heartbeat and, indirectly, also to the way its muscles and bones are shaping themselves. But if the outer influences do not synchronize with its own inner rhythms, the young person will eventually grow into a kind of inner cripple, even if this may not be outwardly discernible in the early stages. Up to its ninth year the child has the strong desire to experience everything that comes toward it inwardly, in the form of beat and rhythm. When a child of this age hears music, it transforms all the outer sounds into its own inner rhythms—and anyone able to observe what goes on in a child's soul will be able to perceive this. The child co-vibrates with the music, reproducing within what it perceives without, for at this stage, it has retained features characteristic of its previous stages at least to a certain extent. Up to the change of teeth, the child is fundamentally like a single sense organ, unconsciously reproducing outer sense impressions, as most sense organs do. The child lives, above all, by imitation, as already shown in previous meetings. If you observe the human eye, you will find that it reproduces outer stimuli by forming afterimages, leaving out of account any mental images resulting from the eye's sense perceptions. These afterimages are then taken up by the activity leading to mental representation. Insofar as the very young child inwardly reproduces all it perceives, especially with regard to the people around it, it is like one great unconscious sense organ. But the images reproduced within do not remain mere images, for they act at the same time as forces, forming and shaping the child even physically.

However, when the second teeth appear, these afterimages enter only as far as the rhythmic system, the system of movement. Something of the previous formative activity remains, but now it is accompanied by a new element. There is a definite difference in the way a child responds to rhythm and beat before and after the change of teeth. Before, through the child's imitation, rhythm and beat directly affected the shaping of bodily organs. After the change of teeth they are transformed into an inner musical element.

From the end of the ninth year until the twelfth year, the child develops an understanding of rhythm and beat, of what belongs to melody in its own right. It now no longer has the same urge to reproduce inwardly all that belongs to this realm, but begins to perceive it as something outside itself. Whereas earlier the child experienced rhythm and beat unconsciously, it now develops a conscious perception and understanding of them. This continues up to the twelfth year, not only for music, but also for everything else coming to meet the child from outside.

Toward the twelfth year, or perhaps a little earlier, the child develops the ability to lead the elements of rhythm and beat, which it previously had experienced only imaginatively, into the thinking realm.

Someone who is able, through insight, to perceive what happens in the realm of the soul can also recognize the corresponding effects in the physical body. I have just spoken of how the child wants to shape its muscles, its bones, in accord with what is happening within its organs. Toward the twelfth year, the child begins to be no longer satisfied with living solely in the elements of rhythm and beat; now it wants to lift this experience more into the realm of abstract and conscious understanding. And this coincides with the hardening of the parts of the muscles that lead into the tendons. Whereas previously all movement was oriented more toward the muscles themselves, it now is oriented toward the tendons. Everything happening in the realm of soul and spirit has its countereffect in the physical realm, and this inclusion of the life of the tendons, the link between muscle and bone, is the outer physical expression of the child's sailing out of a feeling approach to rhythm and beat into the realm of logic, which is devoid of rhythm and beat. A discovery of this kind, an offshoot of a real knowledge of the human being, needs to be made into a guideline in the art of education.

Most adults who think about something in a general way, be it plants or animals—and as teachers you will have to introduce such general subjects to your pupils—will remember what they themselves once learned in botany or zoology, although at a later age than that of the children we are talking about here. Unfortunately, what you find in most textbooks on botany or zoology is unsuitable material for teaching the young. Some of these textbooks may be of great scientific merit, though usually that is not the case, but as teaching material for the age that concerns us here, they are of no use at all. Everything that we, as teachers, bring to our pupils in plant or animal study has to be woven into an artistic whole. We must aim at highlighting the harmonious configuration of the plant's being. We must describe the harmonious relationships of one plant species with another. What children can appreciate through a rhythmical, harmonious, feeling approach has to be of far greater significance for Waldorf teachers than what the ordinary textbooks can offer us. The usual methods of classifying plants are particularly objectionable. Perhaps the least offensive of the various systems is that of Linnaeus, who looks only at the blossom of the plant, where the plant ceases to be merely plant and stretches forth its forces into the entire cosmos. But any of these plant systems is unacceptable for use at school. We shall see later what needs to be done in this respect.

Teachers who enter the classroom, textbook in hand, to teach younger classes what they themselves learned in botany or zoology class are a pitiful sight. If they now stride back and forth in front of the desks, reading from the textbook—which, in itself, is totally unsuitable—to refresh their memory of what they once learned long ago, they become a mere caricature of a teacher. It is absolutely essential for us to learn to talk about plants or animals in a living and artistic way. Only then will our content be attuned to the children's inner musical needs. We must always bear in mind that our teaching must spring from an artistic element. Our lessons must not be merely thought out; an abstract kind of observation, even if correct, is not good enough. Only what is imbued with a living element of sensitive and artistic experience will provide the children with the soul nourishment they need.

When children enter the first grade and we are expected to teach them writing as soon as possible, we might be tempted to introduce the letters of the alphabet as they are used today. But the child of this age, just after the onset of the change of teeth, has not the slightest inner connection with the forms of these letters. How was it, then, at a time when such a direct human relationship to the written letters still existed? To find the answer, we need only look at what happened in early civilizations. In those ancient days primitive humans engraved images on tablets or painted pictures that still bore a resemblance to what they had seen in nature. There still was a direct human link between outer objects and their written forms. As civilization progressed, these forms became more and more abstract until, after many transformations, they finally emerged as today's letters of the alphabet, which no longer have any direct human relationship to the person writing them.

But young children, who in many ways show us how humans of earlier civilizations experienced the world, need a direct connection with whatever we demand from their will activities. Therefore, when introducing writing, we must refrain from teaching today's abstract letter forms straightaway. We must offer the children, especially at the time of the change of teeth, a human and artistic bridge to whatever we teach. This implies that we allow them to link what they have seen with their eyes to the result of their own will activity on paper, which we call writing. Experiencing life through their own will activities is a primary need of children at this stage. We must give them an opportunity to express this innate artistic drive by, for example, letting them run a curve:

When we point out to children that their legs have run such a curve on the floor, we raise their will activity into a semiconscious feeling. The next step would be to ask them to draw in the air the curve they have run, using their arms and hands. Then another form could be run on the floor, again to be "written" into the air.

Thus the form that in the first instance is made by the entire bodies of the running children is subsequently reproduced merely by the use of their hands. This could be followed by the teacher asking the children to pronounce words beginning with the letter *L*.

Gradually, under the teacher's guidance, the children will find the link between the shape they have run and drawn, and the sound of the appropriate letter, *L*.

Only after the children experience their own inner movement are they led to drawing the actual letters. This would be one way of proceeding, but there is also another possibility. After the change of teeth the child is not only an inner musician but also remains, as an echo from earlier stages, an inner sculptor. Therefore we could begin by talking to the children about the fish, gradually leading over artistically to its outer form, which they would draw. Then, appealing to their sense of sound, we could direct their attention from the whole word *fish* to the initial sound "F," in this way relating the shape of the letter to its sound.

This method even follows the historical development of the letter *F*, at least to a certain extent, but there is no need to restrict ourselves to actual historical examples. It is certainly right for us to use our own imagination. What matters is not that the children recapitulate the evolution of the actual letters, but that they find their

way into writing through the artistic activity of drawing pictures
that will lead finally to today's abstract letter forms. For instance, we
could remind the children of how water makes waves, drawing a
picture of this kind:

and gradually changing it into:

Repeating words such as "Washing Waves of Water; Waving,
Washing Water," while at the same time drawing the form, we link
the sound of the letter W to its written form. Starting with the
child's own life experience, we lead from the activity of drawing to
the final letter forms.

Following our Waldorf method, the children will not learn to
write as quickly as they do in other schools. In the Waldorf school
parents, without their children, are invited to regular meetings with
the teachers to discuss the effects of Waldorf education. In these
meetings some parents have expressed their anxieties about their
children still being unable to write properly, even at the age of eight.
We have to show them that our slower approach is really a blessing,
because it allows the children to integrate the art of writing with
their whole being. We try to convince parents that in our school
children learn writing at the right age and in a far more humane
manner than if they had to absorb something essentially alien to
their own nature—alien because it represents the end product of a
long cultural evolution. We must help our parents see the importance of an immediate and direct response within the child to the

introduction of writing. Naturally we have to provide our pupils with the tools of learning, but we must always do so by adapting our content to the nature of the child.

One aspect, so often omitted nowadays, is the relationship of a specific area to life as a whole. In our advanced stage of civilization everything has come to depend on specialization. Certainly this was necessary for a time, but we have now reached a stage where, for the sake of humankind's healthy development, we must never lose sight of the totality of life. This means we must keep an open mind to what spiritual investigation has to tell us about the human being. Believing that anthroposophists always rail against new achievements of technology is a serious misunderstanding of what this movement can contribute to a knowledge of the human being, for it is necessary to look upon the complexities of life from a holistic point of view. To give you an example, I have not the slightest objection to the use of typewriters. Typing is of course a far less human activity than writing by hand, but I do not remonstrate against it. Nevertheless I find it important for us to realize its implications, because everything we do in life has repercussions. Therefore you must forgive me if, to illustrate my point, I say something about typewriting from the point of view of anthroposophic spiritual insight. Anyone unwilling to accept it is perfectly free to dismiss this aspect of life's realities as foolish nonsense. But what I have to say does accord with actual facts.

You see, if one is aware of the spiritual processes that, like those in ordinary life, are always happening around us, typewriting creates a very definite impression. When I have been typing—as you see, I am not fulminating against it at all, but am pleased if I have time for it—the activity continues to affect me for quite a long time afterward. This in itself does not disturb me, but the aftereffects are noticeably there. And when, finally, I reach a state of inner quietude, the activity of typing, seen in imaginative consciousness, is transformed into self-beholding. This seeing of oneself stands there before the seer, who is then able to witness outwardly what is happening inwardly. All this must occur in full consciousness for one to be able to recognize that what has appeared in form on an outer image is only the projection of what is, or has been, taking place, possibly at a much earlier time, as an inner organic activity. One who has reached the stage of clairvoyant Imagination can clearly see what is happening inside the human body. In this objective beholding, every pressing of a typewriter key is changed into a flash of lightning. And what is seen as a human heart during the state of Imagination is constantly being struck and pierced by these flashes of lightning. Now, as you know, the typewriter keys are not arranged according to any spiritual principle, but only according to frequency of use in order to facilitate greater speed in typing. The result is that the flashes of lightning become completely chaotic when the fingers hit the various keys. In short, when typewriting is seen with spiritual eyes, a frightful thunderstorm is raging!

And what does this mean? It is nothing less than an explanation for why so many people walk about with weak hearts, for they are unable to balance the damaging effects of typing by appropriate countermeasures. This is especially the case if people started typing at too early an age, at a time when the heart is most liable to be adversely affected. And if typing spreads more and more, we will soon see an increase in all kinds of heart complaints.

Causes and effects of this kind are part of the pattern of life. We have no wish to run down any of the new technical inventions, but one should be able to look with open eyes at what they do to us. We ought to find the means of compensating for any possible harmful effects. Such matters are of special importance for teachers because they have the task of relating education to practical life. What we do at school or in the company of children is not the only thing that matters. It is of paramount importance that school and everything pertaining to education be related to life in the fullest sense. And this implies that whoever chooses to be an educator must be familiar with what is happening in the big wide world, must know and recognize life in its widest context.

The first railway in Germany was built from Fürth to Nürnberg in 1835. It had always been the custom to seek expert advice before embarking on major projects of this kind, and the health authorities of Bavaria were approached for their opinion about whether, from a medical point of view, building such a railway could be recommended. Their answer was—and documentary evidence is available—that expert medical opinion could not recommend building railways because of the severe strain on the nervous system that travelling on trains would inflict upon passengers and railway staff alike. However, the report continued, should railways be built despite their warning, all railway lines should at least be fenced off by high wooden walls to protect farmers in fields or any others likely to be near moving trains from suffering brain concussion.

These were the findings of medical experts employed by the Bavarian health authorities. Today we laugh about them, and many other similar examples could be quoted. Nevertheless, there are at least two sides to each problem, and from a certain point of view we could even agree with some aspects of this report made not so long ago, in fact not even a century ago. The fact is that people have become more nervous since the arrival of rail travel. And if we investigated the difference between people living in our present age of the train and those who travelled in the old, venerable but rather philistine stagecoach, we would definitely be able to ascertain that the constitutions of the latter were different. Their nervous systems behaved quite differently! Though the Bavarian health authorities have made fools of themselves, from a certain point of view they were not entirely wrong.

When new inventions impact modern life, we must take steps to balance any possible ill effects by finding appropriate countermeasures. We must aim at compensating for any weakening of people's constitutions due to outer influences by strengthening them from within. But, in this age of ever-increasing specialization, this is only possible through a new art of education, based on true knowledge of the human being.

The only safe way to introduce writing to young children is the one just advocated, because at that age all learning must proceed from the will sphere, and the child's inclination toward the world of rhythm and measure springs from the will sphere. We must satisfy this inner urge of the child by allowing it controlled will activities without appealing to its sense of observation and ability to make mental images. From this it follows that it would be wrong to teach reading before the children have been introduced to writing, for reading already represents a transition from a will activity to an abstract observation. The first step is to introduce writing artistically, imaginatively, and then to let the children read what they have written. The last step, since modern life demands it, would be to help the children read from printed texts. Only by applying a deepened knowledge of the human being, based upon the realities of life, is the teacher able to discern what needs to be done.

When children enter the first grade, they are certainly ready to learn how to reckon with simple numbers. But in introducing arithmetic we must also be careful to meet the children's inner needs, which spring from the same realm of rhythm and measure, and from a sensitive apprehension of the harmonizing element inherent in the world of number. However, if we begin with what I will call the additive approach, if we start by teaching the children to count, we again fail to understand their nature. Of course they must learn to count, but additive counting in itself is not in harmony with the children's inner needs.

Our way of dealing with numbers has developed only gradually during the course of civilization into a method of synthesizing, that is, of putting numbers together. Today we have the concept of one unit, of a oneness. We have a second unit, a third unit, and so on, and when we count we mentally place one unit next to the other and add them up. But the child's nature does not experience number this way, for human evolution did not proceed according to this principle. True, all counting began with a unit, with number one. However, the second unit, number two, was not an outer repetition of the first unit, but was felt to be contained within the first unit. Number one was the origin of number two, the two units being concealed within the original number. The same number one, when divided into three parts, gave number three: the three units were felt to be part of the one. Or, in contemporary terms, the bounds of number one were not left upon reaching the concept two, but an inner progression within number one was experienced. The quality of two was inherent in the quality of one. Also three, four, and all other numbers were felt to be part of the all-encompassing first unit; all numbers were experienced as organic members arising out of it.

Due to their musical and rhythmical nature, children experience the world of number in a similar way. Thus, instead of beginning with addition in a pedantic way, it is better to call on a child and give it some apples or any other suitable objects. Instead of giving it, say, three apples, then four more, and finally another two, and then asking that they all be added together, we begin by giving the child a whole pile of apples, or whatever is convenient. This would be the start of the whole operation. Then we call out two more children and say to the first, "Here you have a heap of apples. Give some to the other two children and keep some for yourself. But each one of you must have the same number of apples." In this way we help the children grasp the idea of sharing by three. We begin with the total amount and lead to the principle of division. The child will respond to and apprehend this process quite naturally. By attuning ourselves to the child's nature, according to our picture of the human being, we do not begin by adding numbers, but by dividing and subtracting them. Then, retracing our steps and thus reversing the first two processes, we are led to multiplication and addition. Moving from the whole to the part, we follow the original experience of number, which was one of analyzing, having a divisional quality, and not the contemporary method of synthesizing, of putting things together, of adding.

These are some examples to show that we can read in the development of the child what and how we ought to teach during the different stages. Breathing and blood circulation are the physical bases of the life of feeling, just as the head is the basis for mental imagery, for thinking. With the change of teeth, the life of feeling is liberated; therefore, at this stage one can always reach the child through the element of feeling, provided that the teaching material is artistically attuned to the child's nature. To sum up: Before the change of teeth the child is not yet aware of its separate identity and consequently cannot appreciate the characteristic nature of other persons, whose gestures, manners of speaking, and even sentiments it imitates in an imponderable way. Up to the seventh year the child cannot yet differentiate between its own self and that of another person. It experiences others as intimately connected with it, similar to the way it feels connected with its own arms and legs. It does not yet make a distinction between self and the surrounding world.

With the change of teeth, new soul forces of feeling, linked to breathing and blood circulation, come into their own, and the child begins to distance itself from other people, who are now experienced as individual characters. And this creates a longing in the child to follow the grown-ups in every way and to look up to them in shy reverence. The previous inclination to imitate the more external features changes after the second dentition, and, true to the child's nature, a strong feeling for authority begins to develop.

You will hardly expect a ready sympathy for general obedience to authority from someone who, as a young person, published *Intuitive Thinking as a Spiritual Path: A Philosophy of Freedom* early in the 1890s. But this sense for authority in the child between the change of teeth and puberty must be respected and nurtured, because it represents an inborn need at this age. Only those who experience a shy reverence and feeling for adult authority between their change of teeth and puberty can use their freedom rightly in later life. This is another example showing how education must be seen within the context of social life in general.

Some strange feelings will begin to stir in you if you look back a few decades and see how proud many people then were of their "modern" educational ideas. After Prussia's victory over Austria in 1866, one often heard the opinion expressed in Austria, where I spent half of my life, that the battle had been won by the Prussian schoolmaster! Austria, where the education act was implemented later than in Prussia, was always considered to have an inferior education system, and the Prussian schoolmaster was hailed as having won the victory. However, after 1918 one no longer sang the praises of the Prussian schoolmaster! This is an example to show how "modern" educational attitudes have been praised for the most extraordinary successes. And today we witness some of the results, namely our chaotic social life, which threatens to become more and more chaotic because so many people have replaced a will-controlled and morally strong sense of freedom with indulgence and license. Many of them have forgotten how to use their real, inner freedom. Anyone able to observe life will find definite links between the general chaos of today and educational principles that, though highly satisfying to intellectual and naturalistic attitudes, fail to bring about the full development of the human being. We must become aware of the polar effects in life, such as that human beings can become free in the right way in later life only if they have as children gone through a stage of looking up to and revering their elders. It is wholesome for the child to believe that a thing is beautiful, true, and good—or ugly, false, and evil—if and because the teacher says so.

With the change of teeth, the child gains a new relationship to the world. As its own soul life gradually emerges and is experienced as something in its own right, the child has to meet the world supported, first of all, by the feeling for authority. At this stage the teacher represents the world at large, and the child has to meet it through the teacher's eyes. Therefore we have to say:

From birth to the change of teeth = instinctive imitation
From the change of teeth to puberty = principle of authority

But by authority we mean the child's natural response to its teacher and never an enforced authority. It is the kind of authority that creates, in very intangible ways, the right rapport between child and teacher.

And here we enter the realm of imponderables. I want to show you by way of an example how they work. Let us imagine that we wish to give the children a concept of the immortality of the soul, a much more difficult task than one may suppose. At the age we are talking about, when the child is so open to the artistic element in education, we cannot communicate such a concept by abstract reasoning or by ideas. We must clothe it in pictures. Now, how might teachers who feel drawn to the more intellectual and naturalistic side of life proceed? Subconsciously they may say to themselves that they are naturally more intelligent than the children, who in reality are stupid, and therefore must invent a suitable picture to give the children an idea of the immortality of the human soul. The butterfly's emergence from the chrysalis offers a good metaphor. The butterfly is hidden in the chrysalis. The human soul is hidden in the body. The butterfly flies out of the chrysalis, a visible picture of what happens in death, when the supersensible soul leaves the body to fly into the spiritual world.

This is the kind of idea that a skillful though intellectually inclined person might think out to pass on to children the concept of the immortality of the soul. But children will not feel inwardly touched by such an attitude of mind. They will accept this picture and forget it soon afterward.

However, one could approach the same task in a different way. It is quite wrong to feel that we are intelligent and the children are stupid. We have already seen in the course of our deliberations how cosmic wisdom is still working directly through the child, and from this point of view, it is the child who is intelligent and the teacher who is stupid. I can bear this in mind, and I can fully believe in the picture of the emerging butterfly. A spiritual attitude to the world teaches me to believe in the truth of this picture, which tells me that the same process that, on a higher level, signifies the soul's withdrawal from the body, is repeated on a lower level in a simplified and sense-perceptible form when a butterfly emerges from the chrysalis. This picture is not my invention, but has been placed into the world by powers of cosmic wisdom. Here, before my very eyes, I can behold what, on a higher plane, happens when the soul leaves the body in death.

If this picture makes a deep impression upon my soul, I cannot but feel convinced of its truth. If teachers have such an experience, something begins to stir between them and the pupils, something that can be assigned only to the realm of the imponderables. If, with the warmth and inwardness of their belief, teachers bring this picture to the children, it will create a deep and lasting impression. It will become part of the children's being.

If one can look in a similar light upon the effects of natural authority, then authority will be accepted as something wholesome and positive, leading to an obedience of a most inward kind. Then it will not be resented through a mistaken idea of freedom.

So teachers, artists in the field of education, have to stand before children as artists of life also, because, after the change of teeth, children approach them as artists too, namely as sculptors and musicians.

In certain cases these unconscious and inherent gifts of the child are developed to an especially high degree. Such children never lose these artistic gifts and in later life become virtuosi or geniuses. But inwardly every child is a great sculptor, though entirely unconsciously. Children retain these gifts from the time before the change of teeth. After this, the inner musical activities are woven together with the inner sculptural-formative activities. As educators we must learn to cooperate in a living way with these artistic forces working through the child.

Proceeding along these lines, we can prevent rampant growth in young human beings and enable them to develop their potential in the widest possible sense.

Teaching Children to Write

LECTURE BY RUDOLF STEINER

Stuttgart, August 26, 1919

We have already discussed how the first lesson in school should begin. Obviously I cannot go on to describe every single step, but I would like to indicate the essential course the lessons should take in a way that will enable you to make something in practice of what I say.

You saw that we attached the greatest importance to making the children aware first of all of the reason for coming to school; then they had to be made aware that they have hands. When they have become conscious of this, we should start with some drawing and even make the transition to painting, through which a sense for what is beautiful and not so beautiful can be developed. We saw that this emerging sense can also be observed in hearing, leading to the first elements of a musical sense for what is beautiful and less beautiful.

Let us now turn to the next step. We shall assume that you have continued for a while in the exercises with crayons and paints. If what is learned is to be built on good foundations, it is essential that learning to write be preceded by some concentration on drawing, so that writing can to some extent be derived from drawing. It is furthermore essential that reading print be derived from reading handwriting. Thus we will try to find the transition from drawing to writing, from writing to reading handwriting, and from reading handwriting to reading print. Let us assume that you have reached the stage where the children are finding their feet in drawing and have mastered to some extent how to make the curved and straight forms that will be needed in writing. We now seek the transition to what we have already described as the basis for writing and reading lessons. Today I will start with a few examples of how you might proceed.

We assume, then, that the children have reached the point where they can master straight and curved lines with their little hands. You then try to show them that there are such things as letters, a whole lot of them. We started with the fish and *F.* The sequence you follow is quite immaterial, and you need not proceed in alphabetical order; I will do so now merely so that you have some sort of comprehensive record. Let us see what success we have in evolving writing and reading out of your own free imagination. I would now say to the children, You know what a bath is. (Let me here interpolate another point: It is very important in teaching to be cunning in a rational manner, that is always to have something up your sleeve that can contribute unseen to the children's education. In this sense it is good to use the word *bath* for the step I am about to describe, so that while they are in school the children are reminded of a bath, of washing themselves, of cleanliness as such. It is good always to have something like this in the background without actually mentioning it or concealing it in admonishments. It is good to choose examples that compel the children to think of something that might also contribute to a moral and aesthetic attitude.) Then you continue: You see, when grown-ups want to write down what a bath is they do it like this: BATH. This is the picture of what you express when you say *bath* and mean a bath. Now I again let a number of the children copy this, just copy it; whenever they are given something like this it should go straight into their hands so that they take it in not just by looking but with their whole being. Then I say, Watch how you start to say *bath*; let us look at the beginning of *bath*, B. The children have to be led from saying the whole word *bath* to just breathing the initial sound, as I illustrated with the fish. The next thing to make clear to them is that just as *bath* is the sign for the whole bath, so B is the sign for the beginning of the word *bath*.

Then I explain that a beginning like this can also be found in other words. I say, If you say *band* you also start like this; if you say *bow*, like the bow some people wear in their hair, you again start in the same way. Have you ever seen a bear in the zoo? When you start to say *bear* you again breathe the same sound. All these words start with the same sound. Thus I endeavor to lead the children from the whole word to the beginning of the word by finding the transition to the single sound or letter, always finding the initial letter from the whole word.

It is important that you yourself try to develop the initial letter in a meaningful way out of the drawing element. You will manage this very well if you simply use your imagination and think to yourself: The people who first saw such animals as beavers and bears drew the animal's back, its hind paws on the ground and its forepaws lifted up; they drew an animal in the act of rising on its hind legs, and their drawing turned into a B. You will always find that the initial letter of a word is a drawing, an animal or plant form or some external object. You can give your imagination free reign; there is no need to delve into cultural histories, which are anyway incomplete.

The fact is that if you go back in history to the most ancient forms of Egyptian writing, which was still a sign writing, you find a great many copies of objects and animals in the letters. Not until the transition from the Egyptian to the Phoenician culture did the change take place that brought about the development of the picture into a sign representing a sound. It is this transition that the children must experience over again. Let us therefore gain a clear idea of it ourselves in theory.

When writing first began to develop in ancient Egypt, every detail that was written down was written in picture writing; it was drawn, although the drawing had to be as simplified as possible. If someone employed in copying this picture writing made a mistake, if for instance a holy word was misrepresented, the scribe was condemned to death. We thus see how very, very seriously anything connected with writing was taken in ancient Egypt. All writing at that time consisted of pictures of the kind described. Then cultural life was taken up by the Phoenicians, who lived more firmly in the external world. They retained the initial picture of a word and transferred it to represent the sound. Since we are not here to study Egyptian languages, let me give you an example that is valid for Egyptian and also easily adapted in our own language. The Egyptians knew that the sound "M" could be depicted by watching mainly the upper lip. They therefore took the sign for M from the picture of the upper lip. From this sign the letter that we use for the beginning of the word *mouth* emerged, and the letter is also valid for any other word beginning with the same sound. In this way the picture sign for the beginning of a word became the sign for a sound.

Because this principle was adhered to in the history and development of writing, it is also excellent for teaching, and we shall use it here. That is, we shall endeavor to arrive at letters by starting with drawings: Just as we move from the fish with its two fins to the *F*, and from the bear dancing on its hind legs to the *B*, so do we move from the upper lip to the mouth, and from the mouth to the *M*.

With our imagination we seek to pave the way for the child from drawing to writing. I told you it was unnecessary to make extensive studies of the history of writing in order to find what you need. What you might discover through such studies will serve you far less in your teaching than what you find through your own soul activity and your own imagination. The kind of activity necessary for studying the history of writing would make you so dead that you would have a far less living influence on your pupils than you will have if you yourself arrive at the idea of deriving the *B* from the bear. Working things out for yourself will refresh you so much that what you want to tell your pupils will have a far more living effect than lesson material you find through historical research. Looking at life and your teaching with these two aspects in mind, you must ask, What is more important, to take in a historical fact with great effort and then strenuously seek to weave it into your lessons, or to have such agility of soul that you can invent your own examples to offer your pupils with your own enthusiasm? It will always give you joy, albeit a quiet joy, to transfer to a letter the shape you have made yourself out of some animal or plant. And your joy will live in what you make out of your pupil.

Next we point out to the children that what they have found at the beginning of a word can also appear in the middle. You say, for instance: You have all seen a little baby; when grown-ups want to write the word *baby* they do it like this: BABY. Here you can see that what you had at the beginning in *bear* is now at the beginning and in the middle in *baby*.[4] You always use capital letters to start with so that the children recognize the similarity to the picture. In

---

4. Rudolf Steiner used the German word *Rebe* (vine) as his example here, so I have freely adapted his meaning to an English word. — TRANS.

this way you teach them that what they have learned about the beginning of a word can also be found in the middle of a word. This is another step in the process of dividing the whole into parts for them.

You see how the important thing for us in our endeavor to achieve a living rather than a dead teaching is always to start from the whole. Just as in arithmetic we start not from the addenda but from the sum, which we divide into parts, so here too we proceed from the whole to the parts. The great advantage of this method of teaching and education is that we are thus able to place the children in the world in a living way; the world is a totality and the children maintain permanent links with the living whole if we proceed as I have indicated. Having them learn the individual letters from pictures gives them a link with living reality. But you must never neglect to write the letter forms so that they are seen to arise from the pictures, and you must always take into account that the consonants can be explained as pictures of external objects but never the vowels. Your point of departure for the vowels is that they always render the inner being of human beings and their relationship to the external world. For example, when you are teaching children the letter *A* ["ah"], you will say, Think of the Sun you see in the morning. Can any of you remember what you did when the Sun rose this morning? Perhaps some of the children will remember what they did. If none of them remember, they will have to be helped to recall how they must have stood there and how, if the sunrise was very beautiful, they must have said, "Ah!" A note of feeling must be struck, calling forth the resonance that sounds in the vowel. Then you must try to tell them that when they stood like that and said, "Ah!" it was just as if a beam of sunlight from their inner being spread out from their mouths.

What lives in you when you see the sunrise streams forth out of your inner being when you say, "Ah" (see drawing on left). But you do not let all of it stream out; you keep some of it back and it becomes this sign (see drawing on right). You should try to clothe with a drawing what lies in the breath when a vowel is spoken. You will find drawings that can show in a picture how the signs for the vowels have come about. Primitive cultures do not have many vowels, not even the primitive cultures of today. The languages of primitive cultures are very rich in consonants; these people can express many more things in consonants than we know how to. They even click their tongues and are skilled in articulating all sorts of complicated consonants, with only a hint of vowel sounds in between. You will find African tribesmen who make sounds resembling the crack of a whip, and so on, while the vowels are only faintly heard. European travellers who meet these tribes usually sound their vowels much more strongly than the tribesmen do.

So we can always evolve the vowels out of drawing. For instance, by appealing to the children's feelings you can try to make them imagine themselves in the following situation: Think what would happen if your brother or sister came to you and said something you did not understand at first. After a while you begin to understand what is meant. Then what do you say? One of the children may answer, or you may have to point out that they would say, "Eee" [the letter *I* in German]. When the shape of the sound "Eee" is drawn, it contains a pointing toward whatever has been understood; it is a rather rough expression of pointing to something.

In eurythmy you find it expressed very clearly. So a simple line becomes an *I*; the line should be fatter at the bottom and thinner at the top, only instead we draw a line and express the thinner part with a smaller sign above it. In this way every vowel can be derived out of the shape of the aspiration, of the breath.

Using this method, you will at first be teaching the children a kind of sign writing. You need not be at all shy about employing ideas that arouse feelings that really did live in the process of cultural development. Thus you could say to the children, Have you ever seen a tall building with a dome on top?[5] A dome, *D*. This means you would have to make the *D* like this: ⌒. This was awkward, however, so people upended it and made *D*.

Such ideas really are inherent in writing, and you can make use of them. Now you proceed to the small letters: After a while people did not want their writing to be so complicated, they wanted it to be simpler. So out of this sign *D*, which really ought to be ⌒, they made this sign, the small *d*. You can most certainly evolve the existing letter shapes in this way out of figures you have taught the children in drawing. By always pointing out the transition from form to form and never teaching in an abstract way, you help the children progress so that they can find the genuine transition from the form derived from the drawing to the shape the letter actually has now in handwriting.

There are some individuals today who have recognized such things, though they are few and far between. There are educators who have pointed out that writing ought to be derived from drawing, but they proceed in a different manner from that required here. Their starting point is the shape of the letters as they are today, so instead of proceeding from the sign for the dancing bear to the *B*, they try to lead the children from drawing to writing by carving the *B* up into

5. Rudolf Steiner's example here is *Dach* (roof). *Dome* fits the letter D so well that I have used it here and very slightly altered the text accordingly. — TRANS.

separate lines and curves: I ⊃ . They advocate an abstract version of what we are trying to do quite concretely. These educators are quite right in seeing that it would be practical to proceed from drawing to writing, but people today are too entangled in the dead wood of our culture to hit upon a clearly living way of going about things.

Let me warn you at this point not to be taken in by all sorts of modern endeavors that might tempt you to say efforts are being made here to do this and there to do that. For you will always discover that the intentions do not have very deep foundations. Somehow people are constantly impelled to attempt such things, but they will not succeed until humankind has accepted spiritual science as a part of culture.

So we can always make a connection between the human being and the surrounding world by teaching writing in an organic way and teaching reading by starting with reading handwriting.

Now it is natural to teaching that there is a certain yearning for complete freedom, and we should not leave this out of account. Notice how freedom flows into this discussion of how we might prepare ourselves to be teachers; our discussion intrinsically has something to do with freedom. I have pointed out that you should not make yourselves unfree by toiling away at studying how writing came into being during the transition from Egyptian to Phoenician culture, that you have to develop your own soul capacities. What can be done by this method of teaching will of course differ from teacher to teacher. Not everyone can use a dancing bear; someone might use something much better for the same purpose. The final result, however, can be achieved just as well by one teacher as by another. All teachers give of themselves when they teach. In this their freedom remains inviolate. The more the teachers desire to preserve their freedom, the more they will be able to enter into their teaching by giving of themselves. This is something that has been almost entirely lost in recent times, as you can see from a certain phenomenon.

Some time ago (the younger among you may not remember the matter, but it caused the older ones, who knew what it entailed, a good deal of annoyance), preparations were made to do something in the cultural sphere that very much resembled the introduction of the notorious Imperial German State Gravy in the material sphere. You know how it has often been stressed that there ought to be a standard sauce or gravy for all inns that do not have to reckon with an elite foreign clientele and serve only Germans. Well, just as this Imperial German State Gravy was to be standardized, so spelling, orthography, was to be standardized. Now people have the most curious attitude to this question, as concrete examples demonstrate. There is in German literature an instance of a most beautiful, tender relationship between Novalis and a certain lady. This relationship is so beautiful because when the lady in question had passed away, Novalis continued to live with her quite consciously in the spiritual world, following her through death in an inner meditative activity of soul. He bore witness of this. The relationship between Novalis and his beloved is one of the most entrancing and intimate episodes in the history of German literature. Now a German scholar wrote a highly intelligent (and, seen from its own point of view, also interesting), strictly philological treatise on the relationship between Novalis and the lady. This delicate, tender relationship is "put in its proper light" through the proof that the lady died before she had learned to spell properly. She made spelling mistakes in her letters! In short, we are given, with the strictest scientific accuracy of course, a thoroughly banal picture of this person who had such a special relationship with Novalis. The scientific method is so good that any dissertation made in accordance with it would earn the highest marks! I only want to remind you that people seem to have forgotten that Goethe was never able to spell properly, that all through his life he made spelling mistakes, particularly when he was young. Yet despite this he rose to Goethean greatness! Not to mention the people he knew and thought highly of—their letters, nowadays sometimes published in facsimile, would earn nothing but red corrections from the hand of a schoolmaster! They would get thoroughly poor marks!

All this is linked to a rather unfree aspect of our life, an aspect that ought to play no part in teaching and education. But a few decades ago it was so pronounced that the more enlightened teachers were infuriated. Standard German spelling was to be introduced, the famous Puttkammer orthography. This meant that the state not only exercised the right to supervise and administer the schools but actually laid down the law on spelling. The result is just what you might expect! For this Puttkammer spelling system has robbed us of much that might still have revealed something of the more intimate aspects of the German language. Seeing only the abstract spelling of today, people have lost much in written German of what used to live in the German language.

What matters most in such things is the right attitude of mind. Obviously we cannot let spelling run riot but we can at least recognize what the opposite points of view are. If people, once they had learned to write, were allowed to put down what they heard from others or from themselves just as they heard it, their spelling would be very varied, very individualized. This would make communication more difficult, but it would be extraordinarily interesting. On the other hand, our task is to develop not only our own individuality in community with others but also our social impulses and feelings. A great deal of what could be revealed as our own individuality is rubbed off in what we have to develop for the sake of living together with others. We should feel that this is so; we should be taught to feel that we do such a thing purely for social reasons. Therefore when you begin to orient your writing lessons toward spelling, your starting point must be a quite specific set of feelings. You will again and again have to point out to the children, as I have already said in another connection, that they should respect and esteem grown-ups, that they are themselves growing up into a world already formed and waiting to receive them, and that therefore they must take notice of what is already there. This is the point of view from which the children must be introduced to things like correct spelling. Spelling lessons must run parallel with developing their feeling of respect and esteem for what their predecessors have established. Spelling must not be taught as an abstraction as though it existed as an absolute on the basis of some divine—or shall we say Puttkammer—law or other; you must develop in the children the feeling: the grown-ups whom we are to respect spell like this, so we ought to follow their example. A certain variability in spelling will result, but it will not be excessive; the growing child will make a certain adaptation to the world of the grown-ups. And we must count on this adaptation. It is not our task to create in children the belief that this is right and that is wrong. The only belief we should arouse, thus building on living authority, is that this is the way the grown-ups do it.

This is what I meant when I said we must find the transition from the child's first period, up to the change of teeth, to the second period, up to puberty, by making the transition from the principle of imitation to that of authority. What I mean by this must be introduced everywhere in practice, not by drilling the children to respect authority but by acting in a way that will help their feeling for authority to arise—for instance by teaching spelling in the way I have just described.

Teaching Arithmetic

LECTURE BY RUDOLF STEINER

Torquay, August 16, 1924

It is essential that you have some understanding of the real essence of every subject that you teach, so that you do not use things in your teaching that are remote from life itself. Everything that is intimately connected with life can be understood. I could even say that whatever one really understands has this intimate connection with life. This is not the case with abstractions.

Today we find that teachers' ideas are largely abstractions, so that in many respects the teachers themselves are remote from life. This is a source of great difficulties in education and teaching. Just consider the following: Imagine that you want to think over how you first came to count things and what really happens when you count. You will probably find that the thread of your recollections breaks somewhere, and that you did once learn to count, but actually you do not really know what you do when you count.

Now all kinds of theories are thought out for the teaching of numbers and counting, and it is customary to act upon such theories. But even when external results can be obtained, the whole being of the child is not touched with this kind of counting or with similar things that have no connection with real life. The modern age has proved that it lives in abstractions, by inventing such things as the abacus or bead-frame for teaching. In a business office people can use calculating machines as much as they like—that does not concern us at the moment, but in teaching, this calculating machine, which is exclusively concerned with the activities of the head, prevents you from the very start from dealing with numbers in accordance with the child's nature.

Counting however should be derived from life itself, and here it is supremely important to know from the beginning that you should not ever expect a child to understand every single thing you teach. Children must take a great deal on authority, but they must take it in a natural, practical way.

Perhaps you may find that what I am now going to say will be rather difficult for the child. But that does not matter. It is of great significance that there should be moments in a person's life when in the thirtieth or fortieth year one could say to oneself: Now I understand what in my eighth or ninth year, or even earlier, I took on authority. This awakens new life in a person. But if you look at all the object lessons that are introduced into the teaching of today, you may well be in despair over the way things are trivialized, in order, as one says, to bring them nearer to the child's understanding.

Now imagine that you have quite a young child in front of you, one who still moves quite clumsily, and you say: "You are standing there before me. Here I take a piece of wood and a knife, and I cut the wood into pieces. Can I do that to you?" The child will see that I cannot do it. And now I can say: "Look, if I can cut the piece of wood in two, the wood is not like you, and you are not like the wood, for I cannot cut you in two like that. So there is a difference between you and the wood. The difference lies in the fact that you are a unit, a 'one', and the wood is not a *one*. You are a unit and I cannot cut you in two, and therefore I call you *one*, a unit."

You can now gradually proceed to show the child a sign for this *one*. You make a stroke : "I," so that you show it is a unit and you make this stroke for it.

Now you can leave this comparison between the wood and the child and you can say: "Look, here is your right hand but you have another hand too, your left hand. If you only had this one hand it could certainly move about everywhere as you do, but if your hand were only to follow the movement of your body you could never touch yourself in the way your two hands can touch each other. For when this hand moves and the other hand moves at the same time, then they can take hold of each other, they can come together. That is different from when you simply move alone. In that you walk alone you are a unit. But the one hand can touch the other hand. This is no longer a unit, this is a duality, a *two*. See, you are one, but you have two hands." This you then show like this: "I I".

In this way you can work out concepts of *one* and *two* from the child's own form.

Now you call out another child and say: "When you two walk toward each other you can also meet and touch each other; there are two of you, but a third can join you. This is impossible with your hands." Thus you can proceed to the three:"I I I".

In this manner you can derive numbers out of what the human being is itself. You can lead over to numbers from the human being, who is not an abstraction but a living being.

Then you can say: "Look, you can find the number *two* somewhere else in yourself." The children will think finally of their two legs and feet. Now you say: "You have seen your neighbor's dog, haven't you? Does the dog only go on two feet also?" Then the children will come to realize that the four strokes,"I I I I," are a picture of the neighbor's dog propped up on four legs, and thus will gradually learn to build up numbers out of life.

The teacher's eyes must always be alert and look at everything with understanding. Now you naturally begin to write numbers with Roman figures, because the children of course will immediately understand them, and when you have got to the four you will easily be able, with the hand, to pass over to five — "V". You will soon see that if you keep back your thumb you can use this four as the dog does!: "I I I I". Now you add the thumb and make five— "V".

I was once with a teacher who had got up to this point (in explaining the Roman figures) and could not see why it occurred to the Romans not to make five strokes next to one another but to make this sign "V" for the five. He got on quite well up to "I I I I". Then I said: "Now let us do it like this: Let us spread out our fingers and our thumb so that they go in two groups, and there we have it, 'V'. Here we have the whole hand in the Roman five and this is how it actually originated. The whole hand is there within it."

In a short lecture course of this kind it is only possible to explain the general principle, but in this way we can derive the idea of numbers from real life, and only when a number has thus been worked out straight from life should you try to introduce counting by letting the numbers follow each other. But the children should take an active part in it. Before you come to the point of saying: Now tell me the numbers in order, 1, 2, 3, 4, 5, 6, 7, 8, 9, and so on, you should start with a rhythm; let us say we are going from 1 to 2, then it will be: 1-2, 1-2, 1-2; let the child stamp on 2 and then on to 3 also in rhythm: 1-2-3, 1-2-3. In this way we bring rhythm into the series of numbers, and thereby too we foster the child's faculty of comprehending the thing as a whole. This is the natural way of teaching the children numbers, out of the reality of what numbers are. For people generally think that numbers were thought out by adding one to the other. This is quite untrue, for the head does not do the counting at all. In ordinary life people have no idea what a peculiar organ the human head really is, and how useless it is for our earthly life. It is there for beauty's sake, it is true, because our faces please each other. It has many other virtues too, but as far as spiritual activities are concerned it is really not nearly so much in evidence, for the spiritual qualities of the head always lead back to a person's former earth-life. The head is a metamorphosis of the former life on earth, and the fact of having a head only begins to have a real meaning when we know something of our former earthly lives. All other activities come from somewhere else, not from the head at all. The truth is that we count subconsciously on our fingers. In reality we count from one to ten on our ten fingers, then eleven (adding the toes), twelve, thirteen, fourteen (counting on the toes). You cannot see what you are doing, but you go up to twenty. And what you do in this manner with your fingers and toes only throws its reflection into the head. The head only looks on at all that occurs. The head is really only an apparatus for reflecting what the body does. The body thinks, the body counts. The head is only a spectator.

We can find a remarkable analogy for this human head. If you have a car and are sitting comfortably inside it, you are doing nothing yourself; it is the chauffeur in front who has to exert himself. You sit inside and are driven through the world. So it is with the head; it does not toil and moil, it simply sits on the top of your body and lets itself be carried quietly through the world as a spectator. All that is done in spiritual life is done from the body. Mathematics is done by the body, thinking is also done by the body, and feeling too is done with the body. The bead-frame has arisen from the mistaken idea that reckoning is done with the head. Sums are then taught to the child with the bead-frame, that is to say, the child's head is made to work and then the head passes on the work to the body, for it is the body that must do the reckoning. This fact, that the body must do the reckoning, is not taken into account, but it is important. So it is right to let the children count with their fingers and also with their toes, for indeed it is good to call forth the greatest possible skill in the children. In fact there is nothing better in life than making the human being skillful in every way. This cannot be done through sports, for sports do not really make people skilled. What does make a person skilled is holding a pencil between the big toe and the next toe and learning to write with the foot, to write figures with the foot. This can be of real significance, for in truth a person is permeated with soul and spirit in the whole body. The head is the traveller that sits back restfully inside and does nothing, while the body, every part of it, is the chauffeur who has to do everything.

Thus from the most varied sides you must try to build up what the child has to learn as counting. And when you have worked in this way for a time it is important to pass on and not merely take counting by adding one thing to another; indeed this is the least important aspect of counting and you should now teach the child as follows: "This is something that is ONE. Now you divide it like this, and you have something that is TWO. It is not two ONEs put together but the two come out of the ONE." And so on with three and four. Thus you can awaken the thought that the ONE is really the comprehensive thing that contains within itself the TWO, the THREE, the FOUR, and if you learn to count in the way indicated in the diagram, 1, 2, 3, 4, and so on, then the child will have concepts that are living and thereby come to experience something of what it is to be inwardly permeated with the element of number.

In the past our modern conceptions of counting by placing one bean beside another or one bead beside another in the frame were quite unknown; in those days it was said that the unit was the largest, every two is only the half of it, and so on. So you come to understand the nature of counting by actually looking at external objects. You should develop the child's thinking by means of external things that can be seen, and keep as far away as possible from abstract ideas.

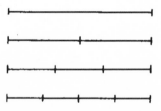

The children can then gradually learn the numbers up to a certain point, first, let us say, up to twenty, then up to a hundred and so on. If you proceed on these lines you will be teaching them to count in a living way. I should like to emphasize that this method of counting, real counting, should be presented before the children learn to do sums. They ought to be familiar with this kind of counting before you go on to arithmetic.

Arithmetic too must be drawn out of life. The living thing is always a whole and must be presented as a whole first of all. It is wrong for children to have to put together a whole out of its parts, when they should be taught to look first at the whole and then divide this whole into its parts; get them first to look at the whole and then divide it and split it up; this is the right path to a living conception.

Many of the effects of our materialistic age on the general culture of humankind pass unnoticed. Nowadays, for instance, no one is scandalized but regards it rather as a matter of course to let children play with boxes of bricks, and build things out of the single blocks. This of itself leads them away from what is living. There is no impulse in the child's nature to put together a whole out of parts. The child has many other needs and impulses that are, admittedly, much less convenient. If you give a child a watch for instance, the child's immediate desire is to pull it to pieces, to break up the whole into its parts, which is actually far more in accordance with human nature—to see how the whole arises out of its components.

This is what must now be taken into account in our arithmetic teaching. It has an influence on the whole of culture, as you will see from the following example.

In the conception of human thought up to the thirteenth and fourteenth centuries very little emphasis was placed upon putting together a whole out of its parts; this arose later. Master-builders built much more from the idea of the whole (which they then split up into parts) rather than starting with the single parts and making a building out of these. The latter procedure was really only introduced into civilization later on. This conception then led to people thinking of every single thing as being put together out of the very smallest parts. Out of this arose the atomic theory in physics, which really only comes from education. For atoms are really tiny little caricatures of demons, and our learned scholars would not speak about them as they do unless people had grown accustomed, in education, to putting everything together out of its parts. Thus it is that atomism has arisen.

We criticize atomism today, but criticism is really more or less superfluous because people cannot get free from what they have been used to thinking wrongly for the last four or five centuries; they have become accustomed to go from the parts to the whole instead of letting their thoughts pass from the whole to the parts.

This is something you should particularly bear in mind when teaching arithmetic. If you are walking toward a distant wood you first see the wood as a whole, and only when you come near it do you perceive that it is made up of single trees. This is just how you must proceed in arithmetic. You never have in your purse, let us say, 1, 2, 3, 4, 5 coins, but you have a heap of coins. You have all five together, which is a whole. This is what you have first of all. And when you cook pea soup you do not have 1, 2, 3, 4, 5 or up to 30 or 40 peas, but you have one heap of peas, or with a basket of apples, for instance, there are not 1, 2, 3, 4, 5, 6, 7 apples but one heap of apples in your basket. You have a whole. What does it matter, to begin with, how many you have? You simply have a heap of apples that you are now bringing home (see diagram). There are, let us say, three children. You will not now divide them so that each gets the same, for perhaps one child is small, another big. You put your hand into the basket and give the bigger child a bigger handful, the smaller child a smaller handful; you divide your heap of apples into three parts.

Dividing or sharing out is in any case such a strange business! There was once a mother who had a large piece of bread. She said to her little boy, Henry: "Divide the bread, but you must divide it in a Christian way." Then Henry said: "What does that mean, divide it in a Christian way?" "Well," said his mother, "You must cut the bread into two pieces, one larger and one smaller; then you must give the larger piece to your sister Anna and keep the smaller one for yourself." Whereupon Henry said, "Oh well, in that case let Anna divide it in a Christian way!"

Other conceptions must come to your aid here. We will do it like this, that we give this to one child, let us say (see lines in the drawing), and this heap to the second child, and this to the third. They have already learned to count, and so that we get a clear idea of the whole thing we will first count the whole heap. There are eighteen apples. Now I have to count up what they each have. How many does the first child get? Five. How many does the second child get? Four. And the third? Nine. Thus I have started from the whole, from the heap of apples, and have divided it up into three parts.

Arithmetic is often taught by saying: "You have five, and here is five again and eight; count them together and you have eighteen." Here you are going from the single thing to the whole, but this will give the child dead concepts. The child will not gain living concepts by this method. Proceed from the whole, from the eighteen, and divide it up into the addenda; that is how to teach addition.

Thus in your teaching you must not start with the single addenda, but start with the sum, which is the whole, and divide it up into the single addenda. Then you can go on to show that it can be divided up differently, with different addenda, but the whole always remains the same. By taking addition in this way, not as is very often done by having first the addenda and then the sum, but by taking the sum first and then the addenda, you will arrive at conceptions that are living and mobile. You will also come to see that when it is only a question of a pure number the whole remains the same, but the single addenda can change. This peculiarity of number, that you can think of the addenda grouped in different ways, is very clearly brought out by this method.

From this you can proceed to show the children that when you have something that is not itself a pure number but that contains number within it, as the human being for example, then you cannot divide it up in all these different ways. Take the human trunk for instance and what is attached to it—head, two arms and hands, two feet; you cannot now divide up the whole as you please; you cannot say: now I will cut out one foot like this, or the hand like this, and so on, for it has already been membered by nature in a definite way. When this is not the case, and it is simply a question of pure counting, then I can divide things up in different ways.

Such methods as these will make it possible for you to bring life and a kind of living mobility into your work. All pedantry will disappear and you will see that something comes into your teaching that the child badly needs: humor comes into the teaching, not in a childish but in a healthy sense. And humor must find its place in teaching.[6]

This then must be your method: always proceed from the whole. Suppose you had such an example as the following, taken from real life. A mother sent Mary to fetch some apples. Mary got twenty-five apples. The apple-woman wrote it down on a piece of paper. Mary comes home and brings only ten apples. The fact is before us, an actual fact of life, that Mary got twenty-five apples and only brought home ten. Mary is an honest little girl, and she really didn't eat a single apple on the way, and yet she only brought home ten. And now someone comes running in, an honest person, bringing all the apples that Mary dropped on the way. Now there arises the question: How many does this person bring? We see him coming from a distance, but we want to know beforehand how many he is going to bring. Mary has come home with ten apples, and she got twenty-five, for there it is on the paper written down by the apple-woman, and now we want to know how many this person ought to be bringing, for we do not yet know if he is honest or not. What Mary brought was ten apples, and she got twenty-five, so she lost fifteen apples.

Now, as you see, the sum is done. The usual method is that something is given and you have to take away something else, and something is left. But in real life—you may easily convince yourselves of this—it happens much more often that you know what

---

6. At this point Dr. Steiner turned to the translator and said: "Please be sure you translate the word *humor* properly, for it is always misunderstood in connection with teaching!"

you originally had and you know what is left over, and you have to find out what was lost. Starting with the minuend and the subtrahend and working out the remainder is a dead process. But if you start with the minuend and the remainder and have to find the subtrahend, you will be doing subtraction in a living way. This is how you may bring life into your teaching.

You will see this if you think of the story of Mary and her mother and the person who brought the subtrahend; you will see that Mary lost the subtrahend from the minuend and that has to be justified by knowing how many apples the person you see coming along will have to bring. Here life, real life, comes into your subtraction. If you say, so much is left over, this only brings something dead into the child's soul. You must always be thinking of how you can bring life, not death, to the child in every detail of your teaching.

You can continue in this way. You can do multiplication by saying: "Here we have the whole, the product. How can we find out how many times something is contained in this product?" This thought has life in it. Just think how dead it is when you say: We will divide up this whole group of people, here are three, here are three more, and so on, and then you ask: how many times three have we here? That is dead, there is no life in it.

If you proceed the other way round and take the whole and ask how often one group is contained within it, then you bring life into it. You can say to the children, for instance: "Look, there is a certain number of you here." Then let them count up; how many times are these five contained within the forty-five? Here again you consider the whole and not the part. How many more of these groups of five can be made? Then it is found out that there are eight more groups of five. Thus, when you do the thing the other way round and start with the whole—the product—and find out how often one factor is contained in it you bring life into your arithmetical methods and above all you begin with something that the children can see before them. The chief point is that thinking must never, never be separated from visual experience, from what the children can see, for otherwise intellectualism and abstractions are brought to the children in early life and thereby ruin their whole being. The children will become dried up and this will affect not only the soul life but the physical body also, causing desiccation and sclerosis. (I shall later have to speak of the education of spirit, soul, and body as a unity.)

Here again much depends on our teaching arithmetic in the way we have considered, so that in old age the human being is still mobile and skillful. You should teach the children to count from their own bodies as I have described—1, 2, 3, 4, 5, 6, 7, 8, 9, 10—first with the fingers and then with the toes—yes indeed, it would be good to accustom the children actually to count up to twenty with their fingers and toes, not on a bead-frame. If you teach them thus then you will see that through this childlike kind of "meditation" you are bringing life into the body; for when you count on your fingers or toes you have to think about these fingers and toes, and this is then a meditation, a healthy kind of meditating on one's own body. Doing this will allow the grown person to remain skillful of limb in old age; the limbs can still function fully because they have learned to count by using the whole body. If a person only thinks with the head, rather than with the limbs and the rest of the organism, then later on the limbs lose their function and gout sets in.

This principle, that everything in teaching and education must be worked out from what can be seen (but not from what are often called "object lessons" today)—this principle I should like to illustrate for you with an example, something that can actually play a very important part in teaching. I am referring to the Theorem of Pythagoras that as would-be teachers you must all be well acquainted with, and that you may even have already come to understand in a similar way; but I will speak of it again today. Now the Theorem of Pythagoras can be taken as a kind of goal in the teaching of geometry. You can build up your geometry lessons to reach their climax, their summit, in the Theorem of Pythagoras, which states that the square on the hypotenuse of a right-angled triangle is equal to the sum of the squares on the other two sides. It is a marvelous thing if you see it in the right light.

I once had to teach geometry to an elderly lady because she loved it so much; she may have forgotten everything, I do not know, but she had probably not learned much at her school, one of those schools for the "Education of Young Ladies." At all events she knew no geometry at all, so I began and made everything lead up to the Theorem of Pythagoras which the old lady found very striking. We are so used to it that it no longer strikes us so forcibly, but what we have to understand is simply that if I have a right-angled triangle here (see diagram) the area of the square on the hypotenuse is equal to the sum of the other two areas, the two squares on the other two sides. So that if I am planting potatoes and put them at the same distance from each other everywhere, I shall plant the same number of potatoes in the two smaller fields together as in the larger one. This is something very remarkable, very striking, and when you look at it like this you cannot really see how it comes about.

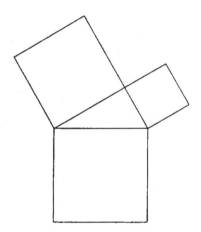

It is just this fact of the wonder of it, that you cannot see how it comes about, that you must make use of to bring life into the more inward, soul quality of your teaching; you must build on the fact that here you have something that is not easily discernible; this must constantly be acknowledged. One might even say with regard to the Theorem of Pythagoras that you can believe it, but you always have to lose your belief in it again. You have to believe afresh every time that this square is equal to the sum of the other two squares.

Now of course all kinds of proofs can be found for this, but the proof ought to be given in a clear visual way.[7] If you use this method of proof, that is, laying one area over the other, you will discover something. If you cut it out instead of drawing it you will see that it is quite easy to understand. Nevertheless, if you think it over afterward you will have forgotten it again. You must work it out afresh every time. You cannot easily hold it in your memory, and therefore you must rediscover it every time. That is a good thing, a very good thing. It is in keeping with the nature of the Theorem of Pythagoras. You must arrive at it afresh every time. You should always forget that you have understood it. This belongs to the remarkable quality of the Theorem of Pythagoras itself, and thereby you can bring life into it. You will soon see that if you make your pupils do it again and again, they have to ferret it out by degrees. They do not get it at once, they have to think it out each time. But this is in accordance with the inner living quality of the Theorem of Pythagoras. It is not good to give a proof that can be understood in a flat, dry kind of way; it is much better to forget it again constantly and work it out every time afresh. This is inherent in the very wonder of it, that the square on the hypotenuse is equal to the squares on the other two sides.

With children of eleven or twelve you can quite well take geometry up to the point of explaining the Theorem of Pythagoras by this comparison of areas, and the children will enjoy it immensely when they have understood it. They will be enthusiastic about it, and will always be wanting to do it again, especially if you let them cut it out. There will perhaps be a few intellectual good-for-nothings who remember it quite well and can always do it again. But most of the children, being more reasonable, will cut it out wrong again and again and have to puzzle it out till they discover how it has to go. That is just the wonderful thing about the Theorem of Pythagoras, and you should not forsake this realm of wonder but should remain within it.

---

7. Steiner then built up a proof for the Theorem of Pythagoras in detail based on the superposition of areas: he gave it in the conversational style used in this lecture course, and with the help of the blackboard and colored chalks.

5

THE MIDDLE ELEMENTARY SCHOOL YEARS

Self and World

LIKE ADAM AND EVE IN PARADISE, young children live in peace and harmony with their environment, intimately connected to their surroundings, full of trust and confidence in the world. When children turn nine, this trusting, secure relationship to the world begins to change. In response, the Waldorf curriculum also changes, and teachers need to establish a new relationship with their students.

The ninth year change is a time when "children, though they do not generally express it in words, nevertheless show through their whole behavior that they have a question—or several questions—that betray an inner crisis in life" (HV, p. 78). When children turn nine, they begin increasingly to have questions about themselves, their place in the world, and their teachers. During the first three grades, the students accepted the authority of their teachers without question; now they need to experience inner justification for that authority. The pupil feels, "Until now I have always looked up to my teacher. Now I can no longer do so, unless I know that my teacher also looks up to something higher—something safely rooted in life" (SE, p. 166).

Steiner urged teachers to be especially sensitive to their students at this time.

Everything depends on the teacher recognizing the significance of this stage and realizing that in the child's tender approach there is a longing for renewed confidence and trust. The way a teacher responds to this situation may be a decisive factor for the child's entire life. Whether the child will grow into an unstable character or into a person strongly integrated in life may well depend on whether the teacher is acting with inner certainty and understanding during this crucial time. (SE, p. 166)

Why do children experience such intense inner questioning at this time? According to Steiner, after the age of nine, children begin to differentiate themselves from the world and to experience their I in a new way. Until this time, the child's I and the outer world interpenetrated each other; as a result the child felt connected to everything. As this connection is severed, the child feels increasingly separate from the world and experiences a new kind of self-consciousness.

The child's new sense of self derives from a change in the relationship between the physical and etheric bodies, on the one hand, and the astral body and I on the other. During the first seven years of life, the etheric body has been working like a sculptor, gradually modeling a second physical body from within, using the inherited physical body as its model. During the second seven years, the astral body, which Steiner characterizes as musical in nature, works more strongly on the child from the periphery. The physical and etheric bodies, which are connected with the child's parents and the stream of inheritance, work from the past into the future. The astral body and the I, which are connected with the stream of individuality and of destiny, work from the future into the past. When these two streams meet during the ninth year, they create a new awareness in the child. The nine-year-old child begins to sense the future, to become aware of the past, and thus, for the first time, to stand fully in the present. With the recognition of the past comes a new sense of responsibility; with the anticipation of the future comes a new sense of freedom. Like Adam and Eve, whose eyes were opened after they ate of the tree of knowledge, children see themselves and the world with new eyes. The nature study curriculum of the middle elementary school addresses their new capacities and their new perspective on the world.

Nature Study

During the first three grades, when students still feel themselves intimately connected to the world, nature study should be introduced through stories and legends, preferably composed by the teacher. "Everything must live," says Steiner. "The teacher must let the plants speak, he or she must let the animals act as moral beings. The teacher must be able to turn the whole world into a fairy tale, into fables and legends" (SE, p. 169). If a teacher works artistically, much of what will be covered in the science curriculum of the upper grades can be introduced through stories and imaginative pictures that capture the essence of the subjects.

After the ninth year change, as the child's picture consciousness changes, nature study is presented through lively descriptions that are deepened by direct observation. Because children are no longer so intimately connected to their surroundings, we must help them develop their sense of connection to the world; this may be achieved by presenting the human being in relation to the animals and the plants in relation to the Earth.

Human Beings and Animals

In Waldorf schools, the study of the animal kingdom begins by considering the human being. As human beings, we reveal a three-fold nature in every aspect of ourselves. We are beings of body, soul, and spirit. We have three soul faculties—thinking, feeling, and willing. We sleep, dream, or live in waking consciousness, and our bodies are divided into three major parts: head, trunk, and limbs.

The major groups of our physiological functions—sense activity, circulation and respiration, metabolism and movement—are centered in the three major parts of the body. The head, which houses our brain and most of the sense organs, serves as the center of the nerve-sense system. The chest, which encloses our heart and the lungs, serves as the center of the rhythmic system. The abdomen, which contains our organs of digestion, excretion, and reproduction, serves as the center of the metabolic system that provides energy for the activities of the limbs. We might draw a further connection between the nerve-sense system and thinking, the rhythmic system and feeling, and the metabolic-limb system and willing. We are most awake in our nerve-sense system; we are dimly conscious in our rhythmic system; and we are almost completely asleep in the work of the metabolic-limb system.

Having established this foundation, we can introduce the children to families of animals. One might think that such studies should provide a foundation for further work in the sciences, but according to Steiner, this is not our goal.

> When we are teaching the children about plants and animals in our grade school lessons, we could hardly imagine a greater mistake in our method of education than to treat the subject as an introduction to the studies needed for that child later to become a botanist or zoologist ... for no one should become a botanist or zoologist through what is learned in grade school; that can come about only through special gifts revealed by the student's choice of vocation, and this would certainly appear in the child's life if there is a true art of education. (BT, p. 4)

Our study of the animals should develop the students' imaginations and nourish their souls. We introduce the animals so that students can recognize that each animal is a reflection of one aspect of the human being. After considering these connections, we must try to awaken in the children the sense that the most perfect parts of our external form are our limbs. Our legs allow us to walk upright, leaving our hands free for work and for creative activity. "There is no more wonderful symbol of human freedom than human arms and hands," (PA, p. 108) says Steiner, for our hands allow us to work not only for ourselves, but on behalf of others and for the world.

In *The Essentials of Education* Steiner indicated another way of looking at animals. Every type of animal shows an enhancement of one pole of our nature—the nerve-sense system, the rhythmic system, or the metabolic-limb system. In cattle the organs of metabolism are the most highly developed; thus cattle are able to draw nourishment from grasses. The image of a cow chewing its cud, even while asleep, is evocative of the work of the metabolic system. In the lion, the chest and the organs of the rhythmic system predominate; we know the lion by its mighty roar. Between periods of intense activity and deep sleep, the lion loves to bask in a semiconscious, dreamlike state; here we have a picture of the rhythmic system. The eagle shows an enhancement of the nerve system of the senses. Soaring aloft, it observes everything below with incredibly keen eyes. When it decides to dive, the eagle swoops down on unsuspecting prey with lightning speed; this is a picture of the nerve system of the senses. In ancient times, these animals represented aspects of the human being. For this reason they were chosen as mythological symbols and are associated with three of the evangelists of the New Testament.

In *The Kingdom of Childhood*, Steiner suggested that we also examine the animals in terms of their soul qualities. In the second grade, children heard fables that illustrated how different animals behaved. They are now ready to explore more consciously the qualities associated with different animals. While it might seem that we are projecting human qualities onto the animals, this is not our aim. We examine the soul qualities of animals in an attempt to recognize the deep truths that are conveyed by myths and legends that ascribe archetypal human qualities to animals. After describing, for instance, the cruelty of the tiger, the patience of the sheep, or the laziness of the donkey, we can show that human beings have all these qualities, and we synthesize and harmonize everything that is spread out in the animal kingdom (KC, pp. 56–57).

When we return to the study of the human being in the seventh and eighth grades,

> the great moment comes when teachers can show their students how what is concentrated within a single human individual,

is spread out over all of the animal kingdom. To allow children to experience very intensely such decisive moments in life is tremendously important in teaching; and one of these moments is the realization, passing through the child's soul, that the human being as seen physically is both the extract and the synthesis of the entire animal world, but on a higher level. The inner experience of such a climb over a childhood peak—if I may use this comparison—is more important than acquiring knowledge step by step. This will have a very beneficial effect for the rest of the child's life. (CCC, pp. 101–102)

By listening to lively descriptions and narratives, the students develop imaginative pictures of the animals, of their form and structure, of their habits and behavior, of their relationship to their environment and to each other. These imaginative pictures are enhanced by direct observation of animals in nature and by artistic work. Clay sculpture can deepen the study of the animals by helping students recognize and express the animals' salient physical characteristics. When students sculpt a mouse, with its large ears, delicate paws, and long, slender tail, or a beaver, with its thick, stocky body, sturdy legs, and flat, scaly tail, they experience the differences between these animals' forms. Through such experiences they come to know the animals in a new way.

Plant and Earth

While the animals are presented in relationship to the human being, Steiner suggested that the plants should be presented in connection to the Earth.

Plant and Earth belong together.... Earth, plant growth, and the influence of the Sun must all be viewed as being part of a complete whole. I would even like to say that the child's idea of the plant should be so steeped in feeling that, if one were to speak of the plant without referring both to the Earth as a whole and to the Sun, the child would experience a twinge of pain inwardly, not unlike that caused by seeing a plant being torn from its earthly home. (SE, p. 171)

To develop this theme, we might study the changing vegetation during the course of the seasons. We can describe how plants sprout in the springtime, blossom and bear fruit in the summer, wither in the autumn, and lie dormant in the winter. We can compare this to the course of a day with its sunrise, midday, sunset, and night, or to the progression of a human life. When we try to apply this analogy to our three states of consciousness, we recognize that

while sleeping, we are actually more at the level of plants. At that time, as individual human beings, we are no different than the Earth with its plant growth. But to which season does our sleep correspond? It corresponds to summer, that is, to that period of the year when the plants are here. To which season does our wakefulness correspond? That is like winter, when plant life ceases and, in a sense, recedes deep within the Earth. In the same way, plant life recedes into the human being and is replaced by something else during the period of wakefulness. If we follow reality instead of some vague analogy, we have to say that we need to compare human sleep with summer, and the period of human wakefulness with the Earth's winter. Thus, the reality of the situation is actually just the opposite of some vague analogy. (RE, p. 109)

We might also examine the distribution of the different types of plants over the globe. The poles and sub-arctic regions have stunted vegetation that grows slowly during the short growing season. In the tropical regions, trees and plants grow in luxurious abundance all through the year. The temperate regions, with their balanced seasons, have rhythmical cycles of growth and dormancy. When we study the families of plants growing on the sides of a tall tropical mountain like

Mount Kilimanjaro, we observe the same progression of plants that are found from the poles to the equator. Once we have established the connections between plants and the Earth, we can deepen the students' appreciation for the plants by developing other themes.

We might follow the rhythm of contraction and expansion in a plant's development. When the plant is a seed, it is in a state of contraction, for all the possibilities of the future lie locked within its shell. When the seed germinates and sprouts, there is the first expansion, as the shoot reaches upward toward the air and light, while the roots reach downward seeking water. As the plant forms its stalk and leaves, it alternates between contraction and expansion, the dense, hard stalk contrasting with the light, airy leaves. When the plant forms buds, there is another contraction, followed by an expansion again when the flowers open. With the formation of the seed there is a final contraction as the cycle ends, waiting to begin again.

We might also examine the different parts of the plant—root, stalk, leaf, blossom, and fruit—and differentiate plant families based on the predominant part. The fungi, for instance, do not have any leaves at all; the mycelia live in the dark Earth, never coming to the light until they send up their fruiting bodies. Algae have no real roots; some kinds of seaweed have a holdfast but most kinds of algae are free-floating. In a fern, the leaf nature is most highly developed, while a tree's trunk shows an enhancement of the stalk. By examining the characteristic features of the different families of plants, students can come to appreciate the features of each individual plant.

The families of plants can also be examined in terms of their soul qualities.

> Now, when you recognize that everything with the nature of a blossom belongs to a certain soul quality, you must also assign other organic parts of the plant to other soul qualities. Thus, whether you associate single parts of the plant with qualities of soul or think of the whole plant kingdom together in this sense, it is the same thing. The whole plant kingdom is really a single plant. (DT, p. 138)

Steiner also suggests that we might draw parallels between the families of plants and the developing soul qualities of a child, comparing, for instance, the mushrooms to a little baby who is barely ready to venture out into the world, or a flowering, fruit-bearing plant to an adolescent, who is ready to take on life's responsibilities and challenges.

These presentations and discussions present opportunities for the students' artistic work. Once they learn how to observe the plants accurately, students strive to render what they have seen artistically through sketching, drawing, and painting. Students may keep a journal that illustrates and describes the development of a bean as it sprouts, grows, blossoms, and forms seeds again, or they might draw a series of tree silhouettes that illustrate various patterns of tree growth. A composition might highlight the differences between the lily and the rose. The same theme might be portrayed by a conversation between the two plants, or by a poem that evokes their contrasting soul qualities. Whatever the assignment or the medium, the goal is the same: to deepen and develop the students' connection to the plants and to the Earth.

In the upper elementary school grades, plants and animals are studied further in connection with geography. Geology and astronomy are introduced in the sixth grade, and the biology curriculum culminates with the study of human anatomy and physiology in grades seven and eight. In the high school, students have several courses in Earth science, and they take courses in the life sciences each year. These courses develop in greater detail the subjects introduced in elementary school. Regardless of their content, all subjects taught in the Waldorf schools are important in their own right as well as a means to a higher end.

Thus, our instruction can teach not only some knowledge about plants and some knowledge about animals, but it can also help develop character. We can develop the entire human being by guiding children to plants, thus developing their intelligence in the proper way, and by guiding them to the animal world and properly developing their will. We can show children between the ages of nine and twelve their connection with the other divine creations, the plants and the animals of the Earth. They will thus be able to find their path through the world through their sound intelligence and through strength in their will. (p. 204)

Studying Geography: Coming to Terms with the World

In the past, the study of geography was not accorded an important place in most educational curricula and was often combined with some other subject, such as history or natural history. This was especially true in the nineteenth century, and according to Steiner, it was partly responsible for the decline in the feeling of brotherhood among people. Geography occupies a prominent place in the Waldorf curriculum. It begins with a study of the students' home surroundings and gradually expands to encompass the entire Earth. The geography curriculum through the grades includes physical, economic, and cultural geography, as well as geology, astronomy, and anthropology.

The study of geography has three major goals: to help students orient themselves in the world by developing their sense of perspective and spatial awareness; to deepen their awareness of their surroundings by awakening their recognition of the connections between the physical world and human activity; and to cultivate their social feeling by heightening their sense of fellowship for other human beings.

Physical Geography

Just as history lessons help students to orient themselves in time, and to view historic events within the context of their own lives, geography lessons help students to orient themselves in space and to extrapolate from their experience of their local surroundings to more distant places.

In "Teaching Geography," Steiner offers many practical suggestions for teachers.

It is particularly important in geography that we start with what the children already know about the face of the Earth and about what takes place on the face of the Earth. We endeavor to give the children, in an artistic way, a kind of picture of the hills and rivers and other features of their immediate surroundings. With the children, we develop an elementary map of the immediate neighborhood where they are growing up and therefore know. (p. 205)

Steiner then describes how to transform the students' knowledge into a map of the local area. Map-making calls on new capacities in the students. Prior to the age of nine, when children are still so intimately connected with their surroundings, they would have difficulty imagining anything from any perspective other than through their own eyes. During the middle elementary grades, however, students can begin to imagine a place from a bird's eye view. Making maps utilizes and develops this capacity.

Map-making also develops the students' ability to use and interpret symbols. By drawing maps that indicate topographical features, agricultural or industrial applications, vegetation, temperature, or weather patterns, students learn to convey information in new ways.

By developing the students' relationship to space, we also help develop their soul capacities. Steiner states that when we teach children geography

the astral body actually grows denser and thicker lower down. We teach about space, and in so doing increase the density of spirit and soul in the lower astral body, toward the ground. In other words, we consolidate, we bring about a certain firmness in the human being when we teach geography in an imaginative way—always stressing the reality of space. (WEA, p. 55)

The astral body allows us to have perceptions and feelings. When it becomes more powerful, it allows students to sense themselves, other people, and the world more deeply. When, through our teaching of geography, we densify the students' souls and spirits, bringing them more fully down to earth, we help students to recognize and embrace their earthly tasks.

Economic Geography

The geography lessons in the middle elementary school grades focus on physical and economic geography, for the relationship between the land and the human activities that it supports are most readily perceptible. In the lecture below, Steiner suggests how a teacher can help students develop a sense of the economic foundations of an area and he explains how a basis for understanding agriculture, manufacturing, and transportation can be established. Steiner suggests that an intensive study of one area will allow students to apply the geographic principles and concepts they have learned to any other area.

The geography curriculum may also develop a theme over a number of years. How might this be done? In their third grade study of farming, students learn about the major grains and see how the farmer must cultivate the earth properly so that it yields a bountiful harvest. In fourth grade geography classes, when they study their neighborhood, students might make maps showing what types of grains are grown on nearby farms, or they might trace the history and development of a local mill. As fifth graders study the geography of North America, they first encounter the vast farms in the Midwest, whose area is measured in square miles, where machines are needed to do the work of an army of workers. In sixth grade, students might study the geographic and climatic conditions that determine what grains can be grown in different areas of the world, and this will help them understand why different cultures rely on different staple crops. In the seventh or eighth grade, when students learn about the physiology and chemistry of nutrition, they will begin to understand why grains have always been vital to human existence. At the same time, they will learn about global distribution of natural resources, about systems of transportation and distribution, and they might consider issues such as conservation and resource management. Through such a course of study spanning a number of years, students begin to develop an awareness of the Earth as a whole, with no aspect of its existence isolated from the rest.

Cultural Geography

In the upper elementary grades, students study cultural geography, which builds upon their study of history. Steiner suggests that

> it is important to show in geography that everything in history depends upon all the things that come from the Earth— the climates, the formations, the structures of the Earth in various places. After giving them an idea about the connection of land, sea, and climate to Ancient Greece, you can move on to what we can portray as a symptom of the inner development of humanity in the characteristics of Ancient Greece. It is possible to find an inner connection between our geographical picture of the Earth and historical developments. (p. 205)

Themes in cultural geography might be developed by examining a culture in depth, tracing its history, delving into language and literature, considering its artistic contributions, and immersing oneself in the characteristic features of daily life. One can also learn much by examining contrasting peoples—North and South Americans, for instance; jungle dwellers such as the Mbuti and inhabitants of the plains, such as the Masai; or people who live on an island, such as England, and those who live in a landlocked country, such as Switzerland. Such studies develop appreciation and tolerance, and help students feel more closely connected to the different peoples of the Earth. According to Steiner,

> Individuals taught geography in this way will have a more loving relation with other human beings than will those who have not learned about spatial relationships. They

learn to take their place next to others and learn to be considerate. These things strongly affect the moral life, whereas a neglect of geography results in an aversion to loving other human beings. (WEA, p. 56)

The study of geography helps students develop a sense of their place in the world and their responsibilities toward other human beings and toward the Earth. It develops their ability to view the world as a whole and to differentiate and distinguish the integral parts of that whole. Through this important subject, Waldorf teachers encourage students to engage more fully in society and inspire them to work toward a better future.

Zoology and Botany in the Elementary School

LECTURE BY RUDOLF STEINER

Basle, May 3, 1920

I have attempted to indicate from various perspectives how we can base curriculum and teaching goals upon human development. In particular, I tried to show that we can characterize the period from around the age of six or seven, characterized by the change of teeth, until puberty, about age fourteen or fifteen, as one stage of life. I also attempted to show that within that stage is a shorter one lasting until approximately the age of nine. Then there is another important change around the age of twelve. We should view these three times, the ages of about nine, twelve, and fourteen or fifteen, (approximately when the students leave school), as important when we create the overall curriculum and teaching goals. You can easily see the importance of comprehending the development of the human being when you realize that what is important in education is that we completely develop these forces that lie buried in human nature.

If we look at things in the proper way, we have to admit that we need to use education and all our teaching material to reveal those hidden forces within human nature. It is not nearly so important to use the forces within children to teach them one detail or another. What is important is that we present the material the children are to learn in such a way that what they learn develops the natural forces within them. We do not do that if we do not take into account how different the children's physical and soul natures are before the age of nine, then again before the age of twelve, and so forth. We need to be aware that the ability to differentiate through reason, which enables human beings to reason independently, actually begins to be present only at puberty, and that we should slowly prepare for it beginning at the age of twelve. We can, therefore, say that until the age of nine children want to develop under authority, but their desire to imitate is still present as well. At nine, the desire to imitate disappears, but the desire for authority remains. At about the age of twelve, while they are still under the guidance of authority, another important desire, the desire to reason independently, begins to develop. If we attempt to exercise the child's independent reasoning too much before the age of twelve, we actually ruin the child's soul and bodily forces. In a certain sense, we deaden human experiencing with reason....

At the age of nine, children experience a truly complete transformation of their being, which indicates an important transformation of their soul life as well as of their physical experience. At that time, human beings begin to feel separated from their surroundings and learn to differentiate between the world and the self. If we can observe accurately, we have to admit that until that transformation, the world and the I are more or less conjoined in human consciousness. Beginning at the age of nine (of course, I mean this only approximately), human beings can differentiate between the self and the world. We must take that into consideration in what and how we teach children beginning at the age of nine. Until that time, it is best not to confuse the children with descriptions and characterizations of things that are separate from the human being, or that we should consider separate from the human being. When we tell young children a story or a fairy tale, we should describe the animals and, perhaps, the plants in the way we would speak about people. In a certain sense, we personify plants and animals. We can justifiably personify them because the children cannot yet differentiate between the self and the world. That is why we should show them the world in a way similar to the way they experience it. You should be clear that what I am suggesting does not diminish childhood before the age of nine, but enriches it.

My last statement may seem quite paradoxical to you. The way I said it has a paradoxical effect. Much of what people say about the life of children is said in such a way that life does not actually become richer, but, instead, poorer. Think for a moment of what modern people often say when children hurt themselves on the corner of a table and hit the table in rage. People say that children's souls have something called animism, so that in a certain sense, the children make the table alive by pushing their souls into the table. This is an impossible theory. Why? Because children do not directly perceive themselves as living beings, beings who can put themselves into the table and personify it. Actually, they do not think of themselves as any more alive than the table is. They look at the table and experience nothing more of themselves than they do of the table. It is not that children personify the table, but, if I can express it this way, they "table" their own personalities. Children do not make their personalities anything more than the table. When you tell children a fairy tale or story, you speak only of what they can comprehend of the external world. That is what must occur until the age of nine. After that, you can count upon the fact that children have begun to differentiate themselves from the world. At that time, we can begin to speak about plants and animals from the perspective of nature.

I have put a lot of effort into studying the effects upon children of teaching about nature too early. Teaching about nature too early really does make children dry; so dry, in fact, that a well-trained observer can see in the changes of someone's skin that he or she was taught about the concepts of nature at too early an age.

At the age of nine we may begin to teach children the concepts of nature, but only through living thoughts. Wherever possible, we should avoid teaching them about minerals, about dead things. What is living, aside from the human being, exists in two domains: the animal realm and the plant realm. However, if we attempt to present the popular scientific descriptions of animals and plants, we will not really be able to teach children about them. You can see in nearly every natural history book that the content is nothing more than a somewhat simplified academic natural science—that is horrible. Of course, people have also attempted to create an illustrative teaching of nature. There are numerous books about that method as well, but they suffer from the opposite mistake. They contain a great deal of trivial information. In that case, the teacher attempts to discuss nothing with the children, nothing more than what they already know. As people say, the teacher tries to create a picture of nature solely out of the nature of the children themselves. We easily fall into triviality that way. We can only throw our hands up in frustration about so many of those method books because they are so terribly trivial. We can only feel that if schools use such things, only triviality will be implanted in children. This triviality will come to expression later as many other things I have already mentioned, as a kind of aridness in later life, or at least make it impossible for people to look back upon their childhood with joy.

That is, however, precisely what human beings need. Throughout life, we need to be able to look back upon our childhood as something like a paradise. It is not just that we had only happy experiences then; it is really not so important that as children we had only happy experiences. Many people may have gone hungry during their childhood, or have been beaten by their teachers out of a lack of understanding, or have been treated unkindly. Of course, nothing but an intent to fight against all such things in the best possible way should ever form the basis of a pedagogy. Nevertheless, such things can occur, and yet, thinking back upon childhood can still be enlivening if, in one way or another, we gained a relationship to the world during childhood. As children, we need to develop that relationship by being taught about nature in the proper way. It is of no help whatsoever to describe the various classes of animals or types of plants and so forth to children, and then, in order not to be too dry, to go on a walk with them to show them the plants outdoors. That is really not at all useful. Of course, through certain instinctive tendencies, one teacher will be able to accomplish more and another less. A teacher can, through his or her own love of nature, bring a great deal to life for children. However, spiritual science can give people something really quite different, a feeling for the living connections between the human being and the remainder of the world.

Today, people laugh about the fact that in the first third of the nineteenth century many people still felt that the entire animal world was an extended human being. We have different groups of animals. One group of animals is one-sidedly developed in one direction, and another group in another direction. We can create an overview of the various groups and kinds of animals for ourselves. The human being contains all the forces, all the inner forms that are spread out over the animals. That was, for example, the view of nature taken by someone like Oken.[1] Oken took that up with a passion. At that time, people looked for the lower animals in nature. Today's materialistic natural science says that these lower animals existed in very early times and that they slowly developed and became more complete. The result was today's human being, a completely developed physical being. We do not need to go into all the details today, since our concern is not with conventional science, but with pedagogy. However, can't we see that the human head, a bony vessel outside with the softer parts inside, looks so similar to certain lower animals? Look at a snail or a mussel and see how similar they are to the human head. If you look at our more or less developed birds, you have to admit that they have adjusted to the air, they have adjusted their entire life to something that corresponds to the inner form of the lungs and such things in human beings. If you remove from your thoughts all those aspects of the human being contained in the limbs, and imagine the entire human inner organization as adjusted to living in air, the result will be the form and function of a bird. You could also compare the organic form of a lion or a cat with

1. Lorenz Oken, 1779-1851, zoologist and professor of medicine.

that of a bovine. You will see everywhere that in one group of animals one part of its form is more developed, and in another group, a different part. Each group of animals is particularly well developed in one direction or another. We can say a snail is almost entirely head. It has nothing except the head aspect, only it is a simple and primitive head. The human head is more complicated. We can say that a bird is, in a certain sense, entirely a lung developed in a particular way because all other aspects are rudimentary. We can say that a lion is, in a certain sense, primarily the blood circulation and the heart. We could say cattle are entirely stomachs. Thus, in external nature we can characterize the various groups of animals by looking toward individual human organs. What I have just said can be said in a very simple and primitive way. If we look at the world of animals and the great diversity there, then compare that with the human organism and see how in the human being everything is well-rounded—how no part of the human being is one-sidedly developed, how each part complements the other—then we can see that in animals the various human organs are adapted to the external world, whereas in human beings the organs do not adapt to the external world, but rather one organ complements another. The human being is a closed totality, a closed entirety, something I can only sketch for you today.

Now imagine that we use everything available to us, the nature exhibits in the school, each walk with the children, everything the children have experienced, to show in a living way how the human being is, in a certain sense, a summary of the animal world. Imagine that we show the children how everything in the human being is formed harmoniously, is well rounded, and how the animals represent one-sided developments and are therefore not fully blessed. We can also show that the human being represents an adaptation of one system of organs to another and thus has a possibility of complete being. If we are completely convinced of this relationship of the human being to the world of animals, if it fully permeates us spiritually, we can then describe that relationship in a lively way so that the description is quite objective, but at the same time children can feel their relationship to the world. Think of what value it is for modern people to be able to say, in our materialistic times, that they are the crown of earthly creation. People do not really understand it—they look at themselves, and they look at individual animals. However, they do not look at each individual animal and try to understand how one system of organs is one-sidedly developed in one animal and another system in another animal. They also do not consider how that all comes together in the human being. If we do that, our knowledge will directly become a feeling, a perception of our position relative to the world. We will then stop experiencing ourselves only egotistically, and our feelings will go out into the universe.

You need only attempt to teach in that sense once, and you will see what value such teaching has for the feelings of the child. Such knowledge is transformed completely into feeling, and under its influence people slowly become more modest. Thus, the material taught becomes a genuine means of education. What is the use of saying that we should not teach in a dry way, that we should not teach the children only facts, if we have no possibility of so transforming the material to be taught that it becomes a direct means of education? Sometimes when people stress that teaching children too many facts hinders their proper development, we want to ask, "Why don't you throw out all the material you teach if it is of no use?" We cannot do that, of course. We must make the material we teach into educational material. Teaching about nature, particularly in connection with the animal world, can become educational material when we shape it in the way I described and do not teach it to children before the age of nine.

With the plant world, we cannot take the individual plants or kinds of plants, present them one-sidedly, summarize everything we find there, and expect to see it again in the human being. This approach, which is so fruitful with animals and gives us such a good basis for an artistic and living presentation of the nature of animals, fails with plants. We cannot consider them in the same way; it does not work. With plants, we need to use a very different approach. We need to consider the entire nature of plants in relationship to the Earth, as something that enlivens the entire Earth.

Our materialism has brought us to the point where we consider the Earth only as a ball made of stones and minerals in which plants are simply placed. We cannot use the same principle with, for instance, the human head and hair. We need to consider the growth of hair as something connected with the human head. In the same way, we must consider plants as belonging to the organism of the Earth. We create an abstract picture if we only think of the Earth as a stone that can at most call gravity its own. We speak of the real Earth when we think of the Earth as an organism with plants that belong to it just as the hair on our heads belongs to us. When we consider it that way, our picture of the Earth grows together with our picture of plants, and we get the proper feeling for how to think of the Earth in connection with the plant world. We can do that when we look at the Earth in the course of the year. If we are to really teach children about plants, we should not compare one class or group of plants with another. Instead, we need to use all the fresh plants we have, the nature exhibits in the school, walks, everything the children remember, and everything we can bring into the classroom as fresh plants. Then we can show the children how spring magically draws the plants out of the Earth. We can show them how various parts of plants are magically drawn out; we then go on to May when the Earth becomes somewhat different, then continue into summer when it looks different again.

We attempt to consider flowers and plants in the same way that children understand the development of the Earth throughout the course of the year. We tell the children how, in the fall, the plant seeds return to the Earth and the cycle begins anew. We consider the Earth as an organism and follow the sprouting, and dying back of the plants. We call a thing by its proper name, which, of course, is simply convention, only after we have taught the child by saying, "Look, here is a plant [under a tree or perhaps somewhere else]. We have this little plant because this kind of plant grows so well in May. It has five little petals. Remember, these plants with five little yellow petals are part of the life of the whole Earth in May. It is a buttercup." You can go on in that way and show them how the world of plants is connected with the yearly cycle of the Earth. You can then go on further to more hidden things, how, for example, some plants bloom at Christmastime, and some plants can live through winter and others much longer. You go from the life of a plant that decorates the Earth for one year and leaves, to others, such as the growth of a tree and so forth. You would never consider simply comparing one plant with another; you always relate the Earth to its plant growth, showing how the growth of plants arises out of the living Earth.

You now have two wonderful poles in the life of nature. Everywhere in the animal realm you find things that point to the human being. People can feel how they are a synthesis of all the one-sided aspects of the animal realm. We do not take up any species of animals without indicating which aspect of the human being that species has developed particularly one-sidedly. The animal kingdom becomes, therefore, a picture of the human being spread out before us—the human being unfolded like a fan. As I said, modern people laugh about such things, but during the first third of the nineteenth century this sometimes took on grotesque forms. People like Oken have said such grotesque things as, "The tongue is a squid," and I certainly to not want to defend them. Of course, Oken had the right principle in mind. He looked at the human tongue and then sought among the animals for something comparable with that human organ. He found the greatest similarity to the human tongue in the squid; thus the tongue is a squid. He went on to say that the stomach is a cow. All that is, as I said, an extreme presentation. We certainly do not need to go that far. At that time, people were really unable to find the proper things. Today, however, we can certainly present the entire animal world as a spread-out human being and the human being as a synthesis of the entire animal world. We thus connect everything the children observe in the animals with the human being. We have, therefore, a possibility of placing all the aspects of a human being in front of the child's eyes by directing the child's eyes outward.

In the plant world we have just the opposite. There, we completely forget the human being and consider the world of plants as entirely growing out of the Earth itself, out of the planet upon which we wander about. In the one case we bring the animal world into a close relationship to the human being, and in the other case we bring the plant world into the same close relationship to something that exists outside the human being. In other words, on the one hand we bring forth a feeling understanding of the world of animals and the human being by observing the animal world itself. On the other hand, we teach children to objectively consider the Earth as an organism from which we live and upon which we run about, and how we can see in the growth of plants, in the life cycle of plants, particularly in how plants live from year to year, something that is separate from ourselves.

Through these two ways of looking at things, we can bring into the human soul a tremendous amount of what we could call balance between intellect and feeling. The result is that we leave simple intellectualism, which is so boring and arid, behind. Once people comprehend annual plants, green plants that grow out of the Earth with their roots in the Earth, and their leaves and stems above it, the green leaves then going on to form the flower and seed; once people perceive a living connection with the Earth and enliven that through their experiences of the yearly cycle; once they experience how the blossom comes forth when sunlight connects itself in love with what pours forth out of the Earth; once they feel the growth from the root through the leaf to the flower and finally to the seed from spring until fall; once people have felt all that throughout their entire being, then they will realize something else. You see, here is the Earth, here is a plant, an annual. This plant that lives only one year is rooted in the Earth. Now let us look at a tree: here, it is wood; here are the branches. What appears on the tree during the course of one year appears similar to an annual plant, and it sits on the tree in a way similar to the way an annual plant sits in the Earth. In a certain sense, the Earth and the woody part of the tree are the same, and through that we can create a picture that will have an enormously strong effect upon us. In the same way a tree grows into wood, the Earth is built upon what lies under the surface. Where no trees grow but only annual plants, the forces that are otherwise in the trunk of the tree are in the Earth itself. We can achieve a living feeling about how to seek the flowing sap in the tree trunk under the surface of the Earth. Just as the sap flowing in a tree brings forth the blossoming of the year, the sap flowing beneath us, which we can see is identical with the sap flowing in the tree, brings forth annual plants. What I want to say is that we can intimately connect what we see in trees with our view of the Earth. We therefore gain an understanding of what is living.

Through such a living characterization of earth, plants, animals, and human beings, you can directly bring something to life in the children that they would otherwise feel as only dead, specifically, in the period from about the age of nine until twelve. During that time, children are particularly interested in gradually differentiating themselves from the world and unconsciously want to learn, on the one hand, about the relationship between the human being and the world of animals, and, on the other hand, about the Earth and earthly life separate from the human being. Through such a presentation, something will grow within them that gives them the proper relationship to the historical life of humanity on Earth. In this way, the appropriate feelings that allow children to properly learn about history will develop. Before the age of ten or eleven, we have told them about history only in the form of stories or biographies. At about the age of ten or eleven, we include history within the teaching of natural history, so that everywhere a feeling will develop in the children through this teaching, that is, in a certain sense, also held in all the concepts and ideas and feelings that can enliven the teaching of history. Only at the age of twelve can we begin to go on to actual reasoning. We will speak more of that tomorrow....

Nature Study in the Elementary School

LECTURE BY RUDOLF STEINER

Ilkley, England, August 13, 1923

If we teach children, as I have described, so that we develop every-thing from the pictorial, we properly raise children so that they can always have flexible concepts instead of inflexible ones. Thus, we notice that when children pass the age of nine or so, after we have told them enough about plants as speaking beings, so that such pic-tures live in the children and they see the plant world in that way, we can guide them organically toward comprehending the world, that is, toward things and events they must differentiate from themselves. We can best teach them what human beings can learn best from the plant world when we begin with children between the ages of nine and ten and then continue into the tenth and eleventh years.

At that age, the human organism is ready to begin working with the plant world as inner ideas. Of course, you will need to give the study of plants a different form in order to offer human develop-ment a more lively and supportive instruction. We often teach what we do about plants only because that is what we ourselves once learned. In reality, there is no meaning for human life in simply placing various plants in front of the children and then giving their names, the number of stamen, the color and number of flower pet-als, and so forth.

Everything we teach to children in this way remains foreign to them. They feel only the imperative of having to learn it. People who want to teach ten- or eleven-year-old children about plants in this way know absolutely nothing about the genuine relation-ships of nature. To simply look at a plant, then pack it away in the botany collection to take home and look at again has no more meaning than pulling out a hair, placing it on a piece of paper, and simply looking at it. A hair as such has no real meaning. It has real meaning only while it is living on a human head or growing on the skin of an animal. It has living meaning only in its context. In the same way, a plant has a real meaning only in its relationship with the Earth and the Sun and, as I will discuss in a moment, with other forces. When working with children we should never consider plants in any way other than in their connection with the Earth and the Sun.

Here, I can only sketch what you can visually and pictorially teach children in a number of class periods. It is important that you teach children something like the following. Here is the Earth.

In conjunction with the Earth, belonging to it, is the root of the plant. You should never awaken any idea other than the living idea that the Earth and the root belong together. Furthermore, you should also never awaken any idea other than that the flower is brought forth from the plant by the Sun and its rays. In this way, you place the children into the universe with life.

Teachers with an abundant inner life can best present in a living way how the plant exists in the universe to children at this age. Such teachers can awaken within the children how the Earth and its minerals penetrate into the root, and how the root wrests itself from the Earth. And, when the root forms a sprout, that sprout is born from the Earth. They can teach how the Sun's light and warmth become the leaf and flower, how the Sun draws the flower to it and how the Earth works with the root.

You can then give the children a lively demonstration of how moist earth, that is, earth that is watery affects the root differently than dry earth. You can show them how the root withers in dry earth, but in earth containing water, the root itself becomes juicy and full of life.

You can go on to show how the rays of the Sun falling perpendicularly upon the Earth draw the yellow petals out of the dandelion, or the blossoms from buttercups or roses. You can also show them that when the Sun rays fall at an angle that glances over the plants, they bring forth the dark violet flowers of the autumn crocus (*colchicum autumnale*). Everywhere you can reveal a living relationship between the root and the Earth and the leaf and flower with the Sun.

When you have thus placed the child's picture into the universe in a living way, you can then teach them how all plant growth draws together in the formation of fruit and how a new plant develops from that.

I now want to anticipate the future a little. You will need to explain a truth, but you will have to prepare it for children at this stage of childhood. Modern people are somewhat ashamed to state this publicly because it is often thought to be some sort of superstition or fantasy, or some nebulous mystical idea. Just as the Sun draws the flower out in all its colors, the forces of the Moon draw together to produce the fruit. The forces of the Moon draw the fruit out of the plant.

Thus, we can livingly place the plant into the effects of the Earth, Sun, and Moon. However, we must still leave out the effects of the Moon since the children would go home and tell about what they have learned, namely, that the development of fruit is connected with the moon. Even if the parents tended to accept what the children said, if there were a naturalist visiting, this might cause the parents to withdraw the child from the school. Thus, we need to keep quiet about this just as we need to keep quiet about many other things in our very externally directed civilization. Nevertheless, I would like to use this radical example to show that you will need to develop living concepts that do not arise out of something that does not really exist. Plants exist not by themselves. Without Sun or Earth they are nothing. We need to develop concepts out of true reality. That is what is important.

We could proceed to teach the children in the following way. We could show that here is the Earth, and the Earth grows a little bump, a hill.

This hill, however, is filled with the forces of the air and also of the Sun. It is no longer simply Earth. Something exists between the juicy leaf of the plant above and the roots and dry Earth below. It is the trunk of a tree. Individual plants grow upon this developed plant and become the branches of the tree. With this, the children can learn how a tree trunk is actually sprouting earth.

In that way, the children will gain an idea of how closely connected wood is with the Earth itself. So that they understand that well, you can show how wood decomposes, how it becomes more and more earthlike and finally disintegrates into dust that is very similar to earth. You can show them how essentially all sand and stone has arisen out of what actually should have become plant, and how the Earth is basically a large plant, a huge tree, and that all other plants are simply the branches that grow upon it. In this way the children will understand that the Earth is truly a living being, and that plants belong to the Earth.

It is extraordinarily important that children do not learn the convoluted concepts of geology. They should not learn that the Earth is made only of stone and only the forces associated with stones are part of the Earth. The growth forces of plants are just as much a part of the Earth as those forces associated with stones. The most important thing at this time is that you do not speak about stones as such. You will notice that the children are very curious in many respects. However, if you teach them this living concept, that the mantle of plants that covers the Earth arises out of the Earth, is drawn out by the Sun, and belongs to the Earth, they will have no curiosity about what stones, as such, are. Children are not yet interested in minerals. It is very fortunate when children before the age of eleven or twelve have no interest in dead minerals, but instead see the Earth as a whole, as a living being, like a tree that brings forth all the plants as its branches. You can see that this gives you a good opportunity for going on to individual plants.

I would say to a child, for example, that the plant's root seeks the soil while the flower is drawn out by the Sun.

Suppose the root that wants to grow on the plant cannot find the soil. It only finds a decayed base, and, for that reason, the Sun makes no effort to develop the flower. Thus, we have a plant that does not actually reach the soil and does not develop a proper root. It also does not develop a proper flower. What we have is a mushroom.

You can go on to help the children understand what takes place when a plant does not properly find the Earth and instead develops into a fungus implanted where the Earth has become a little like a plant. That is, when it is implanted not in the soil but into that plantlike hill, the tree trunk. That becomes lichen. It becomes that gray-green mass we find on the surfaces of trees, a parasite.

Thus, out of the living activity of the Earth, we can form something that all individual plants express. If you guide children into the growth of plants in such a living way, you will be using the study of plants to develop in them a view of how we can perceive the face of the Earth.

The face of the Earth where yellow sprouting plants grow differs from the places where stunted plants exist. In the study of plants, you will find the transition to something else. When you develop it out of plant study, geography is extraordinarily important for the development of children. You should teach children about the face of the Earth by describing the way the Earth presents its surface, how it produces plants at particular places on the surface.

In this way, you develop a living intellect in the child, rather than a dead one. The best time for developing that living intellect is between the ages of nine or ten and eleven or twelve. By guiding children into the living warp and weft of the Earth, by showing them how the inner vitality of the Earth produces the various plant forms, you can give children living, rather than dead, concepts. You can give them concepts that have the same characteristics as human limbs. When we are still very small children, our limbs need to grow. We could not encase our hand in an iron glove, as it would not be able to grow. However, the concepts we teach children should be as sharply contoured as possible. They should be definitions, but the child should do the defining. The worst thing we can teach children are definitions and sharply contoured concepts that cannot grow. Human beings grow organically. Children need flexible concepts that grow as the children become more mature, that can continuously change their form. When we are forty years old and some idea occurs to us, we should not have to remember something we learned at the age of ten. Instead, the concept should have changed within us, just as our limbs and whole organism change.

However, we cannot achieve living concepts by teaching children what people call science, something we can characterize by the fact that although we were required to learn it, it is dead and we know nothing through it. Instead, we should guide children into the life of the natural world. In that way, children will receive flexible concepts, and their souls can grow in the body just as nature grows. Thus, we will not offer to implant what modern education so often implants, namely, a soul aspect that cannot grow into a growing body. We will not implant something dead into the children. For human development, the only beneficial thing we can implant into a living, growing physical organism is a living growing soul, a lively, developing soul life.

We should create this in the way I just described. We can best create it when we see all plant life as having a close connection with the constitution of the Earth. That is, when we present children with the life of the Earth and that of plants as a unity. Children should comprehend the Earth by comprehending plants, by recognizing what is lifeless, that a tree dies and decays and becomes dust, by thus recognizing this lifeless aspect as the remains of something once living. We should certainly not teach children at this age about minerals; rather, concepts and ideas about what is living are important.

[*There was a pause while George Adams translated the preceding section of the lecture.*]

Just as you should connect what you teach about plants with the Earth, so that the plant world appears to be the result of something growing out of the living Earth, so should you bring the entire animal world into a relationship with human beings. In that way, you can give children a living place in nature and the world. They can learn to understand that the carpet of plants covering the Earth belongs to the organism of the Earth. They can also learn to understand that all the types of animals spread out over the Earth are, in a certain way, the path to human growth. Our principle of instruction should be to present plants in relationship to the Earth and animals in relationship to human beings. I can justify this only in principle. What is important though, is that, with a genuinely artistic sense for the details of the animal world, you present this to children of ten to twelve.

Let us look at a human being. If we want to present the nature of the human being in a simple, perhaps even primitive, way to children, we could do that as I described if we have artistically prepared it. Children, though perhaps primitively, can learn to differentiate the three aspects of human beings. We can consider the head, where the most important parts, the soft portions, are within, and how a hard skin grows around the nerves. That is how, in a certain sense, the form of the head reflects the spherical form of the Earth. We can show how the head stands in the cosmos and that it primarily consists of a softer, inner portion, particularly in the area of the brain, surrounded by a hard outer surface. We should guide the children as artistically as possible, using all possible means, toward an understanding of the head. Then we can attempt to guide them to the second portion of human nature, where everything is connected with the rhythmic system of the human being. This includes the breathing organs, the organs for blood circulation, and the heart. Broadly speaking, we will teach the children about the chest. Just as we presented the bowl form of the head which encompasses the softer brain in an artistic and flexible way, so will we consider the vertebrae of the spinal column, set one upon the other, to which the ribs are connected. You can consider the entire chest, including breathing and circulation, in short, the rhythmic nature of the human being in all its characteristics. You can then go on to the third aspect of the human being, to the metabolic and limb aspect. The limbs as organs of movement primarily support the metabolism in that through their movement they regulate combustion. They are connected to the metabolism so that we find a unity in limbs and metabolism.

Thus, we can perceive the human being as having these three aspects. If you as a teacher have the necessary artistic sense and can proceed pictorially, then you can certainly teach children this view of the three aspects of the human being.

We now direct the children's attention to the various animals spread out over the Earth. We first draw the children's attention to the lower animals, to those animals that have soft parts surrounded by a bowl-like form, that is, to shellfish and those lower animals that consist only of protoplasm surrounded by a skin. You can show the children how these lower animals, in their essence, represent a primitive form of the human head.

Our head is the highest development of lower animals. If we consider the human head, particularly the organization of the nerves, we need to look not at mammals, not at the apes. Instead, we must go back to the lowest animals. We must return in the history of the Earth to the oldest forms, where we find animals that, in a certain sense, are only a simple head. We thus make the lower animal world understandable to children as a primitive head. We then need to go on to somewhat higher animals which are grouped around the class of fish, animals in which the spinal column is particularly well developed. The children need to understand those "middle animals" as those beings in which only the rhythmic portion of the human being is strongly developed and the other parts are stunted. When we look at the human head, we find the corresponding aspect in animals at a primitive level, in the lower animals. If we look at the human chest, at the rhythmic system, we find that expressed in a one-sided way in those animals grouped around fish. If we then go on to the metabolic and limb aspects, we arrive at the higher animals. The higher animals have developed the organs of movement in numerous ways. We have such a wonderful opportunity to artistically observe the mechanism for movement in a horse's hoof or in the claws of a lion, and to observe the feet of marsh animals that are more developed for wading. We also have an opportunity to consider the one-sided development of an ape's foot from the perspective of human limbs. In short, when we come to the higher animals, we can begin to comprehend the entire animal through a flexible elaboration of the organs for movement or metabolism. Predators are quite different from ruminants in that the intestines of ruminants are particularly long, whereas in predators the intestines are short, but the heart and circulatory system are particularly strong and well-developed.

When we look at the higher animals, we recognize that what exists in the human being as the metabolism and limbs is one-sidedly developed. We can illustrate that by showing that the head of an animal is actually only the anterior of the backbone. The entire digestive system moves into an animal's head. In animals, the head is closely connected with the digestive organs, with the stomach and intestines. We can actually consider an animal's head only in connection with the stomach and intestines. That portion of human beings that we might say has remained virgin, that is soft and surrounded by a bowl, is set upon the metabolic and limb portion that animals still carry within their heads. In that way the human head is superior to that of animals which is only a continuation of the metabolic and limb systems. The head of the human being goes back to its simplest origins, namely a soft portion surrounded by a bony bowl. You can also show that we can best understand the jaw structure of some animals if we consider the upper and lower jaw as frontal limbs. In that way our understanding of the head of the animal will be the most flexible.

In this way, we can see the human being as a summary or collection of three systems: the head, chest, and limb-metabolic systems. The animal world is a one-sided development of one of those systems or another. Lower animals, for example, shellfish, correspond to the head and we can view others in a similar way. Then we have the limb animals, the mammals, birds, and so forth. We find chest animals, that is, those where the chest is most developed, among fish or other animals similar to fish, reptiles and so forth. We thus have the animal realm as a distributed human being, as a human being spread out like a fan over the Earth.

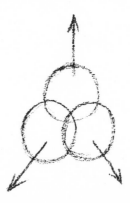

Just as we brought plants into connection with the Earth, we bring the fan-like distribution of the animals on the Earth into connection with the human being, which, in fact, summarizes the entire animal world.

If we begin with the physical form of a human being, we can easily teach children about these three aspects of the human being. If we then go through the animals, we can show that animals exhibit a one-sided development in one way or another of what exists in human beings as a harmonious whole. We can then discover that certain animals have developed their chest organs one-sidedly, others the intestines, still others, the upper digestive organs, and so forth. We can see that transformations of certain organs exist in many animals, for instance, in birds with the digestive organs in the crop. We can thus show that every kind of animal is a one-sided development of a human organ, that the animal world is a fan-like distribution of the human being over the Earth, and that human beings summarize the entire animal world.

If you do that, the children will understand the animal world as a human being whose individual organs have been one-sidedly developed. One system of organs lives in this groups of animals, another system in another group. When the children are approaching the age of twelve, you can return to the human being. Then the children will naturally comprehend that, because human beings carry their spirit within themselves, they are a manifest unity, an artistic summing-up, an artistic expression of all the individual fragments of human beings that are represented by the animals spread out over the world. People are a harmonious summing-up due to the fact that they carry their spirit within themselves. In that way, human beings are a harmonious whole of the lower animals, transformed in a complicated way into the head and correspondingly developed in the chest so that they fit with the other organs. Human beings thus carry, organized into a harmonious whole, what exists within fish as well as what exists in the higher animals. The human being is thus a being who, through the spirit, has gathered together all the individual fragments that exist as animals spread out over the world. In that way, we bring the animal world into connection with the human being, at the same time raising the human above the animal as a carrier of the spirit.

If you teach children that way, and if you have an unprejudiced understanding of humanity, then you will see something. You will see that studying plants results in a living understanding of the world and places people properly into the world. Through that living understanding they become diligent and can find their way through life with living concepts. In the same way, people also strengthen their will by understanding their relationship to the animal world through such a living perspective.

You will need to keep in mind that what I have just discussed in the course of twenty minutes requires a much longer presentation, one that goes from step to step, allowing the children slowly to become used to uniting such ideas with their own nature. In that way, these ideas soak into the way that children perceive their position as human beings upon the Earth. People will have a stronger inner will when they see for themselves how all of these animal fragments flow together through the living spirit that creates this synthesis. That becomes the development of the will in the soul.

Thus, our instruction can teach not only some knowledge about plants and some knowledge about animals, but it can also help develop character. We can develop the entire human being by guiding children to plants, thus developing their intelligence in the proper way, and by guiding them to the animal world and properly developing their will. We can show children between the ages of nine and twelve their connection with the other divine creations, the plants and the animals of the Earth. They will thus be able to find their path through the world through their sound intelligence and through strength in their will.

Our primary goal in education should be to allow young people to develop so that they can find their way through the world with these two capacities. Out of the feeling we develop in children between the ages of seven and nine, we can develop intelligence and strength of will. In that way, we can properly develop something that is often artificially developed in human beings, namely a correct relationship between thinking, feeling, and willing. Everything is rooted in feeling. Children must first feel, and out of that feeling we can develop a thinking that is never dead because it is connected with the plant world. And we can develop a will that properly relates the human being with the animals, but raises human beings above the animals through a study of them.

In that way, we can give young people going out into the world the proper intelligence and proper will. That is what we should do since, in that way, they will become whole human beings, which is the primary goal of all education.

Teaching Geography

LECTURE BY RUDOLF STEINER

Stuttgart, September 2, 1919

I have told you that geography is first introduced during the second of the three stages between the ages of seven and fourteen. We can very well begin with it when the children have passed their ninth year, but it must be arranged in the right way. Geography must encompasses much more in the future than it does now for children up to fourteen, fifteen, and older. It is pushed too much into the background these days, treated like the stepchild of education. In geography the achievements of all the other lessons should meet and flow together in all sorts of ways. And though I have said that mineralogy is not taken up until the third stage, about the twelfth year, it can be woven into geography in a narrative way, combined with direct observation, during the previous stage.

It is particularly important in geography that we start with what the children already know about the face of the Earth and about what takes place on the face of the Earth. We endeavor to give the children, in an artistic way, a kind of picture of the hills and rivers and other features of their immediate surroundings. We develop with the children an elementary map of the immediate neighborhood where they are growing up and which they therefore know. Between the ages of nine and twelve, children can take in an enormous amount from geography if we go about teaching it the right way. We try to teach them what it means when you change your point of view from being within a neighborhood to seeing it from outside, from the air; we take them through the process of transforming a landscape into a map, at first with the landscape they know. We try to teach them how rivers flow through the district by actually drawing the system of rivers and streams on the map of the neighborhood. We also draw in the hills. It is good to work with colors, making the rivers blue and the hills or mountains brown. Then we add the other things linked to the way people live. We put in all the configurations of the district, drawing the children's attention to them as we go: Here is a part where fruit trees are planted, so we draw in the fruit trees.

Then we point out that there are also some parts covered with coniferous trees, so we draw these in too.

We show them that another part of the neighborhood is covered with cornfields, so these too must be included in our map.

There are also meadows to be added. We point out to the children the meadows that can be mown, shown in this drawing.

Meadows that cannot be mown but that do provide grass for the cattle, though it is shorter and sparser, are also included in our map. We tell the children that this is pasture land.

And so we bring the map to life for the children.

From this map the children gain some sort of overall view of the economic foundations of the neighborhood. We also start pointing out that there are many things like coal and ore inside the hills. We show them how the rivers are used to transport things that grow or are made at one place to another place. We unfold for them much of what is connected with this economic structure of the district. Having made clear the economic foundation provided by the rivers and hills, fields and woods, and so on, insofar as these things can be explained to the children, we next put in the villages or towns of the district we are dealing with. And now we begin to point out why it is that a village appears at a particular place and how this is connected with the courses of the streams and rivers, with the hills and what they might have to offer in their depths. In short, by using the map we endeavor to awaken in the children some idea of the economic links that exist between the natural formation of the land and the conditions of human life. This leads into giving them a picture of the difference between country life and town life. We take all this as far as the children are able to grasp it. And finally we show how human beings with their industry meet the conditions nature offers them. That is, we begin to show the children that human beings make artificial rivers known as canals, that they build railways. Then we point out how provisions can be transported with the help of the railways and how people's very situation in life is affected.

After working for a while toward an understanding of the economic relationships between natural conditions and the conditions of human life, we can build on the concepts the children have gained and lead them further into the world at large. If we have taken the first steps in the right way, it will not be necessary to be excessively pedantic in this. The pedant would say at this point that the natural way is to begin with the geography of the immediate neighborhood and then spread out concentrically from there. Even this is too pedantic. There is no need to enlarge in this way. When a firm foundation has been laid in understanding the links between nature and humans, we can quite well turn our attention to something else. In the way we turn to something else, however, we should continue as effectively and intensively as possible to develop the theme of the economic links between human beings and their natural environment.

Here in our district, for instance, after developing the necessary concepts from familiar stretches of land and helping the children find their bearings in their own neighborhood, we can widen their horizon by telling them about the geography of the Alps. We can now extend the map drawing already taught by drawing a line showing where the southern Alps meet the Mediterranean Sea. You also draw the northern part of Italy, the Adriatic Sea, and so on, saying there are great rivers there and drawing in the courses of the rivers. You draw the Rhone, the Rhine, the Inn, and the Danube with their tributaries, and then add the different arms of the Alps. The children will be extraordinarily fascinated when they discover how the different arms are separated by the rivers.

Then along the blue lines of the rivers you can draw red lines, imaginary boundaries, for instance along the Rhone from Lake Geneva back to its source, then along the Rhine, over the top of the Brenner, and so on, dividing the Alps from west to east. You can then say, Look, down below I have drawn a red line along the rivers and at the top I have also drawn a red line. The Alps lying between these red lines are different from those lying above and below them. Now you could bring mineralogy into geography by showing the children a piece of Jura limestone and saying, The mountain ranges above the top red line and those under the lower red line are made of limestone like this. And for what lies in between you show them a piece of granite, gneiss, and say, The mountains in between the red lines are of rock like this, the oldest rock. The children will be tremendously interested in this Alpine massif. You might perhaps also show them a relief map of the area, which gives a more plastic impression of how the river courses divide the Alps into limestone Alps, gneiss, mica, slate, and so on, and of how the whole length of the range is somewhat curved and shows from south to north the differentiation into limestone—granite—limestone, divided by the rivers. Without any pedantic object lessons you can bring much to all this that will greatly extend the children's range of ideas.

Then you go on (you have already prepared for this in your nature lessons) to describe to the children what grows down in the valley, what grows higher up the mountainside, what grows even higher up, and also what at the very, very summit does not grow. You paint a vertical picture of the vegetation.

Next you begin to show the children how human beings establish themselves in a countryside dominated by massive mountains. Help them picture to themselves a really high mountain village and how people must live there. Mark it on your map. Then you describe a village and the roads of a valley, then a town at the confluence of a river and one of its tributaries. You describe in this wider context the relationship between the natural configuration of the land and the way humans build up their economic life. Out of the natural surroundings you in a way build up a picture of human industry, again drawing the children's attention to the places where ore and coal can be found and to how settlements are determined by such things.

Next draw for the children a picture of a landscape with no mountains, a flat plain, and treat this in a similar way. Describe the natural configuration, the structure of the ground, and show them how some things grow on poor soil and others on rich soil. Point out the makeup of the soil in which potatoes grow (you can do this with quite simple means), or wheat, or rye, and so on. You will already have taught them the difference between wheat, rye, oats. Do not hesitate to teach them things that as yet they can understand only in a general way and will only grasp more clearly in later lessons when they return to them from another point of view. Until they are twelve, introduce them chiefly to economic conditions and relations. Make these clear to them. And concentrate more on the geography of their own country than on giving them a complete picture of the Earth. Let them, however, gain an impression of how vast the ocean is. You started drawing it when you showed where the southern Alps meet the Mediterranean. Draw the sea as a blue surface, and draw the outlines of Spain and France, showing how to the west there is an immense ocean. Then introduce gradually in a way that they can understand the idea that America also exists. They should have a mental picture of this before they are twelve.

If you start with this good foundation, you can count on the children having sufficient understanding when they are about twelve for you to proceed more systematically, taking less time to give them a picture of the Earth as a whole by teaching them about the five continents and the oceans (more briefly than has been your method up to now) and describing the economic life of the different continents. You should be able to draw everything out of the foundations you have laid. When you have drawn together in a picture of the whole Earth all the knowledge you have given the children about the economic life of humans and have also taught them history in the manner described for about six months, you can transfer your attention to the cultural environment made by the people who inhabit the different continents. But do not go into this different sphere until you have made the children's souls somewhat adaptable through their first history lessons. Then you can also speak of the geographical distribution of the characteristics of the different peoples. Do not speak any earlier about the characteristic differences of the various peoples, for only now, based on the foundation I have described, will the children bring their best understanding to this subject. You can now speak of the differences between Asiatic, European, and American peoples, and of the differences between Mediterranean and northern European peoples. Thus you gradually combine geography with history. You will be fulfilling a beautiful task that brings much joy to the children if you do what I have just described mainly between their twelfth and fifteenth years.

You see that a great deal must be put into teaching geography so that it can become a kind of summary of everything else we do with the children. And so much can flow together in geography! Toward the end, a wonderful interplay between geography and history will be possible. Because you put a great many things into your geography lessons, you will then be able to draw on them for a great many things. This will of course tax your imaginative abilities and your inventiveness. When you tell the children that here or there certain things are done, for instance that the Japanese make their pictures in such and such a way, you can then encourage them to do the same, albeit in their much more simple and primitive way. When you are telling the children about the links between agriculture and the way humans live, do not miss the opportunity to give them a clear picture of a plough and a harrow in connection with the geographical picture.

Also have the children imitate some of the things you tell them, perhaps in the form of a little plaything or a piece of artistic work. This will give them skills and will prepare them for taking their places properly in life later on. You could even make little ploughs and let them cultivate the school garden, or let them cut with small sickles or mow with small scythes; this will establish a good contact with life. For more important than dexterity is the soul contact made between the life of the child and the life of the world. It is a fact that a child who has cut grass with a sickle or mown it with a scythe, a child who has made a furrow with a little plough, will turn into a different person from one who has not done these things. Quite simply, the soul element is changed. Abstract lessons in manual skills are not really a substitute for this. Paper folding and laying little sticks should be actively avoided, for these things tend to unfit the children for life rather than fit them for it. It is far better to encourage them to do things that really happen in life than to invent things for them to do that do not occur in life.

By building up our geography teaching in the way I have described, we acquaint the children in the most natural way with the fact that human life is brought together from many sides in various ways. At the same time we take care to deal with things that the children are well able to understand. Thus between the ninth and twelfth years we describe economic conditions and external matters in our geography lessons. From this we lead on to an understanding of cultural and spiritual matters pertaining to different peoples. Then, while saving the details for later, we merely hint at what goes on in the rights sphere of the different nations, letting only the very first, most primitive concepts peep through the economic and cultural life. The children do not as yet have a full understanding for matters of the rights sphere, and if they are confronted with these concepts too early in their development, their soul forces will be ruined for the rest of their lives because such things will be so abstract.

It is indeed a good thing if you can use the geography lessons to bring a unity to all the other subjects. Perhaps the worst thing that can happen to geography is for it to be regimented into a strictly demarcated timetable, which is something we anyway do not want.

We arrange things so that each subject can be treated for a longer span of time. When we take children into the school we work first of all toward teaching them to write. That is, we occupy the hours that we claim from them in the morning with painting, drawing, and learning to write. Our timetable will not stipulate that the first lesson be writing, the second reading and so on; we will occupy ourselves with similar things for longer stretches at a time. Not until the children can write a little will we move on to reading. Of course in learning to write they also learn to read a little, but these can be combined in an even better way. We assign definite periods for the other things too, not following one subject with another, lesson by lesson, but staying with one subject for quite some time and only coming back to other things after several weeks. Thus we concentrate our lessons and are in a position to teach much more economically than would be the case if we had to waste our time and energy on adhering to some dreadful timetable, teaching a subject in one lesson and then wiping it out in the next lesson by teaching something quite different. You can see particularly with geography how you can approach it from all sorts of directions. It is not laid down for you that you have to teach geography from the ninth to the tenth year; instead you are left free to decide when the time is ripe to fit geography in with whatever else you have been doing.

This of course imposes a great deal of responsibility on you, but without such responsibility no teaching can be carried out. A curriculum that from the start lays down the timetable and all sorts of other things completely eliminates the art of teaching. And this must not be. The teacher must be the driving and stimulating force in the whole educational system. What I have just shown you about the way to deal with teaching geography is an excellent example that gives you a proper picture of how everything should be done. Geography really can become a great channel into which everything flows and from which a great deal can also be derived. For instance, in the geography lesson you show the children how limestone mountains differ from granite mountains. Later you can show them a lump of granite or gneiss and point out how it contains different minerals, including something that sparkles. Then you show them a piece of mica and tell them that what they see sparkling in the granite is mica. Then you can show them all the other substances hiding in granite or gneiss. You show them a piece of quartz and try to unfold the whole mineral world out of a lump of rock. This is another good opportunity for adding a great deal to the children's understanding of how things that belong together as a whole can be divided into their separate parts. It is far more useful to teach the children about granite and gneiss first and then about the constituent minerals than it is to start with quartz, mica, feldspar, and so on, and then show that they are all mixed up in granite or gneiss. Mineralogy is a very good subject for starting with the whole and moving to the parts, for starting with the way a mountain is constructed and moving on to mineralogy. And this certainly helps the children.

With the animal kingdom you will proceed in the opposite direction, building up from the individual animals. The plant kingdom, as we have seen in our seminar discussions, is to be treated as a totality before we look at the details. And for the mineral kingdom, nature itself often supplies us with the totality from which we can then proceed to the details.

Furthermore, again linking mineralogy with geography, we must not omit a discussion of how all the things of economic value we find in nature are used. Referring to what we have said about the stony structure of the mountains, we then discuss all the things, such as coal, that we have a use for, in industry as well as elsewhere. We describe these things in a simple way, but the starting point is our discussion of the mountains.

Nor should we neglect to describe a sawmill when we are dealing with the forest. We start with the forest, move on to a discussion of wood, and come finally to the sawmill.

We can do a tremendous amount in this direction if we do not have to start with a timetable laid down with military precision but can proceed according to what arises out of the lessons. However, we must have a good idea of what is required by the children in the different stages of their development from the time they start school up to their ninth year, from their ninth year to their twelfth year, and from their twelfth to their fifteenth year.

6

THE UPPER ELEMENTARY SCHOOL YEARS

Cause and Consequence

THE TWELFTH YEAR marks another important turning point in a child's development. At age nine, the child developed a new sense of self, resulting in a sense of separateness from the Earth. At age twelve, a child begins to develop the capacity to perceive other people and the world with new interest and understanding.

The twelfth year change is caused by the beginning of the "birth" of the astral body.[1] The astral body is the bearer of sensation and feeling. When it is liberated from its bodily foundation at puberty, we begin to experience our feelings on a soul level rather than on a purely physical level. This allows us to unite our feelings with our thinking and to form judgments.

After age nine, as the etheric body begins to be permeated by the forces of the astral body, thinking becomes imbued with a feeling element, and thus becomes more vivid. The etheric body can also work reciprocally upon the astral body, illuminating sensations and feelings with the light of thinking so that students can become more objective about their perceptions and experiences and can form judgments. The mutual activity of these bodies makes the child of twelve especially receptive to two realms: the study of literature, history, and geography, which develops empathy and

---

1. See page 24.

understanding; and the study of mathematics, physics, and chemistry, which develops objectivity and clarity.

Young children perceive the world as a reflection of themselves, and the science curriculum of the early grades shows them how the world mirrors human qualities and virtues. After the age of nine, when children begin to experience themselves as increasingly separate from the world, the sciences are presented in relationship to the human being, reinforcing the child's connection to the physical world and the kingdoms of nature. Only when students turn twelve, can they begin to look at themselves more objectively and begin to recognize how physical forces manifesting in the world are also at work in the human being.

The study of physics provides an effective means of introducing children to a new kind of thinking, for physical forces can only be perceived through their effects. In order to understand the working of a physical force, sense experience must be objectified and raised to the conceptual realm. Only in the upper grades of the elementary school are students sufficiently objective to use their senses more consciously and to analyze their perceptions.

Methods for Teaching Science

The physical sciences present teachers with an effective means of helping students to form living concepts. In order to do this, teachers need to develop a thorough understanding of the process of cognition.

In lecture 9 of *The Foundations of Human Experience*, as well as in many other books, Steiner analyzed and described the process of human thinking. In the lectures included here from *Education for Adolescents*, he reviewed what he had presented in *The Foundations of Human Experience* and showed how it might be applied to the organization of the main lesson.

According to Steiner, thinking occurs in three stages: drawing conclusions, passing judgments, and forming concepts. Contrary to what one might expect, only the third of these is connected specifically with the head and thinking. Though it may seem strange, the process of judging is connected with our rhythmic system and feelings, and drawing conclusions relates to the legs and feet and, thus, to the I.

Conclusions, as Steiner characterizes them, are perceptions that are brought to consciousness. Any sense impression can become a conclusion, but only if we become aware of the impression. It is possible to have unconscious impressions. We might hear, for example, but not listen to a sound. Hearing consists of receiving the impressions of the sounds around us, whereas listening requires our active involvement. In order to draw conclusions we must actively listen to what we hear. One of the teacher's primary tasks is to present students with conclusions that can be transformed into concepts, and not present them with concepts that have no possibility of growth.

We begin to form judgments when we become conscious of our perceptions. This process arises out of the human being's innate desire to transform perception into knowledge. While our conclusions live primarily in our sense impressions, our judgments allow us to make sense of our impressions. We do this by weighing our percept against our prior experiences of similar percepts from the past.

Conclusions are complete as soon as we become aware of them, which is well expressed in German by the word *Schluß* (literally, "the end"). The process of passing judgments is not over so quickly. One can continue to ponder and weigh one's impressions for a while, but at some point this process also must come to an end. Concepts, on the other hand, grow gradually in the human being and should never be finished or become fixed. It is the teacher's role to help the students cultivate the process of forming concepts in such a way that the concepts can grow and become increasingly developed and refined. Conclusions develop awareness, judgments result in knowledge, but concepts form the basis for wisdom, allowing us to understand ourselves and the world around us.

The Structure of a Science Main Lesson

In order to engender living concepts in their students, Waldorf teachers need to use methods that address and engage the whole human being. In "Teaching in the Upper Grades," Steiner specified how this might be done by lessons given in a two-day rhythm. This rhythm addresses the human being in thought, feeling, and will, and it allows students to draw conclusions, form judgments, and arrive at concepts.

Let us consider an example that illustrates the rhythms of teaching and learning. In their sixth grade study of acoustics, students learn to identify the origins and qualities of sound and to experience how sound is propagated through air, liquids, and solids. In the seventh grade, students might learn about resonance, forced vibrations, and sympathetic vibration. The teacher might demonstrate these kinds of vibrations by plucking one string of a sonometer. When the string is plucked, the adjacent strings vibrate. Even when the first string is dampened, the other strings continue to make a soft sound. In another demonstration, students might hold a flask up to their ear while the teacher blows in another flask of the same volume. Students hear the note coming both from the teacher's flask and from the flask they are holding.

What is happening during these demonstrations? While they are observing and participating in the demonstration, students draw a series of conclusions from their experiences. The demonstration acts powerfully on each student, affecting the whole human being because it demands that the I bring perceptions to consciousness.

Right after the demonstration, the equipment is laid aside, and the teacher verbally recapitulates the demonstration, objectively recounting what was done and what occurred. Now the students reexperience in their imagination the events they have just observed. Through the recapitulation, the experience that took hold of the whole body is now lifted into the rhythmic system and begins to involve the astral body. After the recapitulation, no further work is done that day with the phenomena that were demonstrated. For the rest of the main lesson the students will work with material presented the previous day or days.

According to Steiner, the I and astral body leave the physical and etheric body during sleep and enter the spirit realm. There the sense impressions of the demonstration and the imaginative pictures that the students formed during the recapitulation are lifted into higher realms. When the students awaken in the morning, these impressions and pictures are present again, but they have been transformed, for they now live in the etheric body as memory pictures and as the seeds of living concepts.

When the students return to school the next day, they will summarize their observations and articulate their judgments. During the review of the previous day's lesson, they will describe what they saw and heard, refining their observations and judgments as they consider the other students' contributions to the review. As the class comes to a deeper understanding of what occurred during the demonstrations, the concept begins to emerge. Once the concept has been stated, students will be able to build upon or develop the concept further by the new demonstrations and activities. They also have opportunities to express the concept in their written and artistic work, and they will begin to recognize and appreciate the concept's manifestations and applications in their daily lives. If a concept has been developed through this living process, it will develop and grow in the students as they mature. Such concepts might even take on new meanings or become transformed into ideals. The acoustical relationship that students experience in the demonstration with resonance, for example, can become an image for human relationships, where hearts and minds may resonate in sympathy with one another.

Coming to Terms with Technology

As students penetrate the laws of the physical universe, the concepts they develop begin to serve as keys to unlock the mysteries of our modern technological existence. Most of us do not understand the principles governing many of the machines and technological processes that surround us. In lecture 12 of *Practical Advice to Teachers* Steiner commented:

Just consider how many people travel today by electric train without the least idea about how an electric train is made to move. Imagine how many people see a steam engine rushing by without any clue concerning the principles of physics and mechanics that propel it. Consider what position such ignorance puts us in regarding our relationship to the environment, the very environment we utilize for our convenience. We live in a world brought about by human beings, formed by human thoughts, a world we use and know nothing about. (pp. 165–166)

Steiner expresses this point again in several other lectures. For instance, in *A Modern Art of Education* he states: "Simply to accept the creations and inventions of the human mind without at least understanding them in a general sense is the beginning of unsocial life" (MA, p. 171). Unless students are helped to understand the world they live in, their soul development will be stunted and they will have difficulty finding their proper place in life. The science curriculum in the upper grades and the high school therefore introduces students to the great discoveries and principles of modern science. Through their courses in biology, geology, organic and inorganic chemistry, and physics, students are helped to come to terms with the applications and implications of science and technology in modern life.

Developing our life of feeling is another antidote to the deadening influences of living in a world that we mostly do not understand. The study of science gives us this possibility, for students will naturally stand in awe of natural phenomena, and they will be curious, interested, and enthusiastic about unveiling nature's secrets. In "The Chld at Twelve," Steiner urges teachers to develop their ability to grasp the processes of physics with their feelings. After describing how the telegraph works, Steiner states:

Whenever you think of how one telegraph station is linked to another you are reminded of the miracles that make the Earth, the whole Earth, into a mediator, taking electric current into its care, as it were, and in turn delivering it to the next station. The Earth itself mediates in this way. All the existing explanations for this are hypothetical. The important thing regarding our human attitude toward this fact, however, is to maintain the ability to feel repeatedly its miraculous nature—that we do not become dulled in our ability to comprehend the processes of physics through our feelings. Then, when we explain these things to children, we again and again find the attitude that allows us to recall how we first took in such a fact and grasped it. Then when we explain a physical phenomenon to a child who is full of wonder, we ourselves become children who are full of wonder. (PA, p. 125)

The study of science in a Waldorf school should be a vital process that addresses the whole human being. It should engage the students' feeling as well as their thinking, and foster their ability to deal with concrete realities as well as abstract concepts. By studying science, students come to know and understand themselves, the natural world, and the world of technology. They learn to recognize the central importance of the human being as a steward of the Earth and its kingdoms. They are inspired to work for the good of the Earth and all that lives upon it.

Studying History: Reading the Script of Time

The formal study of history begins after the twelfth-year change, for only then are students ready to begin considering events in terms of cause and effect. In the fourth grade, students prepare for their history studies by learning about the people and events that have shaped the region and land where they live. In the fifth grade, they examine the ancient cultures of India, Persia, Egypt, Chaldea, and Greece in terms of their outlook, religion, and way of life. In sixth grade, students learn about the classical civilizations of Greece and Rome and about the Middle Ages. In the seventh grade, they study the Renaissance, Reformation, and the Age of Discovery. In eighth grade, students examine the major personalities and events of modern history. The high school history curriculum reviews the span of world history, including contemporary historical trends, and explores the forces underlying the development and transformation of human consciousness, culture, and society.

The history curriculum in Waldorf schools in Europe and North America focuses primarily on the development of western culture, for students growing up in the West need to learn about the forces and personalities that have influenced and shaped their culture and world-view. They also need to understand the relationship of their culture to that of other people. The study of history is therefore complemented by courses in geography, where other cultures and societies are examined in depth. Waldorf schools in other parts of the world adapt the history and geography curricula so that their students will develop an appreciation for their cultural legacy and an understanding of their relationship to other cultures.

The first goal of history teaching is to help students gain an understanding of the deeper forces of historical development. Steiner urged Waldorf teachers not to view history merely as narration or a summary of events presented from the point of view of cause and effect. Whereas, causal relationships may be valid and may reveal important insights,

> people look past what is most important when they look only for cause and effect. They look past the depths of human developmental forces that bring individual events to the surface in the course of time. We simply cannot present those events from the perspective of cause and effect. What occurs in one century is not simply the result of what occurred in previous centuries. It is, in fact, independent and only secondarily an effect. In my opinion, what occurs is independently brought to the surface out of the depths of the stream of human development. (page 309)

To counterbalance our tendency toward viewing history purely in terms of cause and effect, Steiner suggested that teachers cultivate what he called a "symptomatological" approach. This method views historical facts not as essential elements in history but as symbols of a deeper reality that lies behind them. When one examines history in terms of symptoms, one begins to fathom the historical impulses that underlie them.[2] According to Steiner,

> The real essence of humanity lives in historical impulses; what is gathered together in these impulses lives in external historical events, which in turn have their effect on individual human beings. (page 000)

In "Teaching History," Steiner gives a symptomatological interpretation of Gutenberg's invention of printing with moveble type (p. 246). According to Steiner, the invention of the printing press was symptomatic of the fact that humanity had developed the ability to proceed from living concepts to more abstract concepts. The printing press made it increasingly possible for communication to occur through the printed word rather than by direct contact. Consequently, life become more abstract and people began to think more in terms of abstractions. Steiner gives a number of examples that show how concrete experiences in the past became abstractions and how our capacity for abstract thought has been advanced and shaped by the printed word.

The study of historical impulses helps students to develop a keener appreciation of other cultures and a better understanding of the time in which they live. The point of teaching history is not simply to transport children to ancient times but to help students to recognize each age for what it offers to the course of human evolution.

In "Teaching History," Steiner suggests that the teacher introduce a history main lesson block by characterizing the entire historical period that will be studied. In this introduction, the teacher should try to convey the essential nature of that period and show students that we still use and live with the forces originating from that time.

> You should begin with what still exists today, then go on to show the children how such things first developed and took control of human development during the Greek period. This

---

2. See lecture 1 of Rudolf Steiner's *From Symptom to Reality in Modern History.*

will give the children a very solid idea of everything the Greek period gave to the development of humanity.

Through such a presentation, the children should get the idea that historical life is not something that endlessly repeats. Instead, a specific period achieves something very specific for humanity, something that remains. The children should also learn how later periods achieved other things that also remain. In this way, they can gain a firm footing in the present and are able to say to themselves that their own period of history has something specific to accomplish for eternity. (page 304)

During the history lessons, a teacher will help the students gain a sense for how a particular culture or civilization has developed. In *Discussions with Teachers*, Steiner suggests how this might be done, using the Crusades as an example. His presentation is a model of how to encompass the largest and most dramatic historical themes without ignoring interesting historical details. Again and again Steiner stresses that the teacher's presentations must be so graphic, vivid, and dramatic that they evoke living pictures in the children. These pictures provide the kind of soul connection to the subject that will allow the students to form meaningful ideas of the impulses that underlie historical events.

In their study of history, students will examine cultural development as well as the evolution of human consciousness. They will also trace the history of technology, practical life, and language. Through this process, a teacher helps the students develop a sense of historical coherence and teaches them to look at complex developments in a historical context. Students who have learned to view people, events, and ideas in context will, as adults, be able to form their own judgments and to think for themselves rather than having to rely on an external authority.

A second major goal of history teaching is to orient students in time. The study of botany in the fifth grade provides a foundation for a better grasp of time. Whenever we observe a plant we can see only one stage of its development. First there is the seed, then the shoot, then the stem and leaves, then the flower, and finally the fruit, which contains the seeds of the next cycle of the plant's life. In order to grasp the plant as a whole, we need to be able to envision it in time and to condense, as it were, weeks, months, or years, into a single living picture. When young adolescents study history, they also need to be able to condense time in their imaginations in order to perceive the larger themes of historical reality. Rather than making historical leaps, students need to sense the continuity of the human experience and the development of humanity.

In a number of different lecture cycles, Steiner demonstrated how a clearer conception of time could be developed by having the students portray a series of generations. Lecture 3 of *Education for Adolescence* (included in the chapter on adolescence) describes how a student would hold hands with someone who represents his or her father; the one representing the father would hold hands with someone who represents his father; he, in turn, would hold hands with someone who represents his father, and so on, until the generations span the centuries. In the process, the teacher points out the significant personalities and events of the previous generations. Through this experience, students begin to realize that they themselves are part of history; important historical figures can be integrated into the context of the student's ancestors, and the whole of history begins to take on a more human dimension. In Steiner's view,

> history must never be separated from the human being. Children must not think of it as so much book knowledge. Many people seem to think that history is something contained in books—though of course it is not always quite that bad. In any case, we must try in every way possible to awaken a realization of history as living, and that humankind stands within its stream. (MA, pp. 163–164)

The third goal of history teaching is to help students to understand more fully the essential nature of the human being and to recognize the universality of the human experience. This is largely achieved through the study of biography. In lecture 11 of *Soul Economy and Waldorf Education* Steiner states:

Historical ideas and impulses, expressed outwardly in definite historical periods, directly affect social life and social forms; they are like the skeleton of history.... The flesh or the muscles, so to speak, are represented by the historic personalities themselves and their biographies and by concrete, historic events. (SE, pp. 197–198)

When they consider the biography of significant individuals, students develop a better understanding of, and a heightened appreciation for, the course of human development, for the intricacies of human relationships, and for the enduring meaning of a human life. In the process of immersing themselves in the lives of others, students often begin to find answers to their own questions about human existence.

In the seventh grade, for instance, when students are beginning to experience a heightened sense of their own individuality and identity, the biography of Elizabeth I of England can make a deep impression on them. By following the significant events of her life, but also by examining the details of her appearance, habits, and character, the students will gain a thorough understanding of Elizabeth as a person as well as queen.

In their studies, students will develop a vivid mental picture of Elizabeth: her upright stance, her delicate hands and feet, her pale skin, auburn hair, and piercing gaze. They will experience her temperament—fiery and feisty, yet also given to moments of introspection and self-doubt. They will come to appreciate Elizabeth's character and personality—her ability to command and to listen, her impatience and perseverance, and her love of English culture—especially music and dance. They will empathize with her moods—her need to be at the center of attention, her imperial passions and her many fears. Finally, they will be able to identify with Elizabeth's ideals—her aversion to war, her deep abiding love for her people and for England. Through such studies, Queen Elizabeth will come to life, and through her life, the students can experience England at a turning point in its history.

The study of biography develops the students' capacity to look into the being of another and thus more fully into themselves. By arousing their interest in the great individuals of history and by leading them beyond their first impressions into a meaningful encounter with these individuals, Waldorf teachers help their students to see beyond the primary level of existence and to become aware of the deeper relations of human destiny.

The study of history will only be inwardly fruitful for the students if the teachers develop a perspective and insight that allows them to intuit or discover the true significance of what they are teaching. Teachers no less than students should not become dependent on external authorities. They need to develop the inner capacities to discern truth and meaning. When Steiner was asked by the first teachers he trained to suggest historical sources for their preparation, he replied:

> One is often asked these days what history books to read—which historian is best? The reply can only be that, in the end, each one is the best and the worst; it really makes no difference which historical author you choose. Do not read what is written *in* the lines, but read *between* the lines. Try to allow yourselves to be inspired so that, through your own intuitive sense, you can learn to know the true course of events. Try to acquire a feeling for how a true history should be written. You will recognize from the style and manner of writing which historian has found the truth and which has not. (DT, p. 93)

Ultimately, the study of history must nourish the student's life of soul, particularly the life of feeling, for through history, one can participate more meaningfully in life. Feeling must permeate, penetrate, and inform each lesson, because only through feeling can we truly come to understand ourselves and others.

The Child at Twelve

LECTURE BY RUDOLF STEINER

Stuttgart, August 29, 1919

... Another important phase in the child's development is between the twelfth and thirteenth years. During this period the spirit and soul elements in the human being are reinforced and strengthened— that is, the spirit and soul elements are less dependent on the I- being. What in spiritual science we refer to as the astral body per- meates and unites with the etheric body. Naturally, the astral body, as an independent entity, is unborn until puberty; but between the twelfth and thirteenth years it manifests in a particular way through the etheric body by permeating and invigorating it.

Here is another important milestone in the child's development. It expresses itself in the way children—if we treat properly what is now present in them—begin to understand the impulses working in the external world, as, for example, the forces of history, which resemble impulses of spirit and soul. I have given you an example of how the activity of these historical forces can be brought within the scope of teaching at elementary school level. You will have to trans- late what I have said into language for the children, but you can be as childlike as you want in your expressions, and you will still fail to awaken a proper understanding of historical impulses in children if you approach them with historical observations before they have completed their twelfth year. Before this age you can tell them about history in the form of stories—biographies, for example. They will be able to understand this, but they will be unable to grasp historical relationships before they finish their twelfth year. Thus, you will do harm if you fail to observe this turning point. After this, the children begin to develop a longing to have what they took in earlier as stories explained in terms of history. So if you told them stories, for example, about the Crusaders or other his- toric figures, you must now try to transform this material so that they can perceive the historical impulses and historical links involved.

When you observe such a phenomenon and notice unmistakably that when you do things properly, children over twelve will understand you. You will realize that, until the children's ninth year, you will primarily restrict yourself to what we have discussed as the artistic element; you will bring writing and reading, and later arithmetic, out of that. You will not make the transition to natural history until after the point discussed yesterday. And, you will not begin history, except in the form of stories, until the children have reached their twelfth year.

In the twelfth year children begin to take an inward interest in great historical connections. This will be especially important for the future; it will become increasingly obvious that it is necessary to teach an understanding of historical coherence, since the children have never before really achieved a proper concept of history. Until this time, such concepts have been primarily components of economy and nationality, but the children have participated mechanically, coping adequately with their requirements and interests by knowing a few anecdotes about rulers and wars—which is not history—and a few dates of kings and one or two famous people and battles.

Lessons in future will have to be particularly concerned with how the cultural life of humankind has developed and will have to include proper teaching on the impulses of history. These impulses will have to find their proper place in the curriculum so that they are presented at the right moment.

Something else also begins to be comprehensible to children when they have crossed this Rubicon and reached the twelfth year. However clearly you explain the functioning of the human eye to them before this point, they will be unable to understand it properly. For what does it mean to teach children about the functioning of the human eye? It means showing them how beams of light enter the eye and are taken up and refracted by the lens, how they then pass through the vitreous body and work as a picture on the rear wall, and so on. You have to describe all these processes in terms of physics. You are describing a process in physics that takes place in human beings, in one of the human sense organs. If you want to describe this process, you must first teach the concepts that will enable the children to take in this kind of description of the eye. You must first teach them what the refraction of light beams is, which can be done quite simply by showing them a lens, explaining the focus, and demonstrating how light is refracted. But these are facts of physics that have their place outside human beings. We can describe them to the children between the end of the ninth year and the beginning of the twelfth, but we should not apply such descriptions of physics to the organs of the human being before the children have completed their twelfth year because only then do they begin to assess in the right way how the external world is continued in the human being. Before their twelfth year they cannot understand this. They can understand the processes of physics but not how these processes take place within human beings.

The comprehension of the historical impulses of humankind and the comprehension of the working of nature's laws of physics in the human organism are related. The real essence of humanity lives in historical impulses; what is gathered together in these impulses lives in external historical events, which in turn have their effect on individual human beings. And when you describe the human eye you are describing an activity of external nature that is also working within human beings. Both processes require similar powers of comprehension, and these powers only start to develop in the child's twelfth year. So it will be necessary to arrange the curriculum in a way that will include between the ninth and twelfth years lessons on the simple concepts of physics necessary for an understanding of the human being; thus in addition to natural history, simple physics will be taught, but the laws of physics will not be applied to the human being until after the twelfth year. In the same way, stories will be told up to the twelfth year and then transformed into history.

My explanations so far refer to the way subjects are introduced. Of course we can continue to enlarge on physics after the twelfth year. But neither physics nor natural history should be started before the ninth year, and neither history nor lessons involving physiology, that is, descriptions of human functions, should start before the twelfth year is completed. If you take into account that comprehension does not blossom only in the intellect, but also always includes feelings and will, you will find that you are not too remote from what I have just said. When people do not take such things into account it is because they have succumbed to illusions. You can in a makeshift way present the human intellect with historical or physiological facts before the twelfth year, but by doing so you spoil human nature; strictly speaking you make it unsuitable for the whole of life. But between the ninth and twelfth years you can gradually introduce, for instance, the concepts of refraction, and the formation of images through lenses or other instruments. You could perhaps discuss how an opera glass works with the nine- to twelve-year-olds. And you can also talk with them about the way a clock works and explore the difference between a pendulum clock and a pocket watch, anything like this. But before they reach their twelfth year you should not describe how refraction and image formation can also be applied to the human eye.

All this provides points of reference from which you can learn how the material to be taught should be distributed in the curriculum to develop the capacities of the children in the right way....

Teaching in the Upper Grades

LECTURE BY RUDOLF STEINER

Stuttgart / June 14, 1921

In today's lecture we shall consider how the content of a lesson may be adapted to the life of the children. There can be no doubt whatsoever that an education that is not based on a true understanding of the human being cannot possibly succeed in adapting the content of a lesson to the reality of human life.

The spiritual aspect of the human being is not recognized today; it is really only the physical body that is considered. There are some, perhaps, who admit to something of a soul nature that, in a vague way, influences the physical body. But even they do not consider the inner concrete nature of soul and spirit. It is exactly this consideration that anthroposophy is to contribute toward an understanding of the human being. It is only this that will, in a conscious way, make the adaptation of our lessons to the human life processes possible.

Let us assume—it will not be difficult to imagine it—that the children are listening to a story you tell them, or that they are looking at a picture you drew for them on the blackboard, or that they are looking at a diagram of an experiment, or that they are listening to a piece of music you play for them. In each of these activities you are initially in a relation to the outer physical reality of the children. But what you are inserting into the children in a roundabout way through the physical reality—be it through the eyes, the ears, or the comprehending intellect—everything that is thus placed into the children very soon assumes a quite different form of life.

The children go home, they go to bed, they go to sleep; their I-beings and astral bodies are outside their etheric and physical bodies. What you did with the children in this roundabout way through the physical body and also the etheric body continues in the astral body and the I. But the latter two are now, during sleep, in a quite different environment. They experience something that can only be experienced during sleep, and everything you taught the children participates in the experience. The effects of the lesson that remain in the astral body and I are part of the experience during sleep. You must know that you let flow into the astral body and I what you teach the children through this detour of the physical body and that you thus affect the children's sleep experience. The children will present to you on the following morning the results of what they experience between falling asleep and waking.

A simple example will clarify this for you. Think of a child who is doing eurythmy or singing. The physical body is active, and the active physical body and the etheric body impress this activity on the astral body and I. The I and astral body are forced into participating in the movements of the physical and etheric bodies. But they resist, because actually they have other forces to concentrate on. These forces must now, in a way, be subdued. And although the I and astral body resist, they must accept what their own physical and etheric bodies mediate to them—in eurythmy it is more the physical body; in listening to a piece of music, it is more the etheric body.

The I and astral body then enter the world we live in between falling asleep and waking up. Everything that has been impressed on them continues during sleep to vibrate in them. The I and astral body actually repeat—in the more intricate and spiritualized way peculiar to their nature—what they experienced in eurythmy and music. They repeat all of it. And what they thus experience during sleep, this the children take with them to school on the following day. The children incorporate the experience into their etheric and physical bodies, and we have to reckon with that.

Considered in totality, the human being presents an extraordinarily complicated structure for us to come to terms with in our lessons. Let us now take a closer look at these processes. Let us consider a child who is doing eurythmy. The physical body is in movement, and the movements of the physical are transferred to the etheric body. Astral body and I initially resist, but the activities of the physical and etheric bodies are impressed on them. Astral body and I then separate during sleep and connect the impressions to spiritual forces that are quite different. On the following morning astral body and I return the impressions to the etheric and physical bodies. We can then see a remarkable harmony between that which was received from the spiritual world during sleep and what the etheric and physical bodies experienced during eurythmy.

The effect shows itself in the way the sleep experiences adjust to what was prepared and carried out on the previous day. It is only in this complementing of the physical/etheric by the spiritual that we can see the special healing element of eurythmy. Indeed, spiritual substantiality is brought to the human being upon awakening in the morning after a day including eurythmy.

It is similar in singing. When we let a child sing, the essential activity is that of the etheric body. The astral body must strongly adapt to this activity and, again, initially resists before taking it into the spiritual world. The astral body returns, and what it brings back again expresses itself in effectively healing forces. We may say that in eurythmy we have a force that mainly affects the health of the child's physical body, while in singing a force expresses itself that mainly affects the child's mechanism of movement and, through movements, then again the health of the physical body.

We can make very good use of these connections in education. If we organize our curriculum—this is an ideal, but the teachers could at least try to come close to it—so that the eurythmy lesson is given in the afternoon, it will be allowed to continue its life during the following night. On the next day, we can teach a physical education lesson in the way I outlined yesterday. The experience then penetrates the body in such a way that the movements made in physical education have a healing effect. Much can be achieved by this alternation of eurythmy and physical education.

Or again, much can be achieved on any one day when we let the children sing. They take this experience into the spiritual world during sleep. On the following day we let them listen to music—we let them listen to rather than make music. What was done on the previous day is then consolidated in the listening to music—an extraordinary healing process. You can see that under ideal conditions—that is, a curriculum structured to adapt to the conditions of life—we can affect the children's health in an extraordinary way. We shall do still far more in this regard.

Let us take the physics lesson as another example. We make an experiment. Remember what I said yesterday: Our thinking, our mental pictures, are head processes, while it is the rhythmic human being who judges, and the metabolic human being who draws conclusions. It is especially our legs and feet that draw conclusions. If you keep this in mind, if you think of the processes of perception in this way, you will tell yourselves that everything connected with the will, everything we produce out of ourselves during the process of perceiving, is deeply connected to the drawing of conclusions and not only to the forming of mental pictures or ideas. When I look at my body, then this body is itself a conclusion. The idea, the mental image, arises only because I am looking at my body, but in carrying out a definite half-conscious or unconscious procedure, I synthesize the parts in a way, akin to the forming of judgments, that allows me to experience the totality. I then express the experience in the sentence: This is my body. But this is already the perception of a conclusion. As I perceive, perceive intelligently, I am drawing conclusions. And the whole of the human being is within these conclusions.

This is so during an experiment, because in experimenting the whole of the human being is active, receiving information. Conclusions are continuously drawn during the process. Judgments are generally not perceived; they are predominantly inner processes. We may thus say that the whole of the human being is occupied during an experiment.

From an educational point of view, children do not really benefit much at all from such experiments. They may be interested in what they see, but their normal organization as human beings is as such not strong enough for them to exert themselves continuously in every part of their being. That is not possible. I always ask too much of them when I ask them to exert themselves totally. The children always get too far outside themselves when I ask them to observe an experiment or something in the environment. The important aspect in education consists in really paying attention to the three parts of the threefold human being—in allowing each part to receive its due, but also in getting all to the point where they can correspondingly interact.

Let us return to the physics lesson. I make an experiment. The whole of the human being is occupied, is asked to make an effort. This is quite enough to begin with. I then draw the children's attention away from the instruments I experimented with and repeat the various stages. Here I am appealing to their memory of the direct experience. During such a review, or recapitulation—without seeing the experiment—the rhythmic system is especially enlivened. After having engrossed the whole of the human being, I now appeal to the rhythmic system, and to the head system, because the head naturally participates during recapitulation. The lesson can then be concluded. After first having occupied the whole of the human being, then mainly the rhythmic system, I dismiss the children. They go to bed and sleep. What I activated in the whole of their being, then in their rhythmic system, now during sleep continues to live in their limbs when astral body and I are outside the body.

Let us now regard what remains lying on the bed, what allows the content of the lesson to keep on working. Everything that has developed in the rhythmic system and the whole of the human being now streams upward into the head. Pictures of these experiences now form themselves in the head. And it is these pictures that the children find on waking up and going to school. Indeed, it is so. When the children arrive at school on the following morning they have, without knowing it, pictures of the previous day's experiments in their heads, as well as pictures of what—in as imaginative a way as possible—I repeated, recapitulated after the experiment. The children I then confront have photographs of the previous day's experiment in their heads. And I shall now reflect on yesterday's lesson in a contemplative way. Yesterday I experimented, and in reviewing the experiment I then appealed to the children's imagination. In today's lesson I add the contemplative element. In doing so, I not only meet the pictures in the children's heads, but also help to bring the pictures into their consciousness.

Remember the progression: I teach a physics lesson, make an experiment; then I recapitulate the stages of the experiment in a purely narrative form, more for the imagination. On the following day, we discuss the previous experiment, contemplate it, reflect on it. The children are to learn the inherent laws. The cognitive element, thinking, is now employed. I do not force the children to have mere pictures in their heads, pictures they have brought with them from sleep, pictures without substance, without meaning. Just imagine the children coming to school with these pictures in their heads, of which they have no knowledge. If I were to immediately start with a new experiment, without first nourishing them with the cognitive, contemplative element, I would again occupy the whole of their being, and the effort they would have to make would stir up these pictures; I would create chaos in their heads. No, above all, what I must do first is consolidate what wishes to be there, provide nourishment. These sequences are important; they adapt to, are in tune with, the life processes.

Let us take another example, a history lesson. In the teaching of history there is no apparatus, no experiment. I must find a way of again adapting the lesson to the life processes, and I can do this as follows. I give the children the mere facts that occur in space and time. The whole being is again addressed just as during an experiment, because the children are called upon to make themselves a mental picture of space. We should see to it that they do this, that they see what we tell them, in their minds. They should also have a mental picture of the corresponding time. When I have brought this about, I shall try to add details about the people and events— not in a narrative way, but merely by characterization. I now describe and draw the children's attention to what they heard in the first part of the lesson. In the first part, I occupied their whole being; in the second, it is the rhythmic part of their being that must make an effort. I then dismiss them.

When they return on the following day they again have the spiritual photographs of the previous day's lesson in their heads. I connect today's lesson with them by a reflective, contemplative approach—for example, a discussion on whether Alcibiades or Mithradates was a decent or an immoral person. When I make an objective, characterizing approach on the first day, followed on the next day by reflection, by judgments, I shall allow the three parts of the threefold human being to interact, to harmonize in the right way.

These examples show what can be done if the lessons are properly structured, if they are adapted to life conditions. The structuring and adaptation are only possible in our curriculum, which allows the teaching of a subject for several weeks. They are not possible in the traditional schedule, wherein physics is taught on one day and, perhaps, religion on the next. How could one thus consider what the children bring with them? It is difficult, of course, to structure all the lessons in this way, but one can at least come close to doing so. And by taking a good look at our schedule, you will see that we have attempted to make that possible....

Teaching History

LECTURE BY RUDOLF STEINER

Basle, May 7, 1920

When you have taught the children in the way I have indicated, at around the age of twelve—I will explain some details later, for example, working with fractions—you will see they are mature enough to comprehend history, on the one hand, and, on the other hand, to learn about geography, physics, and chemistry. At that age, the children are also mature enough to prepare for genuinely practical life. Today, I would like to give you an outline of this.

Children are not mature enough to understand history before the age of twelve. You can certainly prepare them for learning about history by telling stories or by giving them short biographical sketches, or even by telling them stories with a moral. They become mature enough to learn history through learning about botany and zoology as I described it. You can achieve a great deal in regard to history if, in botany, you have presented the Earth as a unity and shown how the various plants grow upon the Earth's surface during the different seasons of the year, and if they understand the human being as a synthesis of the various groups of animals, that is, if you have presented each of the animal groups as something one-sided which then harmoniously unites with the others in the human being. When children move through such ideas, you prepare them for learning history.

When we begin to teach children history, it is important that we use history to develop and support certain forces of human nature, and, in a certain sense, to fulfill the longings of human nature during this period of life. However, if we use a normal presentation of history, we encounter considerable resistance. Today's usual presentation of history is actually only the telling of certain events, or the summarizing of those events or cultural forms from a particular causal perspective. It is essentially the superficiality of what occurred that prevails. If you remain objective about it, you will feel that form of history does not properly describe the things that really lie at the basis of human development. Recently, we often hear that history should avoid talking about wars or other more external events, and that it should instead present the causal relationships of cultural events. It is very questionable whether we are justified in assuming such causal relationships as, for example, that what occurred in the second half of the nineteenth century resulted from what occurred in the first half, and so forth. We could certainly express the basis of human historical development in a quite different way. In teaching history, it is important not to let ourselves go, so to speak. It is important that we do not try to teach history in a way that we ourselves understand only very little. Of course, we assume that we all learned history at the university, that we understand history as a whole, but that is not what I am talking about. What I mean is that when we begin to teach a particular history class, we normally just start somewhere and assume that what follows that period will be properly taken up at a later time. That is why history is generally taught as just a series of events in time.

Teaching this way does not actually take the forces that emanate from human nature into account. However, that is something we must do. We should, for example, be clear that the most important thing is what we, as human beings living in the present, experience as history. If we take the children back to Greek history in an abstract way, even if they are at a college-preparatory level, that is only an abstract placement in an earlier time. The children will not concretely understand why modern people need to understand anything about the Greek times. They will immediately understand what is important, however, if you begin by describing how we experience the effects of the Greek period in the present. Therefore, we first need to give the children a picture of that, which we can do in various ways. We could have prepared that previously, but in teaching history, we must begin by describing how what existed at a particular historical time still exists in the present.

An objective survey of our culture will easily show you the following. If I were to describe in detail what I now wish to outline, it would take too much time, but each of you can do that for yourself. Here, I want only to indicate the general guidelines. Everything we have as comprehensive and universal ideas, that is, everything we live by in terms of ideas, we essentially have as an inheritance from the Greek period. Certain feelings about art that occupy our souls are only a result of the Greek period. Take any of the most common examples, things we work with every day, for example, the concept of cause and effect, or even the concept of the human being itself. Every universal concept we have, the Greeks developed. Take, for example, the concept of history. It was the Greeks who first developed that concept. Thus, if we look at our entire life of ideas, we will find we inherited it from the Greek period.

We can describe for the students at a quite elementary level our entire universe of ideas and concepts without even mentioning that they arose in Greece. We can speak completely from the perspective of the present, and leave it at that for the time being. We could then attempt to do something dramatic or lyrical with the children, so that we indicate, for instance, how a drama is divided into acts, how the drama is built up, leading to a climax, which then resolves. In that way, we can develop a very elementary concept of catharsis. We certainly do not need to develop any complicated philosophical ideas in the children, but we can give them the concept of catharsis by showing them how a certain feeling of tension is developed in the drama, how we are led into a feeling of sympathy or fear, and then how we can learn to have a balance in our feelings of fear or sympathy. Then we can tell them how the Greeks developed all of that as the most important aspects of drama. All that is possible when we have properly prepared the children for what they are to learn around the age of twelve. We can then show the children some Greek work of art, say, a figure of Aphrodite or something similar, and explain how beauty is revealed in it. We could even go so far as to explain the artistic difference between what is at rest and what is in movement. We can also give them some ideas about public life if we discuss the basic political ideas during the Greek period in connection with modern public life.

After we have discussed all of these things, we can attempt to present the basic character of Greek history to the children, spreading it out before them. We should try to make it clear to the children how the Greek city states worked, and that people with a certain character lived in Greece. Our main task is, therefore, to show that these things we are discussing are still living today and that they arose with the Greeks, that is, to show how sculpture developed during the Greek period or how cities developed, and so forth. Thus, you should begin with what still exists today, then go on to show the children how such things first developed and took control of human development during the Greek period. This will give the children a very solid idea of everything the Greek period gave to the development of humanity.

Through such a presentation, the children should get the idea that historical life is not something that endlessly repeats. Instead, a specific period achieves something very specific for humanity, something that remains. The children should also learn how later periods achieved other things that also remain. In this way, they can gain a firm footing in the present and are able to say to themselves that their own period of history has something specific to accomplish for eternity. Such a presentation of history has a genuine effect upon the soul and excites the will. How you give such a presentation is extremely important. Through the presentation, you have the opportunity to give the children a large number of ideas, a large number of impressions and to show that it was the Greeks who introduced such things into human life.

You may also speak to the children about things that happened a long time ago and are still living, but do not contain any Christian aspects. When we speak about the Ancient Greek culture in such a way that it is perceived as living, we are working with material that contains nothing of Christianity. However, it is precisely in awakening ideas in the children that have remained alive over a long period of time and are neutral in relationship to Christianity that we have the possibility of clearly presenting the effects of the event of Golgotha and the rise of Christianity. After we have presented Greek history by characterizing the entirety of Greek culture, we can go into the details. If we have covered Greek history this way, we will have properly prepared the children for an awakening of a feeling for Christianity.

Many of you may say, with a certain amount of justification, that my suggestion to first avoid discussing the details of history, and instead discuss the great movements and tendencies in Ancient Greece is not the proper method because we would not begin with specific events and then put them together to form a picture of Greek history in its entirety. Here we come to an important question of method, which we cannot answer out of our own desires and prejudices, but instead should answer from a complete understanding of life. I would ask you in return if life is such that the whole is always formed from individual events. If you think for a moment what it would mean to make that demand upon normal perception, then you would have to teach people how to form a human head out of its individual parts, the brain and so on.

In ordinary life, we look directly at the whole. We can gain a living relationship to life only when we look directly at the whole. We should never study the individual parts of the whole in some random fashion. What is important is that we characterize as a whole those things that occur as a whole. For the Greeks themselves, the situation was that they lived in a given decade and experienced as individual human beings the impressions that arose during that decade. The part of Ancient Greece that is alive today is a summarization and forms a whole that the children look past if we do not begin by characterizing what was alive within the entirety of Greek culture.

This also resolves another more practical question. I have experienced time and again what it means in a specific situation when the teacher does not complete the required material in a given grade. It can lead to complete nonsense in two ways. In the first case, you are not finished, which is simply silly. In the second case, you do finish, but you pile things together so much in the last weeks that all the work is really for nothing. However, if you first present the material as a whole, you will have covered the period of history that you want to teach the class. In that way, you don't do nearly so much harm when you skip over some of the details in your discussion. If you have an overview of the subject, it is very simple to later look up the details in an encyclopedia. Not to have learned the overview is, under some circumstances, a lasting loss. You can get a proper overview of a subject only under the guidance of a really lively person, whereas you can learn the details yourself from a book. We will, of course, discuss how to divide the material throughout the curriculum and among the grades later.

That is very important in pedagogy. It should, in fact, be extremely emphasized in testing teachers. I am attempting to do this for the Waldorf School in Stuttgart, which is, of course, only in its beginning stages. You have to admit that what is important in examining teachers is to get an impression of their worldviews and then leave it up to the individual teacher to determine what he or she needs to know to teach on a daily basis. The fact that the teachers' examinations test for details is complete nonsense. What is important is to gain a summary impression of whether someone is appropriate to be a teacher or not. Of course, we should not carry such things to an extreme. We should certainly not believe we should do that. However, what I just said is true in general.

We can consider everything I have just described as living today as a kind of transition into Greece. We could then go on to those things living today that were not yet living in Ancient Greece. You could certainly give a lively presentation about such concepts as general human dignity. You could discuss such concepts as individual human consciousness, of course at an elementary level. The Greeks did not yet have the concept of human dignity. They did have the concepts of polis, of a community to which individuals belonged, but they were divided into groups, the masters and the slaves. The Greeks did not have a fundamental conception of the human being, and you should discuss that with the students. You could also discuss the concept of what is human, a concept that is not very alive because we are not nearly Christian enough in modern times, but that can be very alive for the children through their studies of natural history.

You can awaken the concept of what is universally human in the following way. Describe Leonardo's *Last Supper* to the children, and what he wanted to achieve with that picture—it is actually there only in a sense, there are only some little specks of color left in Milan. Today, unless you can see clairvoyantly, you cannot understand what he wanted to achieve, but the thought of the picture still exists. You can enliven your presentation by placing the picture in front of the children. You can make clear to the children that there are twelve human beings, twelve people pictured by the artist as the twelve apostles surrounding the Lord in the middle, in their positions with various attitudes, from the devoted St. John to the traitorous Judas. In a certain sense, you can develop all human characters from these twelve pictures. You can show the children how different human characters are, and then indicate how the Lord in the middle relates to each of the individuals. You can then have the children imagine someone coming from another planet. Of course, you do not need to say it that way, but say it in some way so it is clear to them. If you imagine someone from a foreign planet coming down to Earth and looking at all the pictures on Earth, that being would need to look only at these twelve people and the transfigured face in the middle to know that that face has something to do with what gives the Earth its meaning.

You can make it clear to the children that there was once a time during which the Earth underwent a developmental preparation, followed by another time that had been awaited and that, in contrast to the preparatory period, provided a kind of fulfillment. You can show them that all of earthly human development is connected with that event of Golgotha, and that the Earth's development would have no meaning if that event had not occurred. That is something that is also alive today and that we can very easily enliven, at least to the extent that it has withered during our half-heathen times. In short, it is important that you explain this second age of humanity. It is an age that developed through the rise of Christianity, through the rise of what is universally human. In contrast, the central purpose of the previous period was the creation of concepts and artistic perception, which could be developed only by an aristocracy, and has remained in its entirety as our inheritance.

When you take up Roman history you can show how it has a tendency toward something that, as such, has hardly any significance. It would be clear to an objective observer of Roman history how great the distance is between the Roman people and those of Greece. The Greeks gave us and the Romans everything that has endured. The Romans were actually students of the Greeks in everything of importance to humanity, and as such were a people without imagination. They were a people who had prepared themselves for the Christian concept of humanity only through the concept of citizen. You can teach children at this age the effects of Christianity upon Roman culture. You can also show them how the old world declined piece by piece, and how Christianity spread piece by piece in the West. In that way, the first millennium of Christianity acquires a kind of unified character, namely, the spreading of the concept of universal humanity. When you teach the children such a living, intense concept as the importance of Christianity in human development, then you also have the possibility of describing the whole modern age for these young human beings.

After the first thousand years of Christian European development, something new slowly begins. Something I would call very prosaic for us clearly begins to enter the development of humanity. Things will look quite different for those who follow us in a thousand years, but today, of course, we need to teach history for our period. We look back at Ancient Greece and at something that may be heathen, namely, art and the life of ideas, and so forth. Then, we look at the first thousand years of Christian development and find that the feeling life of Europe had just developed. What we find when we then look at what occurred after the first thousand years of Christian development is the development of European will. We primarily see that the activities of economics become an object of human thinking, a source of difficulties. Earlier times took care of these activities in a much more naïve way. In connection with that, you can attempt to show how the Earth has become a level stage for human beings due to the voyages of discovery and the invention of printed books. You can also attempt to show that this latter period is the one in which we still stand. You will no longer be able to give a broad overview in the same way that you did for the Greek and Christian-Roman periods and their effects upon life in Middle Europe. You will need to more or less allow everything that occurred from the eleventh or twelfth century forward to fall into the disarray of details. However, in doing that you will be able to awaken in children the proper feeling for the rise of national will during that period of history.

What do we accomplish when we do that? We do not teach causal history or pragmatic history or any of the other wonderful things people have admired at various times. What is causal history? I already described that. It assumes that what follows is always the result of some event preceding it. However, if you have a surface of water and you look at the waves, one following the other, can you say that each wave is the result of the one preceding it? Would you instead not need to look into the depths of the water to find the reasons, the general cause of the series of waves? It is no different in history. People look past what is most important when they look only for cause and effect. They look past the depths of human developmental forces that bring individual events to the surface in the course of time. We simply cannot present those events from the perspective of cause and effect. What occurs in one century is not simply the result of what occurred in previous centuries. It is, in fact, independent and only secondarily an effect. In my opinion, what occurs is independently brought to the surface out of the depths of the stream of human development.

We can give children an impression of that, and we should do that at this stage of their development. If people do not develop that during childhood, they can obstinately remain in their belief of pragmatic or causal history. They remain fixed in their understanding of history and later have little tendency to accept anything that has a real future. In contrast to all other presentations of history, we could call our presentation symptomatological history. Those who try to view history symptomologically do not believe it is necessary to look at each individual event and describe it for itself. Instead, they see such events as symptoms of deeper development. They might say to themselves that if Gutenberg[3] lived and invented the art of printing books during a particular historical time, then that was connected with what existed in the depths of humanity at that time. The invention of book printing is only a symptom that humanity at that time was mature enough to move on from certain simple concrete ideas to more abstract ones. If we come into life during a time that is held together more through printing than through direct and basic content, then we live life in a much more abstract manner.

The way life became more abstract during the course of historical events is seldom taken into account. Think for a moment about a simple example. I can say that my coat is shabby. Everyone can understand it when I say that my coat is shabby, but no one actually knows what that really means. What it means was originally connected with moths,[4] with small insects. At that time, people hung their coats in the closet and did not brush them properly. These little insects lived in them and ate the cloth. The coat then had holes in it, and through the destruction of coats by moths, the word shabby arose. There you have the transition from the concrete to the abstract. That transition continually takes place and is something we should take note of. In the area in Austria where I grew up, the farmers spoke about sleep in their eyes. For them, the sleep in their eyes was not something abstract in the way we think of it today when we say the sleep is in our eyes. The farmer rubbed his eyes, and what he rubbed out of the corners of his eyes in the morning, that specific excretion, he called sleep. Those farmers do not have any other concept of sleep; they must first be taught the abstract idea of sleep. Of course, such things are now dying out. Those of us who are older can remember such things from our youth, if we did not grow up in the city. We can remember how everything was concrete, but with the close of the

---

3. Johannes Gutenberg (Johannes Gensfleisch, 1400-1468) invented movable type around 1445.
4. In German, the word for "shabby" is *schäbig*. A southern German word for moth is *Schabe*. — TRANS.

nineteenth century, such things have more or less died out. I could give you a number of such examples, and you would hardly believe that people in the country thought in such a concrete way. You can experience many curious things in the country. There is an Austrian poet[5] who wrote in dialect and wrote a number of beautiful things that are admired by all the city people. But only city people admire them, since country people do not understand them. He used words the way city people use them—abstractly. People in the country do not understand his poetry at all because they have specific things in mind, so everything has a very different meaning. I recall, for example, that one of his poems speaks about nature. It is completely incomprehensible for farmers, because a farmer does not have the same concept of nature that an educated person has. A farmer understands the word nature to mean something very concrete. In the same way, I can find examples everywhere that would show how the transition from the concrete to the abstract occurs throughout human development, and how a whole wave moving toward abstraction crashed in upon humanity with the rise of book printing. In a way, people began to filter their concepts through the influence of book printing.

It would not be bad to teach children some concepts of modern history that would make them more objective about life. There would be, for example, much less discussion about battling capitalism and so forth if the people who said such things did not speak as though they had never heard anything about capitalism and had no idea that to simply angrily attack capitalism has absolutely no meaning. It has nothing to do with what people today really want; it only shows that such people do not properly understand the significance of capitalism. My books like *Towards Social Renewal* seem so unintelligible to them because they were written about life and not about the fantastic ideas of modern agitators.

A really living consideration of history requires that people understand external events as symptoms of something hidden

---

5. Josef Misson, 1803-1875, priest and writer of poetry in dialect. Rudolf Steiner speaks about him in detail in *The Riddle of Man*, Mercury Press, 1990, GA 20.

within, and they need some idea of what considering those symptoms means. When you consider history from a symptomatological perspective, you will slowly realize that first there is an ascent, then the highest point of a certain event is reached, and then a descent follows. Take, for example, the event of Golgotha. If you look at that part of history and see the external events as symptoms of an inner process, you rise above the purely historical into the religious. The historical thus deepens into the religious. Then, you will find a way that will lead you through feeling into an understanding of what we can teach children at an early age, for instance, the Gospels or the Old Testament. However, we cannot give them an inner understanding of such things, nor is that necessary. You teach them in the form of stories, and when the children have a living, historical feeling for the stories, the material in the Bible takes on a new life. It is good when certain things gain their full liveliness only in stages. Primarily though, considering history symptomatologically deepens a desire for religion, a feeling for religion.

I said before that we should prepare children for learning history by teaching them about nature and that we should proceed in the way I characterized earlier. At the same time, we prepare children for life on Earth by teaching them about botany in the way I described. We can then go on to geography at this stage of childhood. We should base geography upon stories describing various areas, including far distant places, for example, America or Africa. Through our descriptions of natural history, which have presented the plant realm as part of the entire Earth, the children are prepared by about the age of twelve to understand geography. At this time, it is important to show in geography that everything in history depends upon all the things that come from the Earth—the climates, the formations, the structures of the Earth in various places. After giving them an idea about the connection of land, sea, and climate to Ancient Greece, you can move on to what we can portray as a symptom of the inner development of humanity in the characteristics of Ancient Greece. It is possible to find an inner connection between our geographical picture of the Earth and historical developments. Actually, we should always make inner connections between our descriptions of various parts of the Earth and our descriptions of historical developments. We should not, for example, discuss American geography before we have presented the discovery of America in history. We should certainly take into account the fact that the human horizon has extended in the course of development, and we should not try to bring human feelings to some firm absolute point.

In the same way, it is not good in so-called mathematical geography to begin dogmatically with a drawing of the Copernican solar system. Instead, we should begin by describing for the children, at least as a sketch, how people came to such a perspective. In that way, children do not learn concepts that are beyond the level of their human development. Of course, people taught children the fixed Ptolomeic concepts when the Ptolomaic view of the world predominated. Now we teach them those of the Copernican perspective. It is certainly necessary to give children at least some idea about how people determined the positions of the stars in the sky and, from a summarization of those positions, came to some conclusion that then became a description of the planetary system. We do not want the children to believe, for example, that such a description of the planetary system came about by someone sitting in a chair outside of the universe and simply looking at the planets. When you draw the Copernican system on the blackboard as though it were a fact, how can a child imagine how people came to that view? Children need to have some living idea about how such things develop, otherwise they will go through their entire lives with confused ideas, which they believe are absolutely certain. That is how a false belief in authority develops, something that does not occur when you develop a proper feeling for authority between the ages of seven until fourteen or fifteen....

7

THE HIGH
SCHOOL YEARS

Adolescence — The Quest for Self

OF ALL THE STAGES of human development, adolescence is probably the most dramatic. Not only do adolescents change physically, they also experience a profound transformation of their souls. In terms of outlook, behavior, and capacities, the adolescent can sometimes seem like an entirely new person.

According to Rudolf Steiner, the changes that occur at puberty reflect a new relationship between the physical and etheric bodies and the astral body and the I (see p. 24). Until about the age of fourteen, the astral body is closely connected to and working in concert with the etheric and physical bodies. At puberty, the astral body begins to be emancipated from its physiological functions. This "birth" of the astral body echoes the birth of the etheric body at age seven. Just as the child's etheric body is no longer needed purely for the processes of growth and metabolism, but becomes available for the processes of memory and thought, the adolescent's astral body will become available for new capacities. All through our lives, the astral body provides the basis for our perceptions, our sensations, and our feelings. At puberty, our life of feeling becomes increasingly liberated from its bodily foundations. This separation will enable adolescents to become increasingly objective about themselves, other people, and the world, and will allow them to develop the foundation for sound judgment (see p. 40).

The changes at puberty are also a result of the continued working of the etheric body. Throughout childhood, etheric forces slowly penetrate the child's body, working from within outward. These forces penetrate as far as the muscular system at around age nine and the skeletal system at around twelve. By puberty, the etheric forces complete the second stage of development and break through to the outside world, allowing the adolescent to stand fully in the world.

Because adolescents experience life so differently than before, they often feel ill at ease in the world. Steiner describes the reasons for these anxious feelings. He says that what young children brought from pre-earthly existence was gradually interwoven with their whole being, but at the onset of puberty, adolescents feel cast out of the spiritual world. Adolescents unconsciously compare the world that they left behind with the world they have entered; this brings about great inner upheaval. High school teachers need to address adolescents' inner discomfort by being especially sensitive to their feelings, and the high school curriculum must address adolescents' feelings of alienation by strengthening their sense of self and connecting them to other people and to the world.

Forming Connections

An adolescent's interests are much broader and more universal than those of younger children. As the process of separation between self and world (which begins around age nine) nears completion, adolescents develop the ability to appraise humanity as a whole.

At puberty, having found their own way into humanity, children no longer depend on outer support as much as during pre-puberty, and a new feeling arises in them—an entirely new appraisal of humanity as a whole. This new experience of humankind represents the spiritual counterpart to the physical faculty of reproduction. Physically, they acquire the capacity to procreate. Spiritually, they gain the capacity to experience humankind as a totality. (SE, p. 232)

Because adolescents can feel profoundly alone and estranged from the world, their relationships to others become more important, and love and friendship develop new depth and meaning. The capacity for love, which begins to come to the fore at puberty, goes far beyond its sexual dimension. According to Steiner, love between the sexes is a specific and limited aspect of love; only by recognizing this fact can we correctly understand love and its task in the world (SE, p. 231).

While sexuality is a part of human existence, preoccupation or over-involvement with sex indicates a lack of balance in one's soul life. Developing a healthy sense of one's sexuality has become progressively more difficult, due to a barrage of subliminal and explicit sexual messages. With the dramatic rise of teenage pregnancy and sexually transmitted diseases, society has increasingly turned to schools to educate children about relationships and sexual behavior.

Waldorf schools have developed a subtle and effective approach to sex education that addresses the issues of sexuality in the context of relationships—one's relationship to oneself, to other people, and to the world. As our students investigate the miracles of human anatomy and physiology, they develop reverence and respect for the human body and its functions. As they examine the human being in relation to the other kingdoms of nature, they begin truly to understand what it means to be a human being.

Developing the students' sense of beauty also helps them establish the foundations for a healthy relationship to sexuality. In "Working with Adolescents," Steiner states:

A child whose feelings for the beautiful, or esthetic, view of the world have not been stimulated, will during puberty easily become overly sensual, even erotic. There is no better way of counteracting the erotic feelings than through the healthy development of the esthetic sense for the sublime and beautiful in nature. If you succeed in making the children feel deeply the beauty, the colors, in sunrise and sunset, in the flowers, experience the sublime splendor of a thunderstorm—if, as it were, you cultivate in them the esthetic sense—you will do more for them than is done by the often absurdly practiced sex education given to children at an ever younger age. It is the feeling for the beautiful, an esthetic confrontation with the world, that counteracts the erotic feeling. By experiencing the world as beautiful, the human being will also attain the right, healthy relation to his or her body, will not be tormented by it, as happens in eroticism. (p. 263)

Male and Female

Puberty is a process through which the human being begins to become more highly individualized; this is the stage when the polarity between male and female becomes very marked. In the following lecture, Steiner tries to help teachers develop a better understanding of the differences between men and women. Although he sometimes had to generalize about the typical attributes of males and females, Steiner was not trying to stereotype or simplify the qualities of the sexes. He was trying to help teachers become especially aware of and sensitive to the differences between boys and girls so that they could better meet their students' needs and address their inner questions.

What makes men and women so different?

In "Working with Adolescents," Steiner explains that the astral body of a woman, in contrast to that of a man, plays a more significant role and is more highly differentiated and delicately organized. This accounts for the fact that the female organism has a stronger inclination toward the cosmos. During adolescence, the girls' I-being is more under the influence of the astral. Consequently, they sometimes live more in their outer feelings and can seem more confident and self-assured than boys. According to Steiner, the astral body of a male is less differentiated, even crude by comparison. During adolescence, a boy's I is still in concealment, and his astral body does not draw the I in to the same degree. As a result, boys tend to be more reserved and have a need to draw into themselves.

Adolescents experience their inner life as a secret that should not be revealed to the world. This results in a feeling of bashfulness, as a kind of blushing or pallor of soul and spirit. High school teachers need to be sensitive to their students' need for privacy; Steiner urges them to treat their students with a special tact and delicacy, to be conscious of the presence of "something in them they wish to conceal, to preserve—like an unopened flower—then the unspoken effect of one person on another will be soon noticed. To live with just such a feeling will already have a tremendous educational effect" (EA, p. 80).

The Waldorf High School

High school students need an entirely different kind of relationship with their teachers than they had in elementary school. While younger children learn out of love for their teachers, high school students learn because they respect their teachers' knowledge, experience, and expertise. Class teachers who have gained a general wealth of knowledge are no longer appropriate for the high school. Adolescents need to be taught by specialists who are experts in their field.

The Waldorf high school offers a rich and diverse academic curriculum in the sciences, mathematics, and the humanities, which include literature, history, and history of the arts. High school courses address the most basic questions about the nature of the human being, society, and the natural world, and they help students establish a sense of meaning and direction in their lives.

Every subject in the high school curriculum is an opportunity to help students find themselves and, thus, their place in life. A brief description of the content of one of the literature main lesson courses might illustrate how the high school curriculum speaks to the students' inner questions and search for meaning.

In Waldorf high schools throughout the world, students in the eleventh grade study the medieval romance, *Parzival*, by Wolfram von Eschenbach. The reader first meets the noble child Parzival in the forest refuge to which he has been taken after the death of his

father. Removed from the world of chivalry and from his own kingdom by a mother fearful for his well-being, Parzival grows up ignorant of his identity, his heritage, his nobility. His first encounter
with the world outside his cloistered home is a brief meeting with
four bright and shining knights. This encounter arouses such an
intense longing to be like those knights that Parzival abandons his
mother, leaving her to her sorrow and death. In ignorance and dullness of soul, he begins his long quest. It is a quest for glory, a quest
for the highest, a quest for his true being.

What better metaphor can be found for modern humanity than
Parzival, born to achieve the highest honor, yet cut off from his
rightful heritage, forced to find his way alone through suffering,
humiliation, and doubt? Students identify with the bumbling, awkward, simple fool of the early part of the story, who, in his childish
unawareness, fails to ask the question that would heal the wounded
Grail King. They have compassion for the young man of the central
scenes, cursed and condemned for a failing that he does not understand, bereft of hope and faith, and they glory in the triumph of the
noble king Parzival, who has achieved the soul's peace and been
named the Lord of the Grail.

Through his steadfast striving, even in the abyss of darkness
and loneliness, Parzival achieves the goal of his quest and his questioning, and eleventh graders, facing the crises of adolescence that
lead to so many empty answers—drug abuse, sexual promiscuity,
and even suicide—may draw comfort and strength from this age-
less tale.

The Practical Arts

For most students, high school is a preparation for further studies, yet the high school curriculum also strives to prepare students
for life. Especially through the study of technology and practical
human activities, students are led into the world, helped to feel at
home there, and inspired to work responsibly in the world.

Many people today are ignorant of principles utilized by the
machines and processes of daily life. "This fact—that we understand

nothing about something that is formed by human beings and is basically the result of human thinking—is very significant for the whole mood of soul and spirit of humanity." (PA, p. 166).

According to Steiner,

Anyone who uses the products of modern technology without any knowledge of how they work or of how they were made, is like a person in a prison cell without a window through which one would at least be able to *look* at nature and freedom. (SE, p. 243)

Unless students are given the means to understand the world around them, especially the world created and shaped by human beings, they become listless, apathetic, and inured to antisocial conditions of daily life.

We can work against these things only by starting during the last stage of the lower school, by really not letting the fifteen, sixteen-year-olds leave school without at least some elementary ideas about the more important procedures taking place in life. We should teach them in a way that leaves them with a yearning to be curious and inquisitive at every opportunity about what is going on around them so that they use this curiosity and thirst for knowledge to add to whatever they already know. (PA, pp. 167–168)

In various high school courses, students therefore learn about the principles that underlie modern technology. Before they begin to use computers, for example, Waldorf students study electronics so they can understand how computers operate. They learn the mathematical principles that a computer utilizes and investigate the historical background and the industrial, economic, and social impact of computer technology.

In their practical arts courses, Waldorf high school students are taught skills and crafts that will deepen their understanding and appreciation of many of the physical processes of modern life.

Through the study of geometric and technical drawing, surveying, mechanics, metalwork, woodwork, basketry, fabric design and construction, and bookbinding, high school students develop their creativity and practicality. These courses help students to define themselves in new ways, teaching them to relate to the world not only through their thoughts and feelings, but through their will.

The Teacher's Task

High school teachers face immense challenges: to work with, to guide, and to inspire students who are undergoing a profound change in body and soul. In lecture 8 of *The Spiritual Ground of Education*, Steiner spoke in a stirring way about the qualities that allow the teacher to meet the needs of the developing child and maturing adolescent.

> One of the most essential things in training Waldorf school teachers is an openness to changes in human nature.... A Waldorf teacher must be prepared to find things from yesterday completely changed tomorrow. This is the real secret of a teacher's training. For example, in the evening one usually thinks, "Tomorrow the Sun will rise, and things will be just as they are today." Now, using a somewhat extreme means of expression may clarify what I mean. The Waldorf teacher must be ready for the Sun not to rise one day. Only when one views human nature anew in this way, without past bias, is it possible to apprehend growth and development in human beings. We may rest assured that things out in the universe will be somewhat conservative. But speaking of the transition in human nature from early childhood years into the fourteenth to sixteenth years, well, ladies and gentlemen, the sun that rose earlier often fails to rise. Here, in this microcosm—humankind in this *anthropos*—such a great change has happened that we face an entirely new situation, as though nature would one day confront us with a world of darkness, a world where our eyes were useless.

Openness and readiness to receiving new wisdom daily, a disposition that subdues past knowledge to a latent feeling that leaves the mind clear for the new—this is what keeps a person healthy, fresh, and active. And this heart—in openness to life's changes and its unexpected, continuous freshness— must form the essential mood and nature of a Waldorf teacher. (SG, pp. 125–126)

If high school teachers develop this perspective and these quali- ties, then they will truly be able to serve their students as they cross the threshold of adolescence.

Working with Adolescents

LECTURE BY RUDOLF STEINER

Stuttgart, June 16, 1921

Today we shall look at the characteristic features of fourteen- and fifteen-year-old children. We know from our anthroposophical studies that the astral body is born at this age—that it comes into its own at this time. Just as the physical body is especially active from birth to the seventh year, and the etheric body from the sev- enth to the fourteenth or fifteenth year, the astral body (strongly connected with the I) is active from the fourteenth to the twentieth or twenty-first year, when the I can be said to be born.

The fourteenth and fifteenth years are especially important in child development. You can see this importance in the looser con- nection between the astral body and the etheric and physical bodies. Every night, during sleep, we leave our physical and etheric bodies with our astral body and I. On the one side, our physical and etheric bodies are then closely linked; on the other side, we have a close connection between astral body and I. Because of this alternating separation and rejoining, there is a looser connection, on the one hand, between the astral and etheric bodies and, on the other hand, between the I and the physical body.

The transition for the human being at age fourteen or fifteen (earlier for girls) is different from the transition that takes place at seven years. At the change of teeth, when the children are ready for the elementary school, we have a situation that arises, as it were, quite objectively in the physical/corporeal outer nature of the human being, in that part that separates every day during sleep— an objective happening. During the transition at sexual maturity, the adolescent now relates his or her subjective life—the I and the astral body—to the objective sphere, to the etheric and physical bodies. In this transition, the inner (soul) life is affected quite differently than it is during the transition at the change of teeth. During the earlier transition, a physical/etheric connection takes place—which affects the subjective life. During the transition at puberty, the physical and etheric bodies remain as they are, and the astral body and I remain as they are, but there is now, in a certain sense, a different interaction between the two pairs. The physical/ corporeal and the etheric bodies, on the one hand, and the astral body and the I, on the other hand, participate in this transition with equal strength: The inner subjective qualities of the human being participate directly in this process.

The nature of this process accounts for the dramatic changes in character after puberty. The changes can be seen outwardly in a matured capacity for love, which does not immediately show itself in its full sexual form but does show itself, in a general way, in the more intimate, inner relationships in which the children attract each other. Friendships are formed between girls and boys in which the sexual aspects do not initially play a role; rather, the friendships show the beginning of a more conscious development of the forces of love, of the forces needed for relating to and caring for another being at this new stage in development.

We can then see, beginning at puberty, in the outer behavior of both girls and boys, something that often baffles their parents and teachers, something that contradicts their previous character: the teenagers' loutish behavior (especially in boys, differently in girls). This behavior is caused by the feelings of the astral body (which encloses the not yet fully developed I) as it struggles to experience a right relation to the physical body and, through it, to the whole of the environment. Because of the need to discover a relation between the objective and the subjective, this inner struggle is unavoidable. It expresses itself in a denial, as it were, of what the adolescent has so far developed. We sometimes do not recognize the teenagers—they are so different from what they used to be.

I need not go into detailed descriptions; we are all familiar with teenage behavior. But we must understand its nature, because of its significance for education.

What we see initially is that the astral body has a stronger influence in girls than in boys. Throughout life the astral body of women plays a more important role than that of men. The whole of the female organism is organized toward the cosmos through the astral body. Much of what are really cosmic mysteries are unveiled and revealed through the female constitution. The female astral body is more differentiated, essentially more richly structured, than that of the male. Men's astral bodies are less differentiated, less finely structured, coarser.

Girls between the ages of thirteen or fourteen and twenty or twenty-one develop in such a way that their I-being is strongly influenced by what goes on in their astral bodies. We can see how the I of a girl is, one could say, gradually absorbed by the astral body, with the result that during her twentieth and twenty-first years there is a strong counterpressure, a strong effort to come to grips with the I.

The process is essentially different in boys. Their astral bodies do not absorb their I so strongly. Their I-being is more concealed, is not as effective. The I of the boy between the ages of thirteen or fourteen and twenty or twenty-one remains without the strong influence of the astral body. Because of this, because the I of the boy is not absorbed by the astral body and yet lacks independence, boys at this age are less forward than girls. Girls are freer at this age, more at ease in their outer confrontation with the world than are boys. We can notice in those boys especially endowed with these qualities a reserve, a withdrawal from life, the result of this special relation between astral body and I.

Certainly, boys are looking for friendship, for some connection. But they also feel the need to hide their thoughts and feelings. This is characteristic of boys whose I-being is connected to the astral body in this way. Teachers who can empathize with this situation that is present in boys, who can meet it in a subtle, delicate way, will do much to help them. It is this manner of the teacher rather than a direct, crude approach that has a beneficial effect. The boy has a certain love of withdrawal into himself; if this love of withdrawing into himself is not present at this age in a boy we really ought to be cautious. A good teacher will notice this, and he or she will then take care. The teacher will reflect: "There is something I have to look for, something that isn't quite right, something that could cause problems and abnormalities in later life."

It is different with girls. With girls, there are delicate differences, for which it is necessary to develop a certain skill in observation. The girl's I is more or less absorbed by the astrality. Because of this, the girl lives less strongly in her inner being. She takes her I-permeated astral body into her etheric body. Her etheric body—that is, her behavior, her outer mobility—is strongly affected. We can observe in real girls—that is, in girls whose I-being is absorbed by the astral body, who develop in a healthy, correct way—a courageous, firm demeanor during this time. They accentuate their personalities, are self-assured, do not withdraw into themselves. It is natural for them to confront the world freely and unashamedly.

If this demeanor is accompanied by even faint egotistical feelings, it can express itself in showing off, in a wish to display character and personality. But it is characteristic for girls during this time to wish to confront the world in this free uninhibited way and to show their worth. Taken to an extreme, this wish can lead to coquetry and vanity, not only to the display of inner (soul) life but also to self-adornment with jewelry. It is extraordinarily interesting to observe how what later leads to an addiction to makeup and a trivial love of finery can show itself as a delicate esthetic sense during this time. All this is certainly the outward expression of the special relation of the I-permeated astral body to the etheric body: The girls walk differently, their posture changes, they hold their heads more freely. Again, taken to an extreme, they become supercilious, and so on. We should indeed observe these things artistically.

If we bear in mind these differences between boys and girls we shall understand that the blessing of coeducation allows us to achieve much by a tactful treatment of both sexes in the same room. A conscientious teacher who is aware of his or her tasks in approaching such a coeducational situation will still differentiate between girls and boys. We must thus also differentiate with regard to what is so important at this age, what I just now characterized—namely, the way the subjective element has developed in its relation to the outer world. At this age, we are to relate the subjective element to our own body, to the etheric and physical bodies. The condition for doing so is one's relation to the outer world as such.

This can be prepared during the whole of elementary education. It is the task of every teacher; it concerns every teacher. We must, in our lessons, see to it that the children experience the beautiful, artistic, and esthetic view of the world; and their ideas and mental pictures should be permeated by a religious / moral feeling. Such feelings, when they are cultivated throughout the elementary school years, will make all the difference during the thirteenth, fourteenth, and fifteenth years. A child whose feelings for the beautiful, or esthetic, view of the world have not been stimulated, will during puberty easily become overly sensual, even erotic. There is no better way of counteracting the erotic feelings than through the healthy development of the esthetic sense for the sublime and beautiful in nature. If you succeed in making the children feel deeply the beauty, the colors, in sunrise and sunset, in the flowers, experience the sublime splendor of a thunderstorm—if, as it were, you cultivate in them the esthetic sense— you will do more for them than is done by the often absurdly practiced sex education given to children at an ever younger age. It is the feeling for the beautiful, an esthetic confrontation with the world, that counteracts the erotic feeling. By experiencing the world as beautiful, the human being will also attain the right, healthy relation to his or her body, will not be tormented by it, as happens in eroticism.

It is most important during puberty that the children have developed certain moral, religious feelings. Such feelings also strengthen the astral body and I. They become weak if the religious, moral feelings and impulses have been neglected. The children then turn indolent, as though physically paralyzed. This will show itself especially during the years we are now discussing. The lack of moral and ethical impulses also leads to irregularities in the sexual life.

We must consider the differences between girls and boys in our education leading up to this age. We must make the effort to develop the girls' moral and ethical feelings in such a way that they are directed toward the esthetic life. We must take special care that the girls especially enjoy the moral, the religious, and the good in what they hear in the lessons. They should take pleasure in the knowledge that the world is permeated by the supersensible; they should be given pictures that are rich in imagination, that express the world as permeated by the divine, that show the beautiful aspects of the good and moral human being.

In regard to boys, it will be necessary to provide them with ideas and mental pictures that tend toward strength and affect the religious and ethical life. With girls, we should bring the religious and moral life to their very eyes, while with boys we should bring the religious and beautiful predominantly into the heart, the mind, stressing the feeling of strength that radiates from them. Naturally, we must not take these things to an extreme, should not think of making the girls into esthetic kittens that regard everything merely esthetically. Nor should the boys be made into mere louts, as would be the inevitable result of their egotisms being engendered through an unduly strong feeling of their strength—which we ought to awaken, but only by connecting it to the good, the beautiful, and the religious.

We must prevent the girls from becoming superficial, from

becoming unhealthy, sentimental connoisseurs of beauty during their teenage years. And we must prevent the boys from turning into hooligans. These dangers do exist. We must know the reality of these tendencies and must, during the whole of elementary education, see to it that the girls are directed to experience pleasure in the beautiful, to be impressed by the religious and esthetic aspects of the lessons; and we must see to it that the boys are told: "If you do this, your muscles will grow taut, you will become a strong, efficient young man!" The sense of being permeated by the divine must really be kindled in boys in this way.

These now emerging special qualities are indeed founded—very delicately—in human nature. With regard to girls, the I is absorbed in the astral body. This, of course, expresses the situation in a radical and extreme way, but doing so will help you to have a picture of it. There is something in this spiritual/soul process that is akin to physical blushing. The whole development during this time is really a blushing of spirit and soul. The invasion of the I into the astral body is a kind of blushing.

The situation is different in boys. The boy's I is less mobile, does not absorb itself; we are dealing with a spirit and soul growing pale. This situation is easily noticed, is always present. The physical aspects must not deceive us here. When a girl is chlorotic (maidpale), the condition fully corresponds to the blushing of spirit and soul. When a boy turns into a real lout who easily gets excited, this behavior does not contradict the fact that his soul and spirit are growing pale.

This is basically the expression of a new experience or feeling that takes hold of the whole being: the feeling of shame or embarrassment. It permeates the whole being and consists of the feeling: "I must have something in my individual, inner life that is mine, that I do not wish to share with anyone else; I must have secrets." This is the nature of shame or embarrassment. And this feeling reaches every part of the spiritual life and the soul, as far as the most unconscious regions.

If, as teachers and educators, we can feel this development, if we can respect this in our own inner life, and if we then walk past a girl or boy with this delicate feeling in us, a feeling that respects this inwardly reposing feeling of shame—this will already have an effect. There is no need for words. When we move among a group of children with the feeling that there is something in them they wish to conceal, to preserve—like an unopened flower—then the unspoken effect of one person on another will be soon noticed. To live with just such a feeling will already have a tremendous educational effect.

It is a strange fact that in spite of the children's outer manifestations and behavior, everything they do is nothing other than a modified feeling of shame or embarrassment. A girl who blushes in soul and spirit, has an air of confidence, shows herself to the world, confronts it unabashedly. It is peculiar to human nature that the outer manifestation contradicts the inner disposition during this time—this unabashed bearing, this bold confrontation with the world, this rebellious nature, this demand: "I will be treated fairly!" Anyone familiar with girls' boarding schools can tell you this. They don't accept unfair treatment; they insist on being treated fairly. They can now confront a teacher, will show her or him what's what. "We shall not be made use of!" All this is basically nothing other than—let me say—the other side of what reposes quite unconsciously deep down in their soul life as a kind of feeling of shame.

And the boys: The loutish behavior at first, then their rudeness and churlishness during the later teenage years are really nothing other than their reluctance to show the world what they actually are. Wishing to make contact, they move clumsily, lounge about, behave differently from what they actually are. This we ought to consider—boys at this age, due to their special constitution, behave differently from what they really are. They copy other people. While the child during the first seven years imitates naturally, the teenager does so consciously. He imitates somebody in his walk, in his speech, in his rudeness, makes an effort to copy a gentleman. All this expresses his wish to make contact with the world outside—a special characteristic of teenagers. It is basically the embarrassment of revealing their own being, the withdrawal into themselves, the pretense of being different from what they really are.

The worst thing a teacher can do at this time is to confront teen-age boys without humor. The proper humor consists in showing an interest in what they are up to, yet making it clear to them that you, the teacher, do not take it too seriously. You ought to develop these two ways of dealing with the situation. If you allow yourselves to be nettled by the boys' behavior, if you get into a rage, you will lose their respect. If you behave like the teacher who reacted to the boorish behavior of the boys by starting to shout: "If you don't shut up, I'll throw the duster at you!"—the children will no longer respect you.

A different method applies to the girls. The teacher ought to react to their coquetry with a certain delicate grace and then, speaking metaphorically, turn away: gracefully to pay attention, as it were, to what they are doing and, at the same time not to let them notice that one is affected by it. We allow them to exhaust their rage, especially the saucy, impertinent ones. We then leave them to themselves. With the boys, we empathize more with their loutish, rude behavior, at the same time showing them that we don't take it all too seriously, that we laugh a little, but not too much, so that they do not need to be cross.

What matters is that we develop a feeling for meeting the children's needs at this age and that we realize that each child is different. The outer manifestations are those of a metamorphosed feeling of shame or embarrassment that permeates the whole being. We prepare—and we must do so—the children correctly for their life in their twenties by recognizing the fact that the subjective element connects with the astral body in an independent way. Just as the human body needs a solid bone system to prevent it from sagging, so does the astral body, with its enclosed I, need ideals at this age if it is to develop in a healthy way. We must take this seriously. Ideals, strong concepts that are permeated with will, these we must impart into the astral body as a firm, solid support.

We can notice that boys especially feel a strong need at this age—we only have to discover this and understand it correctly—for: "Everybody must choose his own hero, whom he has to follow on his way to Mt. Olympus." And it is especially important for us to present to the boys a fine ideal, a picturesque personality, be it a mythical character or a merely imaginative one, and to elaborate it, together with the boys, or to provide the elements for such elaboration. During a field trip we could have a conversation with one or another of the boys, entering his particular needs. We could say to him: "How would you do this or that?" We point to the future, introduce the idea of purpose, of the aims in life. We, as it were, stiffen the astral body, make it firm—and this is important at this age.

The same applies to girls. If we make use of this knowledge, we shall also educate the girls correctly by recognizing the fact that they are more inclined to the cosmos and boys more inclined to the Earth. Girls incline more toward the cosmic, and this means that their ideals are heroes and heroines; we should tell the girls about them, about their lives and deeds, about actual experiences. Boys need to hear about character, about complete human beings. This is essential; we must differentiate the needs of girls and boys.

It is important during this age to introduce to the students the world outside, so that they come to grips with and understand life as such. It is especially important for us to know this at the time when we are adding the tenth grade class to our school. Our lessons must be directed to the point where the subjective may connect with the objective. And this is certainly not possible if we limit ourselves to the curricula currently practiced in the conventional high schools—because their curricula are the result of the influence of the intellectual world conception. You see, this merely formalistic way of educating our high school students, this one-sidedly cognitive, intellectual approach, this is something we should not continue with in our curriculum. And in not continuing this approach we shall not sin against progress in civilization.

Our curriculum should be such that it allows the children to become practical in life; it should connect them with the world. Our curriculum for the tenth grade class will, therefore, be based on the following: We must, in order to do justice to the social life, have girls and boys together in the room; but we must differentiate by giving them activities suited to their sex. We must not separate them. The boys should watch the girls during their activities and vice versa. There should be a social communication. We should also include the process that takes the thoughts from the head into the movements of the hand, even if this happens to be merely learned or theoretical. It must, as it were, be then a theory of the practical. It is, therefore, necessary to give the boys something that is appropriate for this age: lessons in mechanics—not only theory, as in physics, but practical mechanics, leading to the making of machines. Our curriculum for the tenth grade class must include the basic elements of practical mechanics.

In regard to the girls, we must provide them with something that allows them to have clear ideas of the skills involved in spinning and weaving. Girls must learn to understand the processes in spinning and weaving, must learn how spun and woven material is produced; they must learn to recognize a material that was mechanically produced, must be introduced to the mechanical processes and learn to relate to them. This belongs to this age group.

The boys, on the other hand, must, even if only in an elementary way that allows them to understand it, be taught the principles of surveying and mapping a pasture or forest. This is again essential for this age. Girls must learn the basic elements of hygiene and first aid, the different ways of bandaging.

Both sexes must participate in all these activities. Spinning, weaving, hygiene, and first aid are taught to the girls; the boys will do this later. And the girls must observe the boys handling the surveyance instruments. We can do this in the Waldorf School, can get the boys to draw a precise map of a certain area.

In short, we shall awaken in our students an understanding of what must be done in life if it is to go on. Without such an understanding, we continue to live in a foreign environment.

This, in fact, is the terrible characteristic of our time—that people are living in an environment that is foreign to them. You only have to walk into the street and take a good look at the people boarding a street car or bus. How many of them actually know how this street car is set in motion, know about the natural forces necessary for it? This has an effect on the whole human constitution—

spirit, soul, and body. There is a great difference between having at least an elementary knowledge of the things we use in daily life and not having such knowledge. Traveling in a car, plane, or bus, using an electrical gadget without understanding at least the underlying principles, means blindness of soul and spirit. Just as a blind person is moving through life without experiencing the effects of light, so do people move blindly through the cultural life, because they cannot see, did not have the opportunity to learn to see and understand, the objects around them. This is a defect of spirit and soul. And the damages we see in our advanced civilizations are the result of people's blindness in regard to their environment.

There is something else we have to consider: There is a great difference between learning something before and learning something after the age of nineteen or twenty. People generally learn a trade like surveying at nineteen or later. High school education, especially in grammar schools, does not include such practical subjects. But the long-term effect depends on it. What we learn after the nineteenth year impresses itself more outwardly; what we learn and experience at fifteen permeates our whole being, becomes as one with the human spirit, so that it is not merely a job we can manage, but a job we can identify with, in which our entire being participates. This applies also to the elementary aspects of mechanics, engineering, and the subjects I mentioned in regard to the education of girls.

We must insist on cultivating in our students such feelings and inner qualities that can then live and grow as their limbs are growing. Human development does not proceed by fixing two arms to the body—during the third seven-year period—two arms that then remain the way they are; they must continue to grow. Today's endeavors are such that the students are instructed in a way that what they are learning cannot continue to live but remains unchanged throughout life. The things we learn must continue to live in us. This is only possible if they are learned at the right age. And we have to admit that somebody whose specific skills direct him or her to a certain occupation and who then bases his training on something he already knows—this building on something one already knows will have a tremendous significance for the whole of life.

I have always valued the lectures given by the anatomist Hyrtl. His subject was descriptive and topographical anatomy. Hyrtl belonged to the older generation. He demanded that his students read the relevant chapters in his excellent books prior to the lectures, and he emphasized the fact that he did not wish to lecture on a subject the students had not previously read about. He did this with so much charm that he managed to make his students see the value of this method, and even the lazier ones among them conformed to his wishes—a remarkable achievement, as most of you will appreciate.

··· ···

Translator's note: The difference between students is today no longer understood as necessarily sexually determined—as a difference between boys and girls. Some boys tend to a female astral/I constitution, and some girls to a male astral/I constitution. In most Waldorf schools the students may decide which practical subjects they wish to take. The principle remains: doing activities and observing the other students' activities.

8

THE ARTS IN WALDORF EDUCATION

The Jewels in the Crown

THE ARTS hold a central place in the curriculum of the Waldorf school, for through the arts the whole human being is engaged. Art allows students to experience a subject not only with their intellects, but through their feelings and their will; in this way, art enhances and lends deeper meaning to every subject.

The arts nourish the development of the child's etheric and astral bodies. According to Rudolf Steiner, the pictorial and sculptural arts have a particular connection with the etheric body; the musical and poetical arts are connected to the astral body. In lecture 3 of *The Child's Changing Consciousness*, Steiner states:

> After the change of teeth is complete, all of the forces working through the child are striving toward inwardly mobile imagery, and we will support this picture-forming element if we use a pictorial approach in whatever we bring to the child. And then, between the ninth and tenth years, something truly remarkable begins to occur; the child feels a greater relationship to the musical element. The child wants to be held by music and rhythms much more than before. (CCC, p. 58)

Until puberty, these sculptural and musical forces build up and refine the inner organization of the child's body; after puberty, they become available for the activity of thinking.

The arts are also a path of knowledge. They allow human beings to experience their higher self and to learn to perceive the workings of the spirit in the world.

Art is not a mere human discovery, but a domain wherein the secrets of nature are revealed at a level other than that of ordinary intelligence—a domain where we gaze into the mysteries of the whole universe. Not until the moment when individuals realize that the world itself is a work of art and think of nature as a creative artist—not until then is one's being ready for a deepening in the religious sense. (MA, p. 195)

Throughout the grades, Waldorf students study painting, drawing, modeling, music, speech, drama, and eurythmy. Each of these arts develops specific capacities, and each of them allows Waldorf students to come to know and understand themselves and the world.

Painting

During the elementary grades, Waldorf students usually paint on damp paper with liquid watercolors. Such colors are particularly pure, delicate, and luminous, and the process of working with them nourishes the senses. When students paint, the physical experience of color evokes a soul response that develops the students' inner sense for the nature and nuances of the colors and their combinations. Whereas the experience of color is partly subjective, since each person responds differently to the various colors, Steiner indicates that we can also learn to experience colors more objectively. When we do, we discover that each color has its characteristic quality to which most people respond similarly. In the lecture below, Steiner characterizes the contrasting natures of blue and red, and he describes how one might choose colors to express or evoke certain moods.

By working with fluid colors, children are also able to remain in the realm of color relationships without having to plan or determine how those colors should be formed. In lecture 8 of *The Spiritual Ground of Education*, Steiner speaks about the importance of painting with liquid colors and the value of nonrepresentational painting.

Then children come to feel how one color goes with another, they feel the inner harmony of colors and experience them inwardly. Even if this is difficult and inconvenient ... one may make enormous progress when children develop a direct relationship to color in this way and learn to paint from the living nature of color itself, rather than trying to copy something naturalistically. Colored areas and form seem to come onto the paper on their own. Thus, at Waldorf schools, children initially paint their experience of color. It's a matter of placing one color next to another, or enclosing one color within others. In this way children enter into the color, and little by little, they begin to produce form from color on their own.... The point is not to try to paint some *thing*, but to paint the experience of color; painting an object comes much later. If children begin to paint things too soon, a sense for living reality is lost and is replaced by a sense for what is dead. (SG, pp. 102)

Throughout the grades, painting primarily serves as a form of expression rather than a means of representation. When they first begin to paint, students experience the harmony of colors, and they learn to use color to convey the mood of a story, or to portray the experiences and adventures of red, blue, and yellow. As they become more experienced, students learn how to develop form out of color, and their paintings allow them to express the form and gesture of animals, plants, and minerals. By the upper grades and in the high school, students are able to work with color perspective, light and shadow, and complementary colors to depict landscapes and express nature's moods.

Drawing

Drawing is also taught throughout the grades, both in art classes and as part of the main lesson work. In the early grades, students draw with crayons; in the middle grades they begin to work with colored pencils; and in the upper grades and high school they also draw with charcoal and sometimes with pastels. While painting nourishes the students' faculty of feeling through the experience of color, drawing can develop the faculty of thinking through the experience of form and line. According to Steiner, the process of drawing can become a deadening experience:

> Plain drawing has something untrue about it. The most true is the feeling that comes from the color itself; less true is the feeling that comes from light and dark; and the least true is drawing. Drawing as such approaches the abstract element in nature as something that is dying. We should really draw only in such a way that we are aware of drawing essentially what is dead. And we should paint with colors in such a way that we are aware of invoking the living out of the dead. (p. 289)

To illustrate how drawing tends toward the abstract, Steiner demonstrates how to represent a horizon. If we simply draw a horizon as a line, we are drawing an abstraction, for there are no lines, as such, in nature. The horizon is the boundary where earth and sky or sea and sky meet, so if we want to represent the horizon truthfully, we should draw the colors of land, sea, or sky. Where they meet, the line of the horizon will arise. Steiner suggests that if children can be taught how to draw so that they let forms arise out of color and let lines arise out of the meeting of colors, they will be enlivened and will develop a truer relationship to the external world.

Drawing not only refines the students' perceptions and powers of observation, it also deepens their experience of the curriculum. Through the pictures drawn by students in their art classes and main lesson books, they are better able to express and illustrate the subjects they have studied.

In addition to illustrative drawing, Waldorf students practice form drawing and geometric drawing, both of which require and develop accurate observation, full concentration, and a great deal of coordination. Before learning their letters in first grade, students practice drawing straight and curved lines in many different combinations. Once they become adept at drawing simpler forms and patterns, students in the lower grades work with vertical and horizontal symmetry. They will draw a form on one side and its reflection on the other. In later grades, students draw increasingly complicated shapes and patterns, which develop a sense for harmony, symmetry, movement, countermovement, repetition, and the transformation of forms. In the upper elementary grades, students are introduced to geometric drawing and perspective drawing, and in the high school they learn technical drawing and projective geometry. All of these studies develop the students' imaginations, their sense of spatial relationships, and their mobility of thought.

Modeling and Sculpture

Modeling is taught throughout the grades. In the early grades students use beeswax, in later grades they work with clay and wood and may even learn to carve stone. Modeling enhances a child's experience of the curriculum. By modeling animals as part of their nature study, for instance, fourth graders gain a much more detailed experience of the animals' forms and defining characteristics. By sculpting human figures, high school students gain a much deeper appreciation of the sublime proportions of the human form.

In Steiner's view, modeling has a wonderfully vitalizing effect on the child's physical and inner sight. In lecture 11 of *A Modern Art of Education*, he laments the fact that so many people go through life without noticing even the most significant objects and events in their environment. In order that children learn to observe properly, Steiner says,

> it is very good that they begin as early as possible to model, to guide what they have observed with the head and eyes into hand and finger movements. In this way we not only awaken the children's taste for what is artistic around them—in the arrangement of a room, for example—and a distaste for the inartistic. They will begin to observe the things in the world that should flow into the human heart and soul. (MA, p. 192)

Modeling deepens the students' awareness of the world around them and refines their sense for the relationship of the practical and the esthetic in the physical objects of daily life. Too many of the objects in our lives are impractical or ugly, yet most of us are unconscious of the deadening effect that they exercise on our souls. Waldorf schools work against this modern trend by creating a beautiful working and learning environment. As they work and learn in this environment, the students' sense of beauty is developed, which helps them become adults who are able to bring human qualities into practical life. In lecture 14 of *Soul Economy and Waldorf Education*, Steiner states:

> All this has an important bearing on social issues, which must be tackled from many different angles. Few people are aware of this today. It is certainly possible that all the ugliness around us in almost every European city (you must admit that from an esthetic viewpoint we are surrounded, to a large extent, by all kinds of atrocities in almost every large city) could gradually be transmuted if for a few generations we cultivate the sense of beauty living unspoiled in every child. (SE, p. 253)

Music and Poetry

Music and poetry foster the social life and strengthen the sense of community within the class and the school. While the pictorial and sculptural arts deepen our experience of ourselves as individuals, the musical and poetic arts bring people together.

Music is related to the astral body, the body of feeling and expression. According to Steiner, the very forms of our bodies are shaped out of music.

> Everything happening in nature is permeated with hidden music—an earthly projection of the *music of the spheres*. Indeed, every plant and animal incorporates a tone of the music of the spheres. This is also true of the human body; the

music of the spheres still lives in the forms such as the body, but it no longer lives in human speech, the expression of the soul. Children absorb all of this unconsciously, which is why children are so musical. (BT, p. 19)

Between the change of teeth and puberty, when the astral body is slowly being liberated, music is particularly important, for it aids in this emancipation.

Like every subject in the Waldorf school, the music curriculum addresses and mirrors the stages of child development. In the earliest grades, children are naturally musical and they readily imitate whatever they hear. At this stage, teachers try to lead their students into an experience of the beauty and purity of tone through singing in unison. In lecture 6 of *The Kingdom of Childhood*, Steiner describes how to approach singing classes with young children.

> You must have a feeling that the child is a musical instrument while he is singing, you must stand before your class to whom you are teaching singing or music with the clear feeling: every child is a musical instrument and inwardly feels a kind of well-being in sound....
>
> Sound is brought about by the particular way the breath is circulated. That is inner music. To begin with, in the first seven years of life, the child learns everything through imitation, but should now learn to sing out of the inward joy experienced through building up melodies and rhythms. (KC, p. 96)

After the ninth-year change, students are able to relate to music more consciously. While children in the early grades are deeply affected by and caught up in musical rhythm and beat, students in the middle grades begin to experience these aspects of music as existing outside of themselves. Prior to the third grade, children dwell more in the realm of melody. After age nine, they are ready for rounds and catches, where everyone still sings the same melody, but because groups enter at different times, harmony is created. In the upper grades, students learn to sing songs with three and four parts.

This requires them to be able to hold their own part while listening to and harmonizing with the other parts, and it strengthens their ability to work as individuals within a group.

While singing primarily develops the feeling life of the child, instrumental instruction works more directly on the will. In Waldorf schools, all children, even those who at first seem unmusical, learn to play musical instruments. The process of playing an instrument helps children become more objective by teaching them to listen to, evaluate, and adjust the tones they are creating. In lecture 6 of *The Kingdom of Childhood*, Steiner states:

> As far as circumstances allow, each child should learn to play an instrument. As early as possible the children should come to feel what it means for their own musical being to flow over into the objective instrument....
>
> If you can, you should choose a wind instrument, as the children will learn most from this and will thereby gradually come to understand music ... it is a wonderful thing in the child's life when this whole configuration of the air, which otherwise is enclosed and held along the nerve-fibers, can now be extended and guided. The human being feels the whole organism being enlarged. Processes that are otherwise only within the organism are carried over into the outside world. (KC, p. 98–99)

When children play instruments in ensemble, they must learn to match, blend, and harmonize the sounds they make with those of others. Through this process of reflecting on and objectifying their experience, children learn to consider themselves in relation to others, which in turn fosters and strengthens the social life of the class and of the school.

Music instruction through the grades includes sight singing, ear training, music theory, and music appreciation, all of which call upon and develop the students' thinking. In the earliest grades children simply experience and imitate music, but beginning in the third grade, they learn musical notation and are taught how to take musical dictation. The music curriculum of the upper elementary grades and high school introduces students to the structural and technical aspects of music, which allows them develop musical taste and judgment. In high school, students have a main lesson course on history through music, where they learn how the development of music through the ages reflects and expresses the evolution of society.

The arts of poetry and speech also foster the social life. In the lecture below, Steiner states:

> Poetry is conceived only through a solitary soul; but it is comprehended through human community. It is entirely concrete—not at all abstract—to assert that a person's inner being is revealed through the poetry created, and that this is met by the deepest inner being of another human being who takes in that created work. Consequently, a delight in music and poetry, as well as a yearning for them, should be encouraged in the growing child. (p. 294)

In the lower grades, children should be introduced to poetry through its musical elements: beat, rhythm, and rhyme. The content, imagery, and meaning of a poem need not be stressed. Steiner urges that recitation, even in the upper grades, remain closely linked to the musical element, for the artistic presentation of verse is of paramount importance.

The musical and poetic arts harmonize the human being, bringing us into relation with the harmony of the world. Whereas "in the sculptural and pictorial realm we look at beauty, and we live it; in the musical realm we ourselves become beauty" (p. 297). Although there are many examples of the pictorial and sculptural arts from ancient times, little of their musical arts have come down to us. This gives us the impression that music is something that is still in the process of becoming.

> In all sculptural and pictorial art, people have been imitators of the old celestial order. The highest imitation of a cosmic celestial order is an imitation of the world in sculpture or

painting. But in music humans themselves are the creators. What they create does not come from what is already there, but lays the foundation and firm ground for what is to arise in the future. (p. 297)

The musical and poetic arts are highly developed in their own right all through the grades. They are also encompassed and brought to fuller expression by the art of eurythmy.

Eurythmy

Eurythmy is an art of movement inaugurated by Rudolf Steiner early in this century. During the past eighty years it has been developed as a performance art, as a subject taught in Waldorf schools, and as a form of movement therapy for many types of physical and psychological disorders. *Eurythmy*, which in Greek means "beautiful rhythm," strives to make visible the soul and spirit of language and music through human movement.

As a young man, Steiner edited the scientific writings of the great German poet and scientist, Johann Wolfgang von Goethe. Steiner was deeply impressed and influenced by Goethe, especially by Goethe's perception of how the parts of a living organism express the whole. In Goethe's work with plants, he showed how every part of a plant—root, shoot, stem, leaf, bud, flower, and seed—is a metamorphosis of the primal plant form: the leaf. Steiner perceived this principle in the human speech organs, and in an introduction to a eurythmy performance he states:

> In a remarkable way, everything related to the human vocal organs (the larynx and nearby parts) is a miniature image of the entire structure of the human organism. The complete organic human structure may be found, in the form of cartilage, in the larynx and its neighboring organs. (IE, p. 23)

Goethe also believed that through art human beings could reveal the secrets of nature that lie concealed from our sense perception and our everyday consciousness. The art of eurythmy reveals the invisible forces working through the speech organs. In lecture 6 of *The Renewal of Education*, Steiner states:

> The origin of this art of movement (if I may use Goethe's expression) is based on the perception of the sensible and supersensible activities of the larynx, palate, and lips. According to Goethe's principle of metamorphosis, the movement of a single organ is projected outward, so that the whole human being is engaged. Goethe was also able to see the entire plant as a modified, though complicated, leaf. Similarly, we may see, in all of the self-willed human movements, the representation of the tendencies toward movement (though not the actual movement itself) of the human larynx, palate, and lips. In this sense, a person doing eurythmy becomes a living, moving larynx. (RE, p. 79)

Steiner illuminated these points in another introduction to a eurythmy performance.

> All that can be perceived by supersensible vision—all that can be learned in this way about the nature of these forms and gestures of the air—can be carried into the movements of the arms and hands, and into movements of the whole human being. Thus, the actual counterpart of speech arises in visible form. One may use the entire human body in such a way that it really does the movements otherwise done by the organs related to speech and music. Visible speech and visible music arise in this way—in other words, the art of eurythmy. (LE, p. 16)

Speech and Tone Eurythmy

Speech eurythmy strives to make visible the forces that are working in the human being through language. When we speak, we are constantly expressing the state of our souls. Each sound we make, each word we speak has a soul gesture, which the eurythmist tries to express. According to Steiner, vowels are intimately connected to our feelings. We express wonder, for example, with a long "Ah" and confrontation or resistance with a short "Ay!" The eurythmy gestures for these sounds express these feelings. Consonants, on the other hand, reflect external reality, so the eurythmy gestures for the consonants are more like pictures of things in the world. In eurythmy, whole words, phrases, and sentences can also be depicted through gestures or through series of movements. Because poetry contains so many musical elements, it is well suited to expression through speech eurythmy. The speaker for a performance stresses a poem's rhythm, rhyme, and alliteration to bring out the poem's inner meaning.

Tone eurythmy expresses the tones, intervals, melodies, harmonies, and rhythms of music, as well as the qualities of various instruments, through forms and movements. A two-part invention by Johann Sebastian Bach, for example, might be performed by two eurythmists, one expressing through movement the upper voice, the other the lower. The interweaving of their spatial forms or patterns would clarify the relationship of the two voices through the piece, and their gestures would bring out at times the melodic, at times the harmonic aspect of each voice. In a large orchestral work, such as Franz Schubert's "Unfinished Symphony," groups of eurythmists would carry the voices of different groups of instruments.

Although tone eurythmists move to music, they do not dance with or to the music. The movements are in fact a kind of parallel creation of the music.

> Eurythmy is music translated into movement, and is not dancing in any sense of the word. There is a fundamental difference between eurythmy and dance. People nevertheless often fail to make this distinction when seeing eurythmy on the stage, because eurythmy uses the human body in motion as its instrument.... Accompanied as it is by instrumental music, [tone eurythmy] is clearly distinguishable from ordinary dancing. Essentially, tone eurythmy is not dancing but

singing through movement, which may be done either by a single performer or by many together. (LE, p. 26)

Eurythmy in Education

Because eurythmy encompasses the arts of both music and poetry, it is an ideal subject for students of every age. Although Steiner characterized eurythmy as a kind of "ensouled gymnastics," he distinguished between these two forms of physical education. Gymnastics tends to be somewhat one-sided, since it works primarily on the physical body. Eurythmy also works with the body, but it penetrates far deeper. Every movement is ensouled and permeated with feeling and meaning. In lecture 12 of *A Modern Art of Education*, Steiner contrasts gymnastics and eurythmy.

> In the ordinary gymnastic exercise human beings lend themselves to space; in eurythmy we move in a way that expresses our being according to the principles of our organism. To allow what is within to express itself outwardly in movement is the essence of eurythmy. To fill the outer with the human being, so that the human being is united with the outer world, is the essence of gymnastics. (p. 207)

Eurythmy teaches students to use their bodies as expressive instruments, and it brings balance, harmony, and grace into their movements. It also helps them to work together with others. The execution of a group form—such as a five-pointed star created by five people moving all at once—requires both coordination and cooperation. Eurythmy classes enhance and support the curriculum throughout the grades. The letters that students have learned through pictures and sounds can be rendered through gesture; the geometric shapes that they have drawn can be created in space. Through eurythmy, grammar—including punctuation, syntax, the types of sentences, the parts of speech and parts of the sentence—can take on new life and meaning. Through eurythmy, students can learn to express the characteristic qualities of animals, the gestures of plants, the forms of minerals, and the cosmic movements of the heavenly bodies.

Eurythmy brings students into direct perception of the poetic meters, and it helps them to distinguish and express the qualities of the lyric, epic, and dramatic poetical forms. It also develops the students' understanding and appreciation of music. In the early grades, children move to different musical rhythms and learn how to articulate the structure of musical compositions. As they become better able to perceive the subtler aspects of music, students learn how to express the different tones, intervals, and scales. By representing the different voices or the melody and harmony of a composition, students develop their capacity for musical discernment and judgment.

Through eurythmy, students experience a living synthesis of speech and music expressed through the whole human being in body, soul, and spirit. Steiner beautifully expresses this:

In music one lives in a sea of flowing spirit, so to speak. In speech, it is as though one has reached the shore of such a spiritual sea. Imagination lives on the shore between water and earth. Now, when we come out of the water and give ourselves entirely to the sensory world while perceiving the spirit in it, we reach something that does not become speech but can only be represented by signs that originate within us. We reach eurythmy.

Deep within us an artistic, musical activity weaves and shapes our feeling realm. Somewhat nearer to the periphery, a poetic activity shapes our world of ideas into artistic language. Beyond the periphery, beyond our world of ideas, we have already left ourselves to live in perception. What we experience in perception—not physically but spiritually—is contained in eurythmy. (IE, pp. 90–91)

Education through Art

LECTURE BY RUDOLF STEINER

Stuttgart, August 23, 1919

I have already pointed out that our teaching should proceed from a certain artistic formative quality, so that the child's whole being, especially the will life, can be stimulated to activity in the lessons. Based on our previous discussions, you will not find it difficult to understand how important such measures are. You will also be able to understand that we must give continuous attention to the fact that there is something dead in the human being, something that is dying that must be transformed into something newly alive. When we approach the beings of nature and the world at large, simply observing with our understanding through mental images, we place ourselves within a dying process. If, on the other hand, we approach them with our will, we stand within an enlivening process. As educators it is our task to constantly quicken what is dead and to protect what approaches death in the human being from dying entirely. Indeed, we must fructify this dying with the quickening element we develop out of the will. Therefore, we must not be apprehensive about starting right from the beginning—while the children are still young—with a certain artistic form in our lessons.

Everything artistic that flows toward humankind is divided into two streams—the sculptural, pictorial stream and the musical, poetic stream. These two streams of art, the sculptural and pictorial and the musical and poetic, are indeed polar opposites, though precisely because of their polarity they are also especially capable of a higher synthesis, a higher union. You realize, of course, that in world evolution this duality in the artistic realm finds expression even in terms of race. You need only remind yourselves of certain writings of Heinrich Heine[1] that draw attention to a certain duality:

---

1. Heinrich Heine (1797–1856); one of the greatest German lyric poets and an outstanding satirist and publicist.

All that has emanated from the Greek peoples or is related to them, all that has grown from the being of the Greek peoples in a manner suited to their race, is in the most exalted sense disposed toward the sculptural, pictorial formation of the world; and all that emanates from the Jewish element is disposed toward the musical element of the world. Thus we find these two streams divided even racially; those who are receptive to such things will have no difficulty in tracing this in the history of art.

Naturally, and quite justifiably, there are always efforts to unite the musical with the sculptural and pictorial, but they can only be entirely united in eurythmy, when it is fully developed so that the musical and the visible become one. I mean of course the ultimate aims of eurythmy, not the beginnings of eurythmy we are working with now. We must, then, take into account that there is in the totality of harmonious human nature a sculptural, pictorial element toward which the human will tends to be oriented. How can we properly characterize this tendency in the human being to become sculptural and pictorial?

If we were solely beings of understanding, if we observed the world only through our mental pictures, we would gradually become walking corpses; here on Earth we would indeed give the impression of dying beings. We save ourselves from this mortality only by feeling in ourselves the urge to quicken what is dying in concepts with our sculptural and pictorial imagination. If you wish to be true educators, you must guard against making everything abstractly uniform. Thus you must not allow yourselves to think you should not develop the death processes in the human being and should therefore avoid training the conceptual world of ideas in the children. This would be the same mistake in the realm of soul and spirit that doctors would make if they were to observe cultural evolution as though they were great pedagogues and then pronounce: The bones are the dying part of the human being; let us therefore guard people against this dying element by endeavoring to keep the bones living and soft. The opinion of such physicians would lead to a population of rickety human beings unable to fulfil their tasks properly. It is always wrong to proceed like the many theosophists and anthroposophists who say that we must guard against the influences of Ahriman and Lucifer because they damage human nature and development. This would lead to the exclusion from the human being of everything that ought to constitute it.

We cannot prevent the education of the conceptual, thinking element; we must educate it, but we must also never fail at other times to approach the nature of the child through the sculptural and pictorial element. Out of this, unity will arise; it will not arise by extinguishing one element but by developing both side by side. In this respect people today cannot yet think in terms of unity, which is why they cannot understand the threefold order of the social organism.[2] In social life it is entirely right for the spiritual, the economic, and the rights spheres to stand side by side; unity will then come about, instead of being constructed abstractly. Imagine what it would mean if people thought that, because the head is a unit and the rest of the body also, the human being really ought not to exist, and that we could form the head away from the rest of the human being and let it move about the world freely! We follow the creativity of nature only when we allow the whole to arise out of all the one-sided parts.

So it is a matter of developing, on one side, mental, conceptual education and, on the other side, the sculptural, pictorial element, which quickens what is unfolded in the merely conceptual. We are concerned, in this age that always seeks to destroy consciousness, with raising these things into our awareness without losing our naivete. We need not lose it if we build things up in a concrete and not an abstract way. It would be very good if we started as early as possible with the sculptural, pictorial element, letting the children live in the world of color, and also if we as teachers steeped ourselves in what Goethe presents in the didactic part of *Theory of Colors*,[3] which is based on his permeation of each individual color with

2. See *Towards Social Renewal: Basic Issues of the Social Question*, Rudolf Steiner Press, Bristol, 1992.
3. See Maria Schindler, *Pure Colour*, Rudolf Steiner Press, London, 1989, which contains Goethe's "Theory of Colour."

a nuance of feeling. Thus he emphasizes the challenging nature of red, stressing not only what the eye sees but also what the soul feels in the red. Similarly he emphasizes the stillness and absorption the soul feels in blue. It is possible, without piercing their naivete, to lead the children into the world of color in a way that lets the feeling nuances of this world emerge in a living way. If at first the result is a big mess, it will be a good educational measure to train the child to be less messy.

We should introduce the children to colors as early as possible, and it is good to let them use colored paints on colored as well as white surfaces. And we should endeavor to awaken in them the kind of feelings that can arise only out of a spiritual scientific view of the world of color.[4] Working in the way I have done with friends in the small dome of the Dornach building, one gains a living relationship to color.[5] For instance, you discover when using blue that within the blue color itself the whole realm of inward absorption is characterized. So if we want to paint an angel moved by inwardness, we quite automatically have the urge to use blue because the nuances of blue, the light and dark of blue, call forth in the soul a feeling of movement arising out of the soul element. A yellow-reddish color calls up in the soul the sensation of shining, of outward revelation, so if the effect of something is aggressive, if there is an exhortation, if the angel desires to emerge from his background and speak to us, then we express this in the yellow-reddish nuances. It is perfectly possible, in an elementary way, to show children this inherent living quality of colors.

Next, we must come to be very sure in ourselves that plain drawing has something untrue about it. The most true is the feeling that comes from the color itself; less true is the feeling that comes from light and dark; and the least true is drawing. Drawing as such approaches the abstract element in nature as something that is dying.

---

4. See Rudolf Steiner, *Colour*, Rudolf Steiner Press, London, 1992.
5. See Rudolf Steiner's lecture "The Building at Dornach" in Michael Howard's *Art as Spiritual Activity: Rudolf Steiner's Contribution to the Visual Arts,* Anthroposophic Press, Hudson, NY, 1998.

We should really draw only in such a way that we are aware of drawing essentially what is dead. And we should paint with colors in such a way that we are aware of invoking the living out of the dead.

What is, after all, the line of a horizon? If we simply take a pencil and draw a horizon line, it is something abstract, death dealing, untrue compared with nature, which always has two streams, the dead and the living. We are merely paring off one of the streams and saying that this is nature. If, on the other hand, I say that I can see something green and something blue adjacent to it but separate, then the line of the horizon grows where the two colors meet, and I am saying something that is true.

In this way you will gradually come to appreciate that the forms of nature really arise out of the colors and that therefore drawing is a process of abstraction. We should create in the growing children good mental pictures and feelings for such things because this quickens the whole soul being and gives it a proper relationship with the external world. The reason for the sickness of our culture is that we do not have a proper relationship with the external world. In teaching in this way there is no need for us to become one-sided. It would, for instance, be rather good if we could gradually develop the possibility of passing from purely abstract artistic work, such as that created by human beings out of their delight in beauty, to concrete art, artistic craftsmanship.

Humankind today is urgently in need of really artistic crafts that can find their place in general cultural life. During the nineteenth century we actually finally reached the point of making our furniture to please the eye; we made a chair, for instance, that could delight the eye, whereas in fact a chair should have an inherent character that we feel when we sit on it. This is what ought to govern the shaping of the chair. A chair should not be merely beautiful; it should invite us to feel our way into it; it should have an inherent character that makes it suitable for a person to sit upon. By the way its arms are attached, and so on, the chair should express its growing together with our sense of touch, even our cultivated sense of touch, when we seek support from it. We would be doing today's culture a great service if we introduced artistic craft lessons into the educational system. Consider how those of us who desire the best for humankind are seized today by a tremendous anxiety concerning our culture when we see, for instance, how abstractions, the primitive ideas of socialists, are threatening to flood our culture. (This will not happen if we succeed in achieving our aims.) Nothing will be beautiful in our civilization any more, only utilitarian! And even if people dream of beauty, they will have no feeling for the urgency with which we shall have to stress the necessity for the beautiful the more we drift toward socialism. This must be recognized.

So we should not be sparing with the sculptural, pictorial element in our lessons. In the same way we should not be sparing in our efforts to create a genuine feeling for the dynamic element that finds expression in architecture. It will be very easy to make the mistake of approaching the children with one aspect or another too early, but in some ways it is right if this happens. It fell to me to say a few words to the eighty children from Munich spending their holidays in Dornach, where Frau Kisseleff gave them twelve eurythmy lessons.[6] They demonstrated to some of their teachers and the Dornach anthroposophists what they had learned. The

---

6. Tatjana Kisseleff (1881–1970), eurythmy teacher at the Goetheanum in Dornach from 1914 to 1927, and later a stage eurythmist at the Goetheanum.

children were very keen and after the end of the performance, which included some items by our Dornach eurythmists, they crowded around, asking, "Did you like our performance?" They really wanted to perform well; the whole incident was most heart-warming. Now the people who had arranged the whole event had asked me to say a few words to the children. It was the evening before their return to Munich. I said, literally, "Now I am going to say something you will not yet understand. You will understand it later on. Pay attention in the future when you hear the word *soul*, for now you cannot understand it yet." It is extraordinarily impor-tant to draw attention in this way to things the children cannot yet understand. The principle so much in force today, that one should teach children only what they can understand, is wrong. It is a prin-ciple that makes all education lifeless.

Education comes to life only if what is taken in is carried for a while in the depths and then brought back to the surface later. This is most important for education between the seventh and fifteenth years; a great deal that cannot be understood until later can be allowed to trickle into the children's souls. Please do not feel it is wrong to overstep the children's maturity by touching on things they will only be able to understand later. The contrary principle has brought something deadening into our system of teaching. The children must know, however, that they will have to wait. It is pos-sible to awaken the feeling in them that they must wait until they can understand something they are absorbing. In this sense it was not all bad when in the past children were made to learn by rote, $1 \times 1 = 1$, $2 \times 2 = 4$, $3 \times 3 = 9$, and so on, instead of learning as they do today with the help of an abacus. We ought to break through this principle of holding back the children's understanding. This can of course only be done with the necessary tact, for we must not be too far removed from what the children can love; yet they can become permeated, simply on the authority of their teacher, with a great deal that they will not be able to understand until later.

If you bring the sculptural, pictorial element toward the child in this way, you will find yourself able to quicken much of what is deadening.

The musical element that lives in human beings from birth, finding particular expression during the third and fourth years as an inclination to dance, is inherently a life-carrying will element. Yet strange though this may sound, its initial expression in the child carries life too strongly, life that is too stunning and easily benumbs consciousness. This strong musical element very easily brings about a certain dazed state in the child's development. Therefore the educational influence we exert by using the musical element must consist in a constant harmonizing by the Apollonian element of the Dionysian element welling up out of human nature. While the sculptural, pictorial element has to quicken a deadening influence, the musical element has to be damped down so that something that is alive in the highest degree does not affect the human being too strongly. This is the feeling with which we ought to bring music to the children.

Now the fact is that human nature is developed by karma with a bias toward one side or the other. This is particularly noticeable in the musical element, but it is too much emphasized. We should not stress so sharply that some children are unmusical and others musical. The differences do in fact exist, but it is most definitely wrong to take them as the ultimate reason for excluding unmusical children from everything musical and giving musical education only to children with musical inclinations. At the very least, even the most unmusical children must be present whenever anything musical is done. It is right, of course, that there will be an increasing involvement in musical performances of only the really musical children, but the unmusical children should always be there, and their receptivity to music should be developed. You will notice that even the most unmusical child possesses a remnant of musical talent, although it is rather deeply buried and can only be raised by a loving approach. This should never be neglected, for Shakespeare's words are far truer than we imagine:

> The man that hath no music in himself ...
> Is fit for treasons, stratagems, and spoils;...
> Let no such man be trusted.[7]

This is a fundamental truth. Therefore no effort should be spared in bringing the musical element to the children, even to those considered at first to be unmusical.

Fostering music in an elementary way by teaching the children musical facts without any bemusing theory is of greatest importance for our social life. The children should gain a clear idea of elementary music, of harmonies, melodies, and so on, by applying elementary facts and analyzing melodies and harmonies by ear, so that in music we build up the whole artistic realm in the same elementary way we do by similarly working up from the details in the sculptural, pictorial element. This will help mitigate the amateurishness that plays such a part in music. Mind you, it cannot be denied that musical dilettantism does serve a certain purpose in the social life of the community; we would not progress very well without it, but it should be confined to the listeners. If this could be achieved, it would be possible for those who perform and produce music to find their proper recognition within our social order.

We should not forget that everything in the sculptural, pictorial realm works toward individualizing the human being, while all that is musical and poetical fosters our social life. Human beings are brought together as one through music and poetry; they become individuals through sculpture and painting. The individuality is supported more by the sculptural, pictorial element, and society more by the living and weaving in community through music and poetry. Poetry is conceived only through a solitary soul; but it is comprehended through human community. It is entirely concrete—not at all abstract—to assert that a person's inner being is revealed through the poetry created, and that this is met by the deepest inner being of another human being who takes in that created work. Consequently, a delight in music and poetry, as well as a yearning for them, should be encouraged in the growing child.

The child should early on come to know what is truly poetical. Today we grow up into a social order in which we are tyrannized by the prose element of speech. Countless reciters tyrannize people

---

7. *The Merchant of Venice*, act 5, scene 1.

with prose by giving first place to the prose element in poetry, in other words merely to the actual meaning. Presenting a poem in a manner that gives pride of place to the nuances of content is nowadays regarded as faultless recitation. Really perfect recitation, however, stresses the musical element. In the introductions I sometimes give to eurythmy performances, I have several times pointed out that with a poet like Schiller a poem emerges from the depths of the soul. With many of his poems an undefined melody first held sway in his soul and he only later immersed, as it were, the content, the actual words, into this undefined melody. The content is suspended in the general melody and the creative poetic activity is the forming of the language, not the content, the forming of the beat, the rhythm, the rhyme—in other words the musical element on which poetry is founded. I said that people are tyrannized by the modern manner of recitation because it is always an act of tyranny to place the main emphasis on the prose, the content of a poem taken quite abstractly.

In spiritual science we can supersede this tyranny only by depicting, as I always endeavor to do, a subject from the most varied viewpoints so that our concepts remain fluid in an artistic way. It gave me particular pleasure to be told by one of our artistically gifted friends that some of the lecture cycles I have given could be transcribed into symphonies purely on the basis of their inner structure. Some of the courses are indeed based structurally on something very like this. Take for instance the course given in Vienna on life between death and a new birth: you will see that you could make a symphony of it. This is possible because a lecture concerning spiritual science should not work tyrannically but should arouse people's will. Yet when people meet something like the threefold social order they say it is incomprehensible. It is not incomprehensible; it is only that they are unaccustomed to the manner of its presentation.

It is therefore exceedingly important to draw the children's attention to the musical element on which every poem is founded. The lessons should be arranged in a way that allows the element of recitation in the school to come as close as possible to the musical element. The music teacher should be in close contact with the recitation teacher so that one lesson follows directly on the other and a living relationship between the two is established. It would be particularly useful if the music teacher could stay on when the recitation teacher takes over and vice versa, so that each could continue to point out the links with the other lesson. This would be a way to thoroughly eliminate something really dreadful that is still very much prevalent in our schools: the abstract explanation of poems. This abstract explanation of poetry, verging almost on grammatical dissection, spells the death of everything that ought to work on the child. The interpreting of poems is something quite appalling.

Now you will protest that interpretation is necessary if the children are to understand the poem. The answer to that is that all the lessons must be structured to form a totality. This has to be discussed in the weekly meetings of the teachers. If this or that poem is to be recited, then the other lessons must include whatever might be necessary for its understanding. Care must be taken that the children bring to the recitation lesson whatever they need to help them understand the poem. If, for instance, Schiller's *Spoziergang* is to be recited, the cultural, historical, and even psychological aspects of the poem can quite easily be presented to the children, not by going through the poem line by line but simply by telling them whatever they need to know about the content. In the recitation lesson itself the only important thing is the artistic presentation of something artistic.

If we use the two streams of art in this way to harmonize human nature through and through, we will indeed achieve a tremendous amount. Only consider the fact that something infinitely important in the harmony of human beings with the world is achieved when they sing. Singing is a way of reproducing what is already present in the world. When human beings sing they express the momentous wisdom out of which the world is built. We must also not forget that in singing human beings link the cosmic element of the actual sequence of notes with the human word. This brings something unnatural into singing. We can feel this even in the incompatibility of the sound of a poem with its content. It will be a step in the right direction if we further develop the endeavors we have just started, namely to present each line in recitation form and quicken only the rhyming word with melody, so that the line flows along in recitations and the rhyming word is sung like an aria. This would ensure a clear distinction between the sounding of a poem and the words, which actually disturb the human musical element.

And again, when the musical ear is cultivated the individual is induced to experience in a living way the musical essence of the world itself. This is of the utmost value for the developing human being. We must not forget that, in the sculptural, pictorial realm we look at beauty, and we live it; in the musical realm we ourselves become beauty. This is extraordinarily significant. The further back you go in ancient times, the less you find what we call musical. We can have the distinct impression that music is still in the process of becoming, even though some musical forms are already dying out again. This impression is founded on a most significant cosmic fact. In all sculptural and pictorial art, people have been imitators of the old celestial order. The highest imitation of a cosmic celestial order is an imitation of the world in sculpture or painting. But in music humans themselves are the creators. What they create does not come from what is already there, but lays the foundation and firm ground for what is to arise in the future. Of course a certain musicality can be created by simply imitating in music the sighing of waves or the singing of the nightingale. But all real music and real poetry are new creations, and it is out of this creating anew that the Jupiter, Venus, and Vulcan evolutions of the world will arise later. By starting with music, we in some way rescue what still has to come about; we rescue it for reality out of the present nullity of its existence.

Not until we link ourselves in this way to the great facts of the universe do we gain a real understanding of what teaching means. Only out of such an understanding can the right solemnity emerge so that teaching becomes a kind of service to God, a consecrated service.

What I am presenting to you will be more or less an ideal, but surely what we do in practice can be included in the ideal. For instance, there is something we must not neglect when we take our students (which we shall certainly do) out into the mountains or the fields, out into nature. We must always remember that lessons on natural science have their rightful place only inside the classroom. Let us assume that we step with the children out into nature and draw their attention to a stone or a flower. In doing so we should strictly avoid any allusion to what we teach inside the classroom. Out of doors in natural surroundings we should draw the children's attention to nature in a way totally different from the method we use in the classroom. We should never forget to point out to them: We take you out into the open so that you may feel the beauty of nature, and we bring the products of nature into the classroom so that indoors we can dissect and analyze nature.

Thus we should never speak to the children out of doors about what we show them indoors, for instance about the plants. We should emphasize how different it is to dissect dead nature in the classroom than it is to look upon the beauty of nature out of doors. We should compare these two experiences. It is not right to take the children outside into nature in order to use natural objects to exemplify what we have taught them in the classroom. The kind of feeling we should seek to arouse in the children is how unfortunate it is to have to dissect nature when they bring it into the classroom. But the children should nevertheless feel this as a necessity, for the destruction of what is natural is also necessary in the building up of the human being.

We should certainly not imagine that we are doing any good by giving a scientific explanation of a beetle out of doors in natural surroundings. The scientific description of the beetle belongs in the classroom! When we take the children out into the open we have to arouse in them delight at the sight of the beetle, delight in the way it runs about, in its drollness, delight in its relationship to the rest of nature. Furthermore, we should not neglect to call forth in the children's souls a clear sense of how something creative lies in music, something transcending nature, and of how humans themselves share in the creation of nature when they develop music. This will of course be formed only very primitively as a feeling, but it is the first feeling that must emerge from the will element of music: the human being feels itself within the cosmos!

An Introduction to Eurythmy

BY RUDOLF STEINER

Dornach, May 15, 1920

Today, we offer you a performance of eurythmy. Through this art, we want to place something into the spiritual development of humanity. We can view eurythmy from three perspectives: the purely artistic, the pedagogical, and the hygienic.

As an art, eurythmy represents a kind of voiceless, visible speech. Although it takes the form of gestures and movements, either in groups or individually, you should not confuse it with mime or pantomime, nor with some form of artistic dance. Eurythmy uses the entire human being as its language; this visible unvoiced speech is developed through a study of the laws of voiced speech.

Voiced speech is a way of expressing what lies within the human being. However, Schiller was correct when he said, "When the soul speaks, then, sadly, the soul no longer speaks." In a certain sense, that is correct. Language, aside from the fact that it carries the human soul to the external world, or at least should do that, is also the means of communication between one person and another, and is, therefore, subject to convention. It is also the medium through which we communicate our thoughts to other people. In a certain sense, language is a social effect. The more language must serve as a means of communication and as a means of expressing thoughts, the less it can serve as a means of artistic expression, since art must arise out of the entire human being.

Language has two sides. First of all, the social side. The human being must bow to the social world when speaking. Only in that way does language retain something that is intimately connected with the entirety of the human being. Young children do not learn language from their dreams. They learn it during the time when they need to adjust their entire being to their surroundings. This natural adjustment protects language from being just a means of communication.

When a poet, an artist with words, wants to express something, he or she needs everything that hovers behind language. A poet needs pictures and, above all, musicality. True poetry, the artistic aspect of a poem, is not at all found in the direct content of the words; rather, it is the way the content is formed that is important. In poetry we need most of all to take into account what Goethe expressed in *Faust*: "Consider the what, but even more so, the how." The way the poet shapes the poem is what is most important in poetry.

You can see that much more clearly if you do not use a means of expression that is too strongly permeated by thoughts when you express yourself artistically, but instead use the entire human being. For that reason, we used both sense-perceptible and supersensible observation to study the way the human larynx, tongue, and other organs of speech move when people express themselves through voiced speech. We studied the movements that are transformed into sounds, into vibrations in the air, through normal speaking. We transferred those movements to other human organs, particularly those organs that are most comparable to primitive organs of speech, namely, to the arms and hands.

Upon first seeing eurythmy, people are often surprised that the performers use their hands and arms more than the other limbs of their bodies. You can see this as an obvious outcome if you consider that even in normal speech, when we want to express more than simple conventions, when we want to express someone's own individuality or perception or feelings through speech, we find it necessary to move into these more agile organs, into these spiritual organs. Of course, eurythmy takes the entire human being into account, not just the arms and hands. Eurythmy uses the expressiveness of movements in space, whether of groups or of individuals.

The most important thing to remember is that those movements, whether they are done by individuals or groups, are not at all arbitrary. They are the same movements that are the underlying foundation of what we express through voiced speech, transferred to the entire human being.

I need to emphasize once again that what we see on stage is essentially the entire larynx, represented through the whole human being. What we present is the function, rhythm, and tempo of the larynx. It represents the musical and the pictorial aspects, as well as what is poetic when poetry is genuine art. The entire group reveals it all.

What is presented in eurythmy as voiceless and visible speech is also accompanied by music or recitation. Since music and speech are just other forms of expression for what lives in the human soul, we need to use that good, old-fashioned form of recitation that Goethe had in mind when he was working with actors. So that they would not only understand the content of the words but also learn their rhythms, he kept a conductor's baton in his hand. In our case, we need to avoid the things that our very inartistic age sees as important in recitation, namely, the emphasis upon the literal content of the words. We need to go back to what was artistic in more primitive recitations. That is something rarely seen today, particularly if you live in a city. However, much of it is still alive in people my age who can remember the traveling speakers of their childhood who recited their street ballads.[8] They drew pictures on a blackboard and then spoke the text. They never spoke without keeping time with their feet, and at an exciting point in the story, they marched up and down, or did such things to indicate that not only was the content important, but also the tempo of the verse and its inner form. They wanted the listener to be aware of that.

You will see that we attempt at every turn to emphasize this deeper aspect of art. Even when we attempt to present poetry in humorous or fantastic ways through eurythmy, we do not present the literal content through such things as facial gestures or pantomime.

---

8. This refers to the so-called *Moritaten*, a popular entertainment of the nineteenth century, in which a sensational event such as a murder was described in prose or verse interspersed with songs, often accompanied by a barrel organ. — TRANS.

We do not present the content of the poem through musical or poetic forms expressed solely in space and not in time. Instead, we present what the poet or artist shaped from the content.

Those are a few things I wanted to mention about the artistic aspect of eurythmy Since the human being is the instrument, not a violin or piano, not colors and shapes, eurythmy is particularly able to portray what exists within the microcosm of the human being of the ebb and flow of cosmic forces.

The second aspect of eurythmy is pedagogy. I am convinced that normal gymnastics, which developed during a materialistic period, focuses too much upon only the anatomic and physiological aspects of the human being. In the future, when people can look at such things more objectively, they will recognize that while such gymnastics can strengthen human beings in a certain way, that strengthening does not at the same time strengthen the soul and the will.

From a pedagogical perspective, we can see eurythmy as ensouled gymnastics, ensouled movement. In the small example we will present to you today with the children, you will see how the movements are carried by their souls.

In addition to physical development, what I would like to call a development of the life of the soul and of the will also exists. Those are things we very much need, and simple gymnastics does not at all develop them in the growing human being. It is extremely important for you to understand that.

We also need to say that although we are presenting some children's exercises here, the children can study eurythmy only during the few hours available during school time. However, that is not really right. The pedagogy lying at the basis of our efforts in Dornach, which, to a certain extent, the Waldorf School in Stuttgart has realized, has as its goal that the children will not have to attend any lessons outside of regular school time.

Therefore, it is especially important that we clearly understand the pedagogical significance of eurythmy and completely integrate it into the curriculum of the school. Then the children will have everything that can serve them for normal spiritual, soul, and physical development, in particular what eurythmy contains.

Third is the hygienic element. The human being is certainly a little world, a microcosm. All lack of health essentially stems from the fact that human beings tear themselves from the great laws of the cosmos. We could represent all lack of health pictorially by saying that if I removed my finger from my organism as a whole, it would no longer be a finger. It would wither away. My finger retains its inner function only in connection with my organism as a whole. In the same way, the human being realizes its inner nature only in connection with the universe as a whole. What happens in human beings really is connected with the entirety of the universe. Just consider something that is extremely superficial but shows that human beings are connected with the universe, which is that human beings are not simply enclosed within the boundaries of the skin. Consider for a moment that the air you now have within you was but a moment before outside of you. After you have inhaled it, it becomes part of your organism, and what you now have within, you will exhale, and as soon as you have exhaled it, it will be outside you. Even if we lived only within our skin, we could not prove we are only what is enclosed by our skin. We are not just a part of the air, but of the entire cosmos.

We can, therefore, see that everything unhealthy in human beings results from things they do that are not appropriate, that are not befitting of the entirety of human nature or of the age in which we live, and that do not support the harmony and fulfillment that must exist between human beings and all creation. However, since every movement in eurythmy comes forth naturally out of the entire human organism, just as the movements of the larynx and its associated organs do in normal voiced speech, everything done in eurythmy can bring the human being into harmony with the entire universe.

We can certainly say that what a person, even as a child, can gain from the movements of eurythmy has a healing element. Of course, it must be performed properly and not clumsily.

Eurythmy is something we can certainly consider as an aspect of soul, spirit, and physical hygiene.

Those are, therefore, the three aspects from which we should see eurythmy and from which we have placed eurythmy in our spiritual movement.

Even though many visitors may have been here often and may have seen our recent attempts to move forward in our forms and utilization of space in the groups, we still need to appeal to your understanding for today's presentation. Eurythmy is at its very beginnings. This is an attempt at a beginning, but it is an attempt that we are convinced will improve and become better. Perhaps others will need to join in and take up what we can accomplish with our weak forces and develop it further. In spite of all that, it is certainly possible to see our intent from what will be shown today. Because eurythmy opens the artistic wellsprings, because it uses the entire human being as its means of expression, because it pedagogically develops the soul, spiritual, and physical aspects of the child, and because it places human beings into movements that have a health-giving effect, it is an art, and can be justifiably placed alongside the other, older, arts, especially when our contemporaries turn their interest toward it.

FURTHER READING

Rudolf Steiner

Steiner's autobiography, composed during the final year of his life, covers 1861 until the turn of the century. Published in two translations—*The Course of My Life* and *Rudolf Steiner, An Autobiography*—the second is the more readable and contains hundreds of interesting footnotes. Steiner also gave a short talk about his early years that has been published as *Self-Education: Autobiographical Reflections, 1861–1893*.

Books about Steiner's life and work include: Henry Barnes, *A Life for the Spirit: Rudolf Steiner in the Crosscurrents of Our Time*; Stewart Easton, *Rudolf Steiner: Herald of a New Epoch*; Frans Carlgren, *Rudolf Steiner, 1861-1925*; Johannes Hemleben, *Rudolf Steiner: A Documentary Biography*; and A.P. Shepherd, *A Scientist of the Invisible*.

Books that deal with various aspects of anthroposophy include Robert McDermott, *The Essential Steiner: Basic Writings of Rudolf Steiner;* and Stewart Easton, *Man and World in the Light of Anthroposophy*; Francis Edmunds, *From Thinking to Living*; Rudi Lissau, *Rudolf Steiner: Life, Work, Inner Path and Social Initiatives*; George Adams, *Fruits of Anthroposophy: An Introduction to the Work of Rudolf Steiner*; Gilbert Childs, *Rudolf Steiner: His Life and Work*; and Roy Wilkinson, *Rudolf Steiner: Aspects of His Spiritual World View*. Collections of essays on anthroposophic work include: *Work Arising: From the Life of Rudolf Steiner*, edited by John Davy, and *The Faithful Thinker: Centenary Essays on the Work and Thought of Rudolf Steiner*, edited by George Adams.

Sergei Prokofieff's *Rudolf Steiner and the Founding of the New Mysteries* is a deeply insightful, esoteric examination of Steiner's life and work. Readers who wish to know more about Steiner, the man, should see Friedrich Rittelmeyer's *Rudolf Steiner Enters My Life*, and Friedrich Hiebel's *Time of Decision with Rudolf Steiner: Experience and Encounter.* Other personal recollections of Steiner are included in *A Man Before Others: Rudolf Steiner Remembered, Memories of Rudolf Steiner* by Count Polzer-Hoditz, and *Reminiscences of Rudolf Steiner* by Andrei Belyi, Aasya Turgenieff, and Margarita Voloschin.

Waldorf Education

Many books give an overview of Waldorf education, and each has a different approach, perspective, and flavor. Francis Edmunds's *Rudolf Steiner Education* is a very succinct and readable introduction, but it does not go into much detail. A. C. Harwood's *The Recovery of Man in Childhood*, Gilbert Childs's *Rudolf Steiner Education in Theory and Practice*, and Willi Aeppli's *Rudolf Steiner Education and the Developing Child* go into much greater depth; these books all describe the different stages of child development and illustrate how the Waldorf curriculum and method address the needs of the growing child. Marjorie Spock's *Teaching as a Lively Art* paints a vivid picture of each of the elementary grades, and *School as a Journey*, by Torin Finser, gives a graphic and often moving account of the journey of a teacher and his class through the eight years of elementary school. M. C. Richards's *Toward Wholeness*, provides an overview of Waldorf education in America, while John Gardner's *Education in Search of the Spirit* examines Waldorf education in the context of American culture.

Curative Education

Steiner also spoke about how to work with children with special needs. His course on *Curative Education* provided the basis for a curative education movement and for the establishment of Camphill communities for children and adults with special needs. Karl König, the founder of the Camphill movement, wrote and lectured extensively on the subject of special education; his books include *The Camphill Movement, Being Human: Diagnosis in Curative Education,* and *In Need of Special Understanding.* Michael Luxford's *Children with Special Needs* and Henning Hansmann's *Education for Special Needs* provide useful introductions to the subject of special education, and Walter Holzapfel's *Children's Destinies* examines the subject from the point of view of the school doctor. Carlo Pietzner's *Questions of Destiny* considers the question of special education in the context of Steiner's views of reincarnation, while *To a Different Drumbeat* by F. Clark, H. Kofsky, and J. Lauruol provides a practical guide for parents of children with special needs.

The Nature of the Human Being

Steiner's most thorough descriptions of the nature of the human being can be found in the first chapters of *Theosophy* and the second chapter of *Occult Science.* Lecture 2 of *Theosophy of the Rosicrucian* also provides a succinct and clear summary.

Bernard Lievegoed's *Phases of Childhood* provides a thorough description of the phases of child development, while Victor Bott's *Anthroposophical Medicine* and Friedrich Husemann and Otto Wolff's *An Anthroposophical Approach to Medicine* contain chapters that examine the different stages of child development from a medical point of view. The stages of adult development are described in depth in George and Gisela O'Neill's *The Human Life* and in Bernard Lievegoed's *Phases,* and the anthroposophical view of the human soul is examined in detail in Karl König's *The Human Soul* and by F. W. Zeylmans van Emmichoven's *The Anthroposophical Understanding of the Soul.*

* * * * * *

On the Temperaments

Steiner's most thorough examination of the four temperaments is his essay, *The Four Temperaments,* contained in *Anthroposophy in Everyday Life.* He also examines the temperaments in lecture 7 of *Human Values in Education,* lecture 10 of *A Modern Art of Education,* and in lecture 7 of *The Child's Changing Consciousness.* In lecture 12 of *Soul Economy and Waldorf Education* and lecture 6 of *The Spiritual Ground of Education,* Steiner demonstrates how knowledge of the temperaments will allow the teacher to individualize instruction to meet the needs of different children. In the first five discussions of *Discussions with Teachers,* Steiner considers the temperaments in terms of music, diet, and the temperaments at different ages, and he shows how to vary the style of one's teaching so that it will appeal to the different temperaments. The effects of the teacher's temperament on the child are considered in lecture 1 of both *The Essentials of Education* and *The Roots of Education.*

A number of anthroposophical authors have also written about the temperaments. Gilbert Childs devotes a chapter to the temperaments in *Steiner Education in Theory and Practice,* and deals with the subject in greater depth in *Understand Your Temperament!* In *An Imp on Either Shoulder,* Childs describes how we can work on our temperament. Marieka Anschütz's *Children and Their Temperament* describes how the temperaments were viewed throughout history and examines the changes in temperament between childhood and adulthood.

The temperaments are also described in the following books about Waldorf education: A.C. Harwood's *The Way of a Child* and *The Recovery of Man in Childhood,* Marjorie Spock's *Teaching as a Lively Art,* Francis Edmunds's *Rudolf Steiner Education,* and Caroline von Heydebrand's *Childhood: A Study of the Growing Child.* Betty Staley examines the temperaments and the development of character in adolescence in her excellent book, *Between Form and Freedom,* and Rene Querido considers the temperaments in a lively essay in *Creativity in Education: The Waldorf Approach.* For teachers interested in applying the knowledge of the temperaments in the arts, Magda Lissau's *The Temperaments and the Arts: Their Relation and Function in Waldorf Pedagogy* provides many interesting ideas.

The Task of the Teacher

In almost every educational lecture cycle, Steiner spoke about the inner and outer aspects of the teacher's work. In his closing remarks at the first teacher training course, included in *Practical Advice to Teachers*, Steiner spoke about the qualities that a teacher must cultivate. In the second course he gave to teachers at the original Waldorf School, Steiner returned to this theme; lectures 1 and 2 of *Balance in Teaching* describe the inner attitude of the teacher and show how teachers can work with the three fundamental forces in education. Lecture 9 of *Human Values in Education* and lecture 2 of *A Modern Art of Education* examine the changes in the relationship between students and teachers in different historical epochs; lecture 7 of *The Renewal of Education* describes some of the challenges of teacher training. In lectures 4 and 9 of *The Spiritual Ground of Education*, Steiner speaks movingly about the attitude of the teacher, and he also considers this theme in the final lecture of *A Modern Art of Education*.

How a teacher works with a class of children over a period of eight years is beautifully and lovingly described in Torin Finser's *School as a Journey*. This theme is also described by A.C. Harwood, Gilbert Childs, Marjorie Spock, and Francis Edmunds. Eugene Schwartz considers many aspects of the relationship between teachers and students in his humorous and insightful *Waldorf Teacher's Survival Guide*, and he gives many useful suggestions in *Weaving the Social Fabric of the Class* and in *The Waldorf Teacher's Survival Guide*. The question of discipline is considered in most of the basic books on Waldorf education, the most useful and inspiring of which is Erich Gabert's *Punishment in Self-Education and in the Education of the Child*, which examines the role of punishment from a spiritual perspective. John Gardner's *Youth Longs to Know: Explorations of the Spirit in Education* is also helpful.

Meditation

In his anthroposophic works, Steiner offered a great deal of guidance for the cultivation of the inner life, and the exercises and meditations that he suggested form the basis of the meditative practice of Waldorf teachers. In *Theosophy* and *Occult Science*, Steiner outlined the path of inner development, and he gave a detailed description of the path of self-knowledge and numerous examples of exercises for self-development in *How to Know Higher Worlds*. Many of Steiner's works contain suggestions of how to develop one's inner life, and Paul Eugen Schiller's *Rudolf Steiner and Initiation: The Anthroposophical Path of Inner Schooling* provides a very helpful guide to Steiner's indications on meditation. Steiner's *Verses and Meditations* and *Truth-Wrought Words* are a rich source of meditative material, and his *Calendar of the Soul* traces the cycle of the year in fifty-two mantric verses.

There are a number of other anthroposophical works on meditation that teachers and parents will find helpful. The works of Jörgen Smit, who for many years led the Pedagogical Section of the Anthroposophical Society, are very straightforward and practical. Smit's works include *Meditation: Transforming Our Lives for the Encounter with Christ; How to Transform Thinking, Feeling, and Willing; Lighting Fires: Deepening Education Through Meditation; Spiritual Development; and The Steps Toward Knowledge which the Seeker for the Spirit Must Take*. Other works on meditation and inner development that may prove useful include *Meditation* by Ernst Katz, *Inner Development and the Landscape of the Ego* by Carlo Pietzner, *The Inner Path* by Karl König, *Meditation: Guidance of the Inner Life* by Friedrich Rittelmeyer, and the works of Georg Kühlewind, especially *From Normal to Healthy: Paths to the Liberation of Consciousness*.

The Pedagogical Section Council of North America has published several works for deepening the anthroposophical foundation of Waldorf education. Teachers who are interested in obtaining these works should contact the chairperson of the Pedagogical Section.

* * * * * * *

Early Childhood Education

In addition to the two lectures printed in this volume, there are several other references to early childhood education in the works of Steiner. In *The Education of the Child in the Light of Anthroposophy*, he describes the development of the child before the change of teeth, and he gives a number of practical indications of how to work with young children. In lectures 2 and 3 of *The Child's Changing Consciousness*, Steiner speaks about the relationship that young children have to their environment, and he examines the nature of imitation. In lecture 1 of *The Kingdom of Childhood*, Steiner speaks about the process of incarnation and how the relationship of the body, the soul, and the spirit are established in childhood. The differences in the child's memory before and after the change of teeth are described in lecture 3 of *The Roots of Education*, and the changes in the child's metabolism and circulation after the change of teeth are described in lecture 3 of *The Essentials of Education*. Lecture 4 of *Human Values in Education* and lecture 4 of *the Spiritual Ground of Education* contain brief references to the young child, and lecture 13 of *The Renewal of Education* examines the importance of play for the child's later intellectual development. Kindergarten teachers may also wish to refer to *The Spiritual Guidance of Humanity*, for it explains how the capacities for walking, speaking, and thinking are developed under the guidance of spiritual beings.

Infancy and Early Childhood

In *A Child is Born*, Dr. Wilhelm zur Linden describes pregnancy, birth, and early childhood from an anthroposophical perspective; these are also examined by Norbert Glas in *Conception, Birth and Early Childhood*. Dr. Gilbert Childs and Sylvia Childs also describe the course of pregnancy and the challenges of meeting the needs of the infant in *Your Reincarnating Child*.

In *The Incarnating Child*, Joan Salter provides many inspiring suggestions for making the child's first experiences on the earth nourishing to both body and soul, and Daniel Udo de Haes's *The Young Child* describes the world of the young child and suggests how to help children incarnate gently. Karl König examines the first years of childhood in *The First Three Years of the Child*, and he gives insightful descriptions of how the child develops the capacities to walk, speak, and think. Eva Frommer's *Voyage Through Childhood into the Adult World: A Guide to Child Development* has chapters on the infant and on the young child, and Rahima Baldwin's *You Are Your Child's First Teacher* is a wonderfully insightful and practical guide for parents. Dotty Coplen's books on parenting are also helpful; both *Parenting a Path Through Childhood* and *Parenting for a Healthy Future* give sound advice on raising children.

The Kindergarten

Elizabeth Grunelius, who founded the first Waldorf kindergarten under Steiner's direction, outlines the principles of the Waldorf kindergarten in her booklet, *Early Childhood Education and the Waldorf School Plan*. In *Childhood: A Study of the Growing Child* Caroline von Heydebrand, another of the original teachers in the first Waldorf school, shares her insight and experience gleaned from years of working with young children. Gilbert Childs's *Steiner Education in Theory and Practice* has a chapter on the preschool, and A.C. Harwood has a similar chapter in *The Recovery of Man in Childhood*.

The Association of Waldorf Kindergartens publishes a quarterly newsletter with articles of interest to teachers and parents. Many of these articles are included in *An Overview of the Waldorf Kindergarten* and *A Deeper Understanding of the Waldorf Kindergarten*, edited by Joan Almon. There are also a number of articles about the kindergarten and early childhood reprinted in *Waldorf Schools* vol. 1, *Child and Man Extracts*, and *Educating as an Art*.

Work and Play

Heidi Britz-Crecelius's *Children at Play: Preparation for Life* is a thoughtful and compelling analysis of the importance of children's play for their healthy development. Wil van Haren and Rudolf Kischnick's *Child's Play* offers many examples of finger games, circle games, clapping games, and counting rhymes that are suitable for kindergarten age children. *The Children's Year* by Stephanie Cooper, Christine Fynes-Clinton, and Marye Rowling suggests dozens of craft activities for children and parents, and Susan Smith's *Echoes of a Dream* and Brunhild Müller's *Painting with Children* provide guidance for engaging young children in artistic work. Parents and teachers may also want to refer to the following books on crafts: Freya Jaffke's *Toymaking with Children*, G. Bittleston's *The Healing Art of Glove Puppetry*, Sunnhild Reinckens's *Making Dolls*, and two books of seasonal crafts and decorations by Thomas Berger.

Family Life and Festivals

Gudrun Davy's and Bons Voors's *Lifeways* is a collection of articles that examine family life from many different points of view, and it contains a section on celebrating the festivals. *More Lifeways* by Patti Smith & Signe Schaeffer offers two dozen more articles. Diana Carey and Judy Large's *Festivals, Family and Food* is a marvelous compendium of ideas for parents and children; it gives a background to the Christian festivals and shows how to bring them to life. Two other works deal with the nature and character of the Christian festivals: Brigitte Barz's *Festivals with Children* and Friedel Lenz's pamphlet, *Celebrating Festivals with Children*. For those interested in celebrating festivals from different cultures, Sue Fitzjohn, Minda Weston, and Judy Large's *Festivals Together: A Guide to Multi-Cultural Celebration* is a splendid resource for parents and teachers.

Shea Darien's *Seven Times the Sun* shows parents how to guide their children through the rhythm of the day; Carol Petrash's *Earthways* contains suggestions for nature crafts and seasonal activities that will help children experience the world around them with awe and respect; and M.V. Leeuwen's and J. Moeskops's book *The Nature Corner* shows how to bring the seasons to life for the child in a very special way.

Imagination

Teachers and parents have long recognized the importance of fairy tales in the life of the young child. Steiner's two lectures on the deeper meaning of fairy tales are published as *The Poetry and Meaning of Fairy Tales*. Norbert Glas's fascinating studies of seven classical fairy tales are included in *Once Upon a Fairy Tale*, and Rudolf Meyer provides a most interesting and insightful guide to the language, imagery, and wisdom in fairy tales in his book *The Wisdom of Fairy Tales*.

Waldorf teachers are aware that the media—especially television, videos, and movies—are deleterious to the child's imagination and creativity and consequently recommend that parents limit and guide their young children's exposure to these media. Several anthroposophists have written about the media: Martin Large examines the effects of television on children and families in *Who's Bringing Them Up? Television and Child Development: How to Break the T.V. Habit*, and this theme is also developed by Marie Winn in *The Plug-in Drug* and *Unplugging the Plug-in Drug*.

* * * * * * *

The Seventh-Year Change

Steiner discusses the seventh year change and its implications for the art of education in many lectures. In lecture 4 of *A Modern Art of Education*, he gives a detailed description of the physical changes at seven and fourteen and shows how the physical functions of the etheric and astral bodies are transformed into psychological functions. In the two opening lectures of *Kingdom of Childhood* he describes how the soul of the young child is nourished by the "soul milk" of the teacher during the first school years. Steiner speaks about the importance of the change of teeth in lecture 3 of *The Essentials of Education*, where he also examines how this change is reflected in the development of memory. In lectures 3 and 4 of *The Child's Changing Consciousness* and lecture 3 of *Human Values in Education* Steiner again deals with the stages of child development and suggests how to address the needs of the elementary school child. In lecture 4 of *The Spiritual Ground of Education* and lecture 7 of *A Modern Art of Education*, he describes the changes in the child's rhythmic system between the ages of seven and fourteen and explains why it is important to appeal to the rhythmic system during the elementary school years.

The seventh-year change is also described by Bernard Lievegoed in *Phases of Childhood*, and by Gilbert Childs in *Steiner Education in Theory and Practice*. A.C. Harwood has a chapter about the first school years in *The Recovery of Man in Childhood*, and Marjorie Spock and Torin Finser both conjure vivid pictures of children in the first few years of elementary school. Most of the references given below consider some aspect of the seven-year change in relation to teaching the children in their first school years.

Language Arts

Steiner's educational lectures contain many references to the teaching of language arts. The language arts curriculum for the elementary school is described in "Curriculum Lectures" (in *Discussions with Teachers*) and indications for the high school curriculum are sprinkled throughout *Faculty Meetings with Rudolf Steiner*. A thorough summary of Rudolf Steiner's indications on teaching language arts is given in Stockmeyer's *Rudolf Steiner's Curriculum for Waldorf Schools*, and Heydebrand's *Curriculum* describes the subjects that were taught during the first few years of the original Waldorf School.

Steiner describes the story curriculum for the grades at the end of the first discussion in *Discussions with Teachers*. In discussion 6 he gives an example of how a teacher prepares the children for hearing poems and stories, and in discussions 7 and 8 he makes a few additional comments on this theme. In lecture 5 of *The Renewal of Education* Steiner speaks about the difference between reading a story and making up one's own, and in lecture 4 of *The Kingdom of Childhood* he shows how a teacher might work with a story and respond to the children's questions.

Steiner's most thorough examination of the history and nature of language is presented in *The Genius of Language*. The *Speech and Drama* course also contains many illuminating examples and useful indications. Steiner also deals with the development of language in lecture 4 of *The Child's Changing Consciousness* and lecture 3 of *Human Values in Education*, and he summarizes how to work with aspects of language according to stages of child development in lecture 6 of *The Kingdom of Childhood*. In lecture 9 of *The Renewal of Education* Steiner illustrates the differences between dialect and written language and examines their relationship to the feeling and the will. In lecture 12 of *Soul Economy* Steiner explains how to work with the feeling and thinking elements of language.

Steiner places great stress on the introduction of writing, and he describes this process in the following lectures: lecture 8 of *A Modern Art of Education*, lecture 5 of *The Spiritual Ground of Education*, lecture 2 of *The Kingdom of Childhood*, lecture 4 of *The Child's Changing Consciousness*, lecture 3 of *The Roots of Education*, and lecture 3 of *Human Values in Education*. He comments on composition writing in lecture 10 of *Practical Advice to Teachers* and lecture 7 of *The Kingdom of Childhood*. The relation of writing to reading is often mentioned in the lectures already listed. Steiner also refers to this topic in lecture 8 of *A Modern Art of Education* and lecture 5 of *The Child's Changing Consciousness*. Indications for the teaching of grammar, spelling, and punctuation are given in lecture 11 of *The Renewal of Education* and in lecture 4 of *The Child's Changing Consciousness*.

Several English and American Waldorf teachers have written about the teaching of language arts. Eileen Hutchins provides a detailed summary of the English curriculum in the supplement to Heydebrand's *Curriculum*, and her article on "The Teaching of Writing" is included in *Waldorf Schools*, vol. 1. and in *Child and Man Extracts*. Dorothy Harrer, who taught for many years in the Rudolf Steiner School in New York City, compiled her suggestions for teaching English in *An English Manual*, which is a most useful source for class teachers, and Roy Wilkinson offers helpful hints for language arts teaching in his booklet on *Teaching English*.

Shorter works on teaching language arts include a chapter in Willi Aeppli's *Rudolf Steiner Education and the Developing Child*, Henry Barnes's "The Winged Horse: An Essay on the Art of Reading" in *Educating as an Art*, Christy Barnes's articles "Why Write?" in *For the Love of Literature*, and Betty Staley's article on creative writing in *Waldorf Schools*, vol. 2.

The teaching of grammar is dealt with in a wonderful book by Rudolf Schmid, *An English Grammar: The Language Before Babel*. There are also several excellent articles on teaching grammar, including Dorit Winter's "We Love Grammar" in *Journal for Anthroposophy* Number 35, E.G. Wilson's "The Teaching of Grammar in Younger Classes," and A.C. Harwood's "Grammar and Gramarye," which are included in *Child and Man Extracts*.

Audrey McAllen gives a thorough description of the process of teaching writing in *Teaching Children to Write*, which also includes chapters on writing difficulties and on spelling. *The "Write" Approach: Form Drawing for Better Handwriting* by Joen Gladich and Paula Sassi is also a useful guide. Therapeutic indications for writing, reading, and spelling difficulties are given in Audrey McAllen's *The Extra Lesson*, and in *Take Time: Movement Exercises for Parents, Teachers and Therapists of Children with Difficulties in Speaking, Reading, Writing, and Spelling* by Mary Nash-Wortham and Jean Hunt.

Mathematics

Steiner outlines the mathematics curriculum for the elementary school in the "Curriculum Lectures" in *Discussions with Teachers*. His indications for teaching mathematics are summarized in Stockmeyer's *Curriculum*, and have been expanded in curricula by Amos Franceschelli and R. A. Jarman.

Steiner deals with teaching arithmetic in many of his educational lecture courses. In lecture 1 of *Practical Advice to Teachers*, lecture 9 of *A Modern Art of Education*, lecture 5 of *Spiritual Ground of Education*, and lecture 4 of *The Roots of Education*, he describes the introduction to arithmetic and explains why it is important to work from the whole to the parts. In lecture 10 of *The Renewal of Education* he examines the thought processes of analysis and synthesis and shows how to introduce arithmetic in an analytical way. In discussion 4 of *Discussions with Teachers* he examines the four arithmetic processes in relation to the temperaments.

Steiner describes the teaching of algebra in detail in discussions 13 and 14 of *Discussions with Teachers*. In these discussions he demonstrates how to introduce algebra through the formula for interest; he also shows how to derive powers and roots and how to work with negative numbers. In lecture 9 of *A Modern Art of Education*, Steiner shows how to prepare for the teaching of geometry by working with form drawing. In lecture 6 of *The Renewal of Education*, he shows how developing a feeling for shapes is a good preparation for geometry, and in lecture 12 of that same lecture cycle, he describes how to lead geometry from a static state to a living one.

There are a number of very fine works on the teaching of mathematics in the Waldorf schools. In the early elementary grades, arithmetic is often introduced through movement and reinforced through the arts. Henning Andersen's *Active Arithmetic!* is a wonderful compendium of lively arithmetic activities. Arithmetic teaching should also be pictorial and creative, and Dorothy Harrer's *Math Lessons for the Early Grades* contains many suggestions of how to bring an imaginative element into arithmetic teaching. Roy Wilkinson's booklet on mathematics teaching also contains many suggestions about how to introduce and develop topics in an interesting way.

Educating as an Art contains several short articles on the teaching of arithmetic in the early grades. They include an arithmetic story showing the derivation of the division sign, an article on fractions, and two arithmetic plays. Readers might also refer to W.O. Field's "Early Teaching of Arithmetic" and A.R. Sheen's "Number Work and Arithmetic in the First Two Classes," which are included in *Child and Man Extracts*, and to "Multiplication Tables Can Be Interesting" in *Waldorf Schools* vol. 1, in which William Harrer shows how to bring the times tables to life through geometry.

Another valuable resource for math instruction in the elementary school is Hermann von Baravalle's *The Teaching of Arithmetic and the Waldorf School Plan.* Baravalle was one of the teachers in the first Waldorf School, and he wrote extensively on mathematical subjects. Unfortunately, much of his work has not yet been translated, but this little booklet and the one on *Geometric Drawing and the Waldorf School Plan* are both very clear, practical, and useful.

The mathematics curriculum for the upper elementary school includes algebra and geometry. A.R. Sheen's *Geometry and the Imagination* covers the subject in great detail, and Bengt Ulin's *Finding the Path: Themes and Methods for the Teaching of Mathematics in a Waldorf School* is also a valuable resource, for it traces themes in arithmetic and geometry from the upper elementary grades to the high school. Amos Franceschelli's booklets on *Algebra* and *Mensuration* are both helpful for the upper grades teacher, and his article "Appreciative Thinking: With Special Reference to the Teaching of Mathematics" in *Educating as an Art* deals with the subject of mathematics teaching in a very inspiring way.

Willi Aeppli also has a chapter on the teaching of arithmetic in *Rudolf Steiner Education and the Developing Child*; Gilbert Child addresses the subject in *Steiner Education in Theory and Practice*, and Marjorie Spock, Torin Finser, and A.C. Harwood all give examples in their books of how to work with arithmetic and geometry through the grades.

* * * * * * *

The Ninth-Year Change

Steiner describes the ninth-year change in several of his educational lecture courses. In lecture 5 of *The Child's Changing Consciousness*, Steiner characterizes the crisis around the ninth year, and in the beginning of lecture 6 of *The Spiritual Ground of Education* he describes the physical and physiological changes that occur at this time. In lecture 7 of *Practical Advice to Teachers*, Steiner outlines in detail the curriculum for children of nine and ten, and he considers the subject briefly in lecture 5 of *Human Values in Education*.

Hermann Köpke's *Encountering the Self: Transformation and Destiny in the Ninth Year* is an invaluable resource for parents and teachers. Köpke examines this stage of child development in depth and shows how the Waldorf curriculum addresses the child's needs. Eugene Schwartz's *Rhythms and Turning Points in the Life of the Child* gives a lucid description of the supersensible forces responsible for the changes that the child undergoes, and the books by Torin Finser, Marjorie Spock, A.C. Harwood, and Gilbert Childs characterize the changing relationship between teacher and child at this time. Some shorter works about third grade that may also be useful are "In Third Grade" by Susanne Berlin and "Beginning Bible Stories" by Margaret Peckham, both included in *Waldorf Schools*, vol. 1, Roy Wilkinson's booklet on *Studies in Practical Activities*, and Rudolf Copple's article on Norse mythology in *Educating as an Art*.

Nature Study

Steiner outlines the nature study curriculum in "Curriculum Lectures" in *Discussions with Teachers* and a summary of his indications on teaching nature study is included in Stockmeyer's *Curriculum*. In lecture 7 of *Practical Advice to Teachers*, Steiner illustrates how to teach children about the animals in relation to the human being, and he develops this theme further in lecture 4 of *The Essentials of Education*. In discussions 9, 10, and 11 of *Discussions with Teachers*, Steiner shows how the plants can be introduced, and he suggests a number of themes that the teacher might develop further. Lecture 3 of *The Kingdom of Childhood* gives a wonderful overview of the nature study curriculum; this subject is also considered in lecture 5 of *The Spiritual Ground of Education*, lecture 5 of *Human Values in Education*, and lecture 4 of *The Roots of Education*.

The teaching of botany and zoology is described by Willi Aeppli in *Rudolf Steiner Education and the Developing Child* and in books by Torin Finser, Marjorie Spock, and A.C. Harwood. Shorter works on nature study in the elementary school include Eugen Kolisko's *Natural History*, Francis Edmunds's "Animal Teaching in the Fourth Class," included in *Renewing Education*, William Harrer's "Man and Animal" and Virginia Birdsall's "First Lessons in Botany," which may be found in *Waldorf Schools* vol. 1, and E.G. Wilson's "First Lessons About Plants" and L. Edwards's "Science in the Middle School," reprinted in *Child and Man Extracts*. Roy Wilkinson's booklets *Man and Animal* and *Plant Study* also offer useful indications of how to present these subjects.

Geography

Steiner's suggestions for the geography curriculum are given in "Curriculum Lectures." There are also several references to teaching geography in *Faculty Meetings with Rudolf Steiner*; a summary of his indications on geography is included in Stockmeyer's *Curriculum*. In discussion 12 of *Discussions with Teachers*, Steiner gives additional practical indications to supplement the lecture on geography teaching printed in this volume. In lecture 3 of *Education for Adolescents*, included in chapter 7, he describes how the study of geography helps children orient themselves in space, and he explains how this subject develops moral qualities. The teaching of geography is also considered briefly at the end of the lecture from *The Renewal of Education*, included in chapter 6. Steiner also mentions how geography can be taught in connection with botany in lecture 8 of *A Modern Art of Education*.

A lively summary of the geography curriculum and how to present it to the children is given by René Querido in the chapter "On Teaching Geography: Awakening Our Responsibility for the Earth" in *Creativity in Education*. Roy Wilkinson provides an overview of how to teach geography in his booklet on *Teaching Geography*, and Alan Howard's article "'Mapping Out' a Geography Period," included in *Child and Man Extracts*, is also helpful.

* * * * * *

The Twelfth-Year Change

Steiner's most extensive references to the twelfth year change occur in lectures 11 and 12 of *Soul Economy and Waldorf Education*. In these lectures he describes the physiological and psychological changes between the tenth and fourteenth years and explains how the curriculum of the upper elementary grades meets the needs of children who are about to cross the threshold of puberty. In the beginning of lecture 6 of *The Spiritual Ground of Education*, Steiner speaks about the changes at the ages of nine and twelve in terms of the changing relationship of the rhythmic system and the muscles and skeleton. Lecture 5 of *The Child's Changing Consciousness and Waldorf Education* has a number of illuminating references to the birth of the astral body and to the new capacities that children develop at the age of twelve. Most of the other references to the twelfth-year change occur in the context of discussing the child's capacity to understand causality; these are listed below in the section on history.

Herman Köpke's *On the Threshold of Adolescence: The Struggle for Independence in the Twelfth Year* is an excellent book about the twelfth year change. Köpke presents the twelfth-year change through the story of a young Waldorf teacher who is struggling to come to terms with the changes in her students. Torin Finser's *School as a Journey* and Marjorie Spock's *Teaching as a Lively Art* both paint vivid pictures of the students and the curriculum in the upper elementary grades. A.C. Harwood's *The Recovery of Man in Childhood* also has a chapter devoted to this theme. Other references to the twelfth-year change include Eva Frommer's *Voyage Through Childhood into the Adult World*, Eugene Schwartz's *Rhythms and Turning Points in the Life of the Child*, and Bernard Lievegoed's *Phases of Childhood*.

Science Teaching

Steiner outlines the physical science curriculum for the upper elementary grades in the "Curriculum Lectures," in *Discussions with Teachers*. The two-volume *Faculty Meetings with Rudolf*

Steiner contain several references to the high school curriculum; and Steiner's curriculum indications and references to teaching science are compiled by Stockmeyer in his *Rudolf Steiner's Curriculum for Waldorf Schools*. Readers who wish to delve further into Steiner's work in the physical sciences might wish to refer to the following lecture cycles: *The Light Course, The Warmth Course, The Relation of the Diverse Branches of Natural Science to Astronomy*, and *Anthroposophy and Science: Observation, Experiment, Mathematics*.

In addition to the lectures reprinted here, there are a few additional references to the teaching of science. In *The Spiritual Ground of Education* and in lectures 11 and 12 of *Soul Economy and Waldorf Education*, Steiner speaks about the changes that occur in twelve year olds that allow them to begin to understand the physical sciences. In lecture 10 of *A Modern Art of Education* and lecture 7 of *The Kingdom of Childhood* Steiner mentions the teaching of physics and chemistry, and he stresses how important it is that these subjects be connected to real life.

The Goethean approach is described in *The Marriage of Sense and Thought: Imaginative Participation in Science* by Stephen Edelglass, et. al. and in Henri Bortoft's *The Wholeness of Nature: Goethe's Way toward a Science of Conscious Participation in Nature*. Ernst Lehrs's *Man or Matter* gives a historical overview of the Goethean approach to physics, and Heinrich Proskauer's *The Rediscovery of Color* examines Goethe's color theory. *Catching the Light: The Entwined History of Light and Mind* by Arthur Zajonc is a beautifully written, insightful exploration of our relationship to light through the ages.

A number of works also describe how physics and chemistry are taught in the upper elementary grades. Manfred von Mackensen's *A Phenomena-Based Physics* provides a thorough background to sound, light, heat, magnetism, and electricity and includes many science activities. In *Physics is Fun! A Sourcebook for Teachers*, Roberto Trostli examines the goals, methods, and curriculum for physics in the three upper elementary grades. This book also includes over four hundred demonstrations, activities, and investigations that are interesting, engaging, and easy to perform. A valuable resource is Graham Kennish's *Chemistry in Classes 7 and 8 for Class Teachers of Steiner/Waldorf Schools*; it provides a thorough background with many experiments. Frits H. Julius's *The World of Matter and the Education of Man* is also helpful for chemistry teaching in grades 7, 8, and 9, and his booklet *Sound Between Matter and Spirit* is useful to class teachers. Another good resource is Hermann Baravalle's *Introduction to Physics in the Waldorf Schools*, which describes how acoustics and optics can be presented to upper elementary students. Readers may also wish to refer to a conference report on *Goethean Science in the Waldorf Curriculum*, which outlines the natural science curriculum for the upper elementary grades.

Teaching History

Steiner's suggestions for the history curriculum in the elementary school can be found in the "Curriculum Lectures." *Faculty Meetings with Rudolf Steiner* contains several references to the history curriculum in the high school, and Steiner's indications for teaching history are included in Stockmeyer's *Rudolf Steiner's Curriculum for the Waldorf Schools*.

In most of the lectures listed in the previous two sections, Steiner speaks about the changes at the age of twelve that allow the child to grasp the concept of causality in history. In lecture 3 of *The Kingdom of Childhood*, he describes how the child's new capacity to understand causality is addressed by the study of history. In lecture 9 of *A Modern Art of Education*, Steiner speaks about the teaching of history, and he urges teachers to develop a living relationship to the subject. Steiner describes how to bring the teaching of history to life in discussion 7 of *Discussions with Teachers*, in which he shows how a teacher might engage the students in the study of the Crusades.

Christoph Lindenberg's *Teaching History: Suggested Themes for the Curriculum in Waldorf Schools* is an invaluable resource for elementary and high school history teachers. Lindenberg clearly describes Steiner's symptomatological approach to history and makes excellent suggestions for themes to be considered at each grade level. Werner Glas's *The Waldorf School Approach to History* is also useful, for it examines the history curriculum in the different grades and describes the Waldorf method of history teaching. Readers are also encouraged to refer to Henry Barnes's seminal article on "History Teaching: A Dramatic Art," included in *Waldorf Schools* vol. 2 and in *Educating as an Art*. Notes on historical subjects for fifth and sixth grade by DorothyHarrer have been published as *Chapters in Ancient History* and *Roman Lives*. Charles Kovacs's teaching notes have also been published as *Ancient Mythologies: India, Persia, Babylon, Egypt*, and *Greece: Mythology and History*, and Leo Heirman's study of Greek mythology is very interesting. Roy Wilkinson's three booklets on teaching history provide summaries and practical suggestions for the upper elementary grades.

* * * * *

Adolescence

Steiner's *Education for Adolescents* focuses on this stage of human development and illustrates how the Waldorf curriculum and methods address the needs of the high school student. These lectures are highly recommended for anyone who wishes to read further about this subject. In addition to the lectures reprinted in this volume, readers may wish to refer to lecture 4 of *A Modern Art of Education*, where Steiner describes the changes at puberty and how the physical functions of the astral body are transformed into soul functions. The following lecture, "The Emancipation of the Will in the Human Organism" describes the changes in human development between the ages of 14 and 21.

The most thorough and helpful book about adolescence from an anthroposophical perspective is Betty Staley's *Between Form and Freedom: A Practical Guide to the Teenage Years*. The first section examines the nature of adolescence and its stages, and it includes a thorough description of the temperaments. There is also a chapter on the development of character during adolescence. The second section describes the challenges of adolescence, how the adolescent relates to family, friends, and school. The book concludes with a section on the problems of adolescence: problems of self-esteem, sex, alcohol, drugs, and food. Julian Sleigh's *Thirteen to Nineteen: Discovering the Light: Conversations with Parents* helpfully charts the course of adolescence with advice and encouragement for parents. Michael Luxford's *Adolescence and its Significance for those with Special Needs* has essays on the nature of adolescence and on adolescents with special needs; it also contains three essays by Karl König, founder of the Camphill communities for children and adults with special needs.

A.C. Harwood's *The Recovery of Man in Childhood* has a chapter on adolescence, followed by three chapters that give detailed descriptions of the curriculum and approach of the Waldorf high school. The nature of adolescence is also considered in Eva Frommer's *Voyage Through Childhood into the Adult World*, Gilbert Childs's *Steiner Education in Theory and Practice* and Bernard Lievegoed's *Phases of Childhood*. Both Eugene Schwartz's *Adolescence: The Search For Self* and Erich Gabert's *Educating the Adolescent: Discipline or Freedom* offer valuable insights into this stage of development and give examples of how to deal with its challenges.

The High School Curriculum

In addition to books and articles that illustrate the curriculum and methods of the Waldorf high school, the following list also includes titles that consider some of the subjects in the high school curriculum from an anthroposophical perspective.

Language and Literature

For the Love of Literature and Language: A Celebration of Language and Imagination, Christy MacKaye Barnes, ed.

"Literature with the Upper School," Francis Edmunds.

"Epic, Dramatic, and Lyric Poetry" and "The Appreciation of Poetry," A.C. Harwood, *Child and Man Extracts.*

"Language and Literature for the Adolescent," Eileen Hutchins, *Child and Man Extracts.*

"Teaching Medieval Romances," Jean Hamshaw, *Waldorf School* vol. 2.

"The Adolescent's Approach to Literature," H.L. Hetherington, *Child and Man Extracts.*

Sing Me the Creation, Paul Matthews.

Literature Main Lessons: Parsifal and Shakespeare

"Parzifal: An Introduction," Eileen Hutchins, *For the Love of Literature.*

The Mystery of the Holy Grail: A Modern Path of Initiation, René Querido.

The Holy Grail from the Works of Rudolf Steiner, Stephen Roboz.

The Ninth Century: World History in the Light of the Holy Grail, Walter Johannes Stein.

The Speech of the Grail, Linda Sussman.

From Round Table to Grail Castle, Isabel Wyatt.

Shakespeare's Flowering of the Spirit, Margaret Bennel.

Shakespeare's Prophetic Mind, A.C. Harwood.

The English Spirit, D. E. Faulkner Jones.

History

"History Teaching: A Dramatic Art," Henry Barnes.

The Waldorf Approach to History, Werner Glas.

Teaching History: Suggested Themes for the Curriculum in Waldorf Schools, Christoph Lindenberg.

"History in the Twelfth Class" and "Homer: The Beginning of Greek History," Rudi Lissau, *Child and Man Extracts.*

"Philadelphia: The End of Greek History," Rudi Lissau, *Child and Man Extracts.*

Geography, Earth Science, and Astronomy

China: Ancient Inspiration and New Directions, Judith Blatchford.

Silica, Calcium, and Clay: Processes in Mineral, Plant, Animal and Man, Friedrich Benesch & Klaus Wilde.

China: Ancient Inspirations and New Directions, Judith Blatchford.

The Sun: The Ancient Mysteries and a New Physics, Georg Blattman.

The Living Earth and *The Secrets of Metals*, Walter Cloos.

Astronomy and the Imagination, Norman Davidson.

Living Metals, L.F.C. Mees.

Weather and Cosmos, Dennis Klocek.

The Secrets of Metals, Wilhelm Pelikan.

"Geography and Our Responsibility for the Earth," René Querido, *Creativity in Education* and in *Journal for Anthroposophy*, no. 35, 36.

Europa: A Spiritual Biography, Richard Seddon.

Physics and Chemistry

"Modern Physics in the Waldorf High School" Stephen Edelglass, *Waldorf School* vol. 2.

The Marriage of Sense and Thought: Imaginative Participation in Science, Stephen Edelglass, Georg Maier, Hans Gebert, John Davy.

"Introducing Chemistry to Children in Their Fifteenth Year," H. Friedeberg, *Child and Man Extracts*.

"High School Physics and Chemistry" Hans Gebert, *Educating as An Art*.

The Nature of Substance, Rudolf Hauschka.

"Science in the Upper School," Hans Gebert, *Child and Man Extracts*.

"A Religious Background for the Teaching of Chemistry," Eileen Hutchins.

Nuclear Energy: A Spiritual Perspective, Michael Jones.

The World of Matter and the Education of Man: Chemistry Presented, Simple Phenomena, Frits Julius.

Man or Matter, Ernst Lehrs.

Chemistry, Gerhard Ott.

Catching the Light, Arthur Zajonc.

Mathematics

"Appreciative Thinking: With Special Reference to the Teaching of Mathematics," Amos Franceschelli in *Educating as an Art*.

"Mathematics in the Classroom: Mine Shaft and Skylight," Amos Franceschelli, *Journal for Anthroposophy*, number 35.

"The Teaching of Mathematics," Hans Gebert in *Child and Man Extracts*.

Encounters with the Infinite:Geometrical Experiences through Active Contemplation, H. Keller-von Asten.

Geometry for the Waldorf High School, Herbert Swanson.*Projective Geometry*, Olive Whicher.

Life Sciences

The Plant Between Sun and Earth, George Adams and Olive Whicher.

"The Human Skull: A Lesson with Grade Ten" Francis Edmunds, *Waldorf School* vol. 2; and, *Renewing Education*.

The Vortex of Life: Nature's Patterns in Space and Time, Lawrence Edwards.

The Plant, Gerbert Grohmann.

Nutrition, Rudolf Hauschka.

Genetics and the Manipulation of Life, Craig Holdrege.

The Human Organs: Their Functional and Psychological Significance, Walter Holzapfel.

Nutrition, vols. 1, 2; and *The Twelve Groups of Animals*, Eugen Kolisko.

Sketches for an Imaginative Zoology, Karl König.

Rhythms in Human Beings and the Cosmos, Rudolf Meyer.

Man and Animal; and *Towards a New Zoology*, Hermann Popplebaum.

The Secrets of the Skeleton, L.F.C. Mees.

Man and Mammal, Wolfgang Schad.

The Dynamics of Nutrition; and *The Essentials of Nutrition*, Gerhard Schmidt.

Sensitive Chaos, Theodor Schwenk.

* * * * * *

The Arts in Waldorf Education

Music

Steiner gave many lectures on music, some of which are in *The Inner Nature of Music and the Experience of Tone*. There are also lectures about music and references to music teaching in *Art in the Light of Mystery Wisdom* and in *The Arts and Their Mission*.

Steiner describes the music curriculum for the elementary grades in the "Curriculum Lectures." In *Faculty Meetings with Rudolf Steiner* there are several references to the teaching of music in the high school. Steiner's curriculum indications and suggestions for teaching music are summarized by Stockmeyer in *Rudolf Steiner's Curriculum for Waldorf Schools*.

Many of Steiner's comments about music and music teaching appear in the context of discussing the astral body and the ninth- and twelfth-year changes. In lecture 8 of *Human Values in Education*, Steiner describes the astral body as musical in nature, and he explains how music is important for the emancipation of the astral body. He also considers the relation of music to the astral body in lecture 3 of *The Child's Changing Consciousness and Waldorf Education*, lecture 3 of *The Essentials of Education* and lecture 3 of *The Roots of Education*. In lecture 11 of *A Modern Art of Education*, Steiner considers the same themes and concludes with some interesting remarks about the relation of musical forces to the forms of the animal kingdom.

In lecture 10 of *The Renewal of Education*, Steiner described how to teach singing. He considers the importance of singing and playing musical instruments in lecture 6 of *The Kingdom of Childhood*, and he describes the harmonizing effects of listening to and playing music in lecture 4 of *Education for Adolescents*.

In *The Temperaments and the Arts*, Magda Lissau examines the relationship between musical instruments and the temperaments. In *Steiner Education in Theory and Practice*, Gilbert Childs contrasts the work of the plastic, formative forces with the musical forces, and in *The Recovery of Man in Childhood*, A.C. Harwood briefly summarizes the music curriculum. Articles on music in the Waldorf school include "The Music Lessons in the First Three Classes" by M. Watson in *Child and Man Extracts*, and "The Music Curriculum" by George Rose in *Educating as an Art*.

Readers who wish to explore the art of music from an anthroposophical perspective should refer to *Man, Music, and Cosmos* by Anny von Lange; *Singing and the Etheric Tone* by Hilda Deighton, Gina Palermo, and Dina Winter; *Uncovering the Voice* by Valborg Werbeck-Svärdström; and *Expanding Tonal Awareness* by Heiner Fuland.

Speech and Drama

Steiner gave a lecture course entitled *Speech and Drama*, and a course on the development of language, *The Genius of Language*. At the end of lecture 4 of *Practical Advice to Teachers*, Steiner says that teachers must be profoundly conscious of the power of articulate speech and in *Discussions with Teachers* (discussion 5), he introduces a series of speech exercises to help teachers develop speech and articulation. In lecture 4 of *The Child's Changing Consciousness and Waldorf Education*, Steiner speaks of the difference between vowels and consonants, and returns to this subject in lecture 6 of *The Kingdom of Childhood*. In lecture 8 of *Human Values in Education*, Steiner speaks about the evolution of forms in speech and the importance of teachers developing an inner feeling for language. *The Renewal of Education* contains references to speech and language; lecture 9 focuses on the importance of dialect; lecture 10 on recitation; and lecture 12 on how good speech and breathing may be beneficial for the child's health.

Werner Glas's *Speech Education in the Primary Grades in Waldorf Schools* has a section on choral speaking, and Magda Lissau deals briefly with speech in *The Temperaments and the Arts*. Christy Barnes's excellent articles on speech and recitation may be found *For the Love of Literature*. A wonderful collections of poems suitable for recitation in the different grade levels has been compiled by Heather Thomas.

Many Waldorf teachers write plays for their classes. Published collections of plays for children include *25 Plays Inspired by Waldorf Teachers*, *Plays for Classes and Communities* by Eugene Schwartz; *Pedagogical Theatre*, by Arthur Pittis; *21 Plays for Children* by Pelham Moffat; *Plays for Grades One through Four* by Michael Hedley Burton; and *Collected Plays for Young and Old* by Evelyn Francis Capel. Readers who are interested in the art of drama may also wish to refer to *Liberation of the Actor* by Peter Bridgemont.

Eurythmy

Steiner gave three important courses on eurythmy: *Eurythmy as Visible Speech*; *Eurythmy as Visible Music*; and *Curative Eurythmy*. They may be difficult for most people; Steiner's introductions to various eurythmy performances, published as *An Introduction to Eurythmy*, may prove more accessible.

Stockmeyer summarizes Steiner's indications for a eurythmy curriculum in *Rudolf Steiner's Curriculum for Waldorf Schools*. In lecture 8 of *The Spiritual Ground of Education*, and in lecture 12 of *A Modern Art of Education*, Steiner clearly and concisely describes eurythmy. In lecture 6 of *The Renewal of Education*, he explains how eurythmy and gymnastics affect the students' life of feeling and will. In the first four lectures of *Education for Adolescents*, there are many references to eurythmy and gymnastics, and Steiner describes them in relation to one another and explains how they bring balance to the curriculum. In lecture 7 of *Soul Economy and Waldorf Education* (which is reprinted as part of chapter 1), Steiner explains how physical activity fits into the schedule of the day, and in lecture 15 he describes the effects of play and gymnastics.

A.C. Harwood gives a brief description of eurythmy in *The Recovery of Man in Childhood*, and there are articles on eurythmy in *Educating as an Art*, *Waldorf Schools* vol. 1, and *Child and Man Extracts*. There are two useful anthologies of eurythmy exercises, verses, and plays by Molly von Heider: *And Then Take Hands* and *Come Unto These Yellow Sands*.

For those who wish to know more about eurythmy, Thomas Poplawski's *Eurythmy: Rhythm, Dance and Soul* provides a comprehensive, illustrated introduction; Marjorie Spock's *Eurythmy* is also a good introduction.

Painting and Drawing

Steiner's curriculum indications for painting and drawing in the elementary grades may be found in the "Curriculum Lectures"; relevant quotations from the various educational lectures and conferences have been compiled by Stockmeyer in his *Curriculum*.

Steiner considered painting and drawing crucial activities for the child's development. In the first lecture of *Practical Advice to Teachers*, he stresses the importance of artistic activities in the early school years, and in lecture 4 he shows teachers how to introduce a first lesson in form drawing and how to help children recognize color harmonies.

In lecture 4 of *The Kingdom of Childhood*, Steiner describes what was to become known in Waldorf schools as form drawing. In this lecture he also speaks about developing the children's sense for color harmonies, and in the section that contains questions and answers, he gives an example of how to develop lines out of the boundaries between colors. Steiner also shows examples of form drawing in lecture 9 of *A Modern Art of Education*, and he explains that the forms the child draws continue to work in the child's etheric body during sleep. In lecture 5 of *The Child's Changing Consciousness*, Steiner speaks about the teaching of art and about the importance of teaching color perspective. In lecture 6 of *The Renewal of Education*, he explains how children should be taught to draw, and in lecture 13, he explains how perspective and shadow drawing help children develop a sense for space.

Steiner suggested that art lessons be adapted to the children's particular temperaments and needs. In lecture 6 of *The Spiritual Ground of Education*, he shows how to modify a painting lesson, and in discussion 4 of *Discussions with Teachers* he demonstrates forms and designs for working with the different temperaments. Readers who wish to gain a sense of how Steiner approached painting and drawing should refer to "How Rudolf Steiner Taught Us to Paint in *A Man Before Others*, and *A Drawing Lesson with Rudolf Steiner* by D.J. van Bemelman.

A clear and comprehensive summary of the painting and drawing curriculum and methods may be found in Margrit Jüneman's *Painting and Drawing in the Waldorf School*. Other resources are *Drawing from the Book of Nature* by Dennis Klocek; *New Eyes for Plants* by Margaret Colquhoun and Axel Ewald; and *Black and White Shaded Drawing* by Valerie Jacobs. Hildegard Gerbert describes how art and art history are taught in *Education Through Art*, and Magda Lissau examines drawing and painting in her book on the temperaments. The following articles also describe various aspects of the visual arts: "Experience in Painting," Jean Zay, *Educating as an Art*; "Color in Childhood," Trude Amann, *Waldorf Schools*, vol. 1; "Drawing: From First Grade to High School," Carl Froebe, *Waldorf Schools* vol. 2.

Form Drawing by Hans Niederhauser and Margaret Frohlich provides a most practical introduction to the subject, and *Dynamic Drawing* by Hermann Kirchner describes how to work with form drawing in a therapeutic way. Rudolf Kützli's books on form drawing show how one can develop this subject to a fine art, and, in *Steiner Education in Theory and Practice*, Gilbert Childs shows the transition from form drawing to geometry. Readers should also refer to Hermann von Baravalle's *Geometric Drawing and the Waldorf School Plan* and *Perspective Drawing* for ideas on how these forms of drawing might be presented.

Those who wish to know more about anthroposophic approaches to color and painting should refer to *Colour* by Rudolf Steiner, *The Rediscovery of Color* by Heinrich O. Proskauer, *Pure Colour* by Maria Schindler, *The Individuality of Colour: Contributions to a Methodical Schooling in the Experience of Colour* by Elizabeth Koch and Gerard Wagner, and Collot D'Herbois's two books on color.

Modeling and the Practical Arts

There are only a few references to modeling and the practical arts in Steiner's educational lectures. In lecture 1 of *Practical Advice to Teachers*, Steiner speaks about the differences between drawing and modeling, and he describes how modeling engages the whole child. In lecture 11 of *A Modern Art of Education*, he speaks about the beneficial effects that modeling has on the children's ability to notice what is in their environment. Steiner also discusses modeling in lecture 8 of *Human Values in Education*. After describing how the etheric body models the physical body, he suggests that teachers should practice sculpture in order to understand how etheric forces work.

In lecture 7 of *The Spiritual Ground of Education*, Steiner speaks at length about the practical arts, and he describes the different kinds of woodwork projects that students in the upper grades might make. In lecture 14 of *Soul Economy and Waldorf Education*, he also speaks about the practical arts and describes their importance for the rest of the students' lives.

Hedwig Hauck's book *Handwork and Handicrafts* is an invaluable resource for crafts and handwork teachers. Magda Lissau has a chapter on the plastic arts in her book on the temperaments and the arts, and there are two articles on modeling in *Child and Man Extracts*. Two articles describe the importance of handwork in the early grades: "Handwork in the Early Grades" in *Waldorf Schools* vol. 1, and "Handwork Lessons" by Rosemary Gebert in *Educating as an Art*. Crafts lessons in the upper grades are the subject of an article by Margaret Frohlich in *Educating as an Art*, and her article "Bookbinding in the High School" has been reprinted in *Waldorf Schools*, vol. 2. For description of woodwork classes, readers should refer to the two articles on woodwork in *Child and Man Extracts*.

BIBLIOGRAPHY

Rudolf Steiner: Lectures and Writings on Education

Balance in Teaching (first four lectures of GA; Mercury Press, 1982); *Deeper Insights into Education* (last three lectures of GA; Anthroposophic Press, 1988), *Erziehung und Unterricht aus Menschenerkenntnis*, 9 lectures, Stuttgart, 1920, 1922, 1923 (GA 302a).

The Child's Changing Consciousness As the Basis of Pedagogical Practice (Anthroposophic Press, 1996), *Die pädagogisch Praxis vom Gesichtspunkte geisteswissenschaftlicher Menschenerkenntnis*, 8 lectures, Dornach, 1923 (GA 306).

Discussions with Teachers (Anthroposophic Press, 1997), *Erziehungskunst*, 15 dscussions, Stuttgart, 1919 (GA 295); includes the "Curriculum Lectures."

Education as a Force for Social Change (Anthroposophic Press, 1997), *Die Erziehungsfrage als soziale Frage*, 6 lectures, Dornach, 1919 (GA 296); previously *Education as a Social Problem* .

Education for Adolescents (Anthroposophic Press, 1996), *Menschenerkenntnis und Unterrichtsgestaltung*, 8 lectures, Stuttgart, 1921 (GA 302); previously *The Supplementary Course—Upper School* and *Waldorf Education for Adolescence.*

The Education of the Child and Early Lectures on Education (A collection) (Anthroposophic Press, 1996).

The Essentials of Education (Anthroposophic Press, 1997), *Die Methodik des Lehrens und die Lebensbedingungen des Erziehens*, 5 lectures, Stuttgart, 1924 (GA 308).

Faculty Meetings with Rudolf Steiner, 2 volumes (Anthroposophic Press, 1998), *Konferenzen mit den Lehren der Freien Waldorfschule 1919–1924*, 3 Volumes (GA 300a–c).

The Foundations of Human Experience (Anthroposophic Press, 1996), *Allgemeine Menschenkunde als Grundlage der Pädagogik. Pädagogischer Grundkurs*, 14 Lectures, Stuttgart, 1919 (GA 293); previously *Study of Man.*

The Genius of Language (Anthroposophic Press, 1995), *Geisteswissenschaftliche Sprachbetrachtungen*, 6 Lectures, Stuttgart, 1919 (GA 299).

Human Values in Education (Rudolf Steiner Press, 1971), *Der pädagogische Wert der Menschenerkenntnis und der Kulturwert der Pädagogik*, 10 Public Lectures, Arnheim, 1924 (GA 310).

The Kingdom of Childhood (Anthroposophic Press, 1995), *Die Kunst des Erziehens aus dem Erfassen der Menschenwesenheit*, 7 Lectures, Torquay, 1924 (GA 311).

The Light Course (Steiner Schools Fellowship, 1977), *Geisteswissenschaftliche Impulse zur Entwicklung der Physik. Erster naturwissenschaftliche Kurs: Licht, Farbe, Ton—Masse, Elektrizität, Magnetismus*, 10 lectures, Stuttgart, 1919–1920 (GA 320).

A Modern Art of Education (Rudolf Steiner Press, 1981) and *Education and Modern Spiritual Life* (Garber Publications, 1989), *Gegenwärtiges Geistesleben und Erziehung*, 4 lectures, Ilkley, 1923 (GA 307).

Practical Advice to Teachers (Rudolf Steiner Press, 1988), *Erziehungskunst Methodische-Didaktisches*, 14 lectures, Stuttgart, 1919 (GA 294).

"The Relation of the Diverse Branches of Natural Science to Astronomy" (available in typescript), *Das Verhältnis der verschiedenen naturwissenschaftlichen Gebiete zur Astronomie. Dritter naturwissenschaftliche Kurs: Himmelskunde in Beziehung zum Menschen und zur Menschenkunde*, 18 lectures, Stuttgart, 1921 (GA 323).

The Renewal of Education (Kolisko Archive Publications for Steiner Schools Fellowship Publications, Michael Hall, Forest Row, East Sussex, UK, 1981), *Die Erneuerung der Pädagogisch-didaktischen Kunst durch Geisteswissenschaft*, 14 lectures, Basel, 1920 (GA 301).

The Roots of Education (Anthroposophic Press, 1997), *Anthroposophische Pädagogik und ihre Voraussetzungen*, 5 lectures, Bern, 1924 (GA 309).

Rudolf Steiner in the Waldorf School: Lectures and Conversations (Anthroposophic Press, 1996), *Rudolf Steiner in der Waldorfschule, Vorträge und Ansprachen*, Stuttgart, 1919–1924 (GA 298).

Soul Economy and Waldorf Education (Anthroposophic Press, 1986), *Die Gesunder Entwicklung des Menschenwesens,* 16 lectures, Dornach, 1921–22 (GA 303).

The Spirit of the Waldorf School (Anthroposophic Press, 1995), *Die Waldorf Schule und ihr Geist,* 6 lectures, Stuttgart and Basel, 1919 (GA 297).

The Spiritual Ground of Education (Garber Publications, 1989), *Die geistig-seelischen Grundkräfte der Erziehungskunst,* 12 lectures, 1 special lecture, Oxford 1922 (GA 305).

Waldorf Education and Anthroposophy 1 (Anthroposophic Press, 1995), *Erziehungs- und Unterrichtsmethoden auf Anthroposophischer Grundlage,* 9 public lectures, various cities, 1921–1922 (GA 304).

Waldorf Education and Anthroposophy 2 (Anthroposophic Press, 1996), *Anthroposophische Menschenkunde und Pädagogik,* 9 public lectures, various cities, 1923–1924 (GA 304a).

The Warmth Course (Mercury Press, 1988), *Geisteswissenschaftliche Impulse zur Entwicklung der Physik. Zweiter naturwissenschaftliche Kurs: die Wärme auf der Grenze positiver und negativer Materialität,* 14 lectures, Stuttgart, 1920 (GA 321).

Rudolf Steiner: Other Writings and Lectures

Agriculture: Spiritual Foundations for the Renewal of Agriculture, Bio-Dynamic Farming and Gardening Association, Kimberton, PA, 1993.

Anthroposophical Leading Thoughts: Anthroposophy as a Path of Knowledge and The Michael Mystery, Rudolf Steiner Press, London, 1985.

Anthroposophy (A Fragment), Catherine Creeger & Detlef Hardorp, trans., Anthroposophic Press, Hudson, NY, 1996.

Anthroposophy in Everyday Life, Anthroposophic Press, Hudson, NY, 1995 (contains "The Four Temperaments").

The Apocalypse of St. John, Rudolf Steiner Press, 1985.

Art as Seen in the Light of Mystery Wisdom, Rudolf Steiner Press, London, 1996.

Aspects of Human Evolution, Anthroposophic Press, Hudson, NY, 1987.

The Boundaries of Natural Science, Anthroposophic Press, Spring Valley, NY, 1983.

The Calendar of the Soul, William & Liselotte Mann, trans., Hawthorn Press, Stroud, UK, 1990.

The Calendar of the Soul, Ruth & Hans Pusch, trans., Anthroposophic Press, Hudson, NY, 1988.

Christianity as Mystical Fact, Andrew Welburn, trans., Anthroposophic Press, Hudson, NY, 1986.

Colour, Rudolf Steiner Press, Sussex, 1992.

Curative Education, Rudolf Steiner Press, London, 1981.

Curative Eurythmy, Rudolf Steiner Press, London, 1983.

The East in the Light of the West & "Children of Lucifer," a Drama by Edouard Schuré), Spiritual Science Library, Blauvelt, NY, 1986.

Economics: The World as One Economy, New Economy Publications, Bristol, 1993.

Education as an Art (with other authors, Paul Allen, ed.), Steinerbooks, Blauvelt, NY, 1988.

Egyptian Myths and Mysteries, Anthroposophic Press, Hudson, NY, 1997.

Extending Practical Medicine: Fundamental Principles Based on the Science of the Spirit (Dr. Ita Wegman, co-author), Rudolf Steiner Press, London, 1996 (previous trans., *Fundamentals of Therapy*).

Eurythmy as Visible Music. Rudolf Steiner Press, London, n.d.

Eurythmy as Visible Speech. Rudolf Steiner Press, London, 1984.

The Evolution of the Earth and Man and the Influence of the Stars, Anthroposophic Press, Hudson, NY, 1987.

The Foundation Stone / The Life, Nature, and Cultivation of Anthroposophy, Rudolf Steiner Press, London, 1996 (previously published as separate volumes).

The Fruits of Anthroposophy, Rudolf Steiner Press, London, 1986.

Health and Illness: Lectures to the Workmen, 2 vols. Anthroposophic Press, Hudson, NY, 1983.

How to Know Higher Worlds: A Modern Path of Initiation, Christopher Bamford, trans., Anthroposophic Press, Hudson, NY, 1994.

Human and Cosmic Thought, Rudolf Steiner Press, London, 1991.

The Human Being in Body, Soul, and Spirit, Anthroposophic Press, Hudson, NY, 1989.

The Inner Nature of Music and the Experience of Tone, Anthroposophic Press, Hudson, NY, 1983.

An Introduction to Eurythmy, Anthroposophic Press, Hudson, NY, 1984.

Intuitive Thinking as a Spiritual Path: A Philosophy of Freedom, Michael Lipson, trans., Anthroposophic Press, Hudson, NY,1995.

Karmic Relationships: Esoteric Studies, 8 vols., Rudolf Steiner Press, London, 1974–1997.

A Lecture on Eurythmy, Rudolf Steiner Press, London, 1967.

Light: First Scientific Lecture-Course (Light-Course), Steiner Schools Fellowship Publications, East Sussex, 1987.

Man and the World of Stars: The Spiritual Communion of Mankind, Anthroposophic Press, New York, 1963.

Occult Science, An Outline, George & Mary Adams, trans., Rudolf Steiner Press, London, 1989.

An Outline of Esoteric Science, Catherine Creeger, trans., Anthroposophic Press, Hudson, NY, 1997.

An Outline of Occult Science; Henry Monges, trans., Anthroposophic Press, Hudson, NY, 1972.

Pastoral Medicine, Mercury Press, Spring Valley, NY, 1987.

The Philosophy of Spiritual Activity: A Philosophy of Freedom, Rita Stebbing, trans., Rudolf Steiner Press, Bristol, 1988.

Polarities in the Evolution of Mankind: West and East, Materialism and Mysticism, Knowledge and Belief, Rudolf Steiner Press, London, 1987.

The Portal of Initiation: A Rosicrucian Mystery Drama / Fairy Tale of the Green Snake and the Beautiful Lily (by Johann W. von Goethe), Spiritual Science Library, Blauvelt, NY, 1981.

Prayers for Parents and Children, Rudolf Steiner Press, London, 1995.

The Principle of Spiritual Economy in Connection with Questions of Reincarnation, Anthroposophic Press, Hudson, NY, 1986.

Psychoanalysis & Spiritual Psychology, Anthroposophic Press, Hudson, NY, 1990.

Reincarnation and Karma: Two Fundamental Truths of Human Existence, Anthroposophic Press, Hudson, NY, 1992.

Rudolf Steiner: An Autobiography, Steinerbooks, Blauvelt, NY, 1977.

The Social Future, Anthroposophic Press, Spring Valley, NY, 1972.

Social Issues: Meditative Thinking and the Threefold Social Order, Anthroposophic Press, Hudson, NY, 1991.

Speech and Drama, Anthroposophic Press, Hudson, NY, 1959.

The Spiritual Guidance of the Individual and Humanity, Anthroposophic Press, Hudson, NY, 1992.

Spiritual Science and Medicine, Steinerbooks, Blauvelt, NY, 1989.

Theosophy: An Introduction to the Spiritual Processes in Human Life and in the Cosmos, Anthroposophic Press, Hudson, NY, 1994.

Theosophy of the Rosicrucian, Rudolf Steiner Press, London, 1981.

Therapeutic Insights: Earthly and Cosmic Laws, Mercury Press, Spring Valley, NY, 1984.

Toward Imagination: Culture and the Individual, Anthroposophic Press, Hudson, NY, 1990.

Truth-Wrought-Words: with Other Verses and Prose Passages, Anthroposophic Press, Spring Valley, NY, 1979.

The Twelve Moods, Mercury Press, Spring Valley, NY, 1984.

The Universal Human: The Evolution of Individuality, Anthroposophic Press, Hudson, NY, 1990.

Universe, Earth and Man, Rudolf Steiner Press, London, 1987.

Verses and Meditations, Rudolf Steiner Press, Bristol, 1993.

Warmth Course, Mercury Press, Spring Valley, NY, 1988.

Wonders of the World, Ordeals of the Soul, Revelations of the Spirit, Rudolf Steiner Press, 1983.

The World of the Senses and the World of the Spirit, Rudolf Steiner Research Foundation, 1990.

The Younger Generation, Anthroposophic Press, Hudson, NY, 1984.

Other Authors

A Man Before Others: Rudolf Steiner Remembered. London: Rudolf Steiner Press, 1993.

Adams, George and Olive Whicher. *The Plant Between Sun and Earth*. London: Rudolf Steiner Press, 1980.

Aeppli, Willi. *Rudolf Steiner Education and the Developing Child*. Hudson, NY: Anthroposophic Press, 1986.

Andersen, Henning, *Active Arithmetic! Movement and Mathematics Teaching in the Lower Grades of a Waldorf School*. Fair Oaks, CA: Association of Waldorf Schools of North America, 1995.

Anschütz, Marieka. *Children and Their Temperament*. Edinburgh, Scotland: Floris Books, 1995.

Baldwin, Rahima. *You Are Your Child's First Teacher*. Berkeley, CA: Celestial Arts, 1989.

Baravalle, Hermann von. *The Teaching of Arithmetic and the Waldorf School Plan*. Englewood, NJ: Waldorf School Monographs, 1967.

———— *Introduction to Physics in the Waldorf Schools: The Balance Between Art and Science.* Englewood, NJ: Waldorf School Monographs, 1967.

———— *Perspective Drawing.* Englewood, NJ: Waldorf School Monographs, 1968.

———— *Geometric Drawing and the Waldorf School Plan.* Englewood, NJ: Waldorf School Monographs, 1959.

Barnes, Christy MacKaye, ed., *For the Love of Literature: A Celebration of Language and Imagination,* Hudson, NY: Anthroposophic Press, 1996.

Barnes, Henry, *A Life for the Spirit: Rudolf Steiner in the Crosscurrents of Our Time,* Hudson, NY: Anthroposophic Press, 1997.

Belyi, Andrei, Aasya Turgenieff, Margarita Voloschin. *Reminiscences of Rudolf Steiner.* Ghent, NY: Adonis Press, 1987.

Bennel, Margaret. *Shakespeare's Flowering of the Spirit.* Isabel Wyatt, ed. Sussex, England: Lanthorn Press, 1971.

Blatchford, Judith. *China: Ancient Inspiration and New Directions.* Fair Oaks, CA: Rudolf Steiner College Publications, 1989.

Blatmann, Georg. *The Sun: The Ancient Mysteries and a New Physics.* Hudson, NY: Anthroposophic Press, 1985.

Bott, Victor. *Spiritual Science and the Art of Healing.* Rochester, VT: Inner Traditions, 1984.

Burton, Michael Hedley. *In the Light of a Child: A Journey through the 52 Weeks of the Year in Both Hemispheres for Children and for the Child in Each Human Being.* Ghent, NY: Adonis Press, 1989.

Capel, Evelyn Francis. *The Mystery of Growing Up: Childhood and the Spiritual Life: Practical Ideas for Parents and Teachers.* London: Temple Lodge Press, 1990.

———— *Celebrating Festivals Around the World.* London: Temple Lodge Publishing, 1991.

———— *Collected Plays for the Young and Old.* London: Temple Lodge Publishing, 1992.

Carey, Diana & Judy Large. *Festivals, Family and Food.* Stroud, UK: Hawthorn Press, 1982.

Carlgren, Frans. *Education Towards Freedom.* Joan & Sigfried Rudel, eds. East Grinstead, England: Lanthorn Press, 1976.

Childs, Gilbert. *Understand Your Temperament!* London: Sophia Books, 1995.

———— *Steiner Education in Theory and Practice.* Edinburgh, Scotland, 1991.

———— *Rudolf Steiner: His Life and Work.* Hudson, NY: Anthroposophic Press, 1995.

Childs, Gilbert & Sylvia Childs. *Your Reincarnating Child.* London: Rudolf Steiner Press, 1995.

Clark, F. and H. Kofsky and J. Lauruol. *To a Different Drumbeat: A Practical Guide for Parenting Children with Special Needs.* Stroud, UK: Hawthorn Press, 1981.

Cloos, Walter. *The Living Earth: The Organic Origin of Rocks and Minerals.* East Grinstead, England: Lanthorn Press, 1977.

Clouder, Christopher & Martyn Rawson. *Waldorf Education: Rudolf Steiner's Ideas in Practice,* Hudson, NY: Anthroposophic Press, 1998.

Cooper, Stephanie, Christine Fynes-Clinton, Marye Rowling. *The Children's Year.* Stroud, UK: Hawthorn Press, 1986.

Coplen, Dotty Turner. *Parenting a Path Through Childhood.* Edinburgh, Scotland: Floris Books, 1982.

———— *Parenting for a Healthy Future.* Stroud, UK: Hawthorn Press, 1995.

Davidson, Norman. *Astronomy and the Imagination: A New Approach to Man's Experience of the Stars.* London: Routledge and Kegan Paul, 1985.

———— *Sky Phenomena: A Guide to Naked Eye Observation of the Stars.* Hudson, NY: Lindisfarne Press, 1993.

Davy, Gudrun. *Lifeways.* Stroud, UK: Hawthorn Press, 1983.

Davy, John. *Work Arising: From the Life of Rudolf Steiner.* London: Rudolf Steiner Press, 1975.

de Haes, Daniel Udo. *The Young Child: Creative Living with Two to Four-Year-Olds.* Edinburgh, Scotland: Floris Books, 1986.

Easton, Stewart, C. *Man and World in the Light of Anthroposophy.* New York: Anthroposophic Press, 1983.

———— *Rudolf Steiner: Herald of a New Epoch.* New York: Anthroposophic Press, 1980.

———— *The Way of Anthroposophy.* Rudolf Steiner Press, 1985.

Edelglas, Stephen and Georg Maier, Hans Gebert, and John Davy. *The Marriage of Sense and Thought: Imaginative Participation in Science.* Hudson, NY: Lindisfarne Press, 1997.

Edmunds, Francis. *Anthroposophy: A Way of Life.* Hartfield, E. Sussex: Carnant Books, 1982.

———— *From Thinking to Living: The Work of Rudolf Steiner.* Longmead, Dorset, England: Element Books, 1990.

———— *Renewing Education*. Stroud, UK: Hawthorn Press, 1992.

———— *Rudolf Steiner Education: The Waldorf Impulse*. Rudolf Steiner Press, London, 1962.

Edwards, Lawrence. *The Vortex of Life: Nature's Patterns in Space and Time*. Edinburgh, Scotland: Floris Books, 1993.

Ege, Karl. *An Evident Need of Our Times: Goals of Education at the Close of the Century*. Ghent, NY: Adonis Press, 1979.

Elium, Jeanne & Don. *Raising a Daughter: Parents and the Awakening of a Healthy Woman*. Berkeley, CA: Celestial Arts, 1994.

———— *Raising a Family: Living on Planet Parenthood*. Berkeley, CA: Celestial Arts, 1997.

———— *Raising a Son: Parents and the Making of a Healthy Man*. Berkeley, CA: Celestial Arts, 1992.

Faulkner-Jones, D.E. *The English Spirit: A New Approach through the World Conception of Rudolf Steiner*. London: Rudolf Steiner Press, 1982.

Finser, Torin. *School as a Journey: The Eight-Year Odyssey of a Waldorf Teacher and His Class*. Hudson, NY: Anthroposophic Press, 1994.

Fenner, Pamela Johnson & Karen Rivers. *Waldorf Education: A Family Guide*. London: Rudolf Steiner Press, n.d.

Fitzjohn, Sue, Minda Weston & Judy Large. *Festivals Together: A Guide to Multi-Cultural Celebration*. Stroud, UK: Hawthorn Press, 1993.

Franceschelli, Amos. *Mensuration: Mathematics for Grades 6, 7, and 8*. Spring Valley, NY: Mercury Press, 1985.

Franceschelli, Amos. *Elementary Algebra*. Spring Valley, NY: Mercury Press, 1985.

Frommer, Eva A. *Voyage Through Childhood into the Adult World: A Guide to Child Development*. Stroud, UK: Hawthorn Press, 1994.

Gabert, Erich. *Educating the Adolescent: Discipline or Freedom*. Hudson, NY: Anthroposophic Press, 1988.

———— *The Motherly and Fatherly Roles in Education*. Hudson, NY, Anthroposophic Press, 1977.

———— *Punishment in Self-Education and in the Education of the Child*. E. Sussex, UK: Steiner Schools Fellowship Publications, 1951.

Gardner, John F. *Education in Search of the Spirit: Essays in American Education*. Hudson, NY: Anthroposophic Press, 1995.

———— *Youth Longs to Know: Explorations of the Spirit in Education*. Hudson, NY: Anthroposophic Press, 1997.

Glas, Norbert. *Conception, Birth and Early Childhood.* Spring Valley, NY: Anthroposophic Press, 1972.

Glas, Werner. *Speech Education in the Primary Grades of Waldorf Schools.* Detroit: Sunbridge College Press, 1974.

—— *The Waldorf School Approach to History.* Spring Valley, NY: Anthroposophic Press, 1981.

Glöckler, Michaela & Wolfgang Goebel. *A Guide to Child Health.* Edinburgh, Scotland: Floris Books, 1984.

Grohmann, Gerbert. *The Plant: A Guide to Understanding its Nature,* vols. 1 & 2. London: Rudolf Steiner Press, 1974.

Grunelius, Elizabeth M. *Early Childhood Education and the Waldorf School Plan.* Englewood, NJ: Waldorf School Monographs, 1966.

Hahn, Herbert. *From the Wellsprings of the Soul: Towards the Religious Teaching of the Young.* Sussex, UK: Rudolf Steiner Schools Fellowship, 1966.

Haller, I. *How Children Play.* Edinburgh, Scotland: Floris Books, 1991.

Hansmann, Henning. *Education for Special Needs.* Edinburgh, Scotland: Floris Books, 1992.

Haren, Wil Van and Rudolf Kischnick. *Child's Play: Games for Life.* Stroud, UK: Hawthorn Press, 1995.

Harrer, Dorothy. *An English Manual.* Spring Valley, NY: Mercury Press.

—— *Chapters From Ancient History.* Spring Valley, NY: Mercury Press, 1996.

—— *Math Lessons for Elementary Grades.* Spring Valley, NY: Mercury Press, 1985.

—— *Nature Stories.* Spring Valley, NY: Mercury Press, 1982.

—— *Roman Lives.* Spring Valley, NY: Mercury Press, 1996.

Harwood, A.C. *The Recovery of Man in Childhood: A Study in the Educational Work of Rudolf Steiner.* New York: Myrin Institute, 1958.

—— *The Way of a Child: An Introduction to the Work of Rudolf Steiner for Children.* London: Rudolf Steiner Press, 1967.

Hauck, Hedwig. *Handwork and Handicrafts.* Sussex, England: Steiner Schools Fellowship, 1968.

Hauschka, Rudolf. *Nutrition.* London: Rudolf Steiner Press, 1983.

—— *The Nature of Substance.* London: Rudolf Steiner Press, 1983.

Heirman, Leo. *Pictures of Initiation.* Roselle, IL: Schaumburg Publications.

Hemleben, Johannes. *Rudolf Steiner: A Documentary Biography.* London: Henry Goulden, 1975.

Heydebrand, Caroline von. *Childhood: A Study of the Growing Child.* Hudson, NY: Anthroposophic Press, 1988.

—— *Curriculum of the First Waldorf School.* Sussex, England: Steiner Schools Fellowship, 1972.

Hiebel, Frederick. *Time of Decision with Rudolf Steiner.* Hudson, NY: Anthroposophic Press, 1989.

Holtzapfel, Walter, M.D. *Children's Destinies: The Three Directions of Human Development.* Spring Valley, NY: Mercury Press, 1977.

—— *The Human Organs: their Functional and Psychological Significance,* Cornwall, UK: Lanthorn Press, 1993.

Hutchins, Eileen. *Parzival: An Introduction.* Temple Lodge Publishing, 1979.

Husemann, Friedrich, M.D.& Otto Wolff, M.D. *The Anthroposophical Approach to Medicine: An Outline of a Spiritual-Scientifically Oriented Medicine.* vol. 1, Spring Valley, NY: Anthroposophic Press, 1982.

Jacobs, Valerie. *Black and White Shaded Drawing: A Course of Exercises.* London: Rudolf Steiner Press, 1975.

Jaffke, Freya. *Toymaking with Children.* Edinburgh, UK: Floris Books, 1988.

Julius, Frits H. *The World of Matter and The Education of Man: Chemistry Presented by Simple Phenomena.* Sussex, UK: Steiner Schools Fellowship, n.d.

—— *Sound Between Matter and Spirit.* Spring Valley, NY: Mercury Press, 1993.

Keller von Asten, H. *Encounters with the Infinite: Geometrical Experiences Through Active Contemplation.* Dornach, Switzerland: Walter Keller Press, 1971.

Kennish, Graham. *Chemistry in Classes 7 and 8 for Class Teachers in Steiner / Waldorf Schools,* Shaddon, Gloucester, UK: Wynstones Science Training Course, 1997.

Kirshner, *Dynamic Drawing: Its Therapeutic Aspects.* Spring Valley, NY: Mercury Press, 1977.

Kischnick, Rudolf. *Games, Gymnastics, Sport in Child Development.* London: Rudolf Steiner Press, 1979.

Klocek, Dennis. *Weather and Cosmos.* Fair Oaks, CA: Rudolf Steiner College Publications, 1990.

Klocek, Dennis. *Drawing from the Book of Nature.* Fair Oaks, CA: Rudolf Steiner College Publications, 1990.

König, Karl. *Being Human: Diagnosis in Curative Education.* Hudson, NY: Anthroposophic Press, 1989.

———— *Brothers and Sisters: A Study in Child Psychology.* Edinburgh, Scotland: Floris Books, 1983.

———— *Earth and Man.* Wyoming, RI: Biodynamic Literature, 1982.

———— *Elephants, Bears, Horses, Cats and Dogs: Sketches for an Imaginative Zoology.* Edinburgh, Scotland: Floris Books, 1992.

———— *Eternal Childhood.* North Yorkshire, UK: Camphill Books, 1994.

———— *In Need of Special Understanding.* North Yorkshire, UK: Camphill Books, 1986.

———— *Penguins, Seals, Dophins, Salmon and Eels: Sketches for an Imaginative Zoology.* Edinburgh, Scotland: Floris Books, 1984.

———— *Swans and Storks, Sparrows and Doves: Sketches for an Imaginative Zoology.* Edinburgh, Scotland: Floris Books, 1984.

———— *The Camphill Movement.* North Yorkshire, UK: Camphill Books, 1993.

———— *The First Three Years of the Child.* Spring Valley, NY: Anthroposophic Press, 1984.

———— *The Human Soul.* Spring Valley, NY: Anthroposophic Press, 1973.

———— *The Inner Path.* North Yorkshire, UK: Camphill Books, 1994.

Koepke, Hermann. *Encountering the Self: Transformation and Destiny in the Ninth Year.* Hudson, NY: Anthroposophic Press, 1989.

———— *On The Threshold of Adolescence.* Hudson, NY: Anthroposophic Press, 1992.

Kolisko, Eugen, M.D. *Zoology for Everybody* vols. 1–6. Bournemouth, England: Kolisko Archive Publications, 1978.

———— *Geology.* Bournemouth, England: Kolisko Archive Publications, 1978.

———— *Elementary Chemistry.* Bournemouth, England: Kolisko Archive Publications, 1978.

———— *Natural History.* Bournemouth, England: Kolisko Archive Publications, 1979.

———— *Nutrition.* vols. 1 & 2. Bournemouth, England: Kolisko Archive Publications, 1979.

———— *The Threefold Human Organism.* Bournemouth, England: Kolisko Archive Publications, 1943.

Kühlewind, Georg. *From Normal to Healthy: Paths to the Liberation of Consciousness.* Hudson, NY: Lindisfarne Press, 1988.

——— *Stages of Consciousness: Meditations on the Boundaries of the Soul.* Hudson, NY: Lindisfarne Press, 1984.

——— *Working with Anthroposophy.* Hudson, NY: Anthroposophic Press, 1992.

Kutzli, Rudolf. *Creative Form Drawing,* vols. 1, 2, 3, & 4. Stroud, UK: Hawthorn Press, 1983.

Large, Martin. *Who's Bringing Them Up? Television and Child Development: How to Break the T.V. Habit.* Stroud, UK: Hawthorn Press, 1990.

Lauenstein, Dieter. *Biblical Rhythms in Biography.* Edinburgh, Scotland: Floris Books, 1983.

Leeuwen, M.V. & J. Moeskops. *The Nature Corner.* Edinburgh, Scotland: Floris Books, 1990.

Lindenberg, Christoph. *Teaching History: Suggested Themes for the Curriculum in Waldorf Schools.* Fair Oaks, CA: Association of Waldorf Schools of North America, 1989.

Lindenberg, Christoph-Andreas. *The Child's Praise of the Seasons: Festival Music to Sing.* Chatham, NY: Rose Harmony Association, 1995.

——— *In Praise of the Seasons: Festival Music to Sing and Play.* Chatham, NY: Rose Harmony Association, 1995.

Lievegoed, Bernard. *Man on the Threshold: The Challenge of Inner Development.* Stroud, UK: Hawthorn Press, 1985.

——— *Phases of Childhood.* Edinburgh, Scotland: Floris Books, 1987.

——— *Phases: Crisis and Development in the Individual.* London: Rudolf Steiner Press, 1979.

Lissau, Magda. *The Temperaments and the Arts: Their Relation and Function in Waldorf Pedagogy.* Chicago, 1983.

Lissau, Rudi. *Rudolf Steiner, Life, Work, Inner Path and Social Initiatives.* Stroud, UK: Hawthorn Press, 1987.

Logan, Arnold, arr. & ed. *Building the Chorus: Exercises and Songs for All Voices.* Chatham, NY: Rose Harmony Association, 1994.

——— *Building the Chorus: Arrangements of Folk Songs.* Chatham, NY: Rose Harmony Association, 1994.

Luxford, Michael. *Adolescence and its Significance for those with Special Needs.* Botton Village, U.K.: Camphill Books, 1995.

——— *Children with Special Needs: Rudolf Steiner's Ideas in Practice.* Hudson, NY: Anthroposophic Press, 1994.

Mackensen, Manfred von. *A Phenomena Based Physics,* 3 vols. Fair Oaks, CA: Association of Waldorf Schools of North America, 1987.

Matthews, Paul. *Sing Me the Creation*. Stroud, UK: Hawthorn Press, 1994.

McAllen, Audrey E. *The Extra Lesson: Exercises in Movement, Drawing and Painting for helping Children in difficulties with Writing, Reading and Arithmetic*. Sussex, UK: Steiner Schools Fellowship, 1985.

McAllen, Audrey E. *Teaching Children to Write*. London: Rudolf Steiner Press, 1977.

McDermott, Robert. *The Essential Steiner: Basic Writings of Rudolf Steiner*. San Francisco: Harper & Row, 1984.

Mees, L. F. C., M.D. *Living Metals: Relationship between Man and Metals*. New York: Regency Press, 1974.

———— *Secrets of the Skeleton: Form in Metamorphosis*. Spring Valley, NY: Anthroposophic Press, 1984.

Meyer, Rudolf. *Rhythms in Human Beings and the Cosmos*. Edinburgh, UK: Floris Books, 1985.

———— *The Wisdom of Fairy Tales*. Hudson, NY: Anthroposophic Press, 1981.

Müller, Brunhild. *Painting with Children*. Edinburgh, Scotland, 1987.

Müller, Heinz. *Healing Forces in the Word and its Rhythms*. Sussex, England: Rudolf Steiner Schools Fellowship Publications, 1983.

Niederhauser, Hans R. & Margaret Frohlich. *Form Drawing*. Spring Valley, NY: Mercury Press, 1984.

O'Neill, George and Gisela. *The Human Life*. Florin Lowndes, ed. Spring Valley, NY: Mercury Press, 1990.

Piening, Ekkehard & Nick Lyons, eds. *Educating as an Art: Essays on the Rudolf Steiner Method-Waldorf Education*. New York: Rudolf Steiner School Press, 1979.

Pelikan, Wilhelm. *The Secrets of Metals*. Spring Valley, NY: Anthroposophic Press, 1973.

Petrash, Carol. *Earthways: Simple Environmental Activities for Young Children*. Beltsville, MD, Gryphon Press, 1992.

Polzer-Hoditz, Ludwig Graf. *Memories of Rudolf Steiner: Reminiscences of an Austrian*. Spring Valley, NY: St. George Press, 1987.

Poplawski, Thomas, *Eurythmy: Rhythm, Dance and Soul*, Hudson, NY: Anthroposophic Press, 1998.

Poppelbaum, Hermann. *A New Zoology*. Dornach: Philosophischer-Anthroposophischer Verlag, 1961.

———— *Man and Animal: Their Essential Difference*. London: Rudolf Steiner Press, 1982.

Pusch, Ruth, ed. *Waldorf Schools*. vols. 1 & 2. Spring Valley, NY: Mercury Press, 1993.

Prokofieff, Sergei. *Rudolf Steiner and the Founding of the New Mysteries*. London: Rudolf Steiner Press, 1986.

Proskauer, Heinrich O. *The Rediscover of Color*. Spring Valley, NY: Anthroposophic Press, 1986.

Querido, René. *Creativity in Education: The Waldorf Approach*. San Francisco, CA: H.S. Dakin, 1984.

———— *The Esoteric Background of Waldorf Education: The Cosmic Christ Impulse*. Fair Oaks, CA: Rudolf Steiner College Press, 1995.

———— *The Mystery of the Holy Grail: A Modern Path of Initiation*. Fair Oaks, CA: Rudolf Steiner College Press, 1991.

Richards, Mary Caroline. *Opening Our Moral Eye: Essays, Talks, & Poems Embracing Creativity & Community*. Hudson, NY: Lindisfarne Press, 1995.

Richter, Gottfried. *Art and Human Consciousness*. Spring Valley, NY: Anthroposophic Press, 1985.

Rittelmeyer, Friedrich. *Meditation: Letters on the Guidance of the Inner Life, According to the Gospel of St. John*. Edinburgh, Scotland: Floris Books, 1983.

Rittelmeyer, Friedrich. *Rudolf Steiner Enters My Life*. Edinburgh, Scotland: Floris Books, 1982.

Roboz, Stephen. *The Holy Grail: From the Works of Rudolf Steiner*. North Vancouver, BC: Steiner Book Centre, 1984.

Schad, Wolfgang. *Man and Mammals: Toward a Biology of Form*. Garden City, NY: Waldorf Press, 1977.

Schiller, Paul Eugen. *Rudolf Steiner and Initiation: The Anthroposophical Path of Inner Schooling: A Survey*. Spring Valley, NY: Anthroposophic Press, 1981.

Schmidt, Gerhard, M.D. *The Dynamics of Nutrition: The Impulse of Rudolf Steiner's Spiritual Science for a New Nutritional Hygiene*. Wyoming, RI: Bio-Dynamic Literature, 1980.

———— *The Essentials of Nutrition*. Wyoming, RI: Bio-Dynamic Literature, 1980.

Schmid, Rudolf. *An English Grammar: The Language Before Babel*. Fair Oaks, CA: Association of Waldorf Schools of North America, 1995.

Schwartz, Eugene. *Adolescence: The Search for Self and Weaving the Social Fabric of the Class: Two Lectures on Waldorf Education*. Fair Oaks, CA: Rudolf Steiner College Publications, 1991.

———— *Gratitude, Love, and Duty: Their Unfolding in Waldorf Education.* Association for a Healing Education, 1989.

———— *Rhythms and Turning Points in the Life of the Child.* Fair Oaks, CA: Rudolf Steiner College Publications, 1991.

———— *Seeing, Hearing, Learning: The Interplay of Eye and Ear in Waldorf Education.* Fair Oaks, CA: Rudolf Steiner College Publications, 1990.

Schwartz, Eugene. *Plays for Children and Communities: Grades 1–7.* Association for a Healing Education, 1989.

Schuré, Edouard. *From Sphinx to Christ: An Occult History.* Blauvelt, NY: Garber Communications, 1977.

———— *The Great Initiates: A Study of the Secret History of Religions.* Blauvelt, NY: Garber Communications, 1977.

Schwenk, Theodor. *Sensitive Chaos: The Creation of Flowing Forms in Water and Air.* London: Rudolf Steiner Press, 1996.

Seddon, Richard. *Europa: A Spiritual Biography.* London: Temple Lodge Press, 1995.

Sheen, A. Renwick. *Geometry and the Imagination: The Imaginative Treatment of Geometry in Waldorf Education.* Fair Oaks, CA: Rudolf Steiner College Press, 1991.

Shepherd, A. P. *A Scientist of the Invisible: An Introduction to the Life and Work of Rudolf Steiner.* New York: Inner Traditions, 1983.

Sleigh, Julian. Thirteen to Nineteen: Discovering the Light: Conversations with Parents. Edinburgh, Scotland: Floris Books, 1989.

Sloan, E. Douglas. "Waldorf Education: An Introduction." *Teachers College Record.* New York: Columbia University, spring 1980.

Smit, Jörgen. *Lighting Fires: Deepening Education Through Meditation.* Stroud, UK: Hawthorn Press, 1992.

———— *How to Transform Thinking, Feeling and Willing.* Stroud, UK: Hawthorn Press, 1989.

———— *Meditation.* London: Rudolf Steiner Press, 1991.

———— *The Steps Toward Knowledge Which the Seeker for the Spirit Must Take.* David Mitchell, ed. & trans. Fair Oaks, CA: Association of Waldorf Schools of North America, 1991.

Smith, Patti & Signe Eklund Schaeffer. *More Lifeways: Finding Support and Inspiration in Family Life.* Stroud, UK: Hawthorn Press, 1997.

Smith, Susan. *Echoes of a Dream: Creative Beginnings for Parent and Child.* London, Ontario: Waldorf Schools Association of London, 1982.

Spock, Marjorie. *Eurythmy.* Spring Valley, NY: Anthroposophic Press, 1980.

———— *Teaching as a Lively Art.* Spring Valley, NY: Anthroposophic Press, 1978.

Staley, Betty. *Between Form and Freedom: A Practical Guide to the Teenage Years* Stroud, UK: Hawthorn Press, 1988.

Stein, Walter Johannes. *The Ninth Century: World History in the Light of the Holy Grail.* London: Temple Lodge Press, 1991.

Stockmeyer, Karl E. A., *Rudolf Steiner's Curriculum for the Waldorf Schools.* Sussex, England: Steiner Schools Fellowship, 1982.

Stoehr, Shaina. *Eurythmy: An Art of Movement for Our Time.* Stourbridge, England: Robinswood Press, 1993.

Sussman, Linda. *Speech of the Grail: A Journey toward Speaking that Heals and Transforms.* Hudson, NY: Lindisfarne Press, 1995.

Swanson, Herbert J. *Geometry for the Waldorf High School.* Fair Oaks, CA: Association of Waldorf Schools of North America, 1987.

Trostli, Roberto. *Physics is Fun! A Sourcebook for Teachers.* New York: Octavo Editions, 1995.

Wachsmuth, Günter. *The Life and Work of Rudolf Steiner from the Turn of the Century to his Death.* Blauvelt, NY: Spiritual Science Library, 1989.

Whicher, Olive. *Projective Geometry.* London: Rudolf Steiner Press, 1971.

Wilkinson, Roy. *Commonsense Schooling: Based on the Indications of Rudolf Steiner.* Sussex, UK: Henry Goulden, 1975.

———— *Man and Animal.* Sussex, UK: Roy Wilkinson, 1973.

———— *Nutrition, Health, Anthropology.* Sussex, UK: Roy Wilkinson, 1973.

———— *Plant Study & Geology.* Sussex, UK: Roy Wilkinson, 1973.

———— *Studies in Practical Activities.* Sussex, UK: Roy Wilkinson, 1973.

———— *Teaching English.* Sussex, UK: Roy Wilkinson, 1973.

———— *Teaching Geography.* Sussex, UK: Roy Wilkinson, 1973.

———— *Teaching History: The Ancient Civilizations* vols. 3, 4, & 5. Sussex, UK: Roy Wilkinson, 1973.

———— *Teaching Mathematics.* Sussex, UK: Roy Wilkinson, 1973.

———— *The Physical Sciences,* vols 1 & 2. Sussex, UK: Roy Wilkinson, 1973.

Wolff, Otto. *The Etheric Body: A Report of a Lecture.* Spring Valley, NY: Mercury Press, 1990.

————— *Home Remedies: Herbal and Homeopathic Treatments for Use at Home*. Edinburgh, Scotland: Floris Books, 1991.

Wyatt, Isabel. *From Round Table to Grail Castle*. Sussex, UK: Lanthorn Press, 1979.

Zajonc, *Arthur. Catching the Light: The Entwined History of Light and Mind*. New York: Bantam Books, 1993.

Zur Linden, Wilhelm. *A Child Is Born: Pregnancy, Birth and First Childhood*. London: Rudolf Steiner Press, 1973.

Zelymans van Emmichoven, F. W. *The Anthroposophical Understanding of the Soul*. London: Rudolf Steiner Press, 1963.

INDEX

RUDOLF STEINER
(1861–1925)

During the last two decades of the nineteenth century the Austrian-born Rudolf Steiner became a respected and well-published scientific, literary, and philosophical scholar, particularly known for his work on Goethe's scientific writings. After the turn of the century he began to develop his earlier philosophical principles into an approach to methodical research of psychological and spiritual phenomena. His multifaceted genius has led to innovative and holistic approaches in medicine, science, education (Waldorf schools), special education, philosophy, religion, economics, agriculture (Biodynamic method), architecture, drama, new arts of eurythmy and speech, and other fields. In 1924 he founded the General Anthroposophical Society, which today has branches throughout the world.

. . . .

ROBERTO TROSTLI, has been active in Waldorf education for almost two decades, teaching, lecturing, leading workshops, consulting, and writing. He is the author of numerous articles, a dozen plays for children, and *Physics is Fun! A Sourcebook for Teachers*. He received his B.A. from Columbia University, which awarded him a fellowship for graduate study in medieval languages and literature at the University of Cambridge, England. When he returned, he worked for several years as a violinmaker before becoming a class teacher at the Rudolf Steiner School in New York City, which he attended as a child. After ten years, he moved to western Massachusetts where he is a class teacher at The Hartsbrook School.

ROBERT MCDERMOTT, president of the California Institute of Integral Studies since 1990, has been professor of comparative philosophy and religion since 1964. His published writings include *Radhakrishnan* (1970), *The Essential Aurobindo* (1974) and *The Essential Steiner* (1984), the "Introduction" to William James, *Essays in Psychical Research* (1986), and "Rudolf Steiner and Anthroposophy" in Antoine Faivre and Jacob Needleman, eds., *Modern Esoteric Spirituality* (1992). He was president of the Rudolf Steiner Institute (1983-94), served as chair of the board of Sunbridge College (1986-1992) and Rudolf Steiner College (1990-1996), and currently serves on the Council of the Anthroposophical Society in America.

. . . .

For an informative catalog of the work of Rudolf Steiner
and other anthroposophical authors please contact

ANTHROPOSOPHIC PRESS
3390 Route 9, Hudson, NY 12534
TEL: 518-851-2054
FAX: 518-851-2047
website: www.anthropress.org